Mint Chocolate

3

MAMI ORIKASA

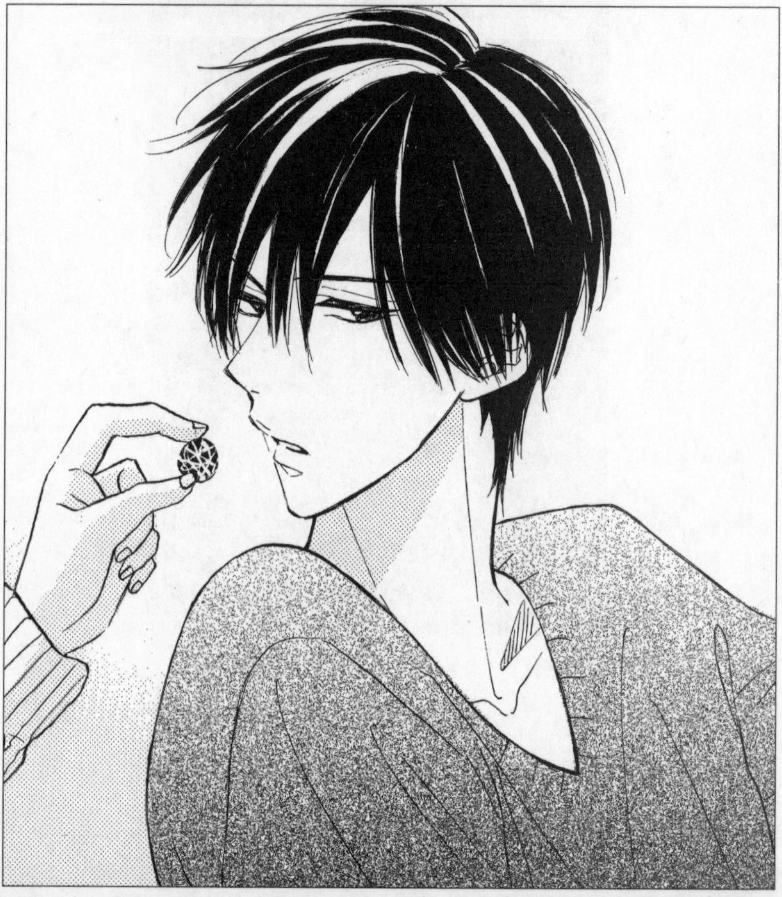

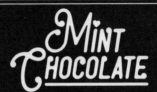

Mint Chocolate

CONTENTS

ROOM: 13
—003—

ROOM: 14
—035—

ROOM: 15
—067—

ROOM: 16
—097—

ROOM: 17
—127—

VOICE DRAMA COMIC ADAPTATION
—157—

BONUS CHAPTER
—187—

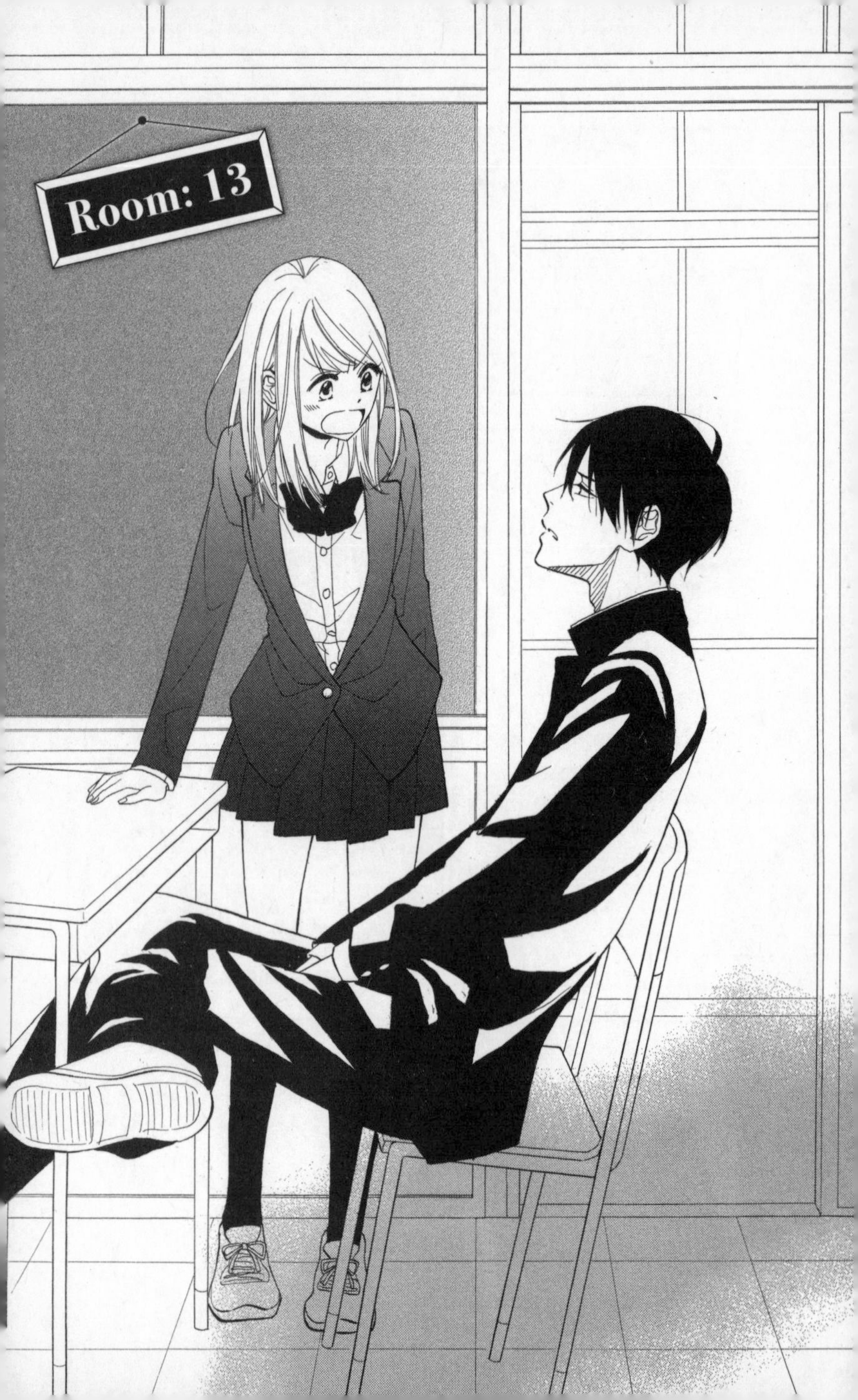
Room: 13

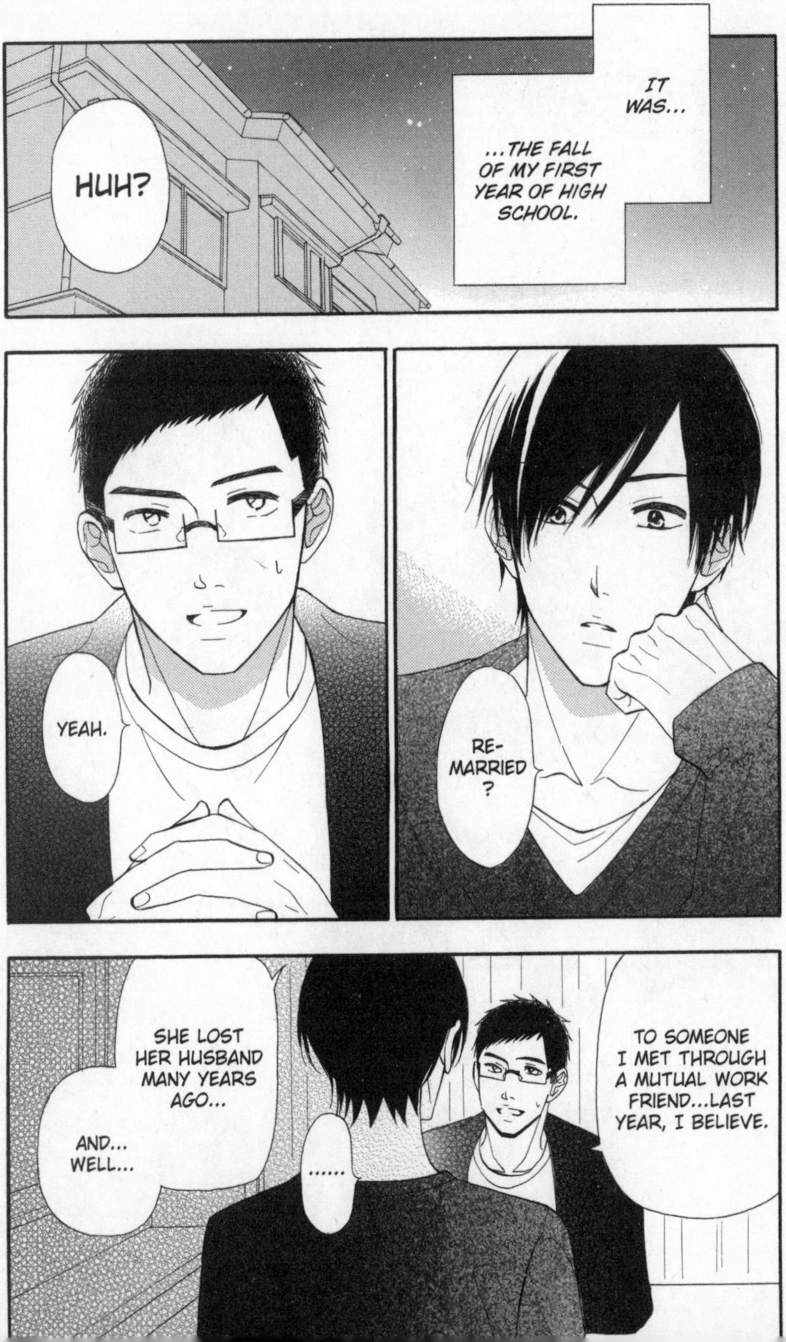
IT WAS...
...THE FALL OF MY FIRST YEAR OF HIGH SCHOOL.
HUH?
RE-MARRIED?
YEAH.
TO SOMEONE I MET THROUGH A MUTUAL WORK FRIEND...LAST YEAR, I BELIEVE.
......
SHE LOST HER HUSBAND MANY YEARS AGO...
AND... WELL...

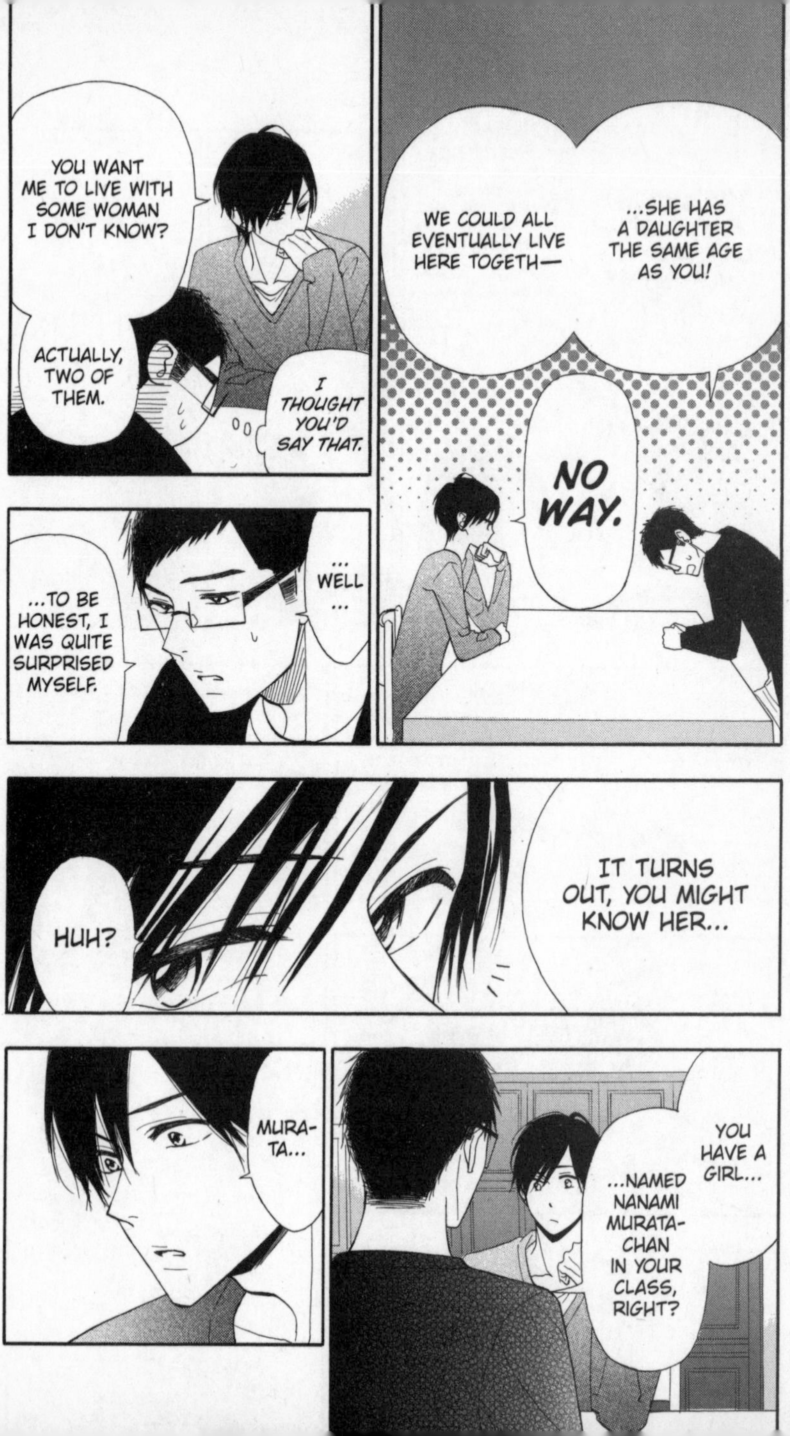
...SHE HAS A DAUGHTER THE SAME AGE AS YOU!
WE COULD ALL EVENTUALLY LIVE HERE TOGETH—
NO WAY.
YOU WANT ME TO LIVE WITH SOME WOMAN I DON'T KNOW?
I THOUGHT YOU'D SAY THAT.
ACTUALLY, TWO OF THEM.
...WELL...
...TO BE HONEST, I WAS QUITE SURPRISED MYSELF.
IT TURNS OUT, YOU MIGHT KNOW HER...
HUH?
YOU HAVE A GIRL...
...NAMED NANAMI MURATA-CHAN IN YOUR CLASS, RIGHT?
MURA-TA...

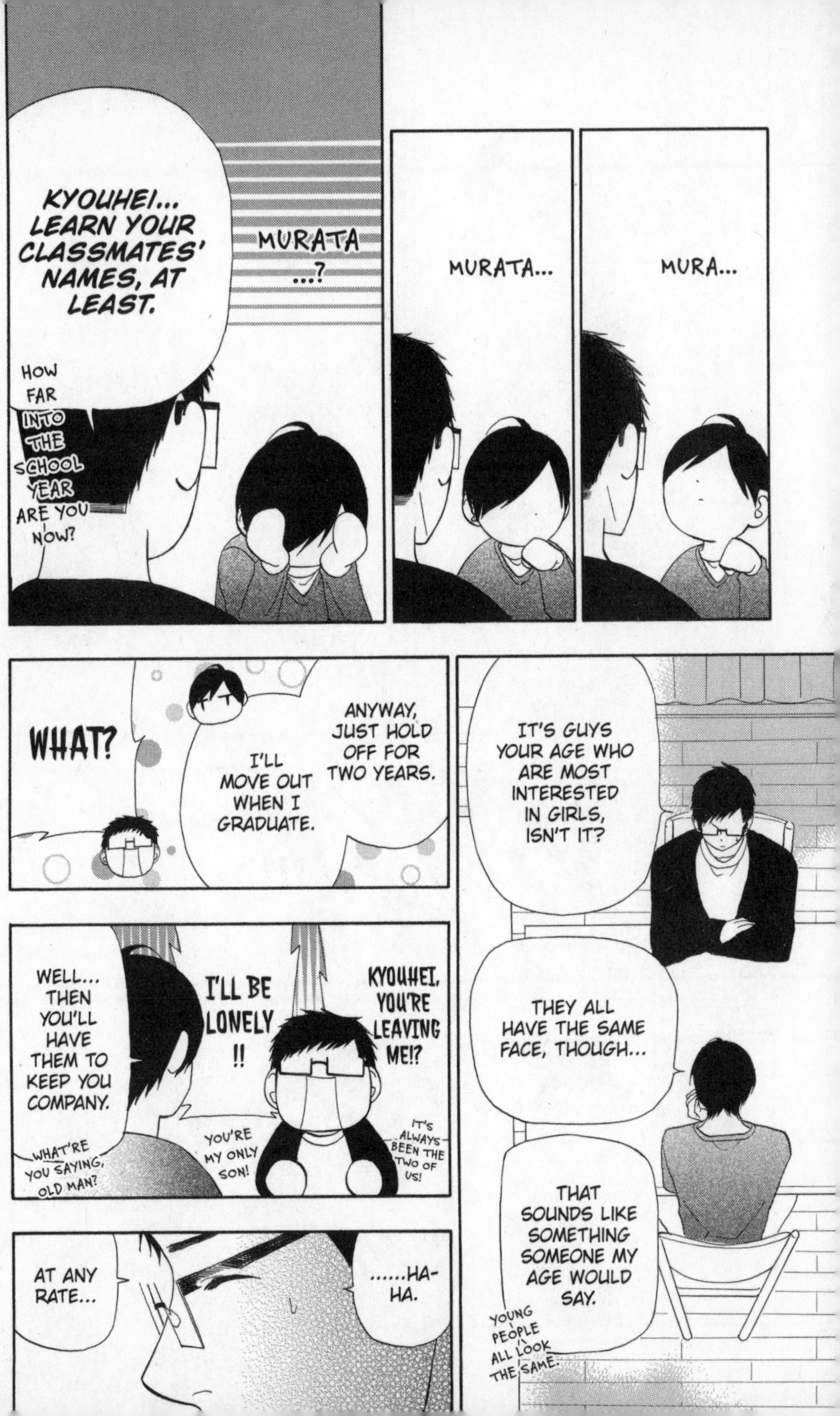
MURA...
MURATA...
MURATA ...?
KYOUHEI... LEARN YOUR CLASSMATES' NAMES, AT LEAST.
HOW FAR INTO THE SCHOOL YEAR ARE YOU NOW?
IT'S GUYS YOUR AGE WHO ARE MOST INTERESTED IN GIRLS, ISN'T IT?
THEY ALL HAVE THE SAME FACE, THOUGH...
THAT SOUNDS LIKE SOMETHING SOMEONE MY AGE WOULD SAY.
YOUNG PEOPLE ALL LOOK THE SAME.
ANYWAY, JUST HOLD OFF FOR TWO YEARS.
I'LL MOVE OUT WHEN I GRADUATE.
WHAT?
KYOUHEI, YOU'RE LEAVING ME!?
IT'S ALWAYS BEEN THE TWO OF US!
I'LL BE LONELY !!
YOU'RE MY ONLY SON!
WELL... THEN YOU'LL HAVE THEM TO KEEP YOU COMPANY.
WHAT'RE YOU SAYING, OLD MAN?
......HA-HA.
AT ANY RATE...

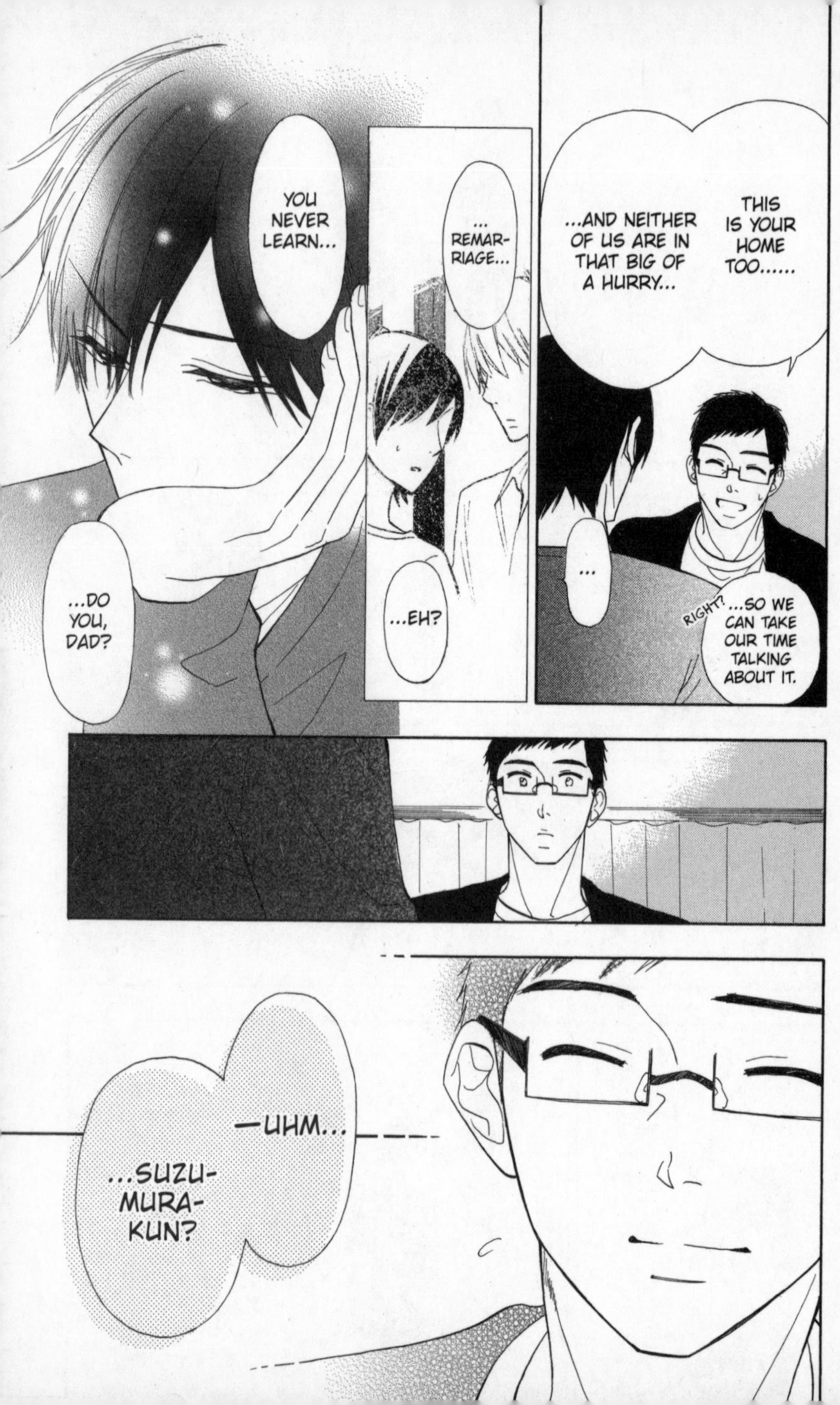
THIS IS YOUR HOME TOO......
...AND NEITHER OF US ARE IN THAT BIG OF A HURRY...
...
RIGHT?
...SO WE CAN TAKE OUR TIME TALKING ABOUT IT.
...REMARRIAGE...
...EH?
YOU NEVER LEARN...
...DO YOU, DAD?
—UHM...
...SUZUMURA-KUN?

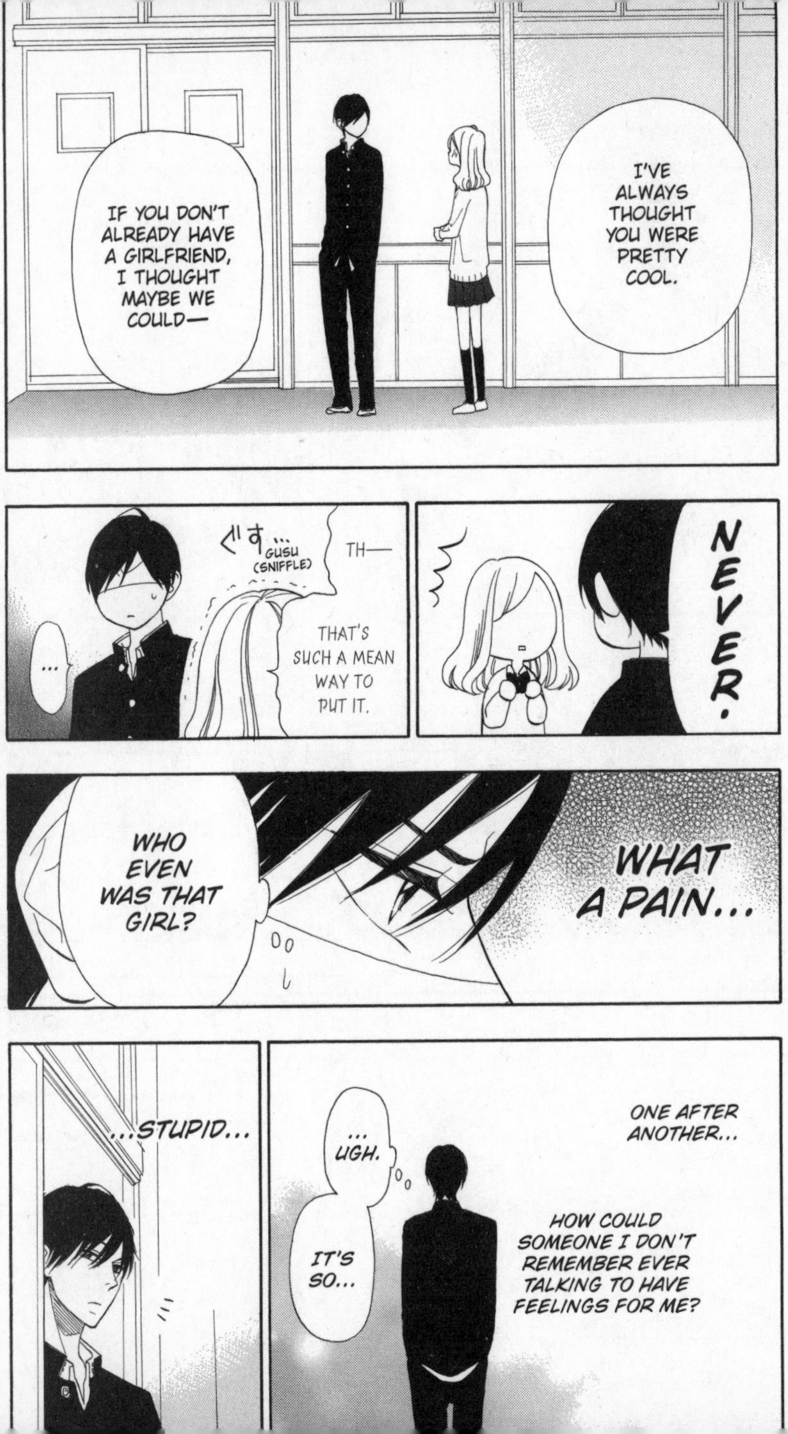
I'VE ALWAYS THOUGHT YOU WERE PRETTY COOL.
IF YOU DON'T ALREADY HAVE A GIRLFRIEND, I THOUGHT MAYBE WE COULD—
NEVER.
TH—
ぐす… GUSU (SNIFFLE)
THAT'S SUCH A MEAN WAY TO PUT IT.
…
WHAT A PAIN...
WHO EVEN WAS THAT GIRL?
ONE AFTER ANOTHER...
HOW COULD SOMEONE I DON'T REMEMBER EVER TALKING TO HAVE FEELINGS FOR ME?
... UGH.
IT'S SO...
...STUPID...

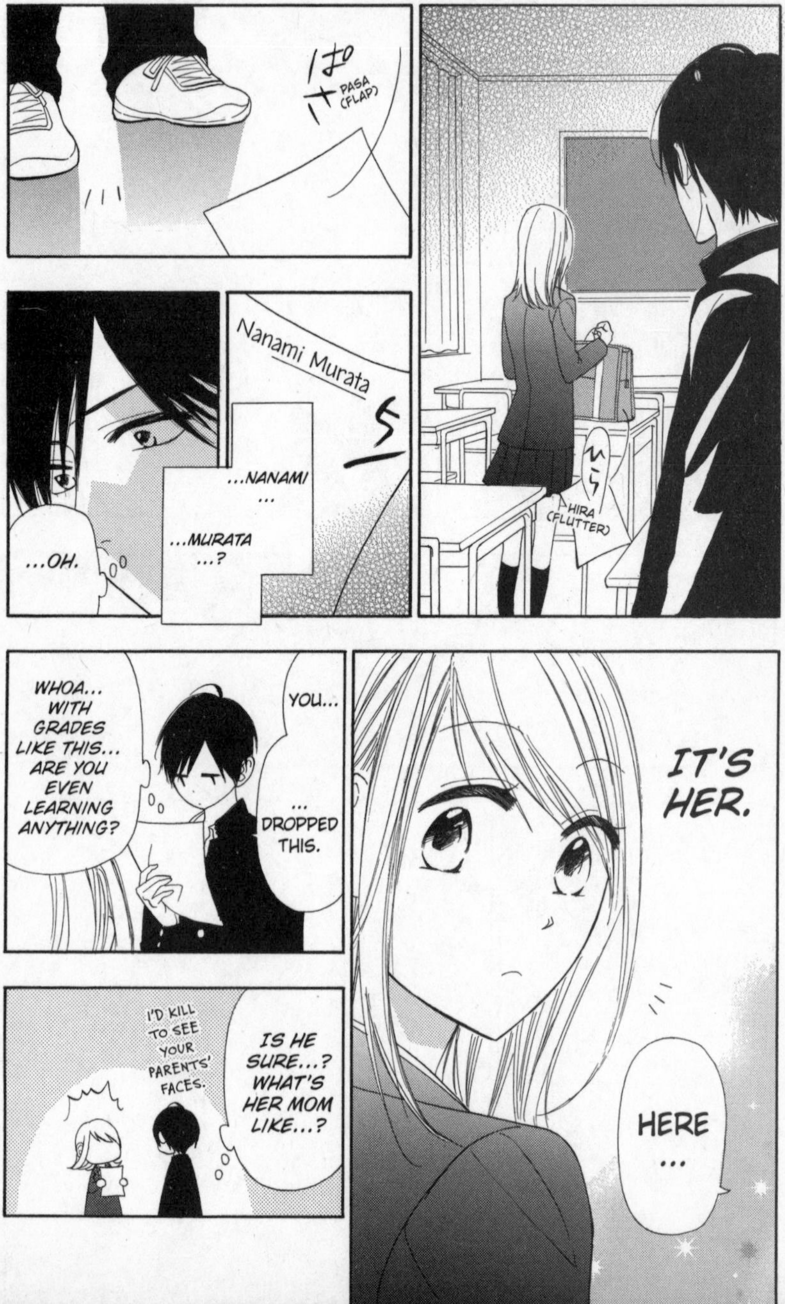
ひら
HIRA (FLUTTER)
ぱサ
PASA (FLAP)
Nanami Murata
...NANAMI...
...MURATA...?
...OH.
IT'S HER.
HERE...
YOU... ...DROPPED THIS.
WHOA... WITH GRADES LIKE THIS... ARE YOU EVEN LEARNING ANYTHING?
IS HE SURE...? WHAT'S HER MOM LIKE...?
I'D KILL TO SEE YOUR PARENTS' FACES.

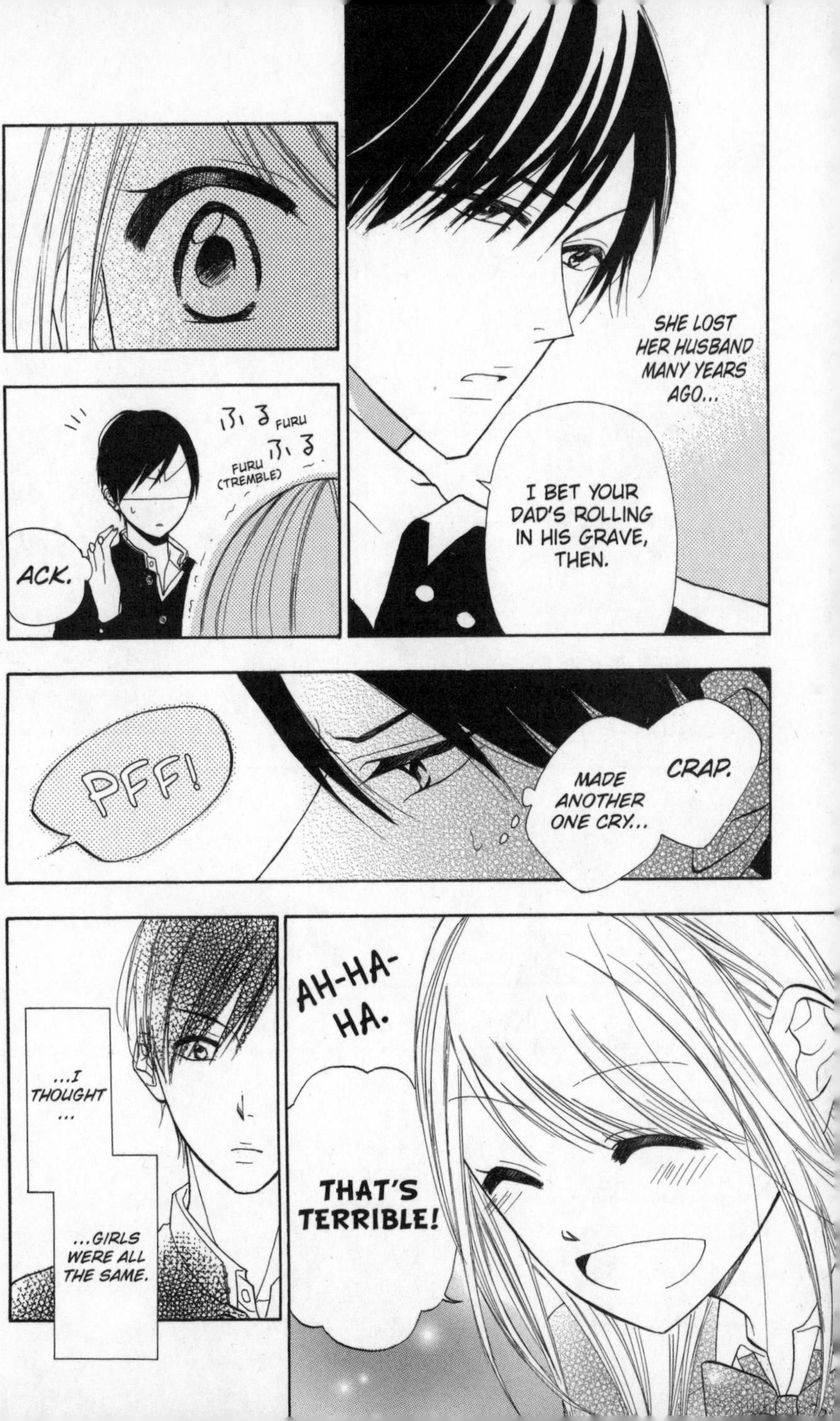
SHE LOST HER HUSBAND MANY YEARS AGO...
I BET YOUR DAD'S ROLLING IN HIS GRAVE, THEN.
ふる FURU ふる FURU (TREMBLE)
ACK.
CRAP.
MADE ANOTHER ONE CRY...
PFF!
AH-HA-HA.
THAT'S TERRIBLE!
...I THOUGHT...
...GIRLS WERE ALL THE SAME.

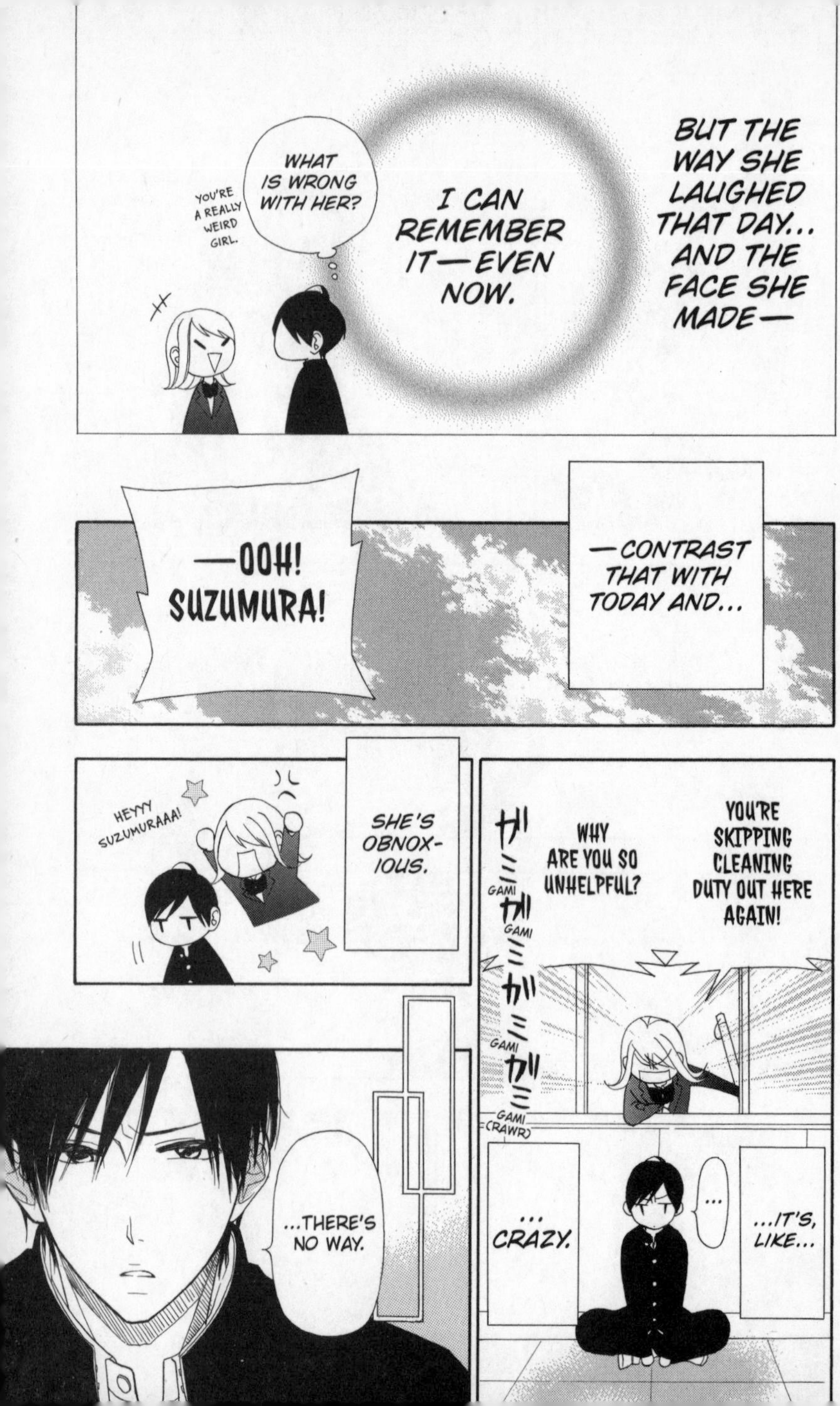
BUT THE WAY SHE LAUGHED THAT DAY... AND THE FACE SHE MADE—
I CAN REMEMBER IT—EVEN NOW.
WHAT IS WRONG WITH HER?
YOU'RE A REALLY WEIRD GIRL.
—CONTRAST THAT WITH TODAY AND...
—OOH! SUZUMURA!
YOU'RE SKIPPING CLEANING DUTY OUT HERE AGAIN!
WHY ARE YOU SO UNHELPFUL?
GAMI GAMI GAMI GAMI (RAWR)
...IT'S, LIKE...
...
...CRAZY.
SHE'S OBNOX-IOUS.
HEYYY SUZUMURAAA!
...THERE'S NO WAY.

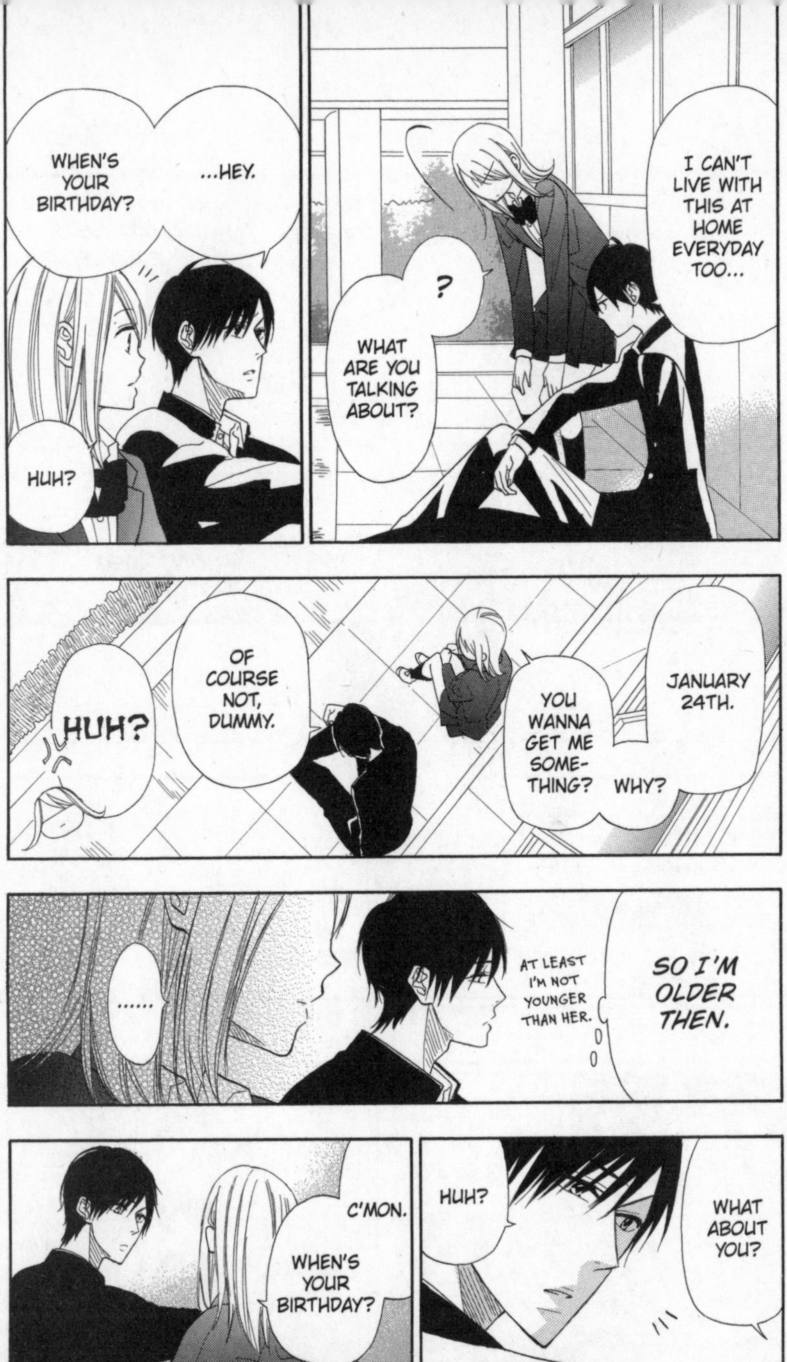
I CAN'T LIVE WITH THIS AT HOME EVERYDAY TOO...
?
WHAT ARE YOU TALKING ABOUT?
...HEY.
WHEN'S YOUR BIRTHDAY?
HUH?
JANUARY 24TH.
WHY?
YOU WANNA GET ME SOME-THING?
OF COURSE NOT, DUMMY.
HUH?
SO I'M OLDER THEN.
AT LEAST I'M NOT YOUNGER THAN HER.
......
WHAT ABOUT YOU?
HUH?
C'MON.
WHEN'S YOUR BIRTHDAY?

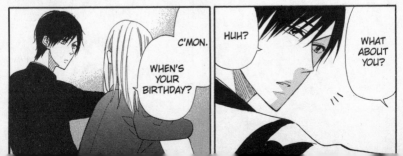

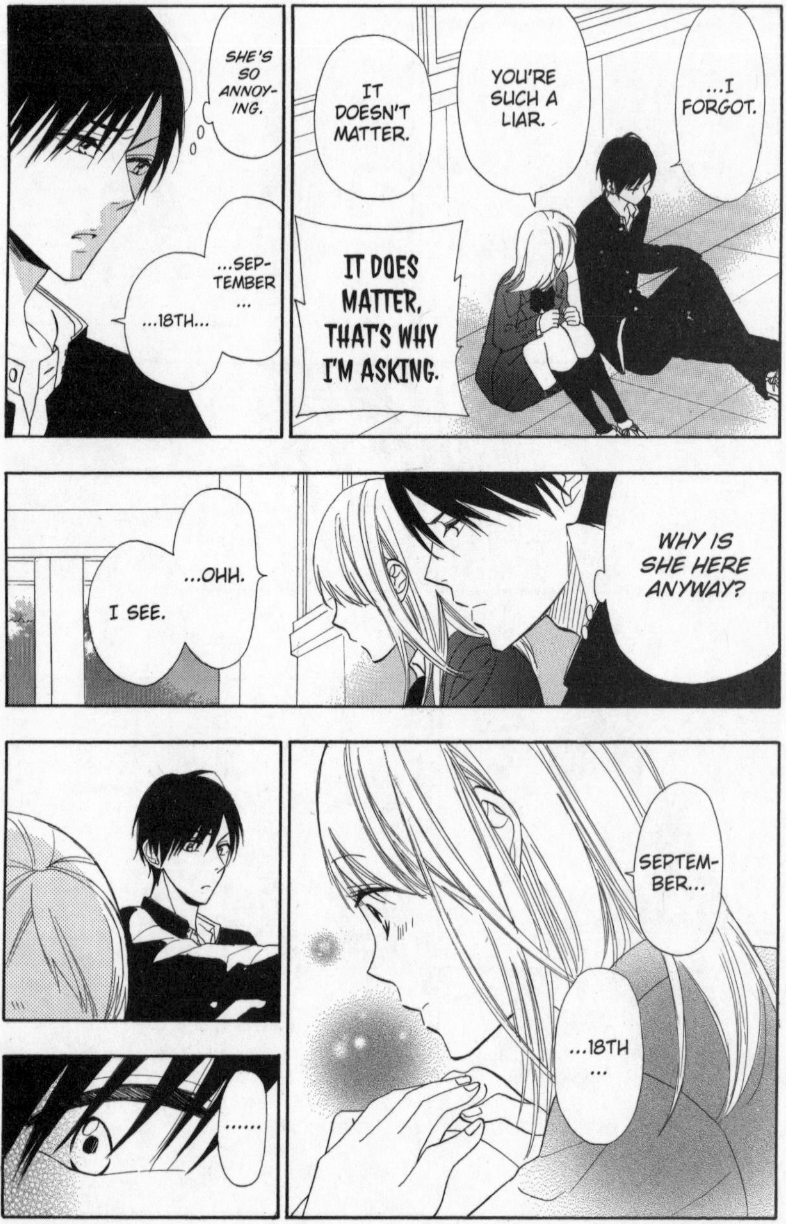
...I FORGOT.
YOU'RE SUCH A LIAR.
IT DOESN'T MATTER.
IT DOES MATTER, THAT'S WHY I'M ASKING.
SHE'S SO ANNOY-ING.
...SEP-TEMBER...
...18TH...
WHY IS SHE HERE ANYWAY?
...OHH.
I SEE.
SEPTEM-BER...
...18TH...
......

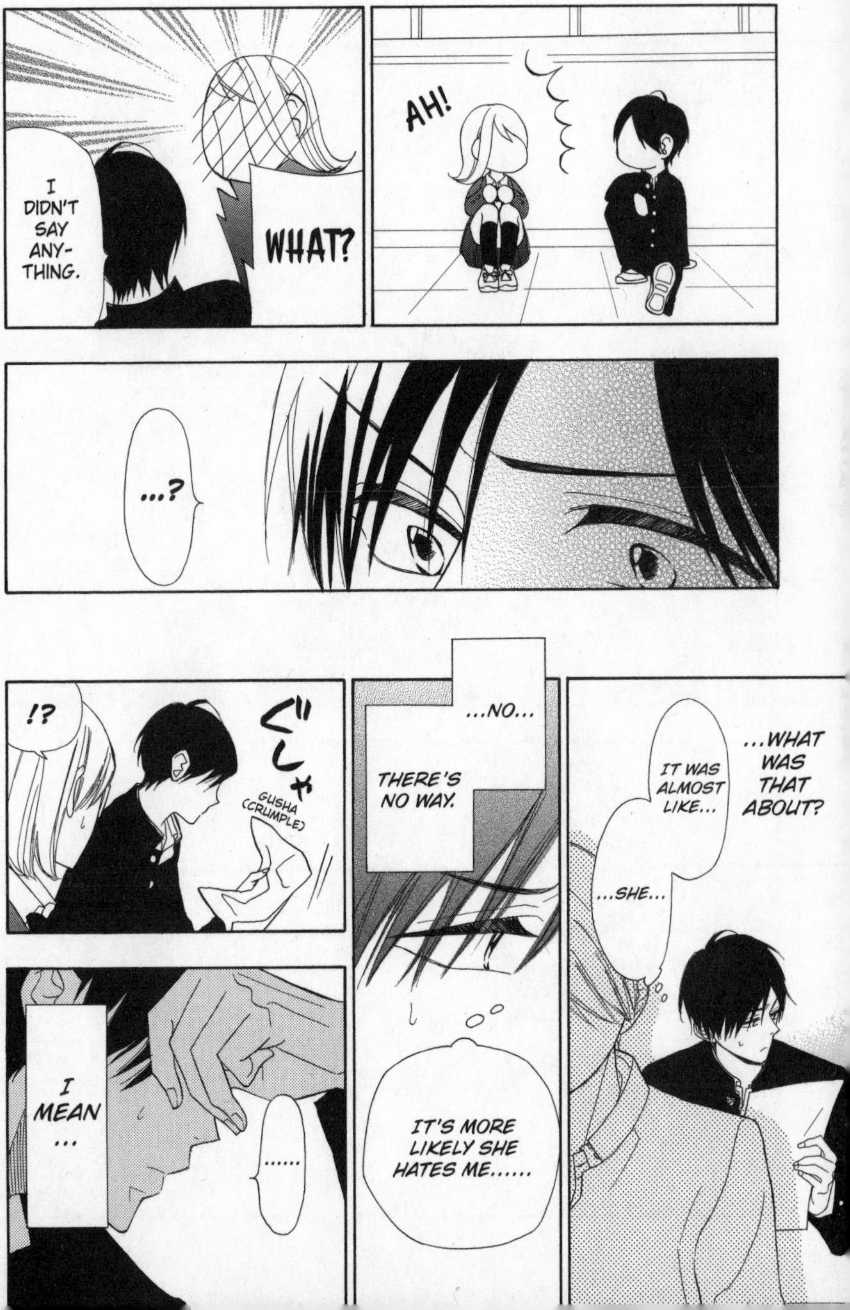
AH!
WHAT?
I DIDN'T SAY ANYTHING.
...?
...WHAT WAS THAT ABOUT?
IT WAS ALMOST LIKE...
...SHE...
...NO...
THERE'S NO WAY.
IT'S MORE LIKELY SHE HATES ME......
!?
ぐしゃ
GUSHA (CRUMPLE)
I MEAN ...
......

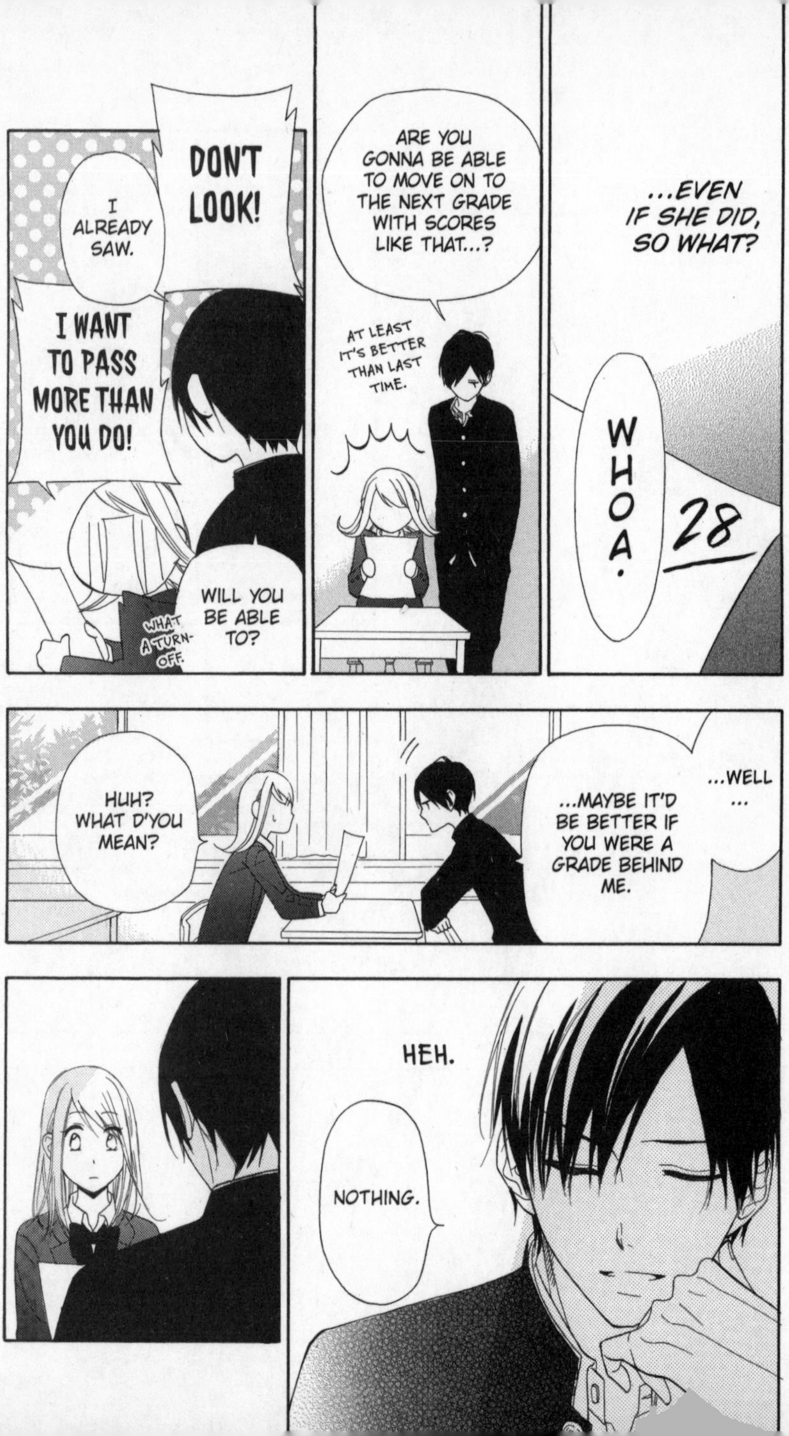
...EVEN IF SHE DID, SO WHAT?
WHOA.
28
ARE YOU GONNA BE ABLE TO MOVE ON TO THE NEXT GRADE WITH SCORES LIKE THAT...?
AT LEAST IT'S BETTER THAN LAST TIME.
DON'T LOOK!
I ALREADY SAW.
I WANT TO PASS MORE THAN YOU DO!
WILL YOU BE ABLE TO?
WHAT A TURN-OFF.
...WELL ...
...MAYBE IT'D BE BETTER IF YOU WERE A GRADE BEHIND ME.
HUH? WHAT D'YOU MEAN?
HEH.
NOTHING.

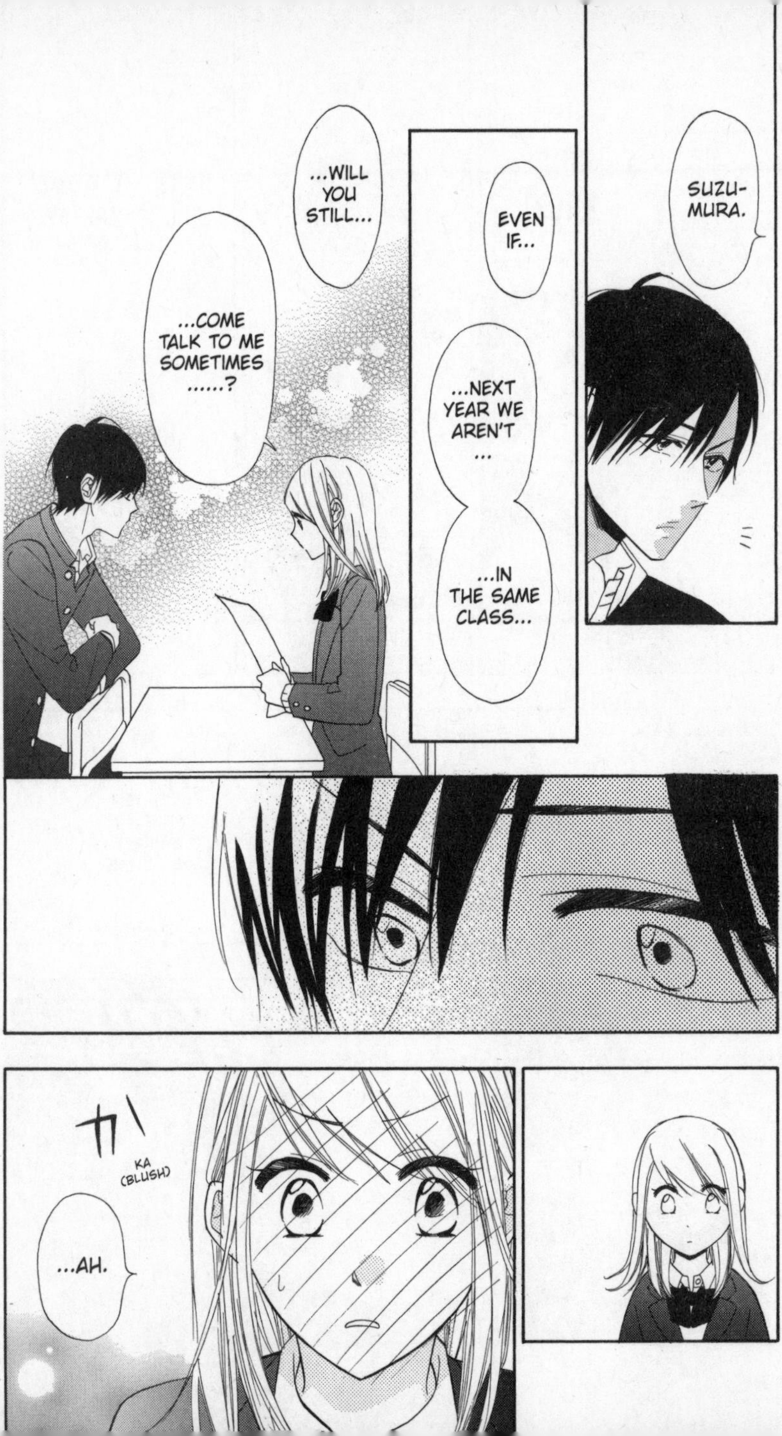
SUZU-MURA.
EVEN IF...
...NEXT YEAR WE AREN'T ...
...IN THE SAME CLASS...
...WILL YOU STILL...
...COME TALK TO ME SOMETIMES ......?
カ
KA (BLUSH)
...AH.

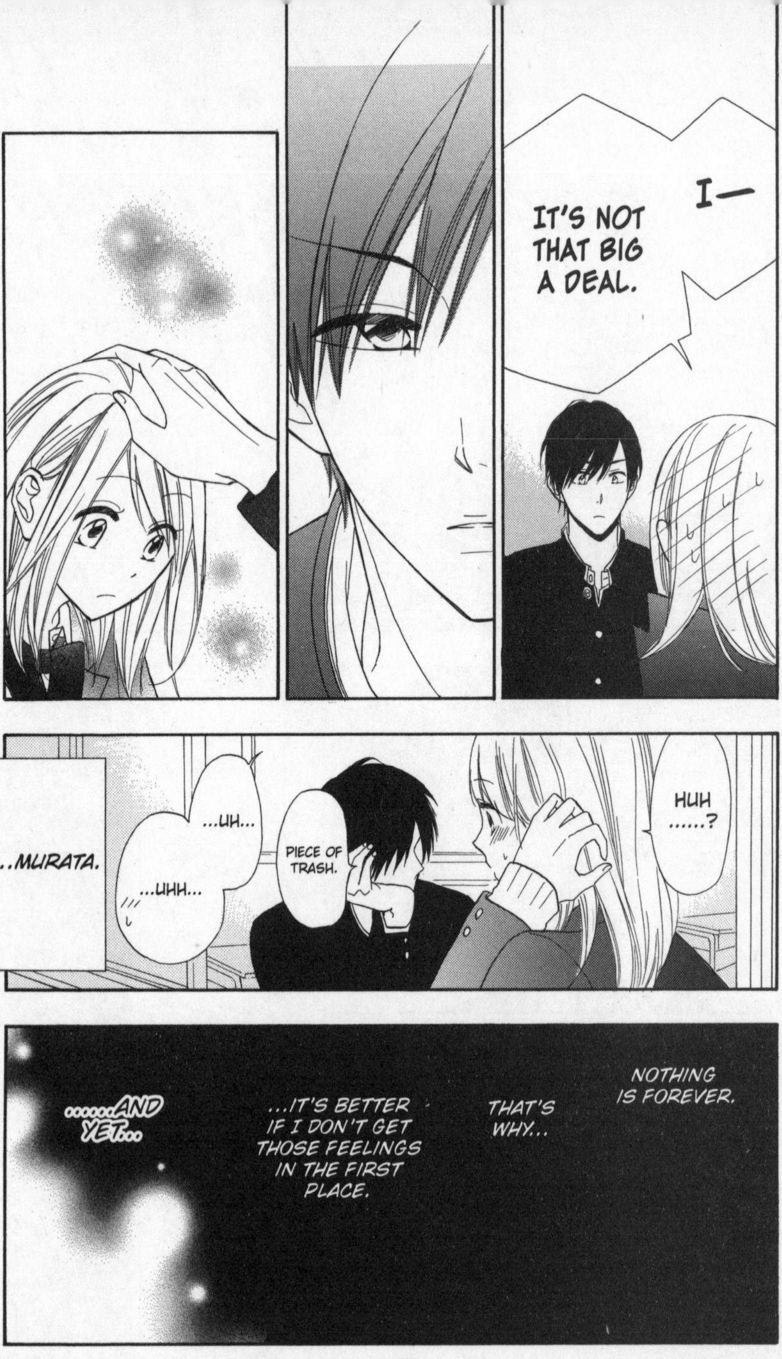
I—
IT'S NOT THAT BIG A DEAL.
HUH ......?
PIECE OF TRASH.
...UH...
...UHH...
...MURATA.
NOTHING IS FOREVER.
THAT'S WHY...
...IT'S BETTER IF I DON'T GET THOSE FEELINGS IN THE FIRST PLACE.
......AND YET...

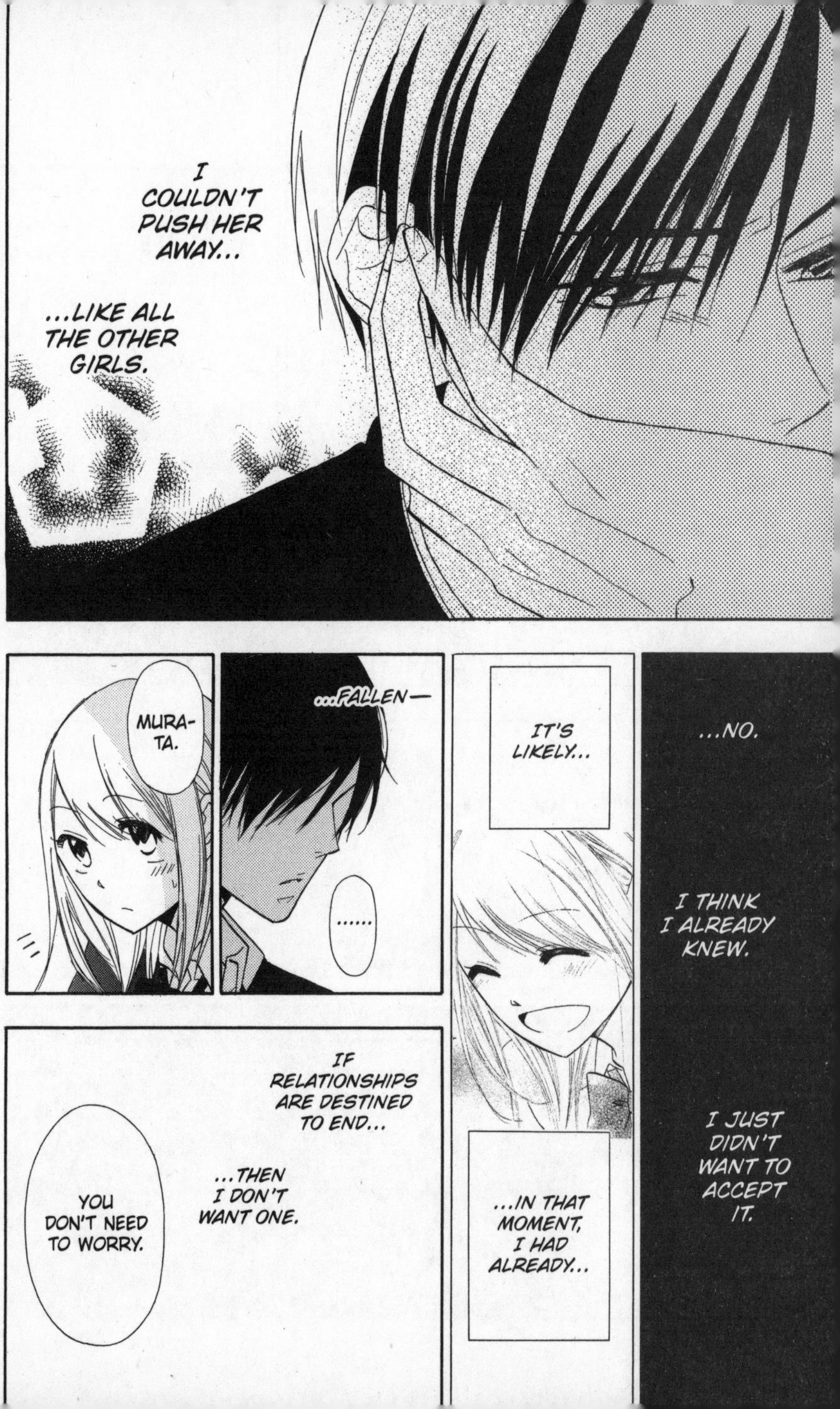
I COULDN'T PUSH HER AWAY...
...LIKE ALL THE OTHER GIRLS.
...NO.
I THINK I ALREADY KNEW.
I JUST DIDN'T WANT TO ACCEPT IT.
IT'S LIKELY...
...IN THAT MOMENT, I HAD ALREADY...
...FALLEN—
......
MURA-TA.
IF RELATIONSHIPS ARE DESTINED TO END...
...THEN I DON'T WANT ONE.
YOU DON'T NEED TO WORRY.

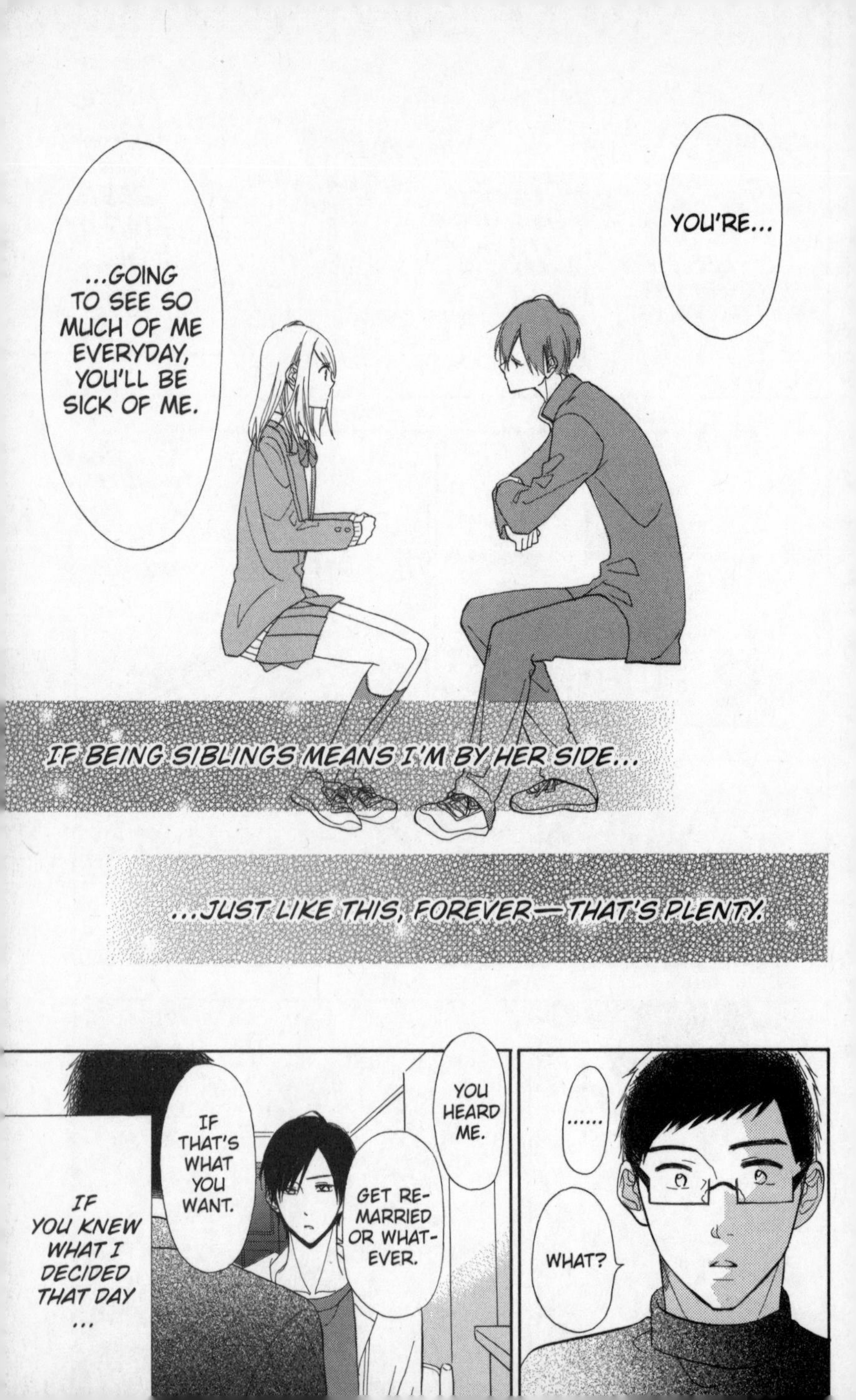
YOU'RE...
...GOING TO SEE SO MUCH OF ME EVERYDAY, YOU'LL BE SICK OF ME.
IF BEING SIBLINGS MEANS I'M BY HER SIDE...
...JUST LIKE THIS, FOREVER—THAT'S PLENTY.
......
WHAT?
YOU HEARD ME.
GET RE-MARRIED OR WHAT-EVER.
IF THAT'S WHAT YOU WANT.
IF YOU KNEW WHAT I DECIDED THAT DAY ...

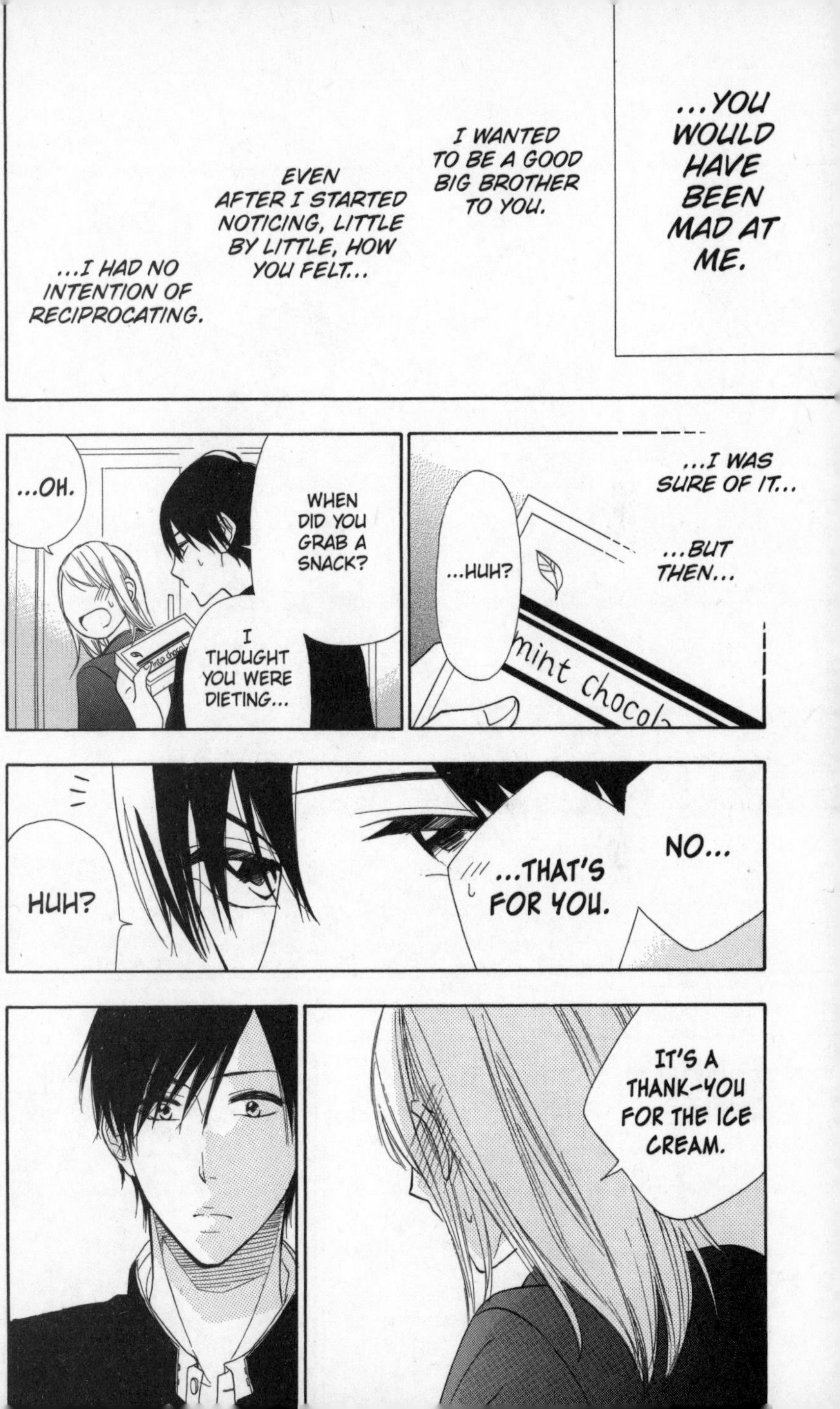
...YOU WOULD HAVE BEEN MAD AT ME.
I WANTED TO BE A GOOD BIG BROTHER TO YOU.
EVEN AFTER I STARTED NOTICING, LITTLE BY LITTLE, HOW YOU FELT...
...I HAD NO INTENTION OF RECIPROCATING.
...I WAS SURE OF IT...
...BUT THEN...
...HUH?
WHEN DID YOU GRAB A SNACK?
I THOUGHT YOU WERE DIETING...
...OH.
NO...
...THAT'S FOR YOU.
HUH?
IT'S A THANK-YOU FOR THE ICE CREAM.

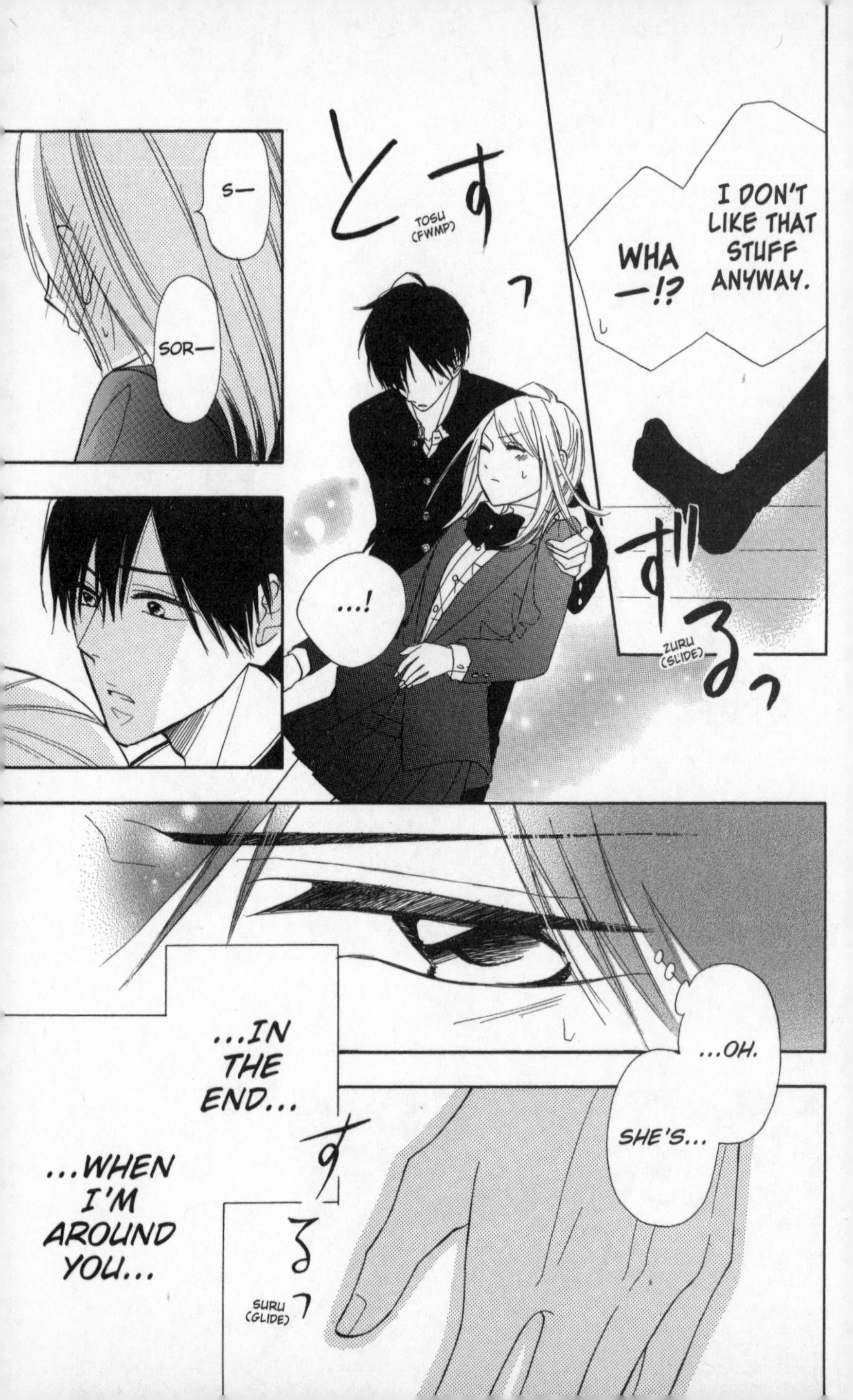
I DON'T LIKE THAT STUFF ANYWAY.
WHA—!?
とすっ
TOSU (FWMP)
ずるっ
ZURU (SLIDE)
S—
SOR—
...!
...OH.
SHE'S...
...IN THE END...
するっ
SURU (GLIDE)
...WHEN I'M AROUND YOU...

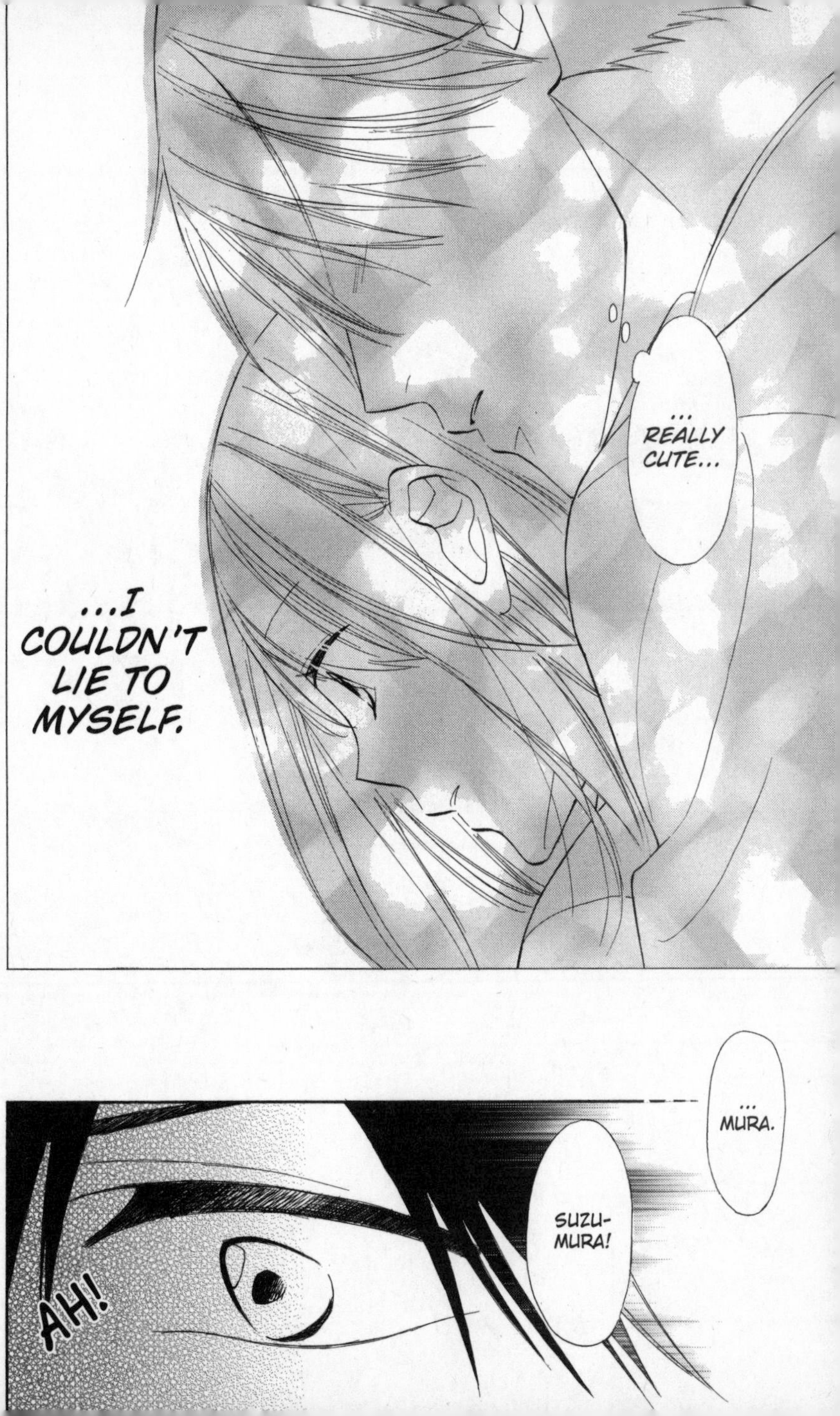
...REALLY CUTE...
...I COULDN'T LIE TO MYSELF.
...MURA.
SUZU-MURA!
AH!

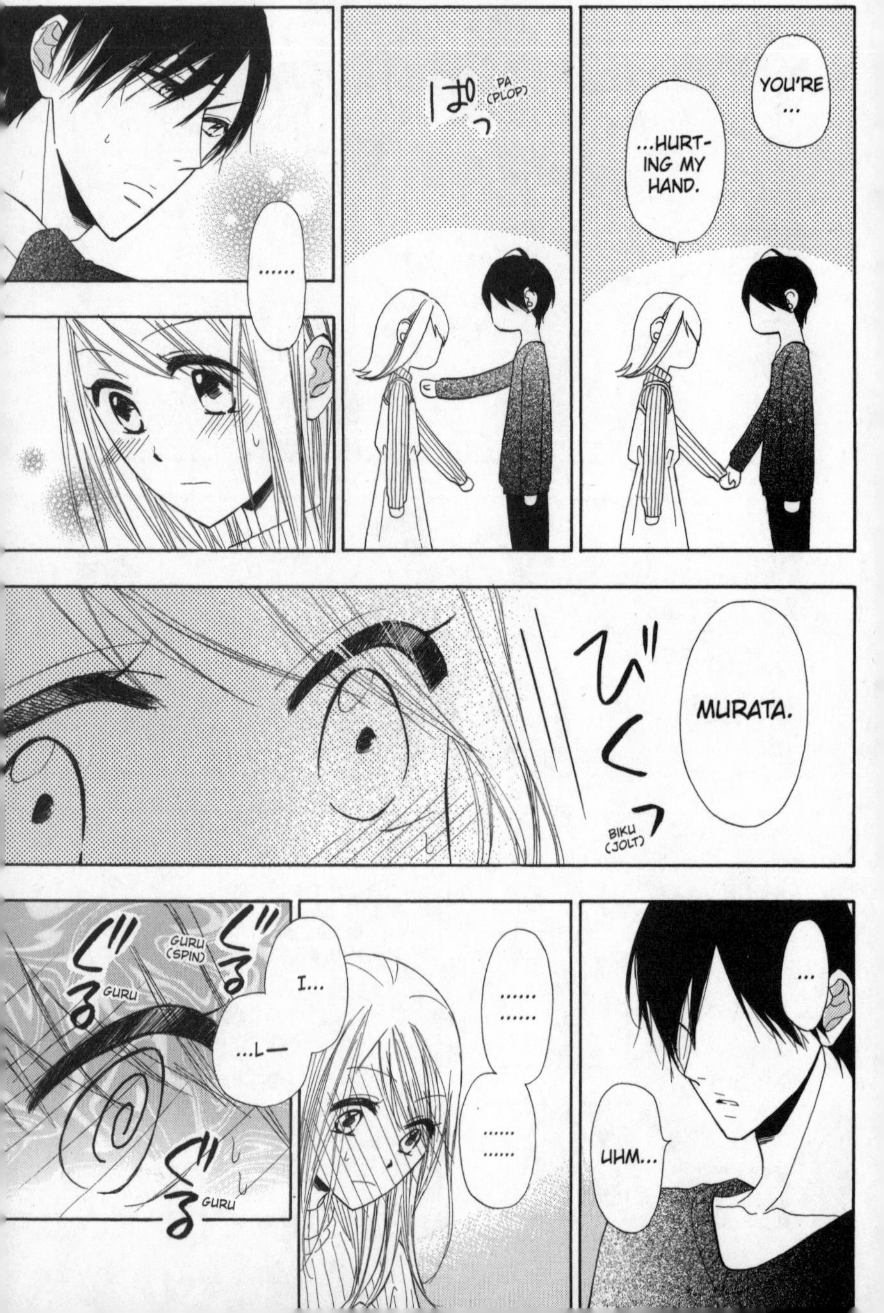
YOU'RE ...
...HURT-ING MY HAND.
ぱっ
PA (PLOP)
......
MURATA.
びくっ
BIKU (JOLT)
...
UHM...
......
......
......
......
I...
...L—
ぐる
GURU (SPIN)
ぐる
GURU
ぐる
GURU

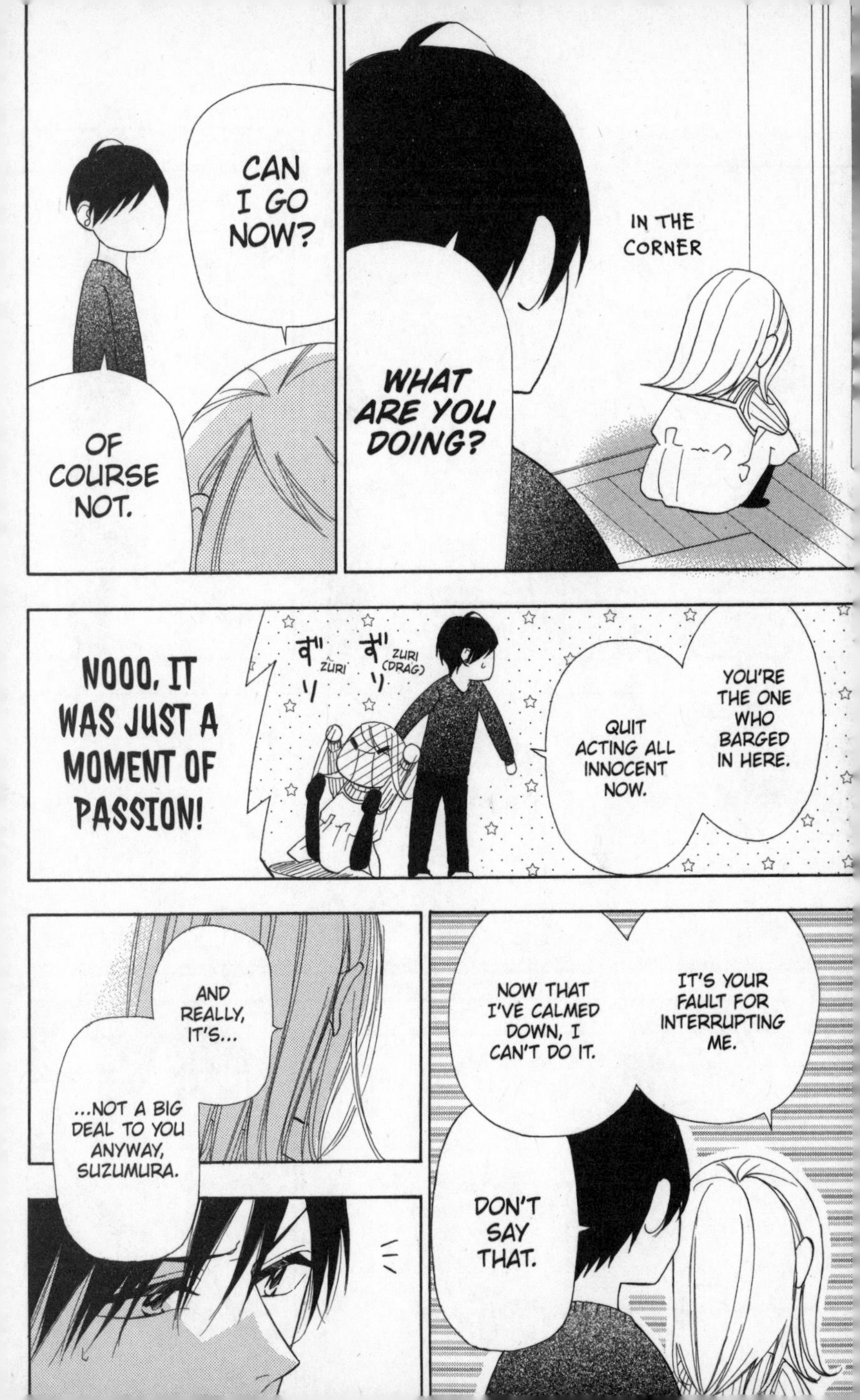
IN THE CORNER
WHAT ARE YOU DOING?
CAN I GO NOW?
OF COURSE NOT.
YOU'RE THE ONE WHO BARGED IN HERE.
QUIT ACTING ALL INNOCENT NOW.
ずり ZURI (DRAG)
ずり ZURI
NOOO, IT WAS JUST A MOMENT OF PASSION!
IT'S YOUR FAULT FOR INTERRUPTING ME.
NOW THAT I'VE CALMED DOWN, I CAN'T DO IT.
DON'T SAY THAT.
AND REALLY, IT'S...
...NOT A BIG DEAL TO YOU ANYWAY, SUZUMURA.

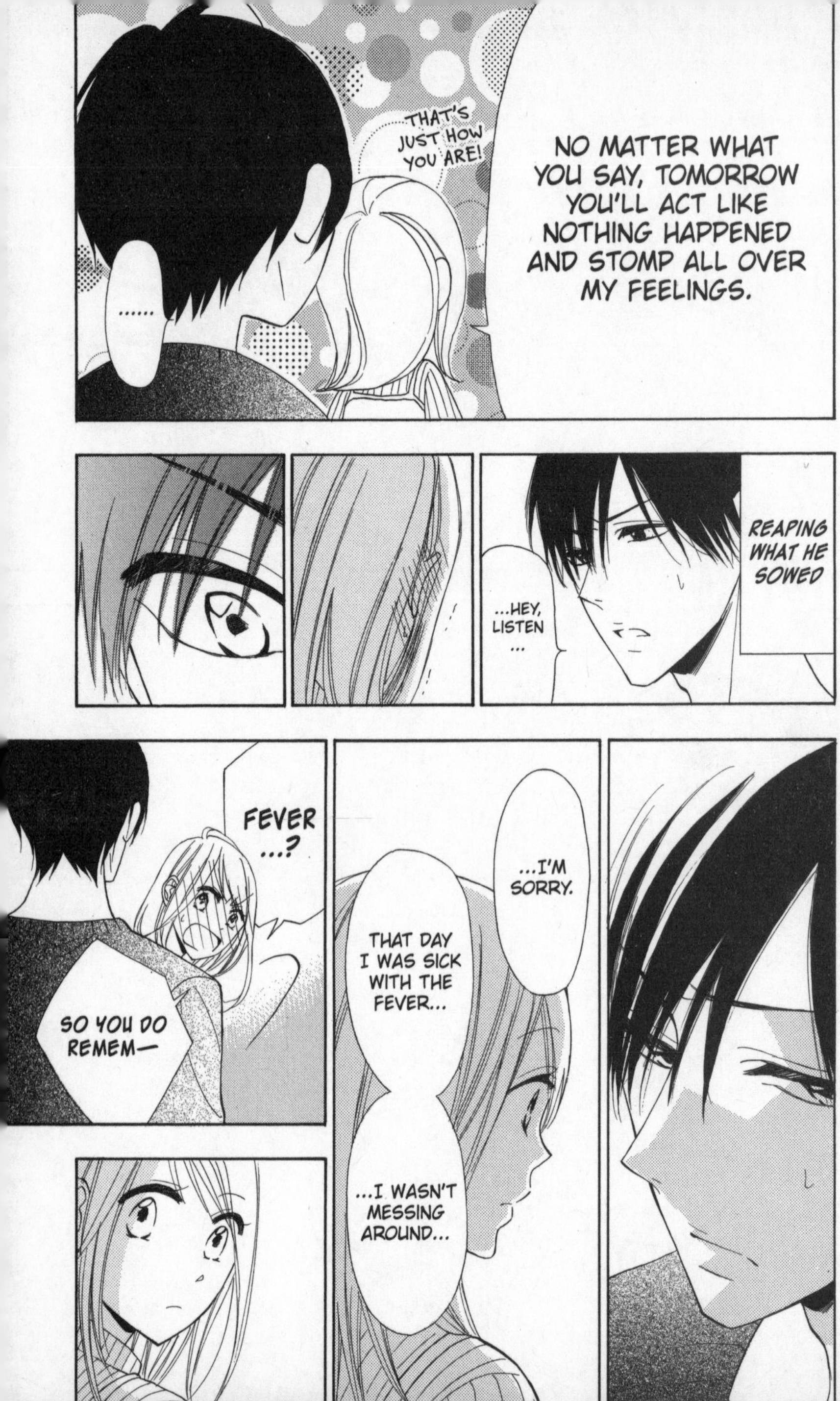
NO MATTER WHAT YOU SAY, TOMORROW YOU'LL ACT LIKE NOTHING HAPPENED AND STOMP ALL OVER MY FEELINGS.
THAT'S JUST HOW YOU ARE!
......
REAPING WHAT HE SOWED
...HEY, LISTEN ...
...I'M SORRY.
THAT DAY I WAS SICK WITH THE FEVER...
...I WASN'T MESSING AROUND...
FEVER ...?
SO YOU DO REMEM—

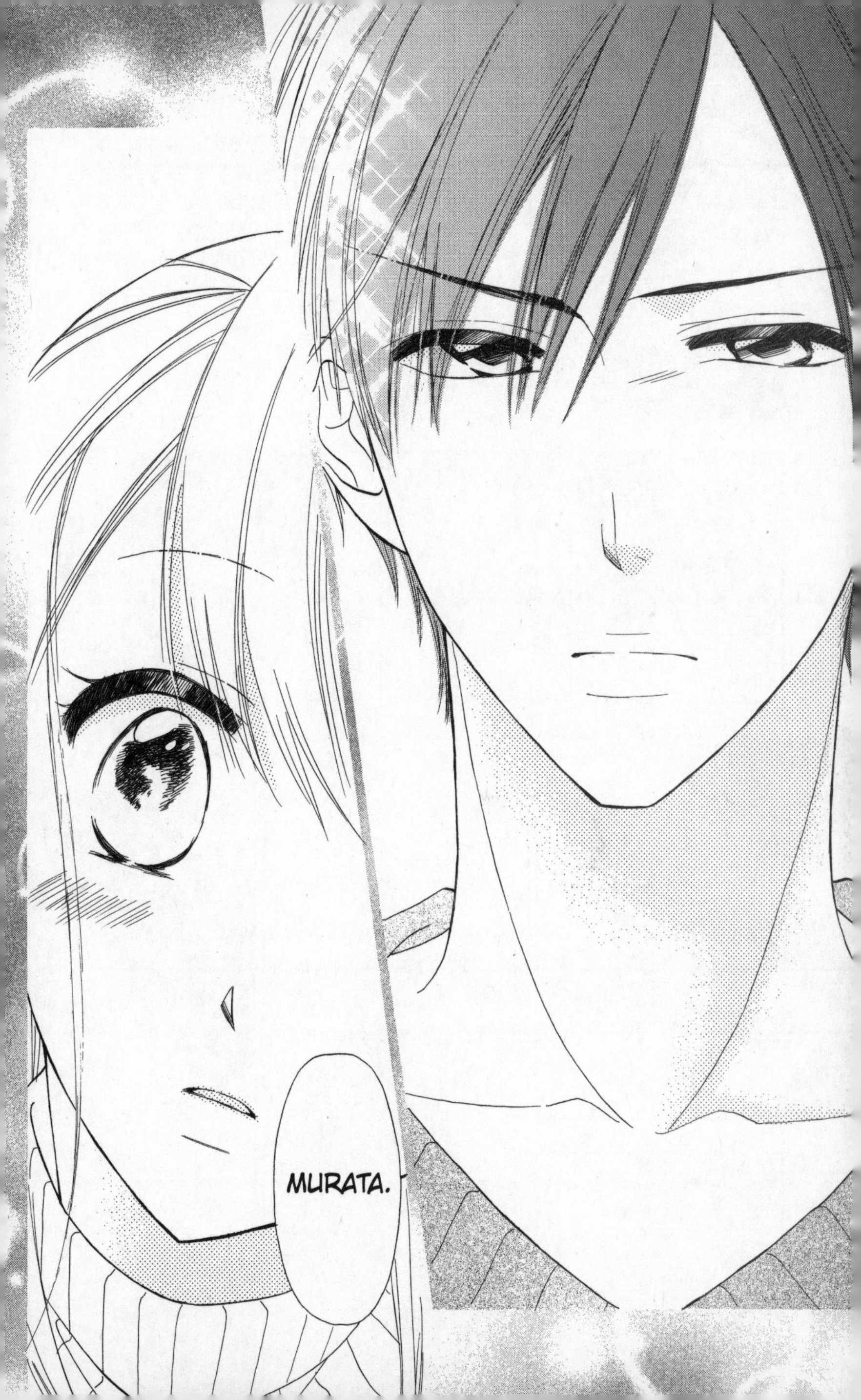
MURATA.

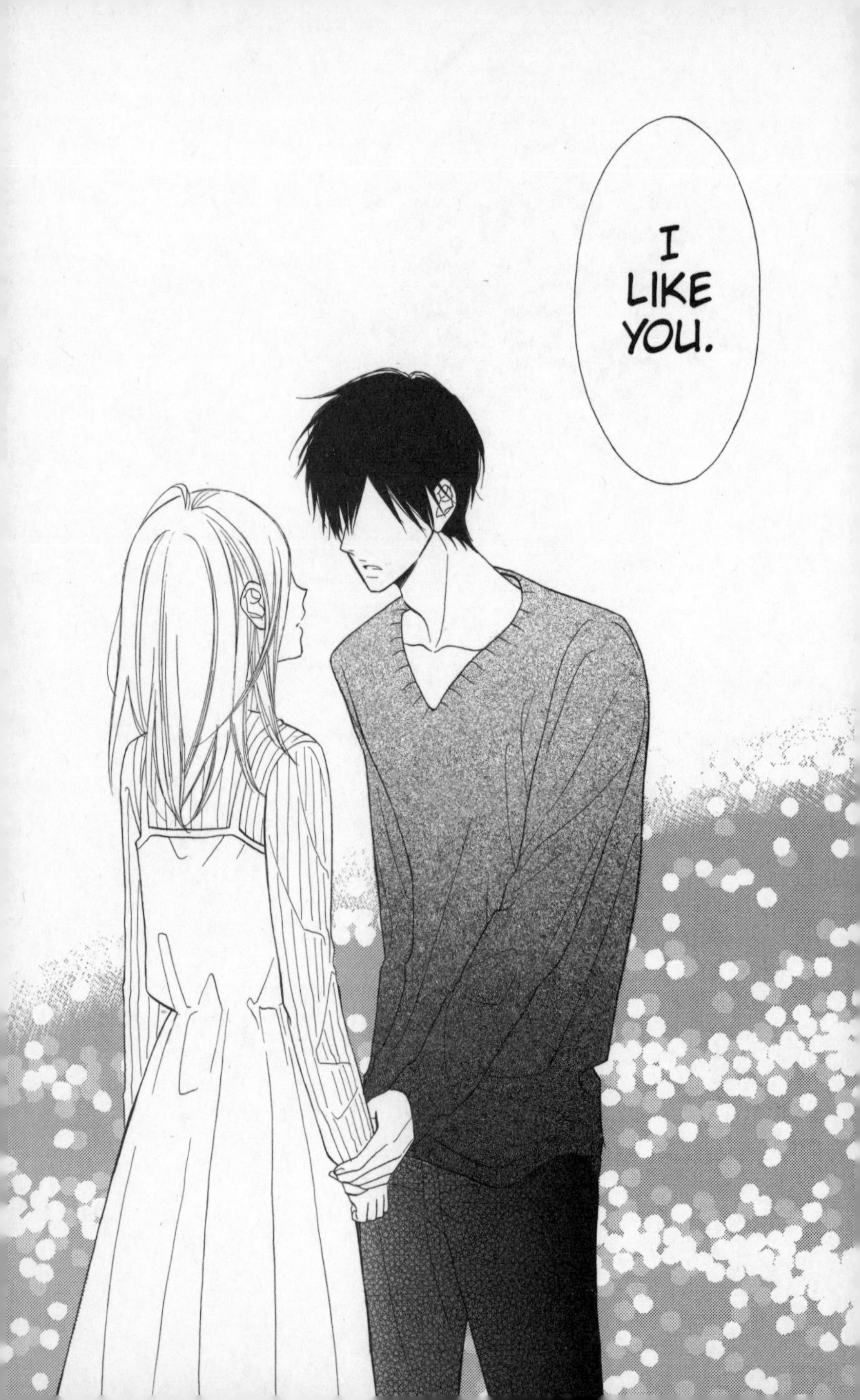
I LIKE YOU.

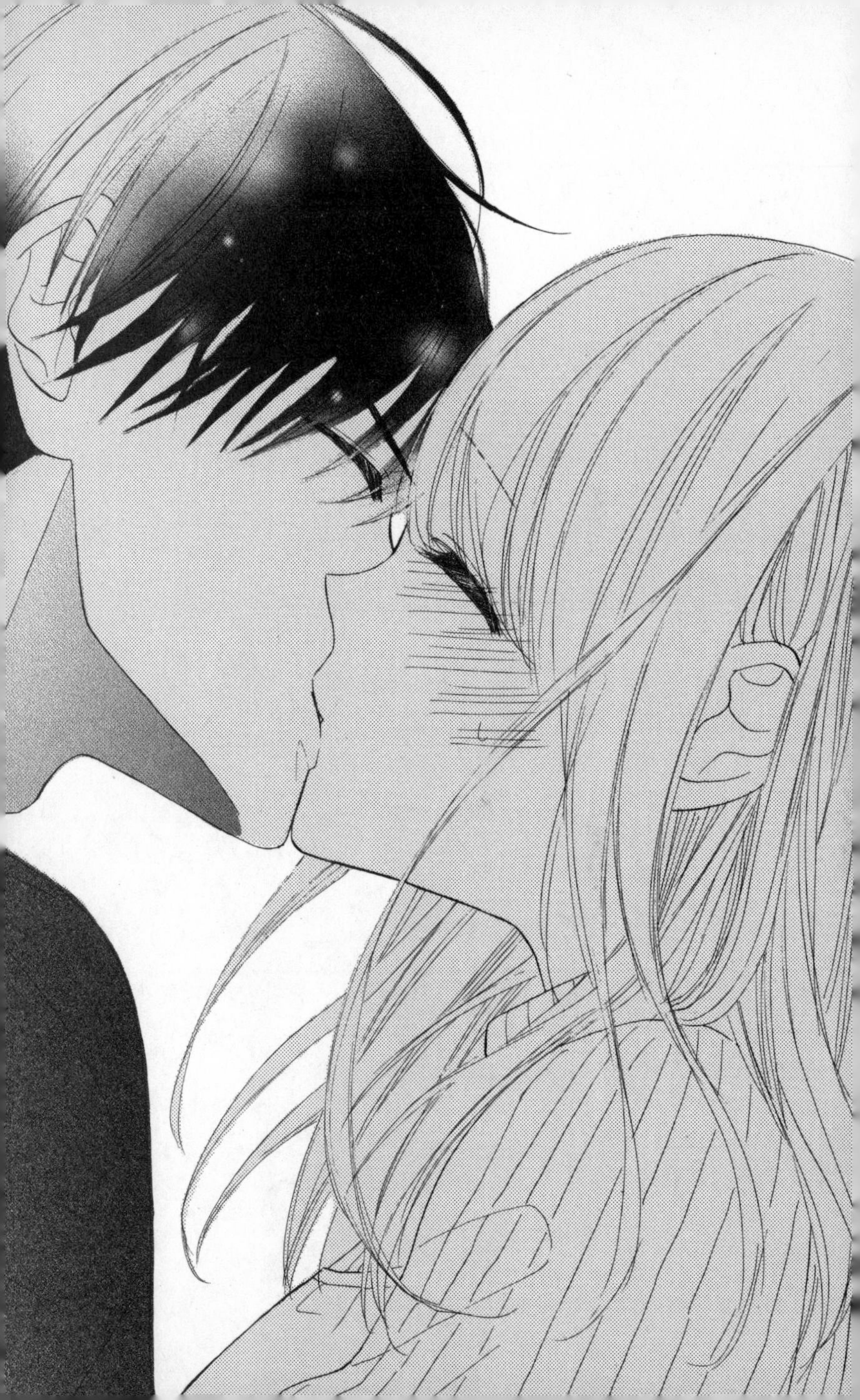

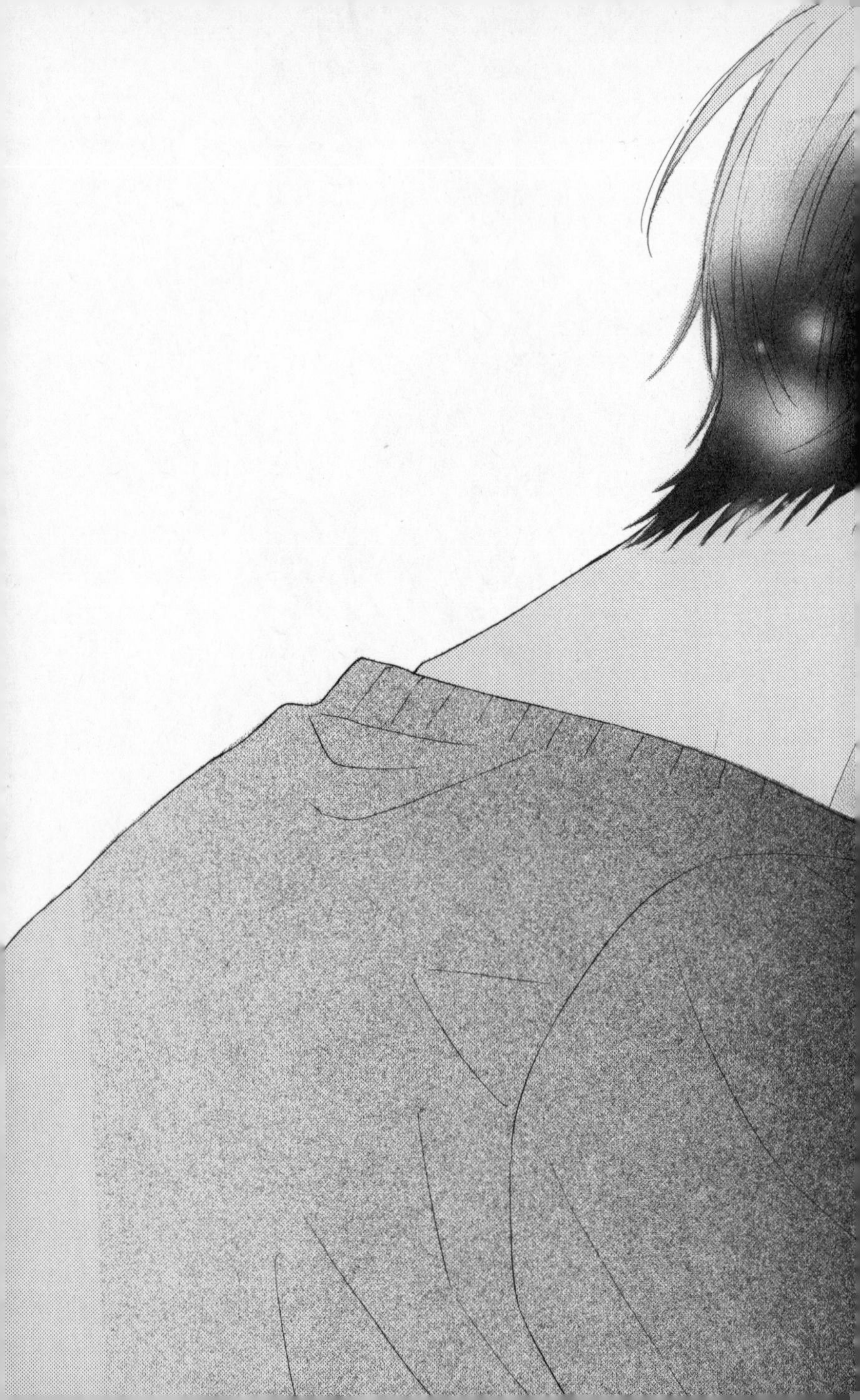

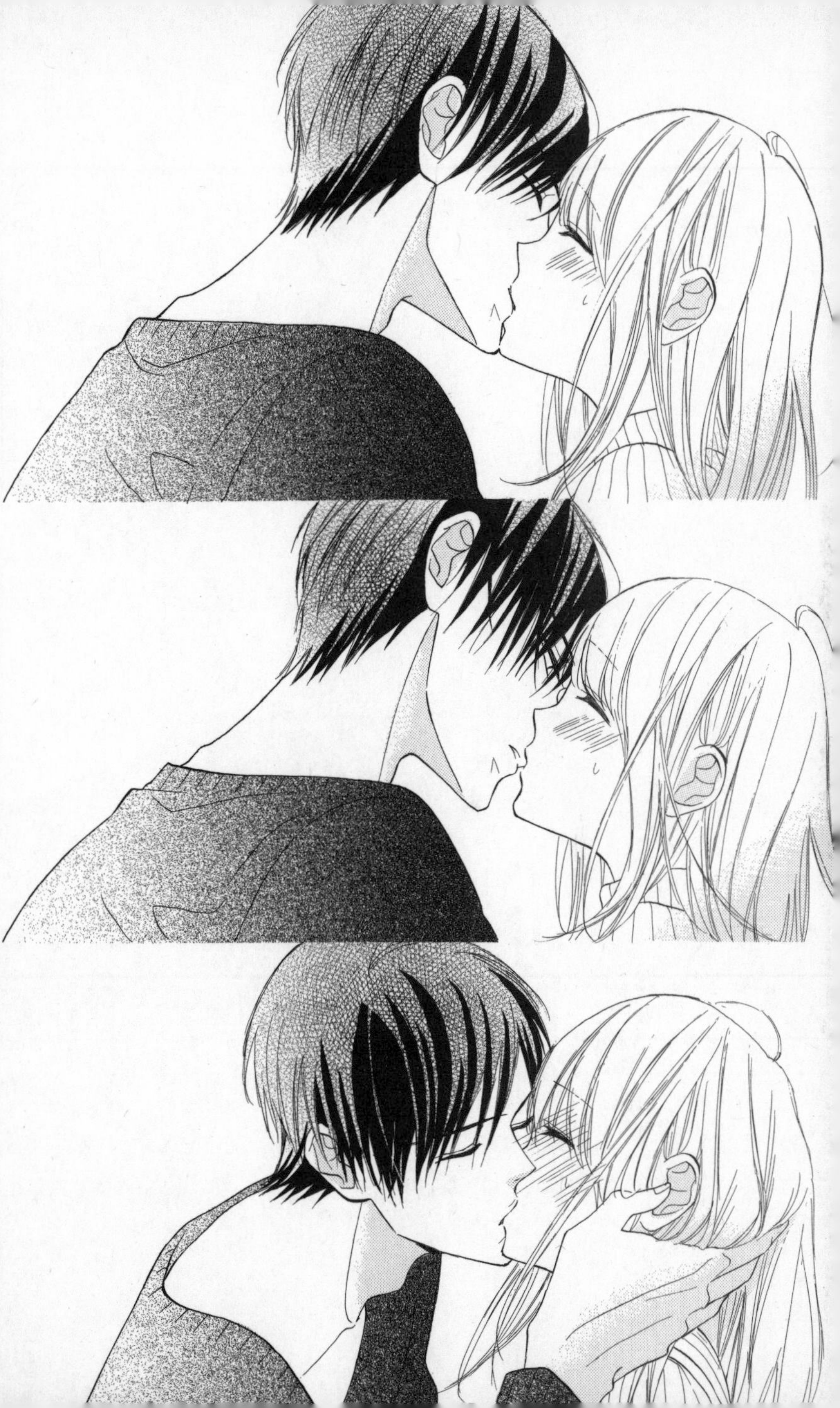

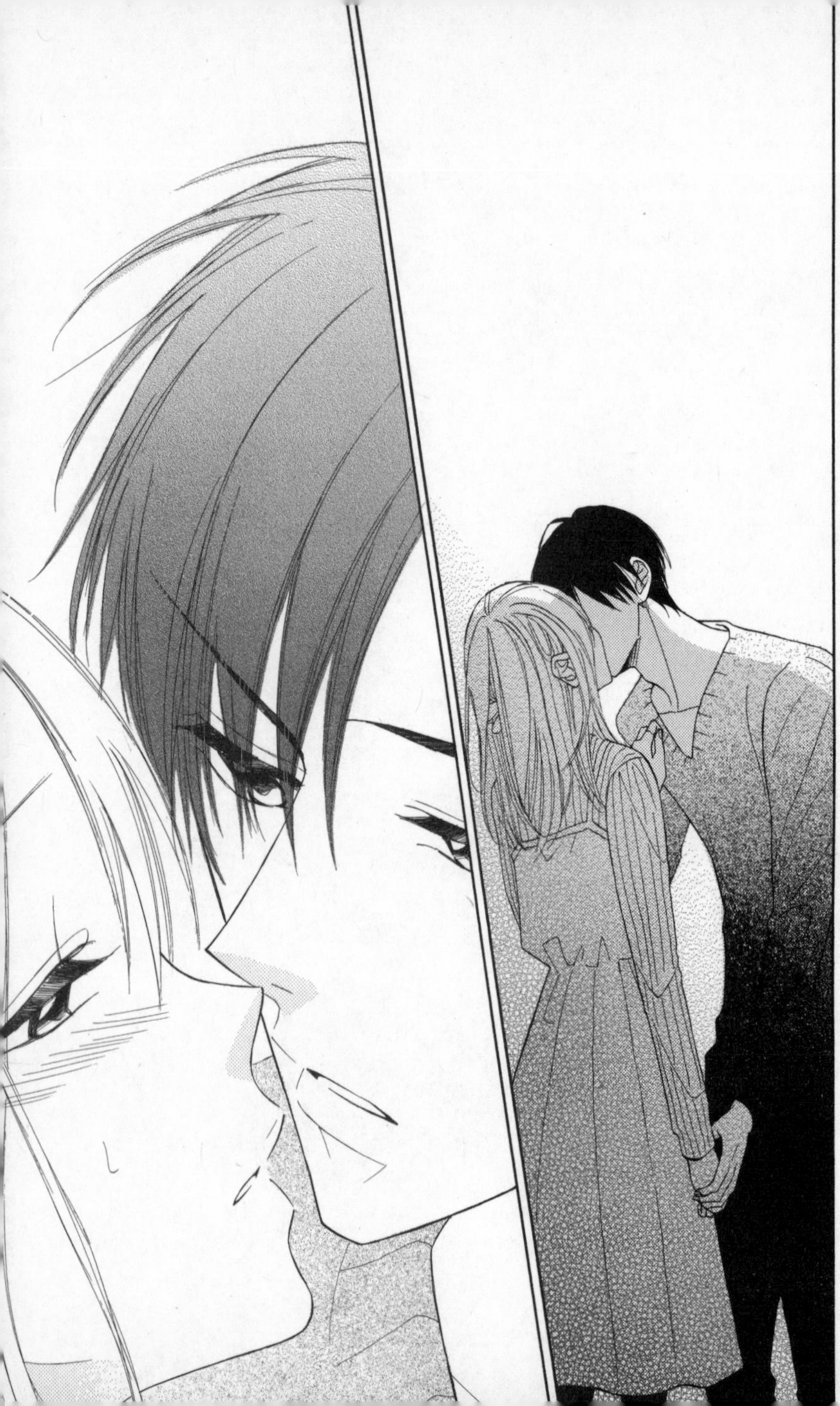

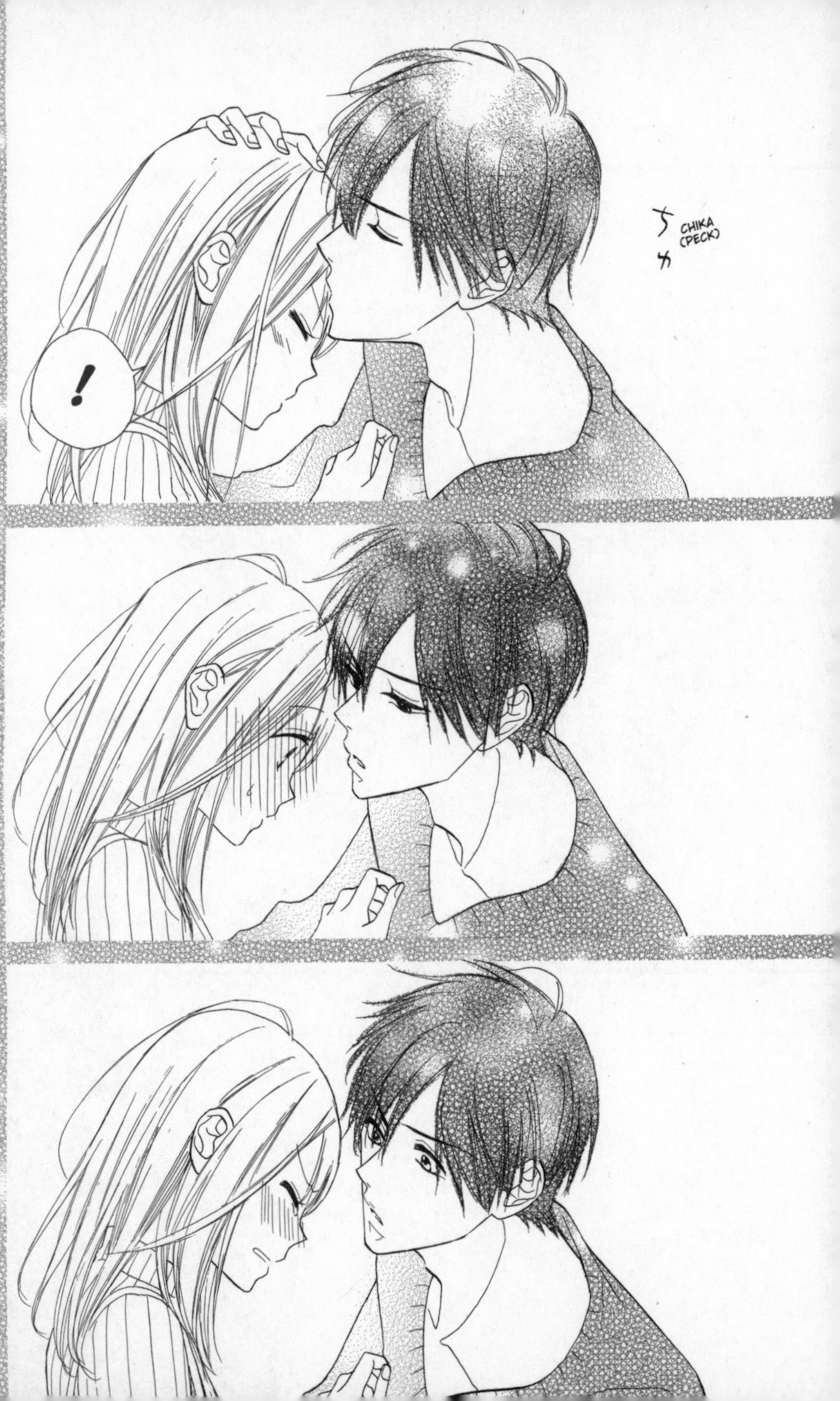
ちゅ
CHIKA (PECK)
!

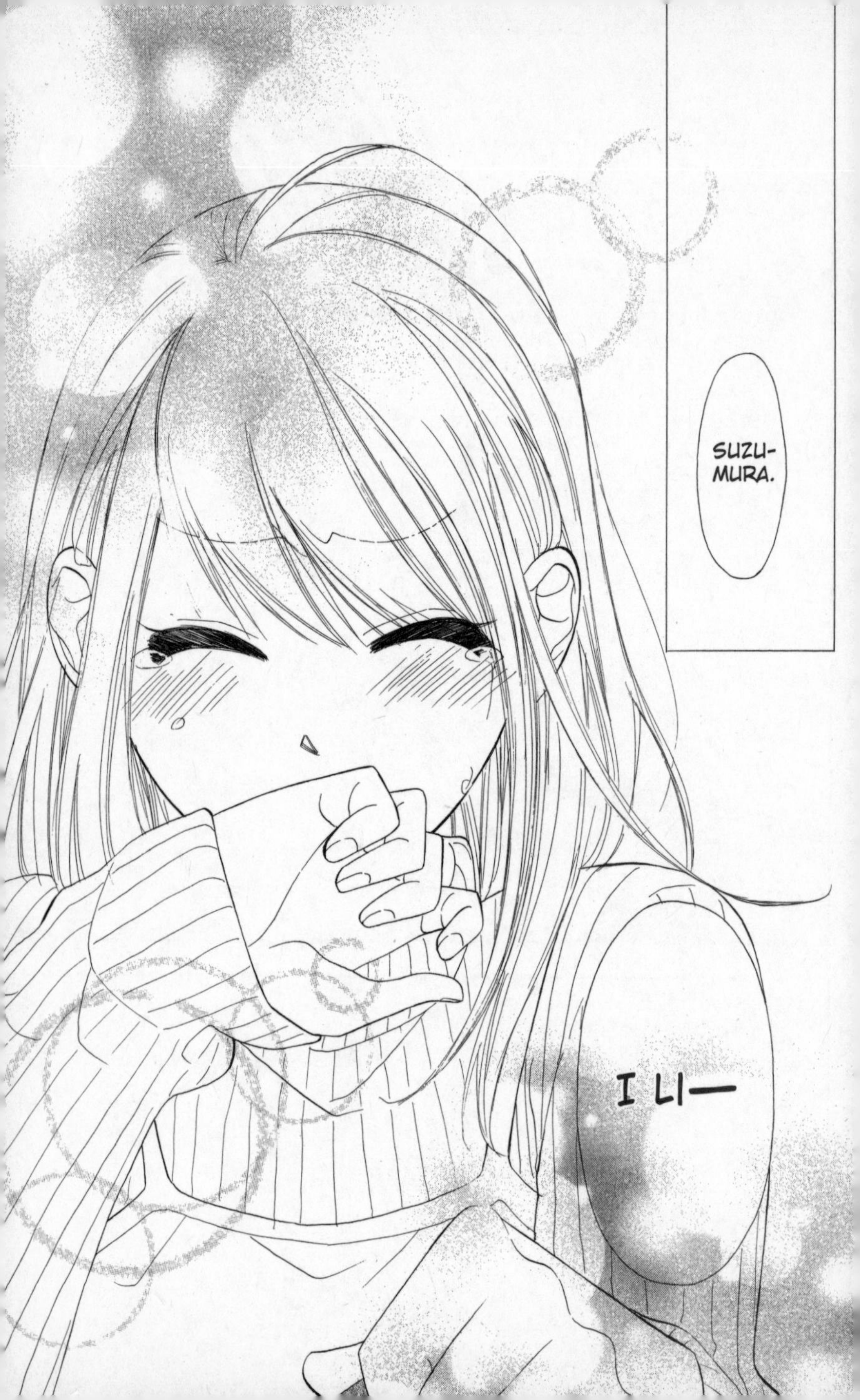
SUZU-
MURA.
I LI—

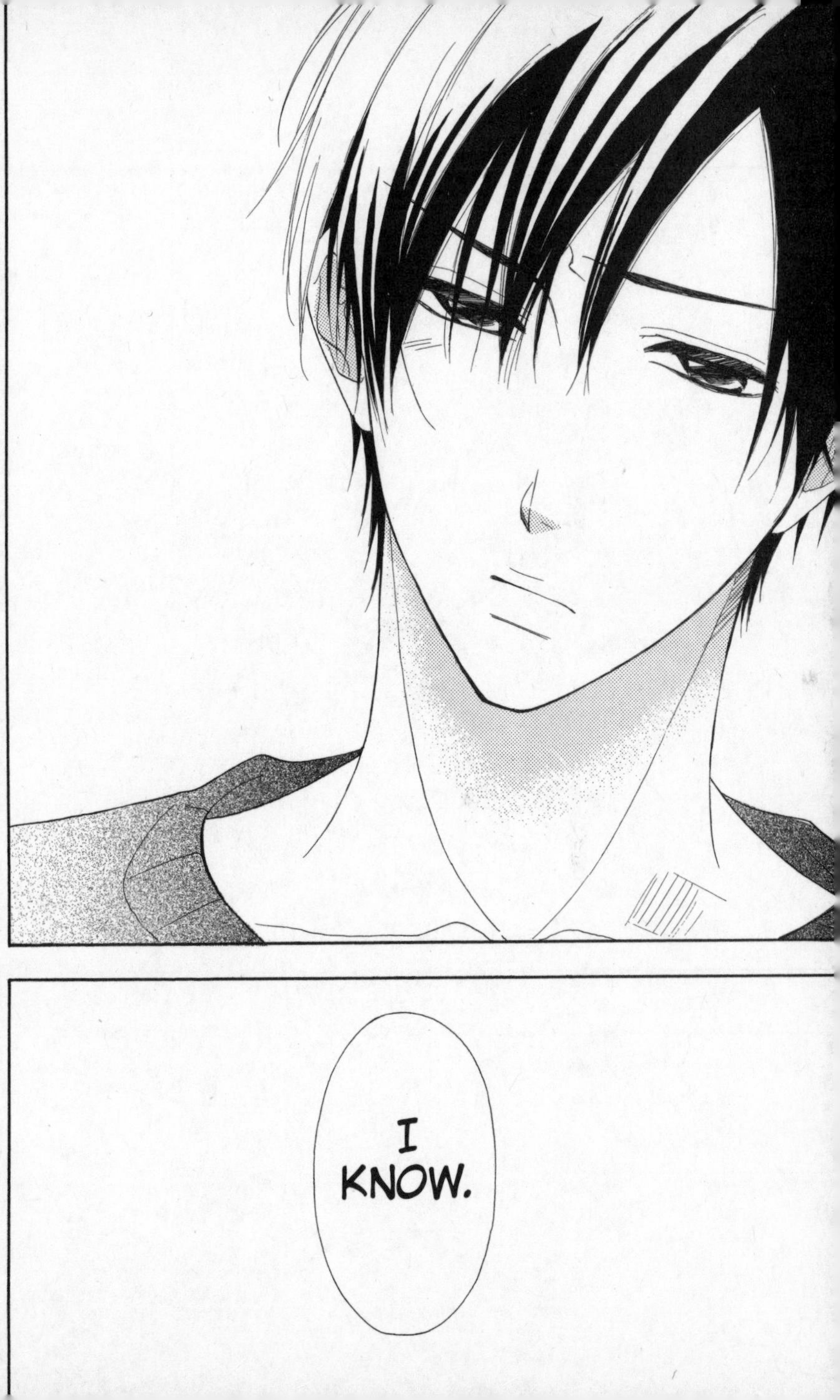
I KNOW.

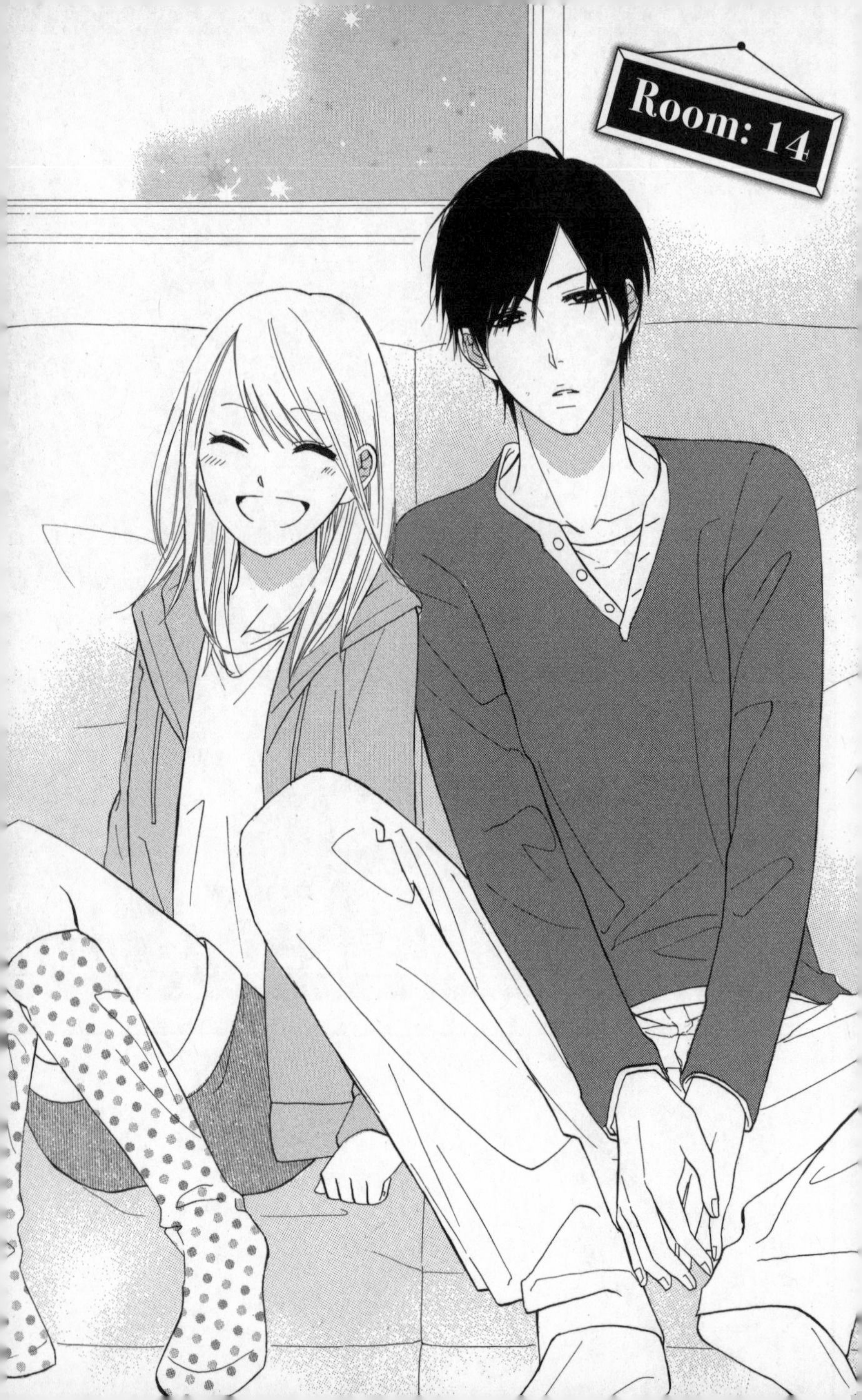
Room: 14

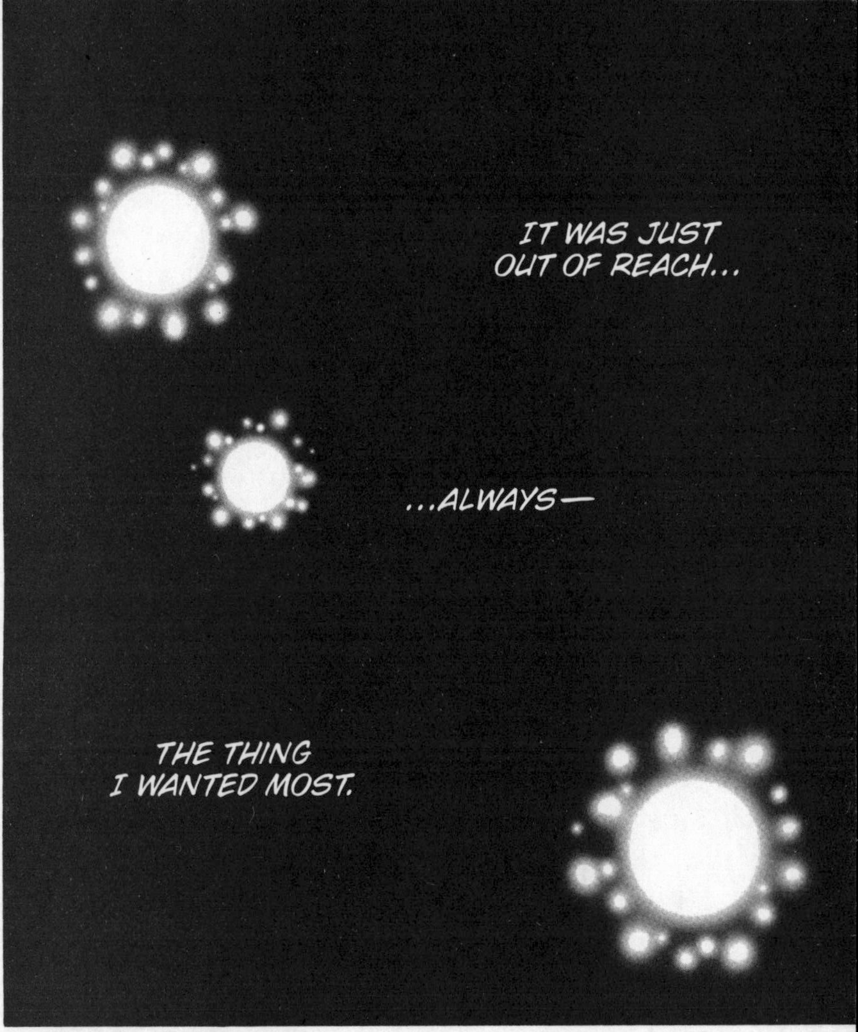
IT WAS JUST OUT OF REACH...
...ALWAYS—
THE THING I WANTED MOST.
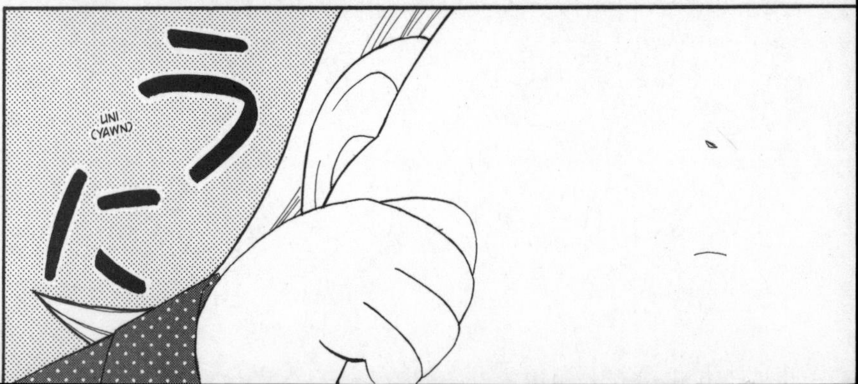
UNI (YAWN)

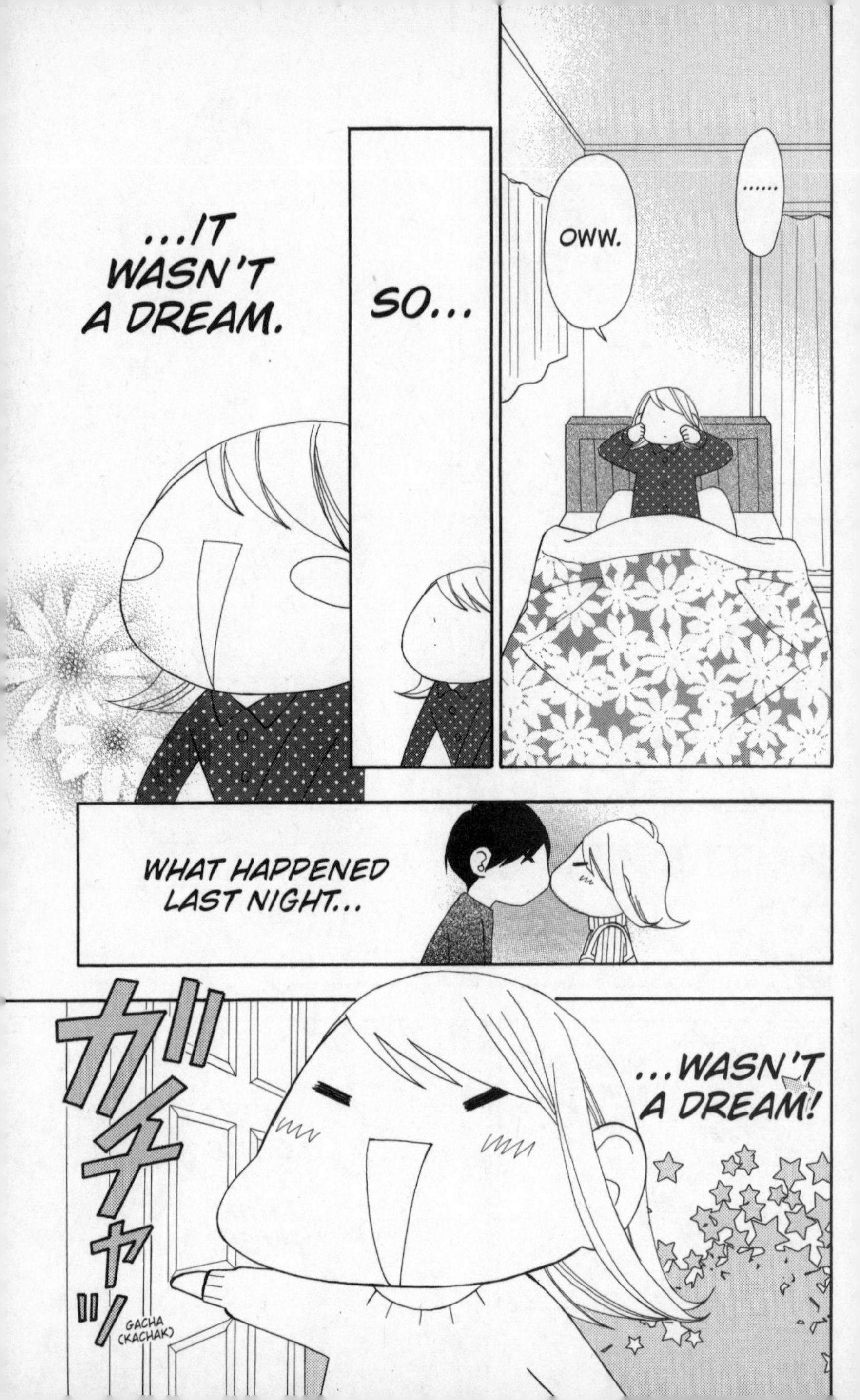
......
OWW.
SO...
...IT WASN'T A DREAM.
WHAT HAPPENED LAST NIGHT...
...WASN'T A DREAM!
ガチャッ!!
GACHA (KACHAK)

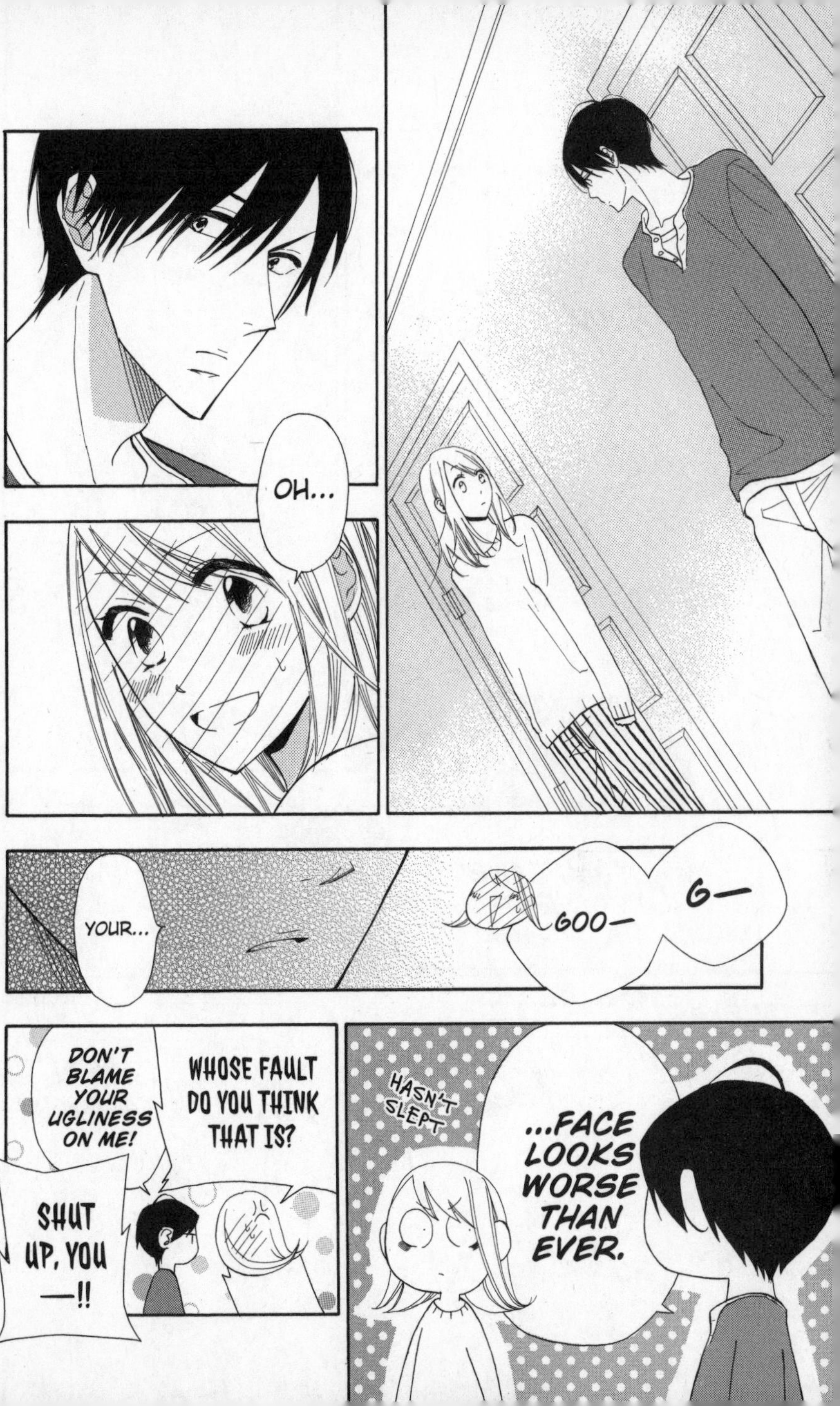
OH...
G—
GOO—
YOUR...
...FACE LOOKS WORSE THAN EVER.
HASN'T SLEPT
WHOSE FAULT DO YOU THINK THAT IS?
DON'T BLAME YOUR UGLINESS ON ME!
SHUT UP, YOU—!!

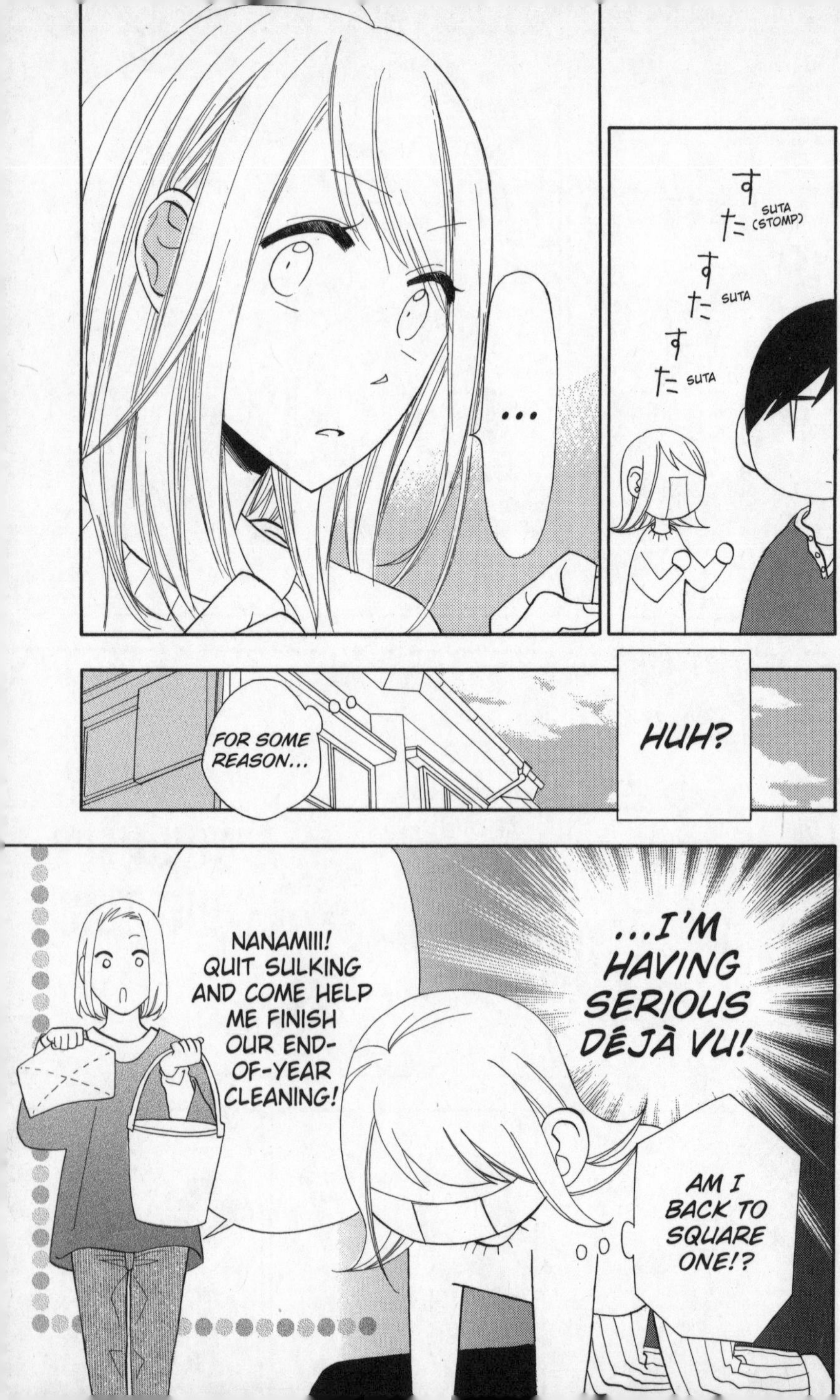

すたすたすた
SUTA (STOMP)
SUTA
SUTA
...
HUH?
FOR SOME REASON...
...I'M HAVING SERIOUS DÉJÀ VU!
NANAMIII! QUIT SULKING AND COME HELP ME FINISH OUR END-OF-YEAR CLEANING!
AM I BACK TO SQUARE ONE!?

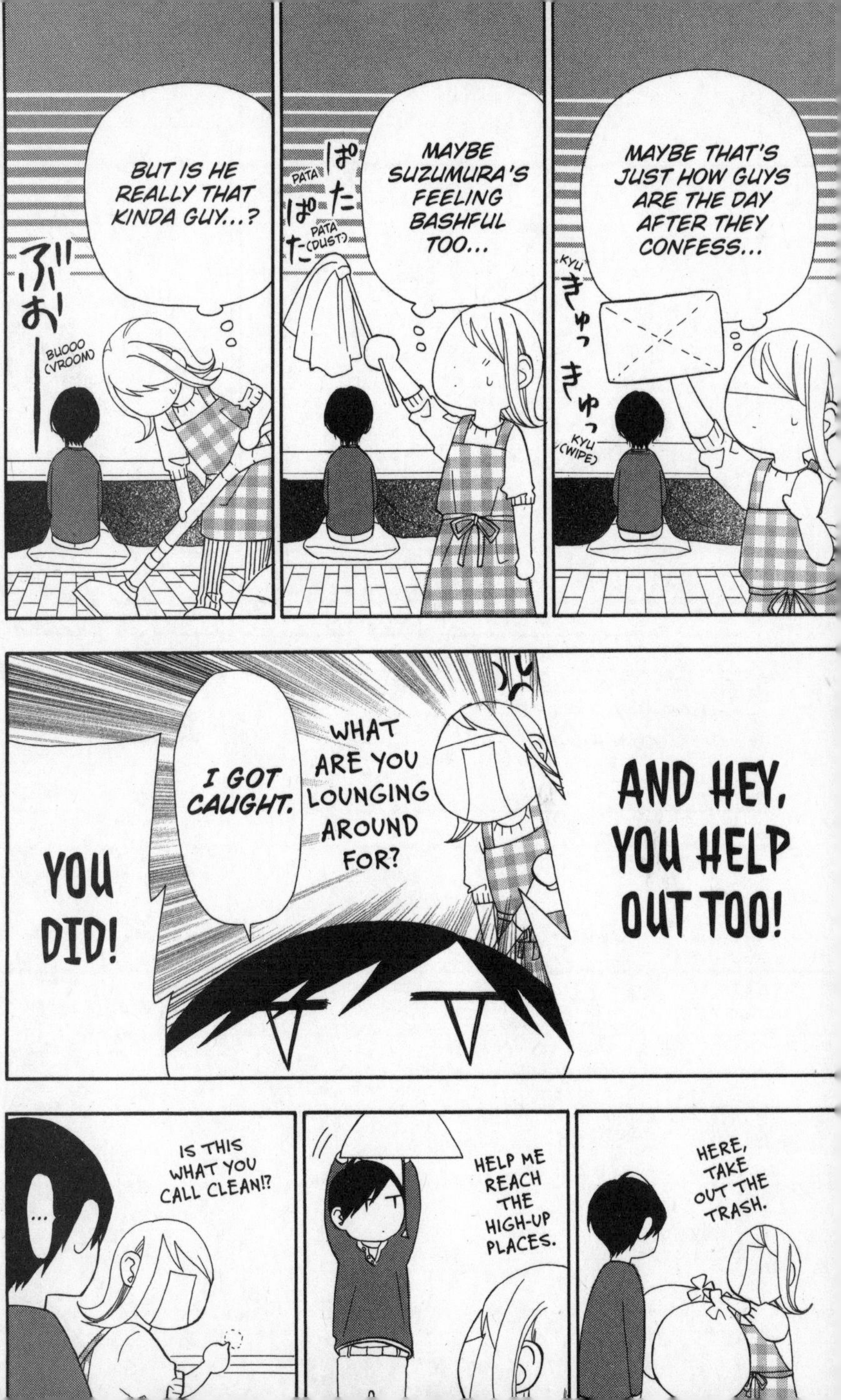
MAYBE THAT'S JUST HOW GUYS ARE THE DAY AFTER THEY CONFESS...
きゅっ
KYU
きゅっ
KYU (WIPE)
MAYBE SUZUMURA'S FEELING BASHFUL TOO...
ぱた
PATA
ぱた
PATA (DUST)
BUT IS HE REALLY THAT KINDA GUY...?
ぶぉー
BUOOO (VROOM)
AND HEY, YOU HELP OUT TOO!
WHAT ARE YOU LOUNGING AROUND FOR?
I GOT CAUGHT.
YOU DID!
HERE, TAKE OUT THE TRASH.
HELP ME REACH THE HIGH-UP PLACES.
IS THIS WHAT YOU CALL CLEAN!?
...

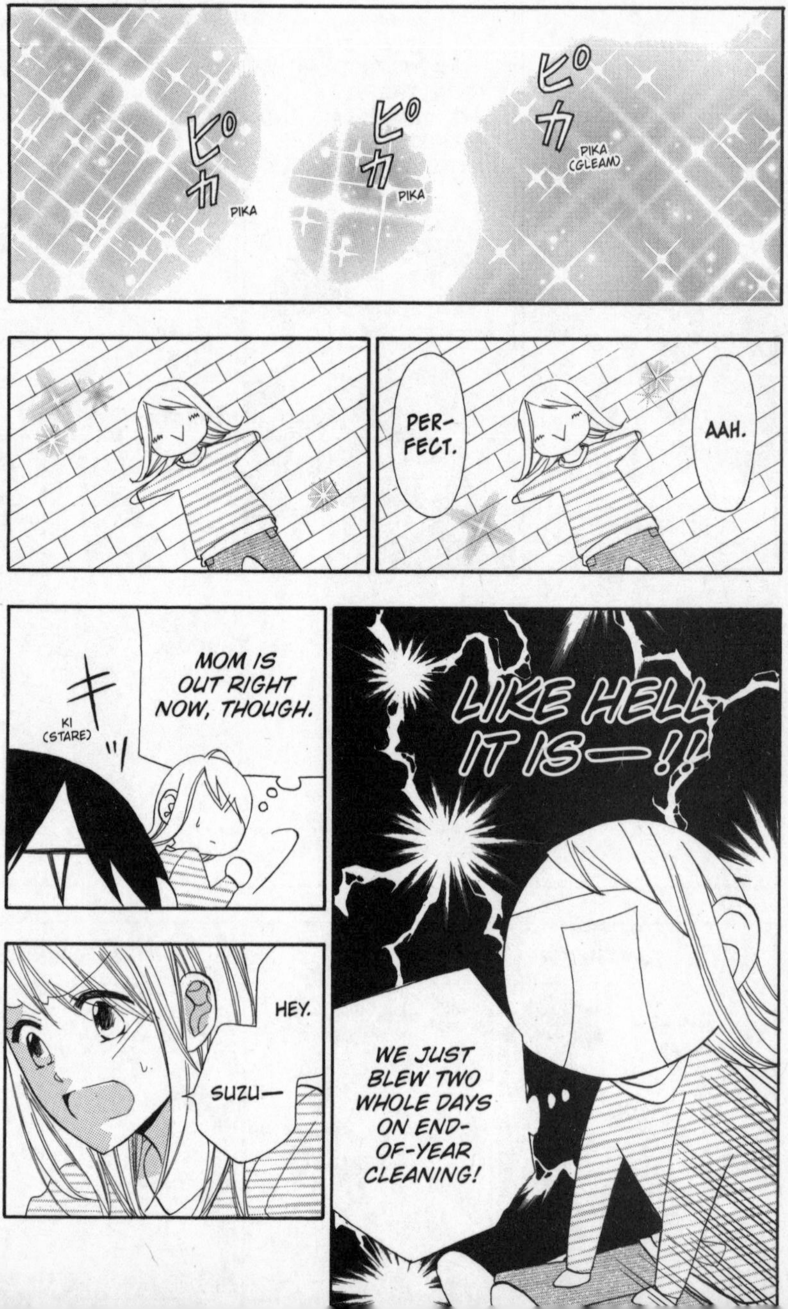
ピカ
PIKA (GLEAM)
ピカ
PIKA
ピカ
PIKA
AAH.
PER-FECT.
LIKE HELL IT IS—!!
WE JUST BLEW TWO WHOLE DAYS ON END-OF-YEAR CLEANING!
MOM IS OUT RIGHT NOW, THOUGH.
キ
KI (STARE)
HEY.
SUZU—

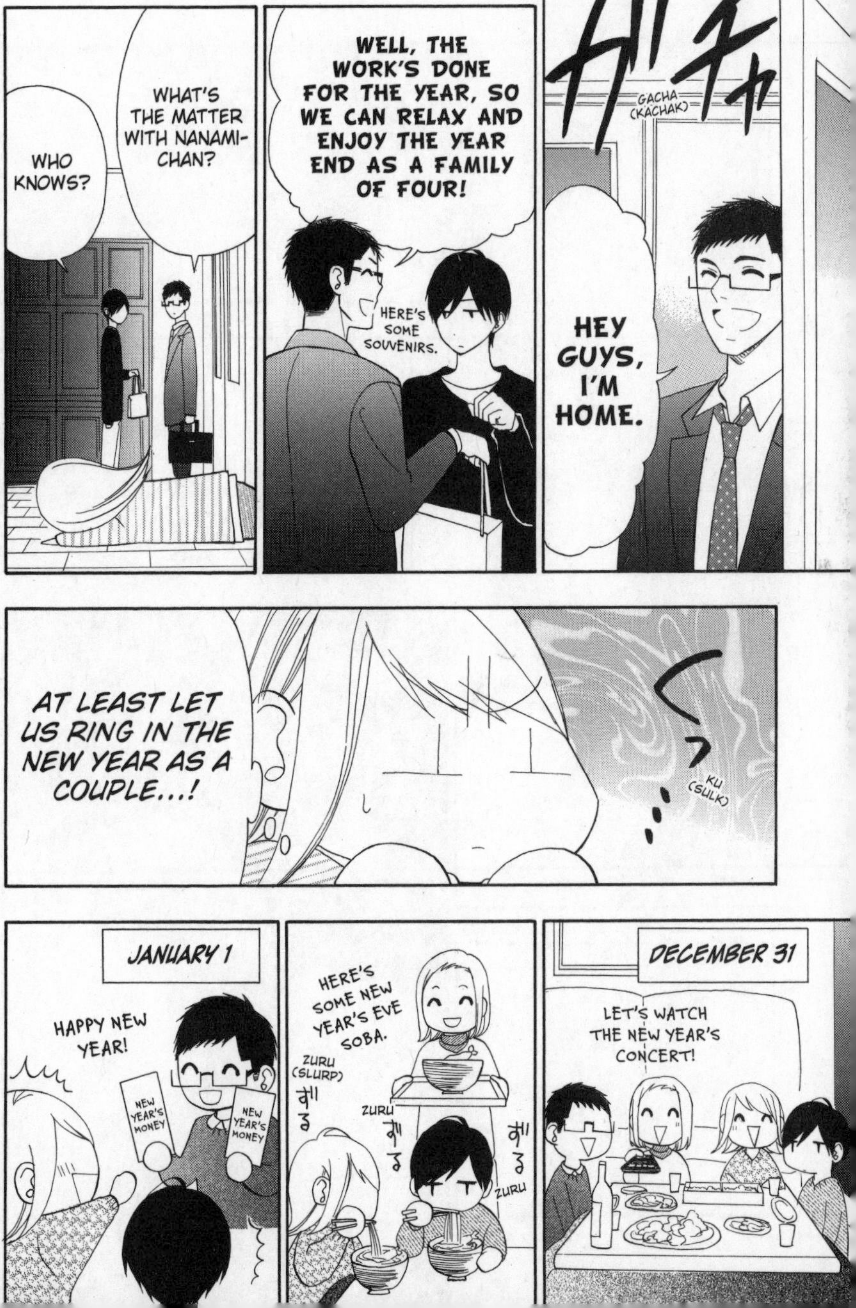
ガチャ
GACHA (KACHAK)
HEY GUYS, I'M HOME.
WELL, THE WORK'S DONE FOR THE YEAR, SO WE CAN RELAX AND ENJOY THE YEAR END AS A FAMILY OF FOUR!
HERE'S SOME SOUVENIRS.
WHAT'S THE MATTER WITH NANAMI-CHAN?
WHO KNOWS?
くっ
KU (SULK)
AT LEAST LET US RING IN THE NEW YEAR AS A COUPLE...!
DECEMBER 31
LET'S WATCH THE NEW YEAR'S CONCERT!
HERE'S SOME NEW YEAR'S EVE SOBA.
ずる
ZURU
ずる
ZURU
ずる
ZURU (SLURP)
JANUARY 1
HAPPY NEW YEAR!
NEW YEAR'S MONEY
NEW YEAR'S MONEY

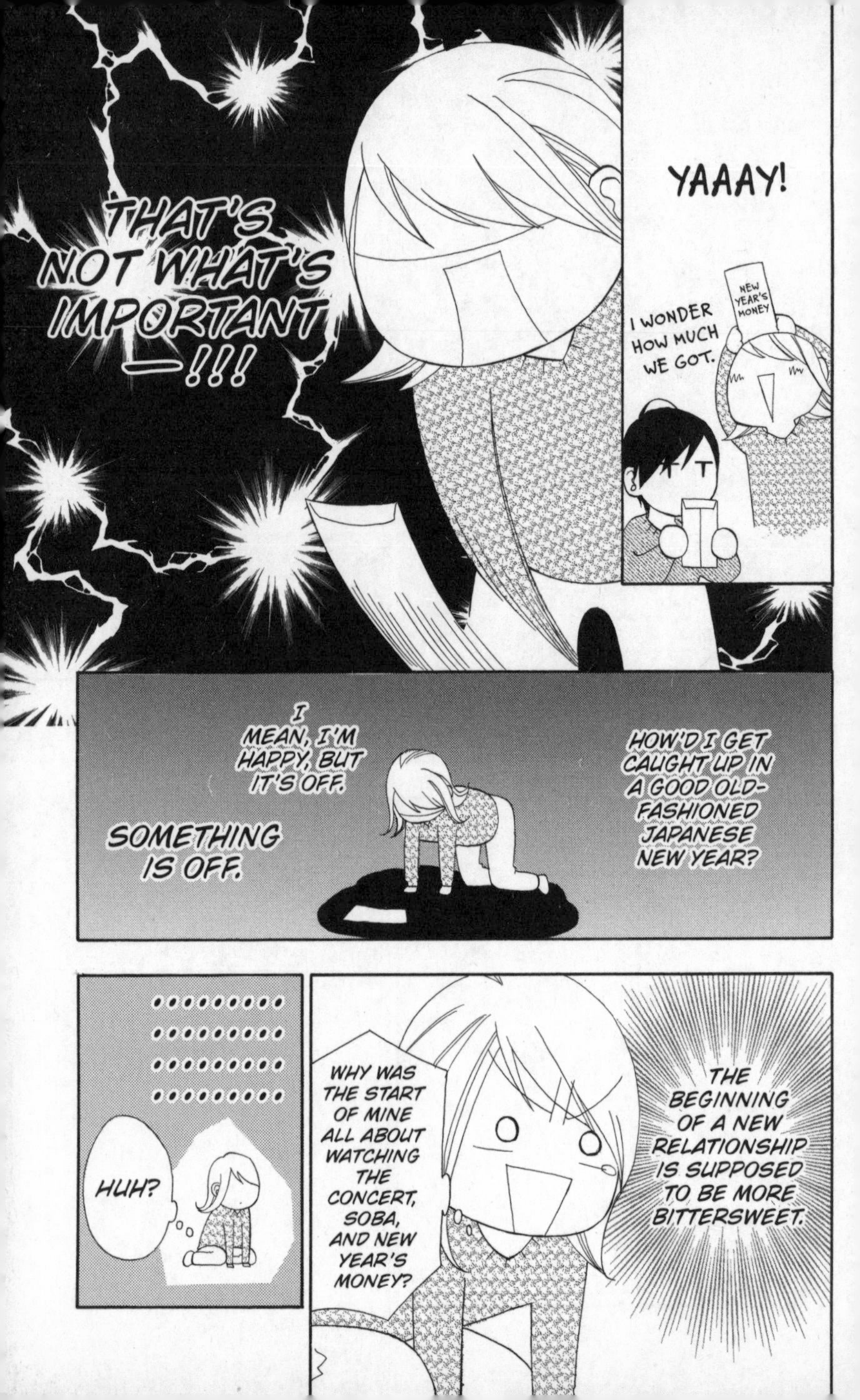
YAAAY!
NEW YEAR'S MONEY
I WONDER HOW MUCH WE GOT.
THAT'S NOT WHAT'S IMPORTANT—!!!
HOW'D I GET CAUGHT UP IN A GOOD OLD-FASHIONED JAPANESE NEW YEAR?
I MEAN, I'M HAPPY, BUT IT'S OFF.
SOMETHING IS OFF.
THE BEGINNING OF A NEW RELATIONSHIP IS SUPPOSED TO BE MORE BITTERSWEET.
WHY WAS THE START OF MINE ALL ABOUT WATCHING THE CONCERT, SOBA, AND NEW YEAR'S MONEY?
....
....
....
....
HUH?

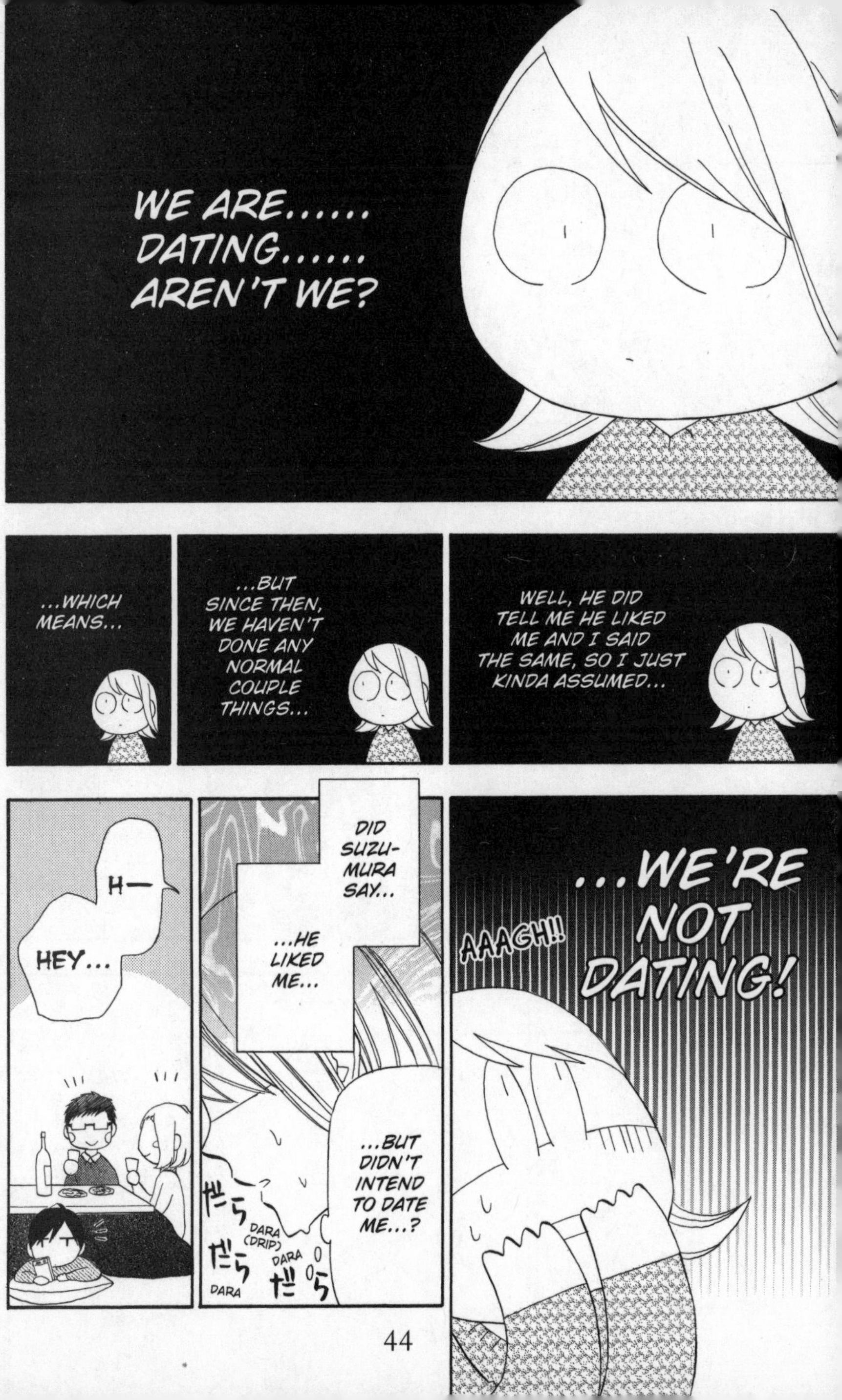
WE ARE...... DATING...... AREN'T WE?
WELL, HE DID TELL ME HE LIKED ME AND I SAID THE SAME, SO I JUST KINDA ASSUMED...
...BUT SINCE THEN, WE HAVEN'T DONE ANY NORMAL COUPLE THINGS...
...WHICH MEANS...
...WE'RE NOT DATING!
AAAGH!!
DID SUZUMURA SAY...
...HE LIKED ME...
...BUT DIDN'T INTEND TO DATE ME...?
だら
DARA (DRIP)
だら
DARA
だら
DARA
H—
HEY...

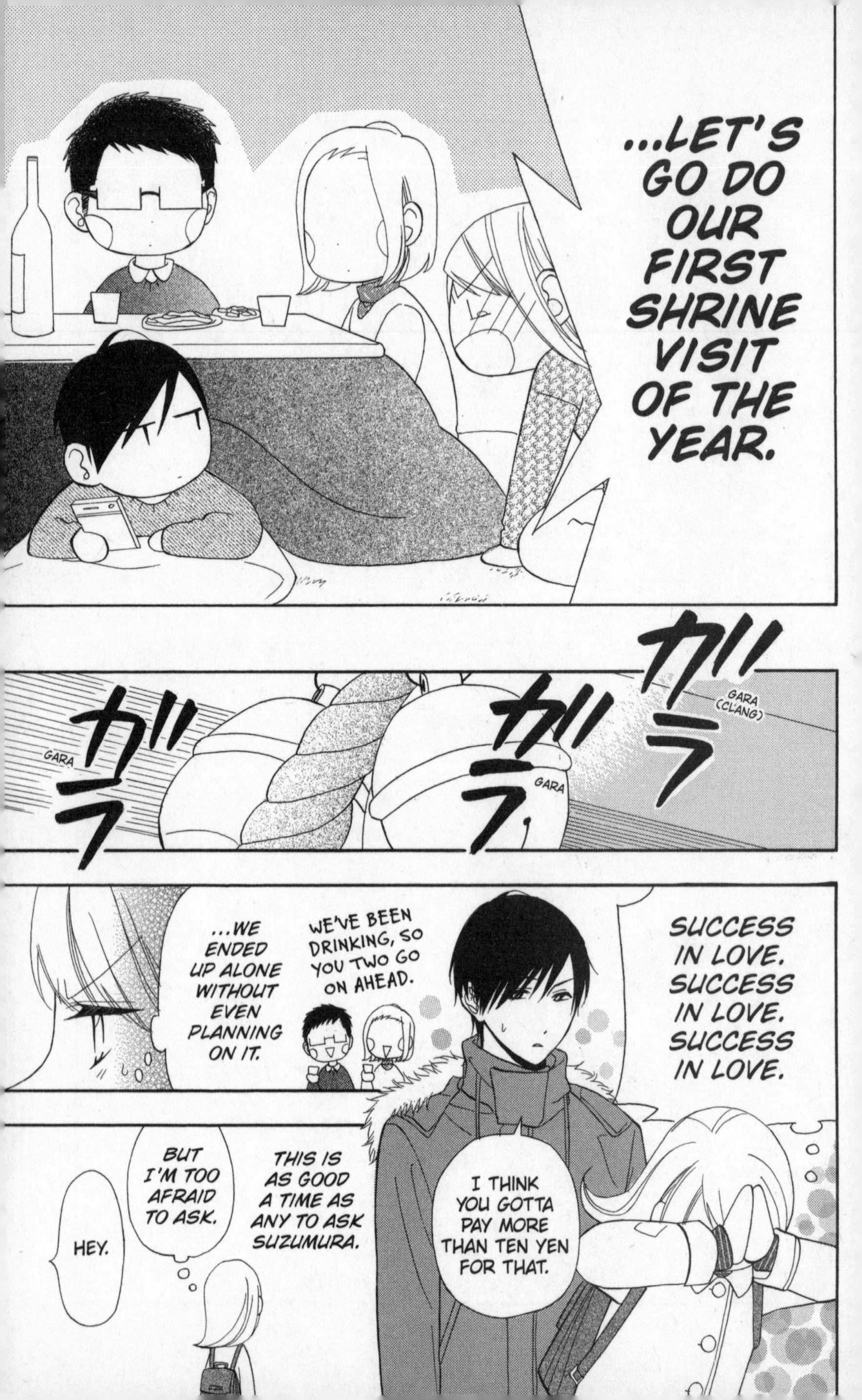
...LET'S GO DO OUR FIRST SHRINE VISIT OF THE YEAR.
GARA (CLANG)
GARA
GARA
SUCCESS IN LOVE. SUCCESS IN LOVE. SUCCESS IN LOVE.
WE'VE BEEN DRINKING, SO YOU TWO GO ON AHEAD.
...WE ENDED UP ALONE WITHOUT EVEN PLANNING ON IT.
I THINK YOU GOTTA PAY MORE THAN TEN YEN FOR THAT.
THIS IS AS GOOD A TIME AS ANY TO ASK SUZUMURA.
BUT I'M TOO AFRAID TO ASK.
HEY.

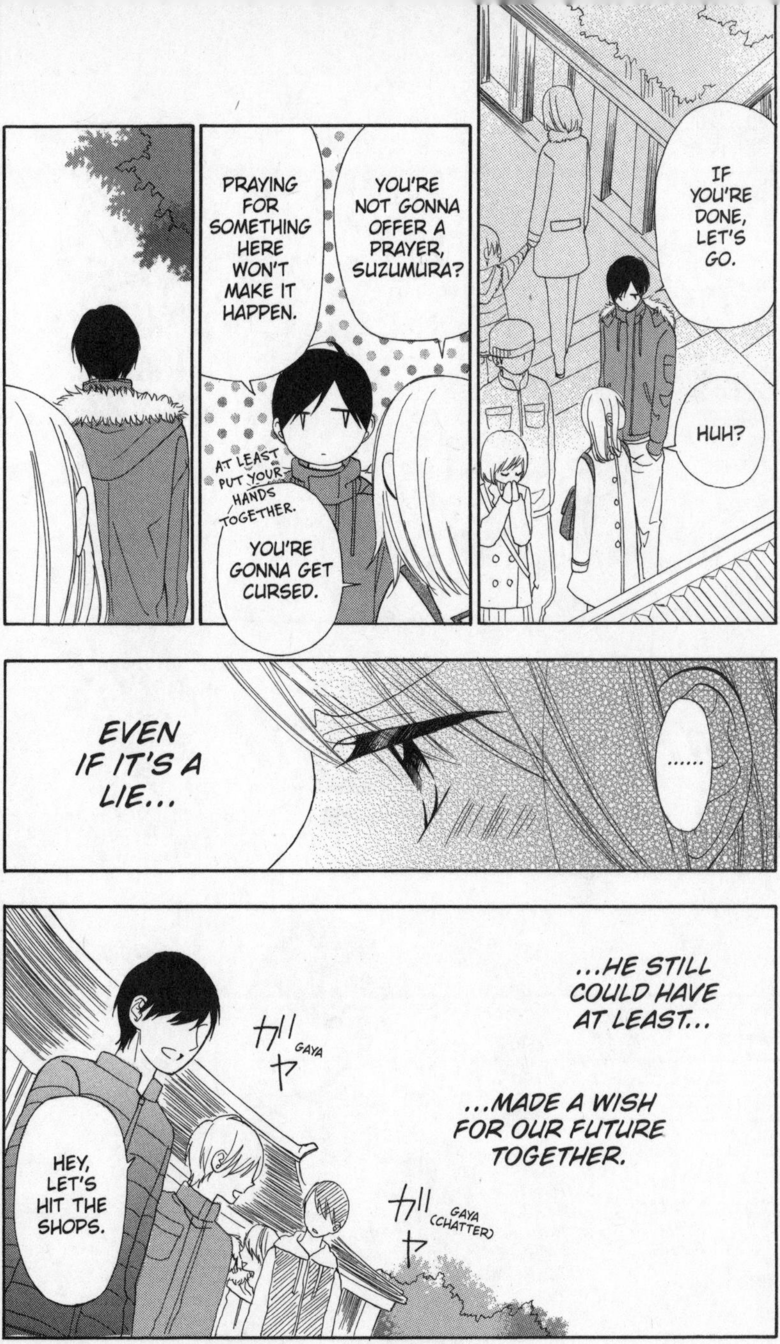
IF YOU'RE DONE, LET'S GO.
HUH?
YOU'RE NOT GONNA OFFER A PRAYER, SUZUMURA?
PRAYING FOR SOMETHING HERE WON'T MAKE IT HAPPEN.
AT LEAST PUT YOUR HANDS TOGETHER.
YOU'RE GONNA GET CURSED.
......
EVEN IF IT'S A LIE...
...HE STILL COULD HAVE AT LEAST...
...MADE A WISH FOR OUR FUTURE TOGETHER.
ガヤ GAYA
ガヤ GAYA (CHATTER)
HEY, LET'S HIT THE SHOPS.

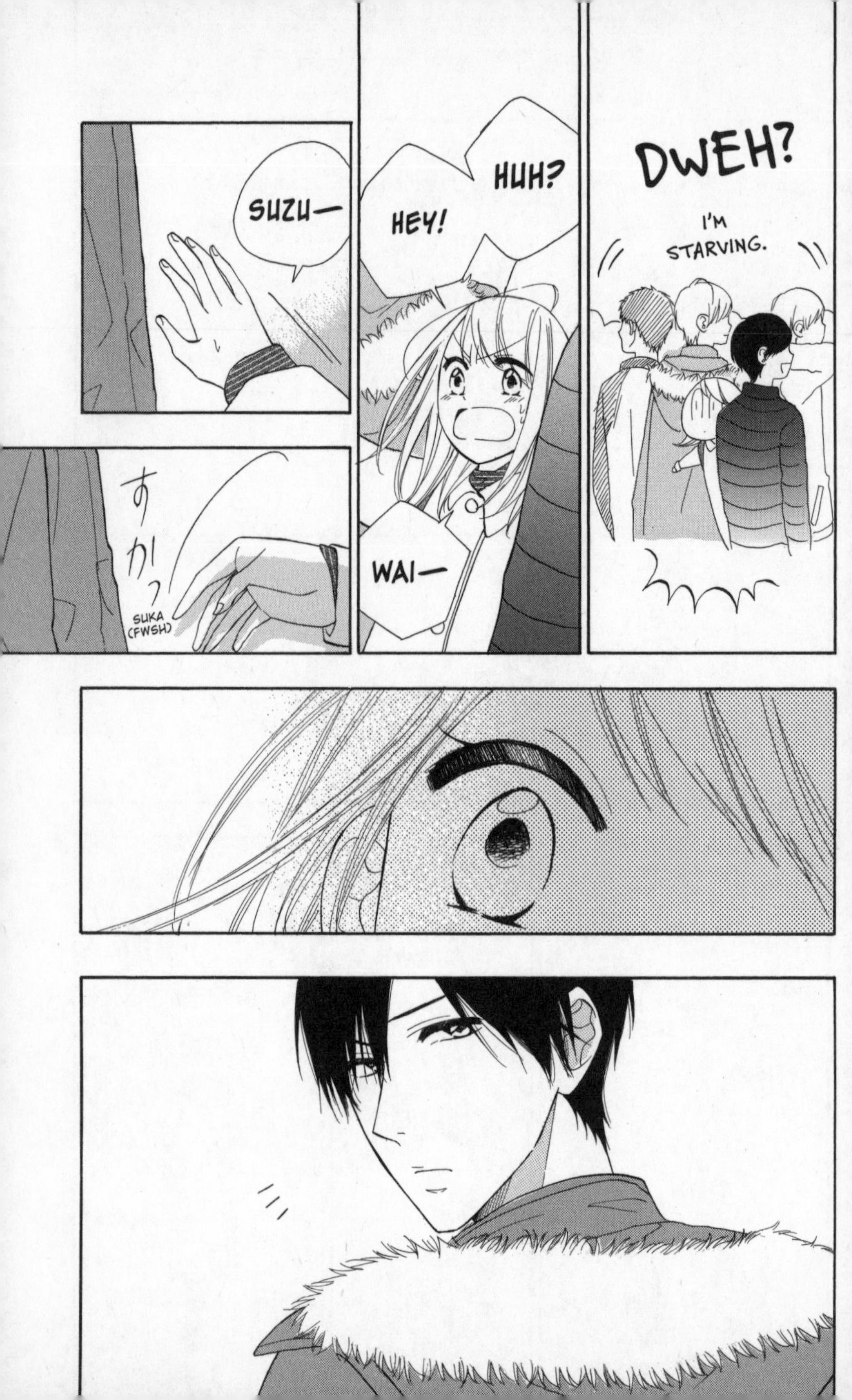
DWEH?
I'M STARVING.
HUH?
HEY!
WAI—
SUZU—
すかっ
SUKA (FWSH)

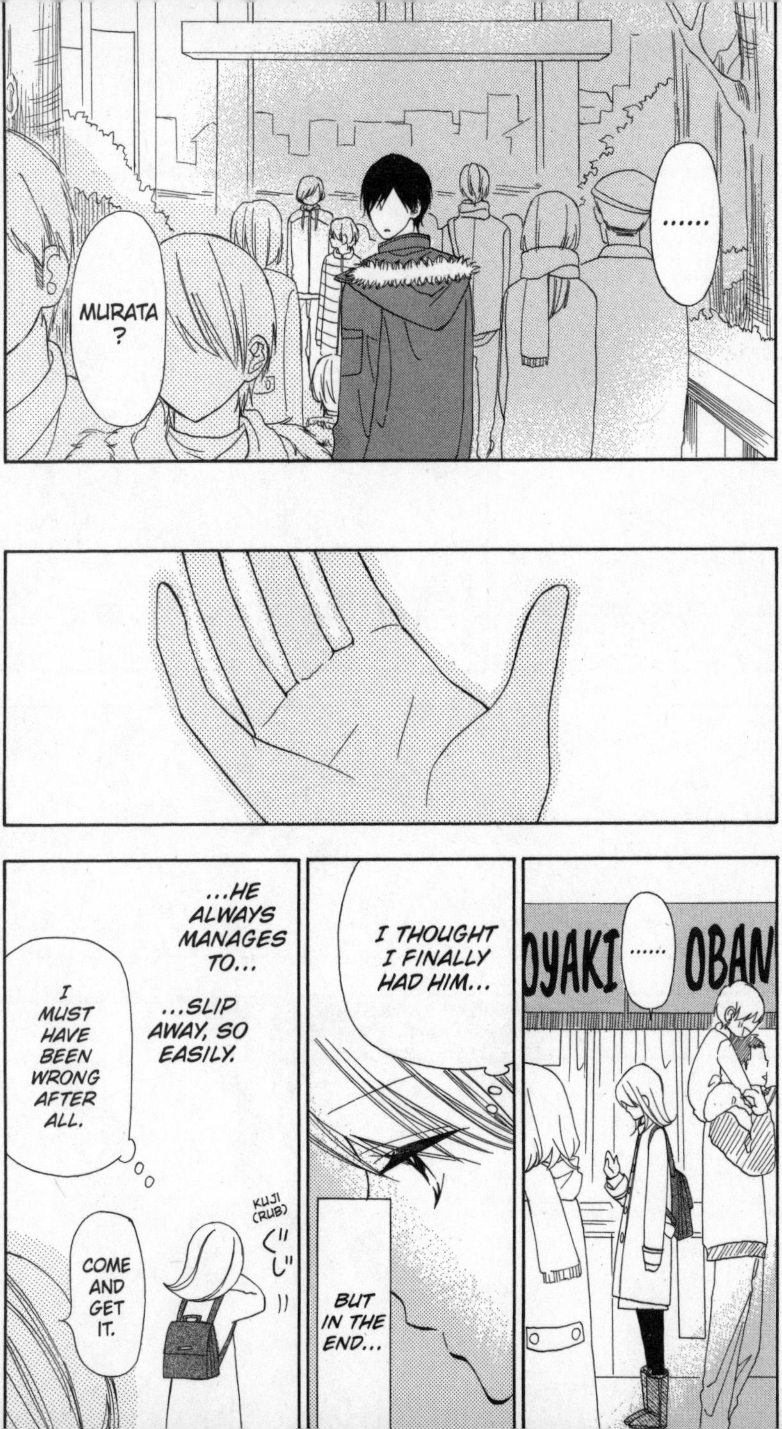
......
MURATA?
......
DYAKI OBAN
I THOUGHT I FINALLY HAD HIM...
BUT IN THE END...
...HE ALWAYS MANAGES TO...
...SLIP AWAY, SO EASILY.
I MUST HAVE BEEN WRONG AFTER ALL.
KUJI (RUB)
ぐじ
COME AND GET IT.

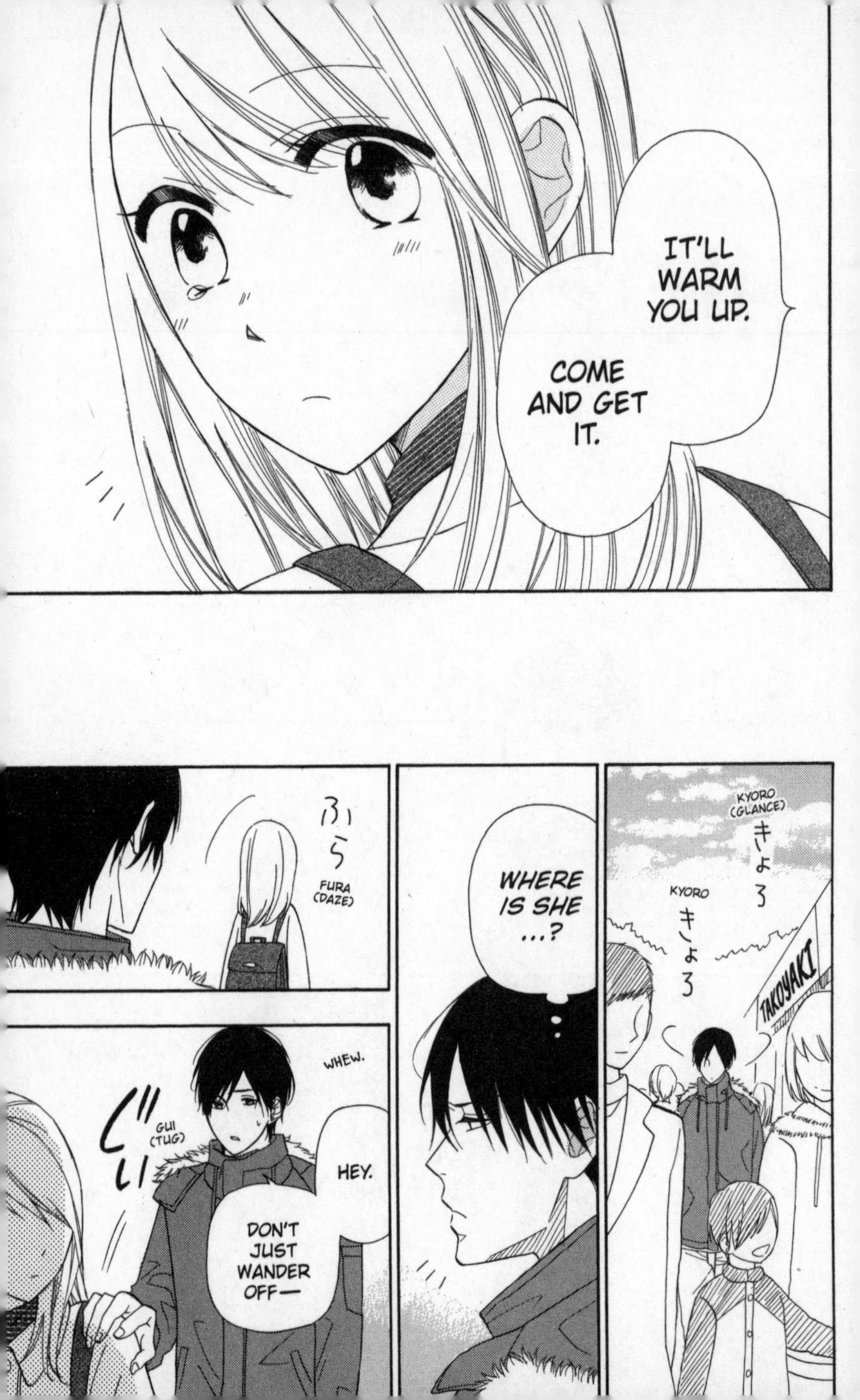
IT'LL WARM YOU UP.
COME AND GET IT.
KYORO (GLANCE)
きょろ
KYORO
きょろ
TAKOYAKI
WHERE IS SHE ...?
ふら
FURA (DAZE)
WHEW.
HEY.
GUI (TUG)
ぐい
DON'T JUST WANDER OFF—

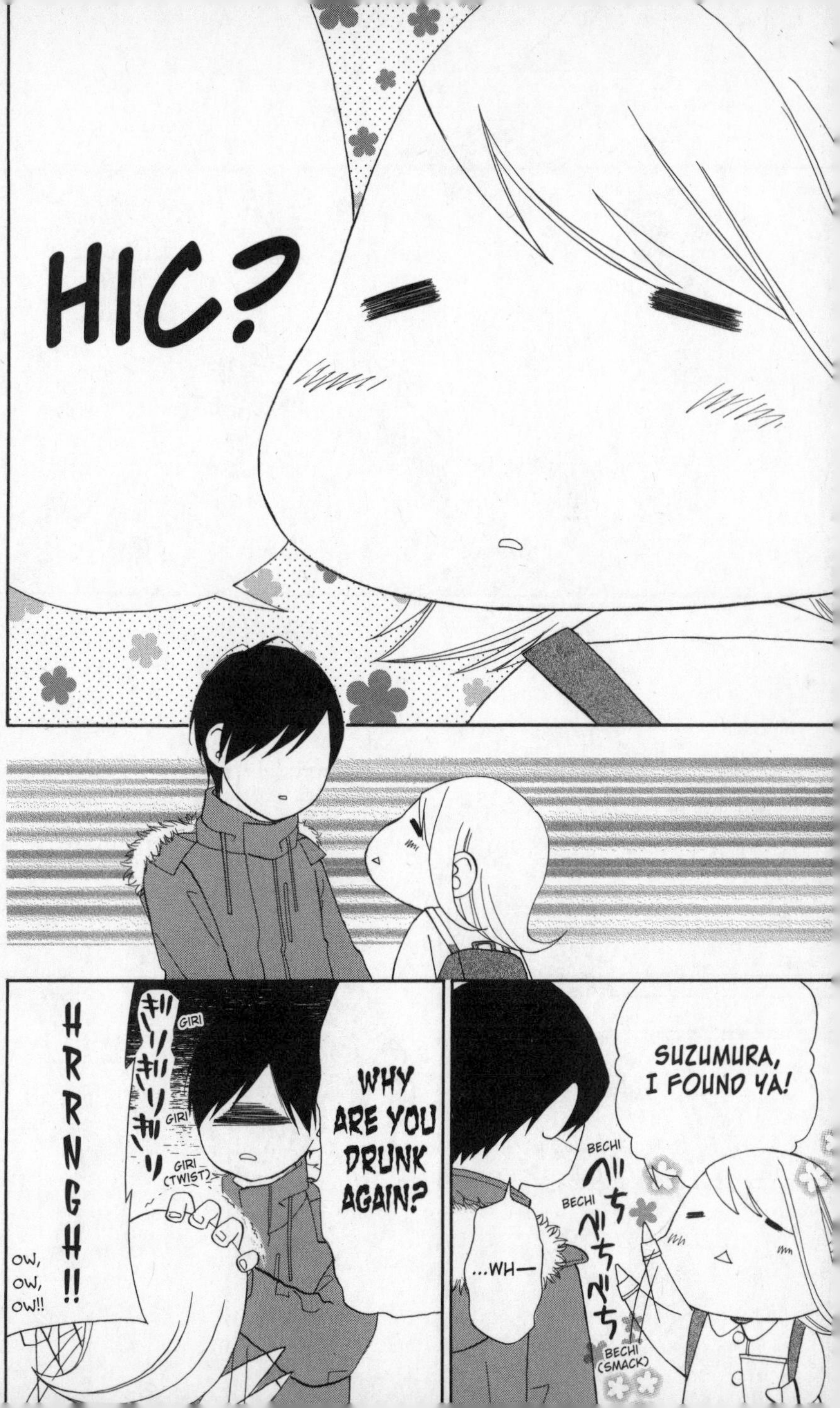
HIC?
SUZUMURA, I FOUND YA!
べちべちべち
BECHI
BECHI
BECHI (SMACK)
...WH—
WHY ARE YOU DRUNK AGAIN?
ギリギリギリ
GIRI
GIRI
GIRI (TWIST)
HRRNGH!!
OW, OW, OW!!

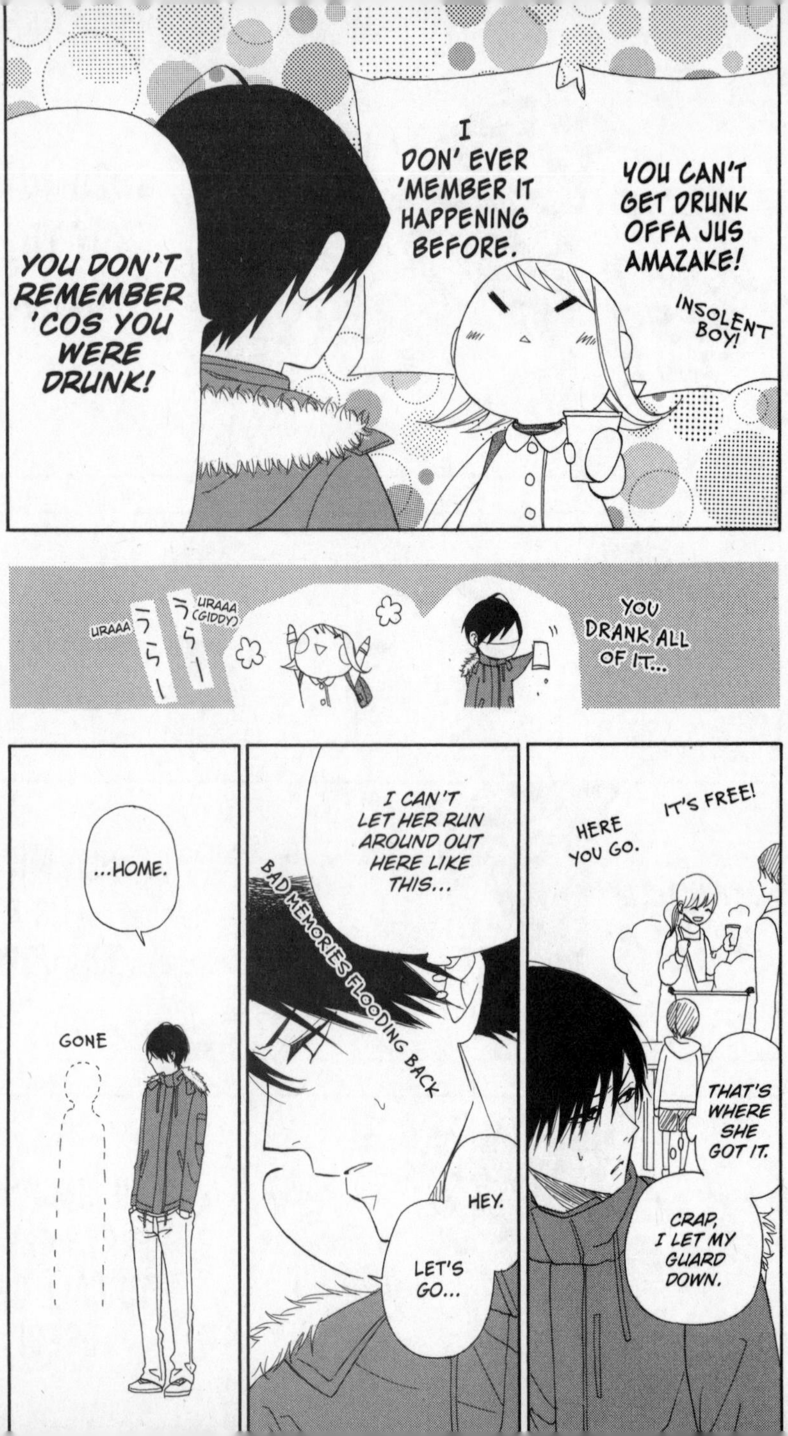
YOU CAN'T GET DRUNK OFFA JUS AMAZAKE!
I DON' EVER 'MEMBER IT HAPPENING BEFORE.
INSOLENT BOY!
YOU DON'T REMEMBER 'COS YOU WERE DRUNK!
YOU DRANK ALL OF IT...
うらー
URAAA (GIDDY)
うらー
URAAA
IT'S FREE!
HERE YOU GO.
THAT'S WHERE SHE GOT IT.
CRAP, I LET MY GUARD DOWN.
I CAN'T LET HER RUN AROUND OUT HERE LIKE THIS...
BAD MEMORIES FLOODING BACK
HEY.
LET'S GO...
...HOME.
GONE

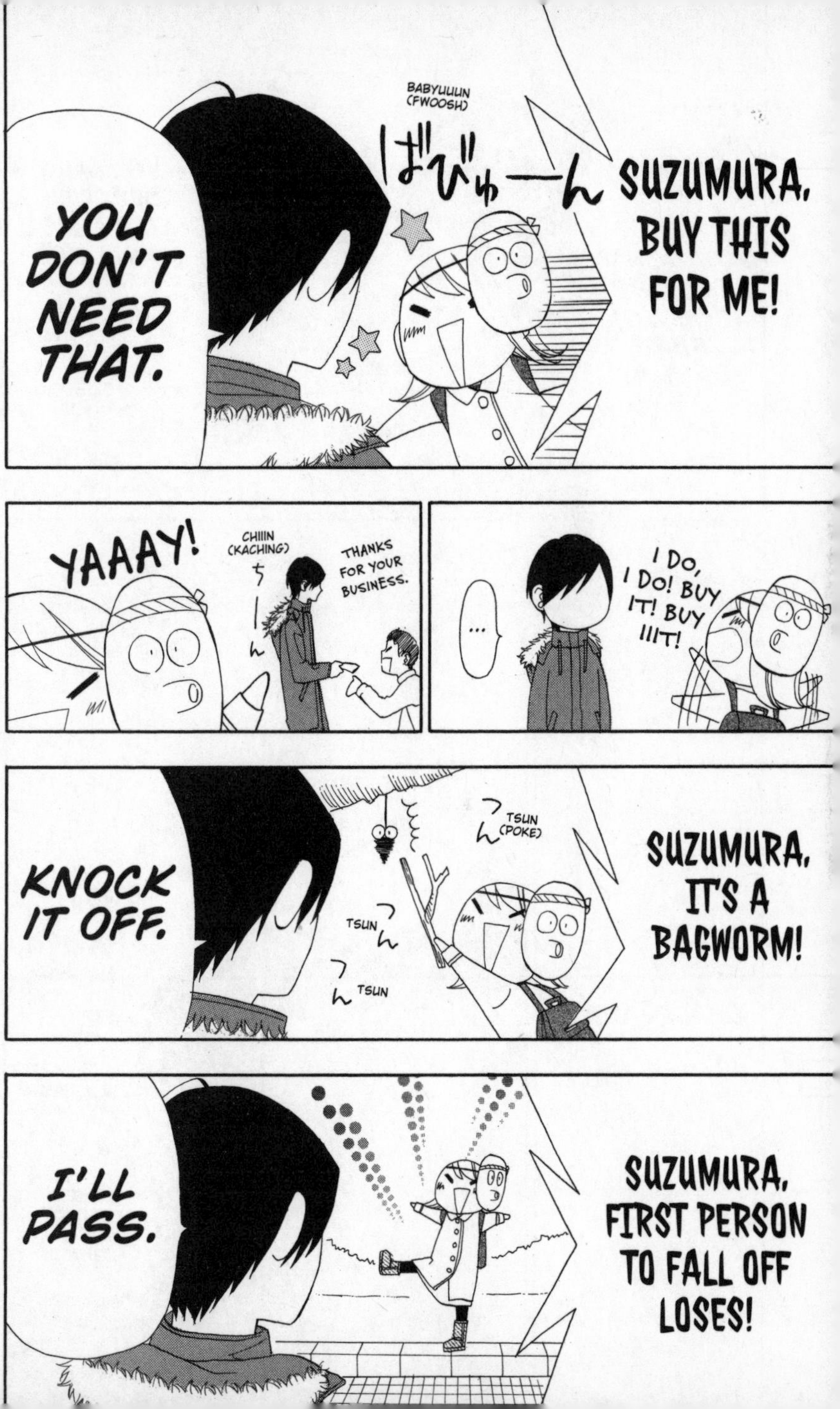
SUZUMURA, BUY THIS FOR ME!
BABYUUUN (FWOOSH)
ばびゅーん
YOU DON'T NEED THAT.
I DO, I DO! BUY IT! BUY IIIT!
...
THANKS FOR YOUR BUSINESS.
CHIIIN (KACHING)
ちーん
YAAAY!
SUZUMURA, IT'S A BAGWORM!
TSUN (POKE)
つん
TSUN
つん
TSUN
つん
KNOCK IT OFF.
SUZUMURA, FIRST PERSON TO FALL OFF LOSES!
I'LL PASS.

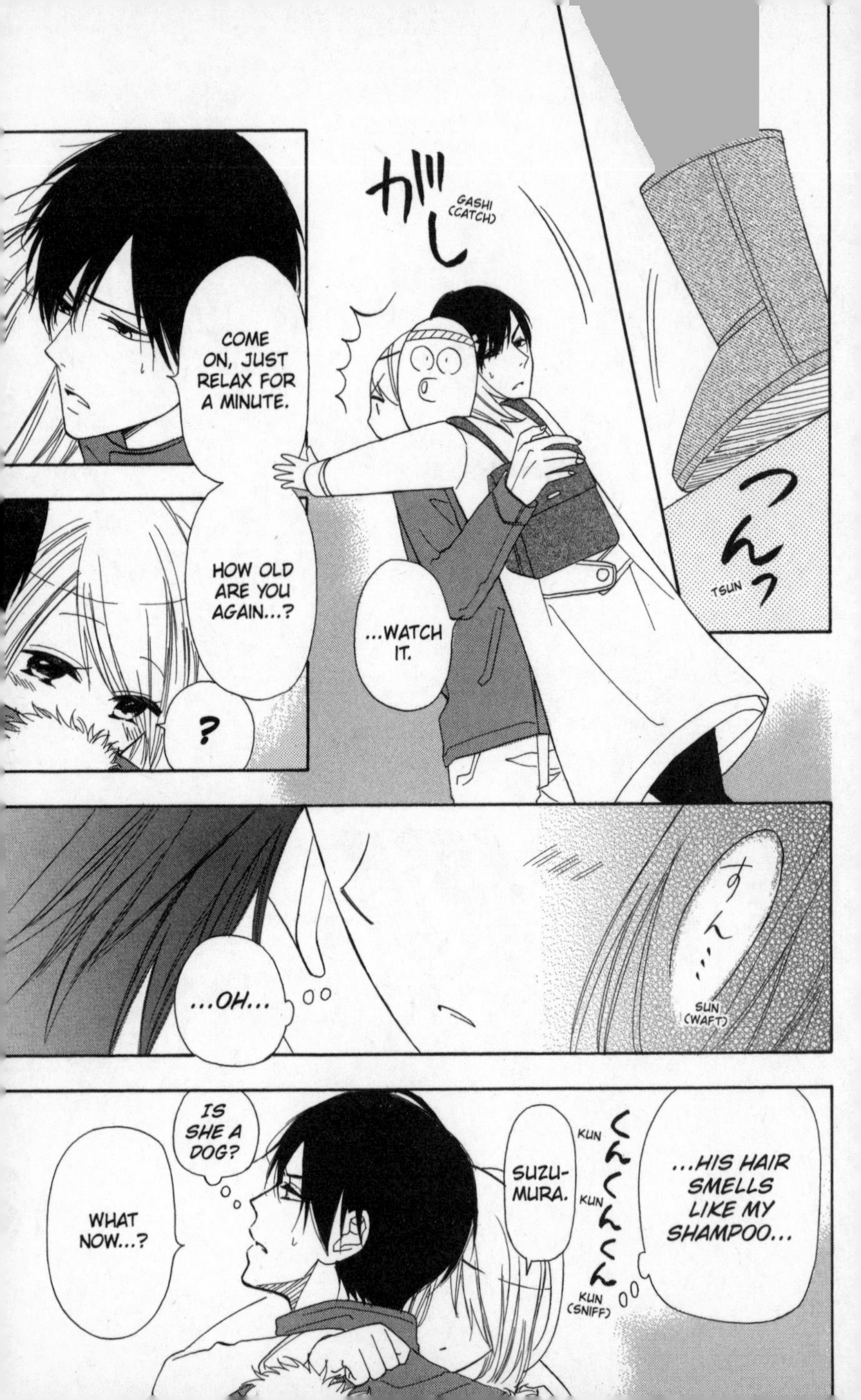
つんっ
TSUN
がし
GASHI (CATCH)
...WATCH IT.
COME ON, JUST RELAX FOR A MINUTE.
HOW OLD ARE YOU AGAIN...?
?
すん…
SUN (WAFT)
...OH...
...HIS HAIR SMELLS LIKE MY SHAMPOO...
くんくんくん
KUN KUN KUN (SNIFF)
SUZU-MURA.
IS SHE A DOG?
WHAT NOW...?

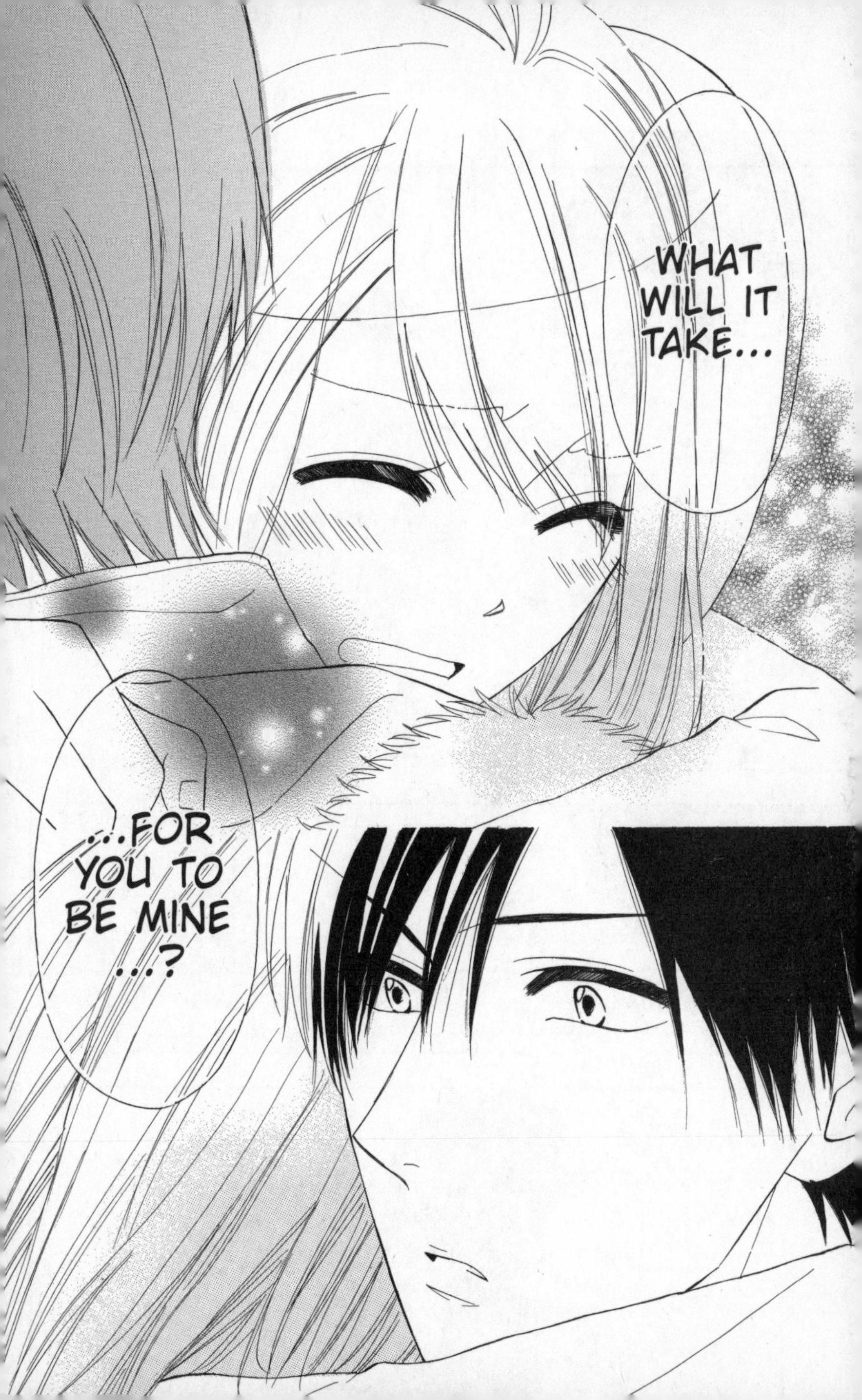
WHAT WILL IT TAKE...
...FOR YOU TO BE MINE ...?

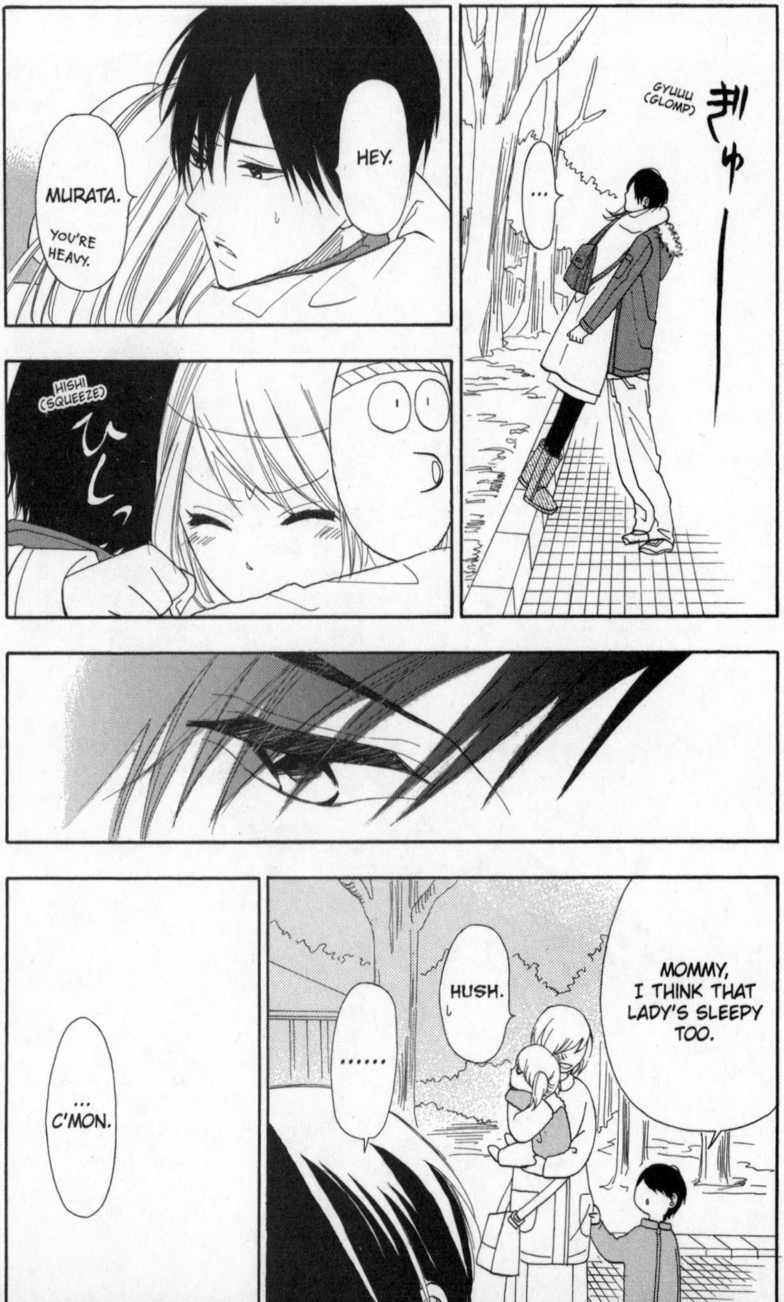
GYUUU (GLOMP)
ぎゅー
...
HEY.
MURATA. YOU'RE HEAVY.
HISHI (SQUEEZE)
ひしっ
MOMMY, I THINK THAT LADY'S SLEEPY TOO.
HUSH.
......
... C'MON.

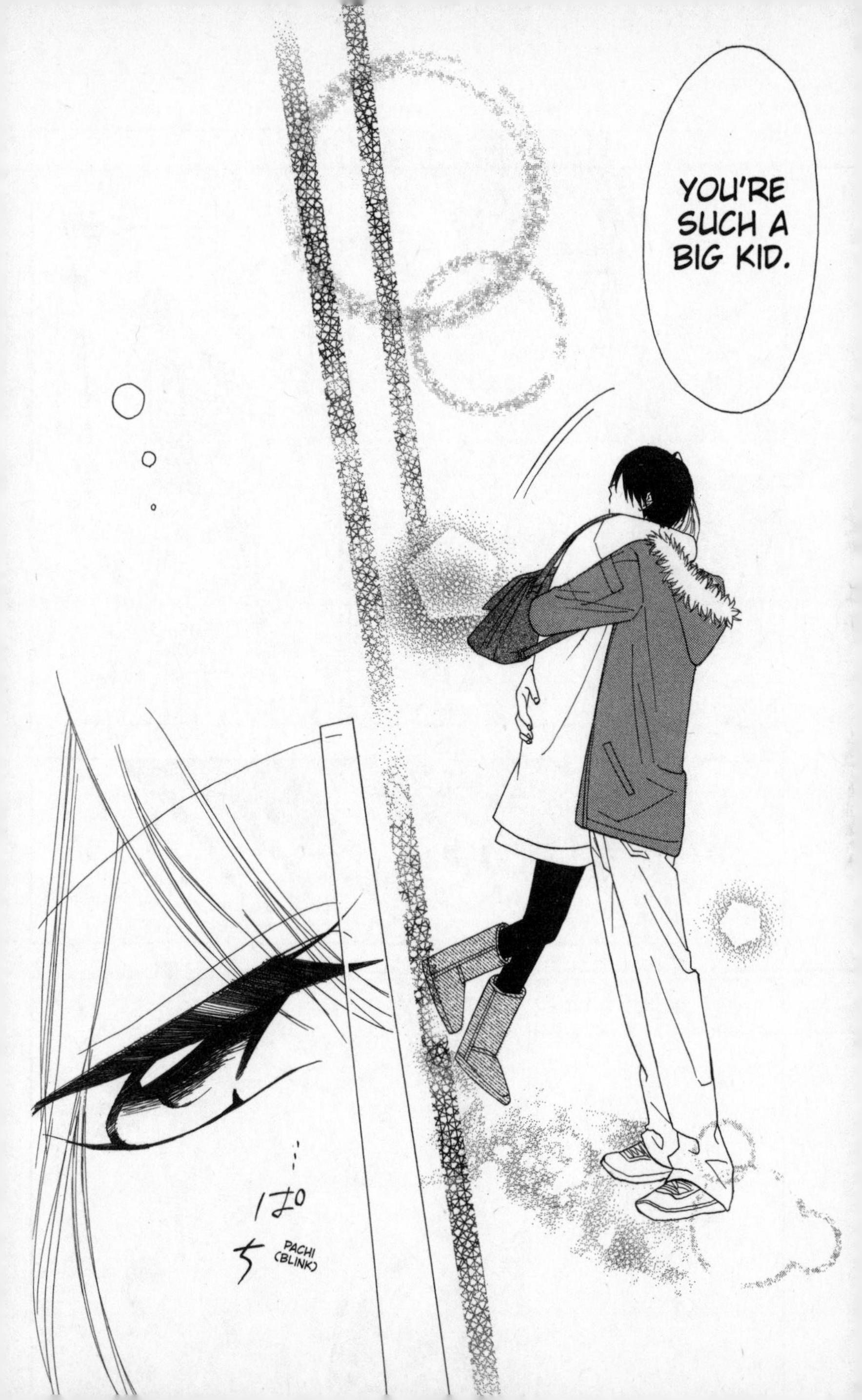
YOU'RE SUCH A BIG KID.
...
ぱち
PACHI (BLINK)

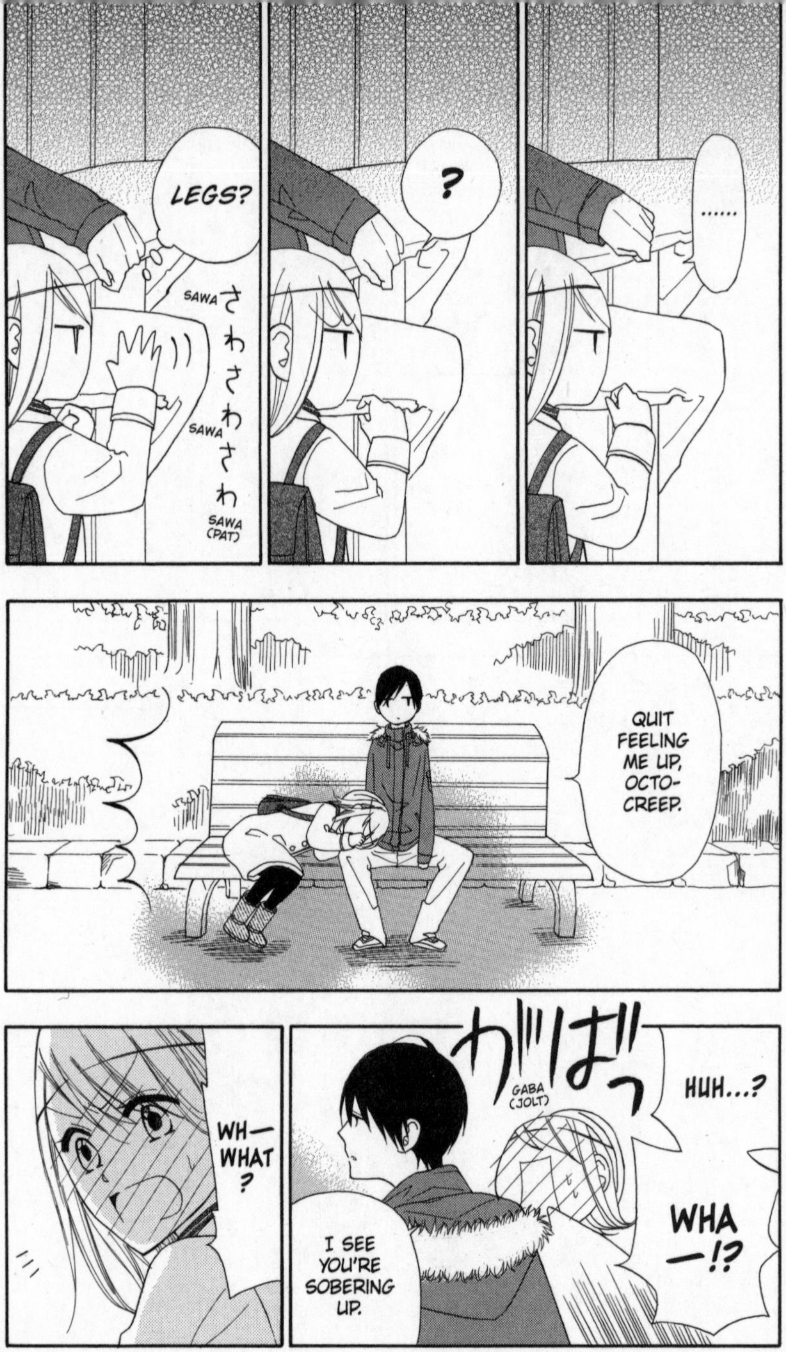
......
?
LEGS?
さわさわさわ
SAWA SAWA SAWA (PAT)
QUIT FEELING ME UP, OCTO-CREEP.
HUH...?
がばっ
GABA (JOLT)
WHA—!?
I SEE YOU'RE SOBERING UP.
WH—WHAT?

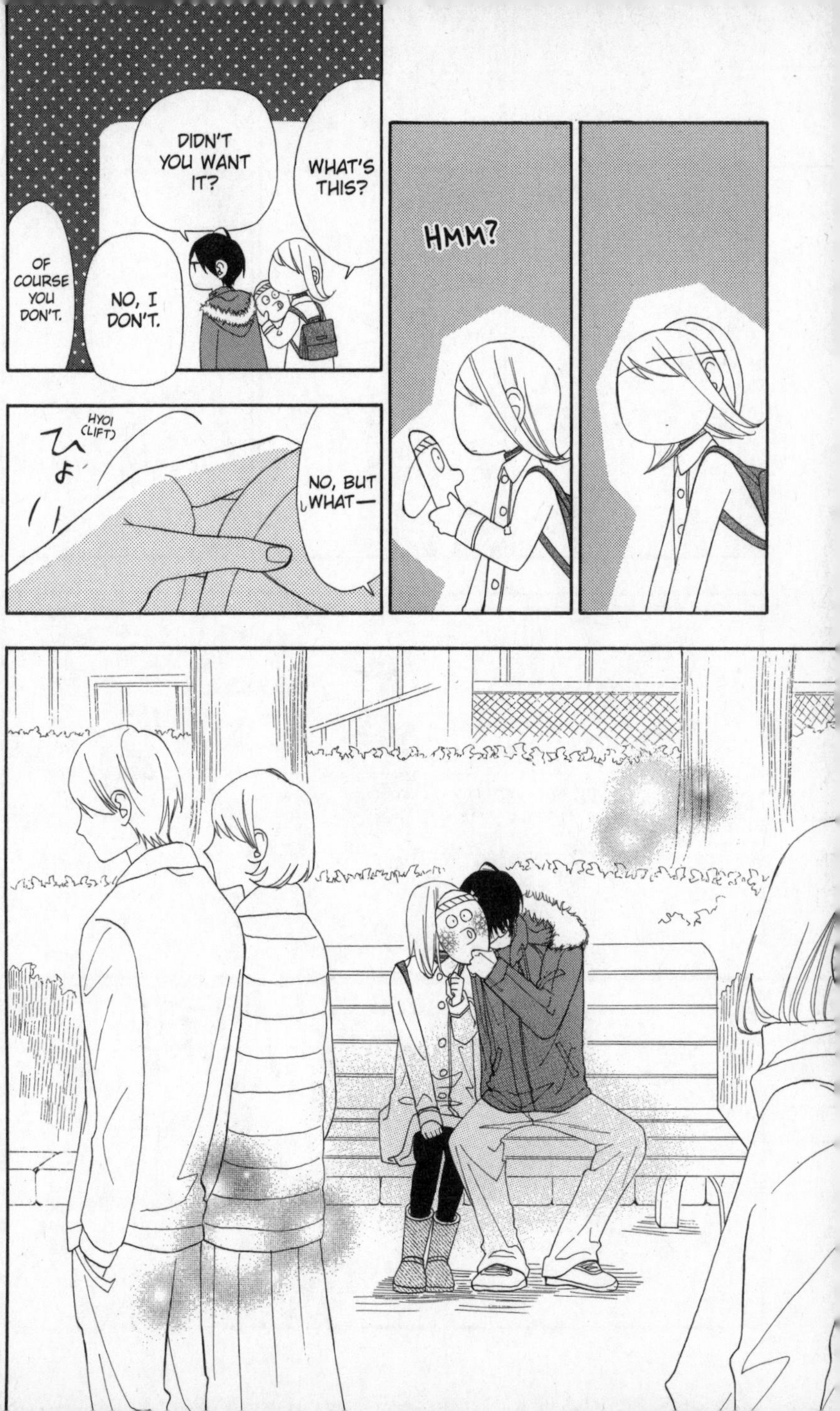

WHAT'S THIS?
DIDN'T YOU WANT IT?
NO, I DON'T.
OF COURSE YOU DON'T.
HMM?
NO, BUT WHAT—
HYOI (LIFT)
ひょい

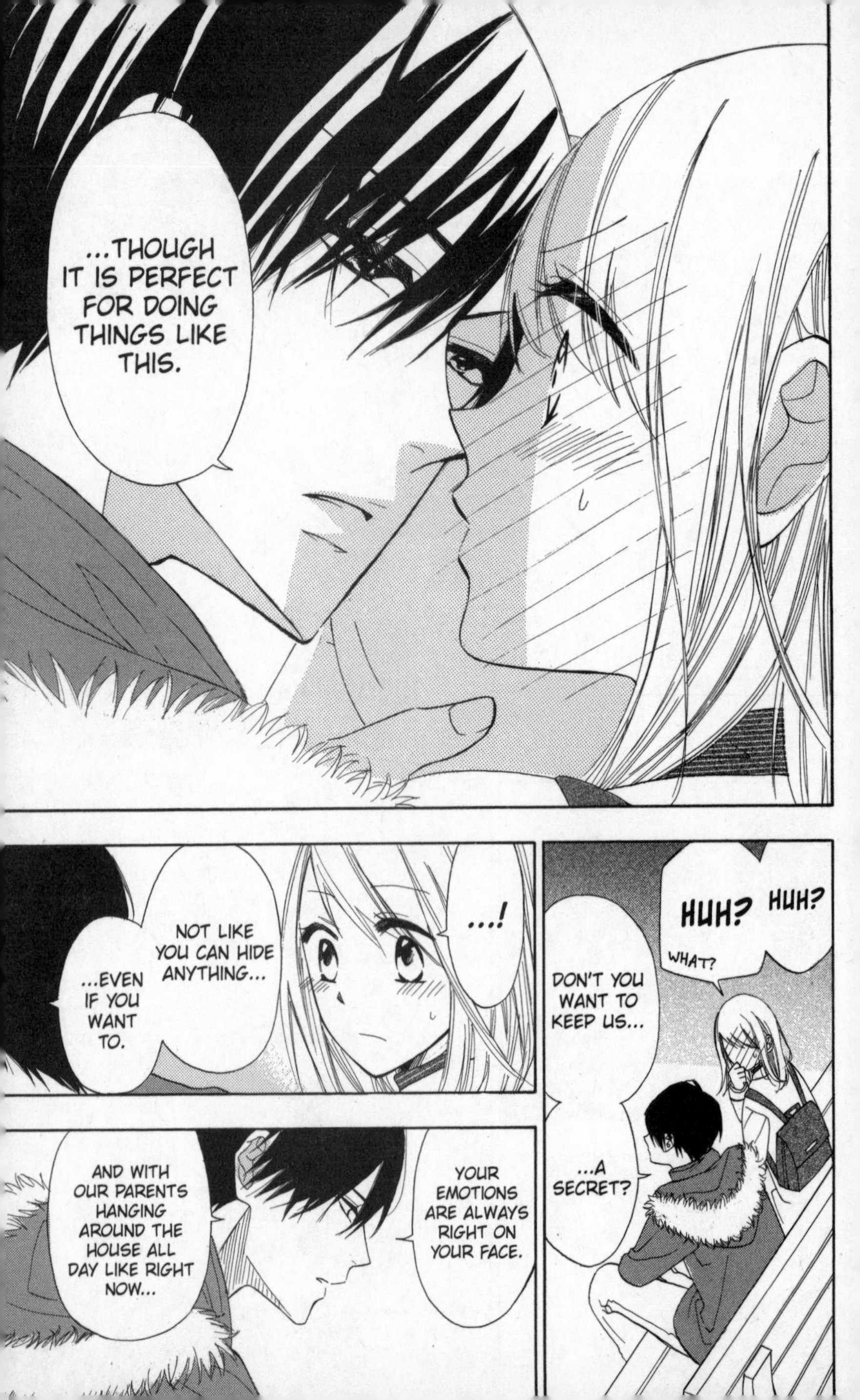
...THOUGH IT IS PERFECT FOR DOING THINGS LIKE THIS.
HUH? HUH?
WHAT?
DON'T YOU WANT TO KEEP US...
...A SECRET?
...!
NOT LIKE YOU CAN HIDE ANYTHING...
...EVEN IF YOU WANT TO.
YOUR EMOTIONS ARE ALWAYS RIGHT ON YOUR FACE.
AND WITH OUR PARENTS HANGING AROUND THE HOUSE ALL DAY LIKE RIGHT NOW...

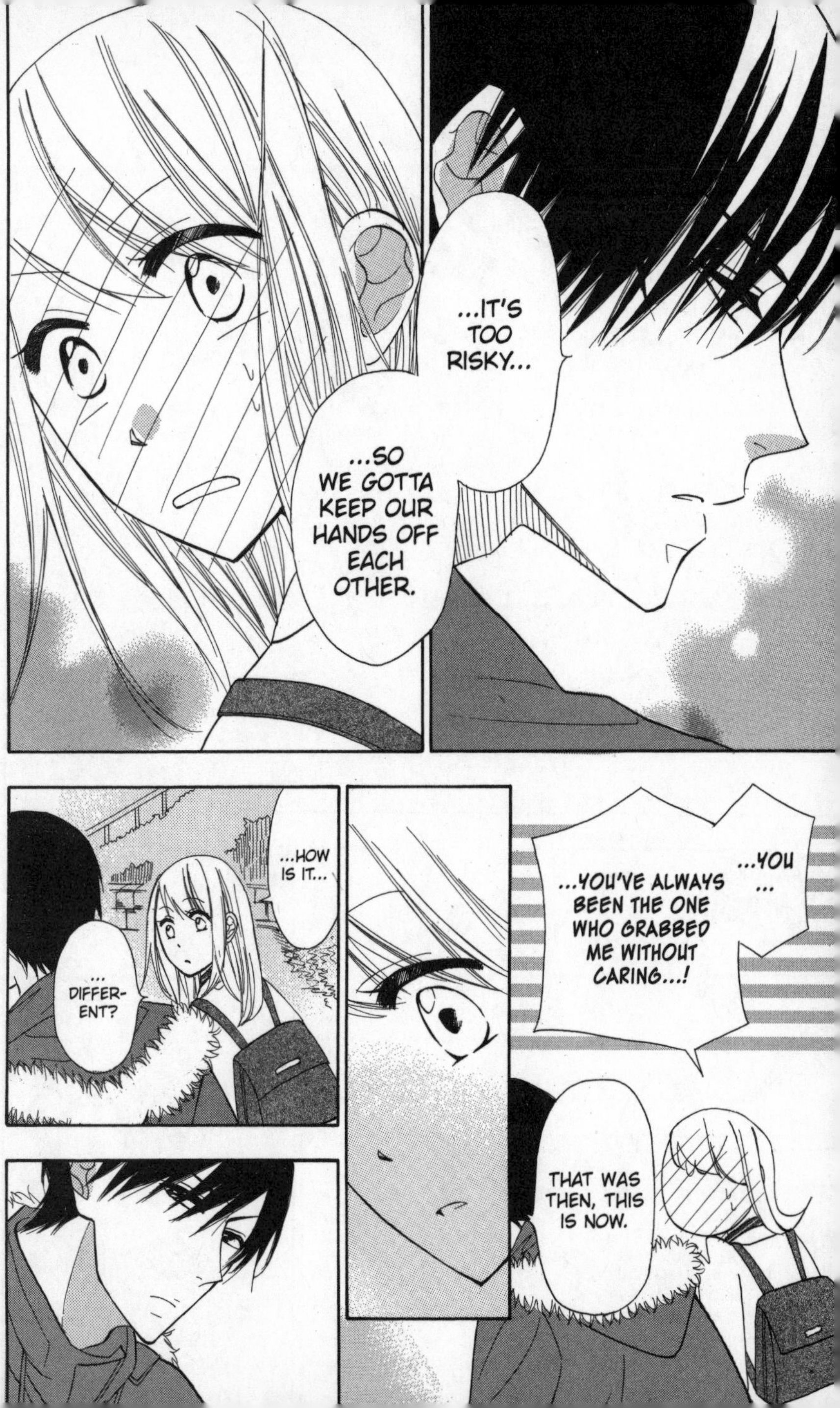
...IT'S TOO RISKY...
...SO WE GOTTA KEEP OUR HANDS OFF EACH OTHER.
...YOU ...
...YOU'VE ALWAYS BEEN THE ONE WHO GRABBED ME WITHOUT CARING...!
THAT WAS THEN, THIS IS NOW.
...HOW IS IT...
... DIFFER-ENT?

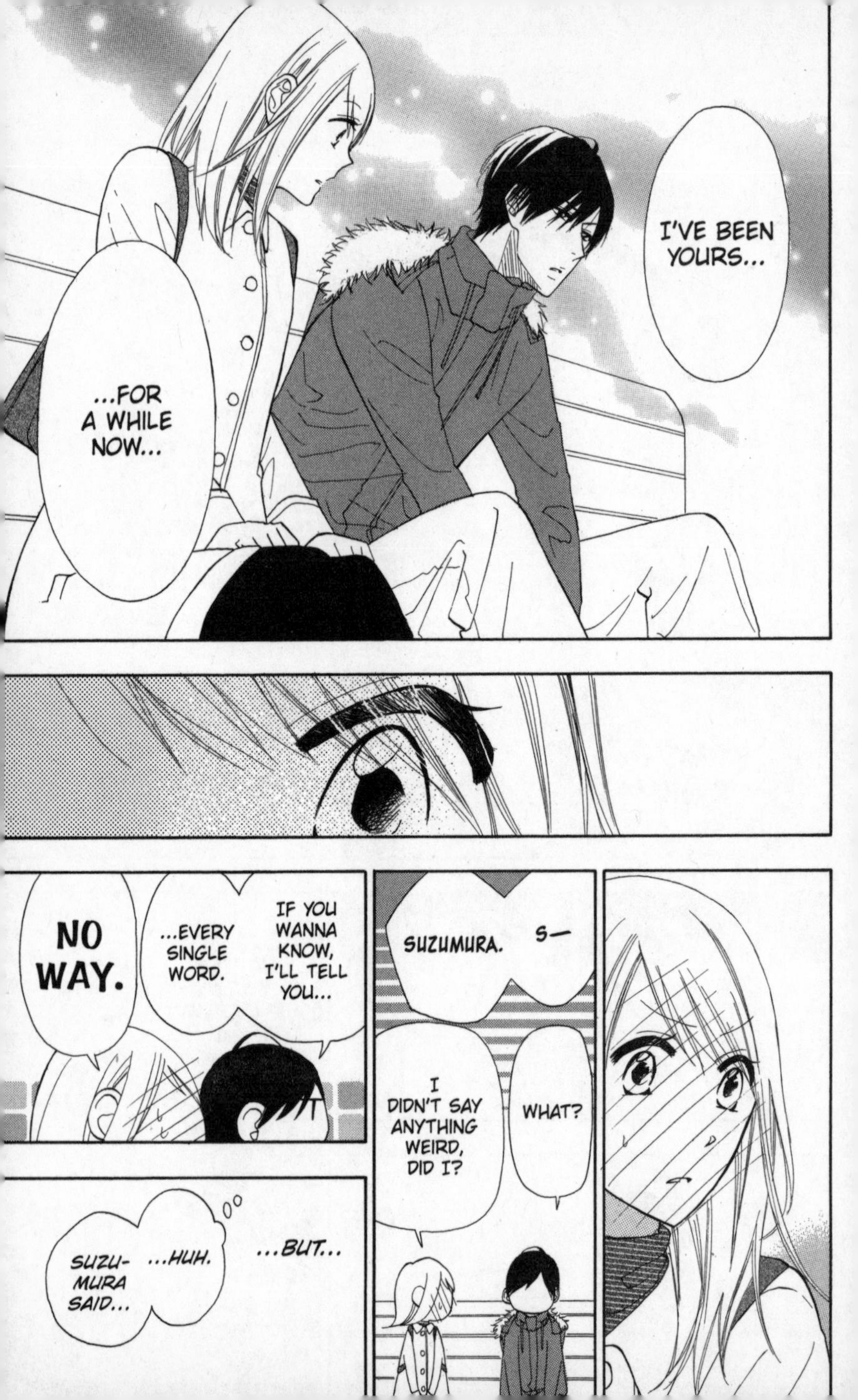
I'VE BEEN YOURS...
...FOR A WHILE NOW...
S—
SUZUMURA.
WHAT?
I DIDN'T SAY ANYTHING WEIRD, DID I?
IF YOU WANNA KNOW, I'LL TELL YOU...
...EVERY SINGLE WORD.
NO WAY.
...BUT...
...HUH.
SUZU-MURA SAID...

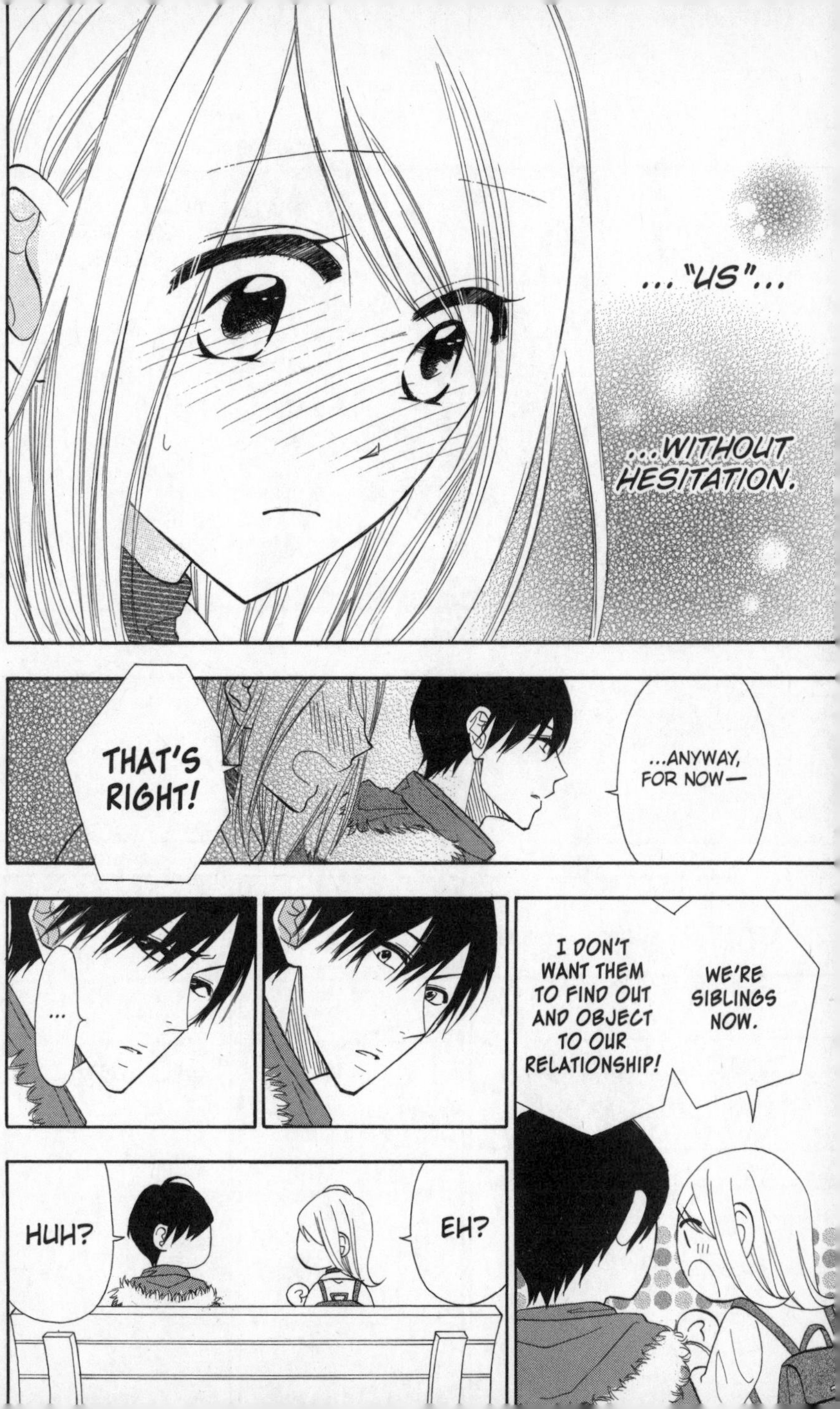
..."US"...
...WITHOUT HESITATION.
...ANYWAY, FOR NOW—
THAT'S RIGHT!
WE'RE SIBLINGS NOW.
I DON'T WANT THEM TO FIND OUT AND OBJECT TO OUR RELATIONSHIP!
...
EH?
HUH?

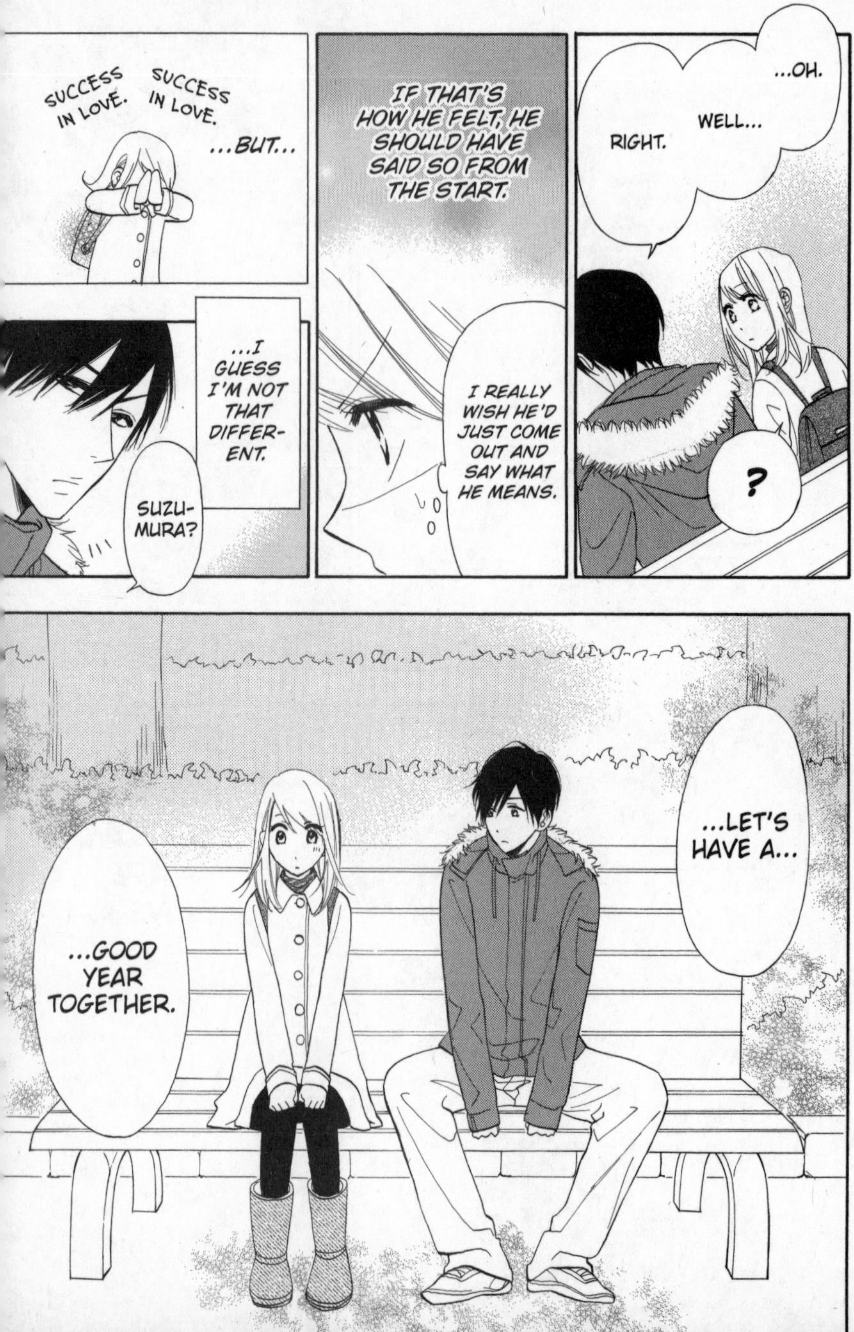
...OH. WELL... RIGHT.
?
IF THAT'S HOW HE FELT, HE SHOULD HAVE SAID SO FROM THE START.
I REALLY WISH HE'D JUST COME OUT AND SAY WHAT HE MEANS.
SUCCESS IN LOVE.
SUCCESS IN LOVE.
...BUT...
...I GUESS I'M NOT THAT DIFFER-ENT.
SUZU-MURA?
...LET'S HAVE A...
...GOOD YEAR TOGETHER.

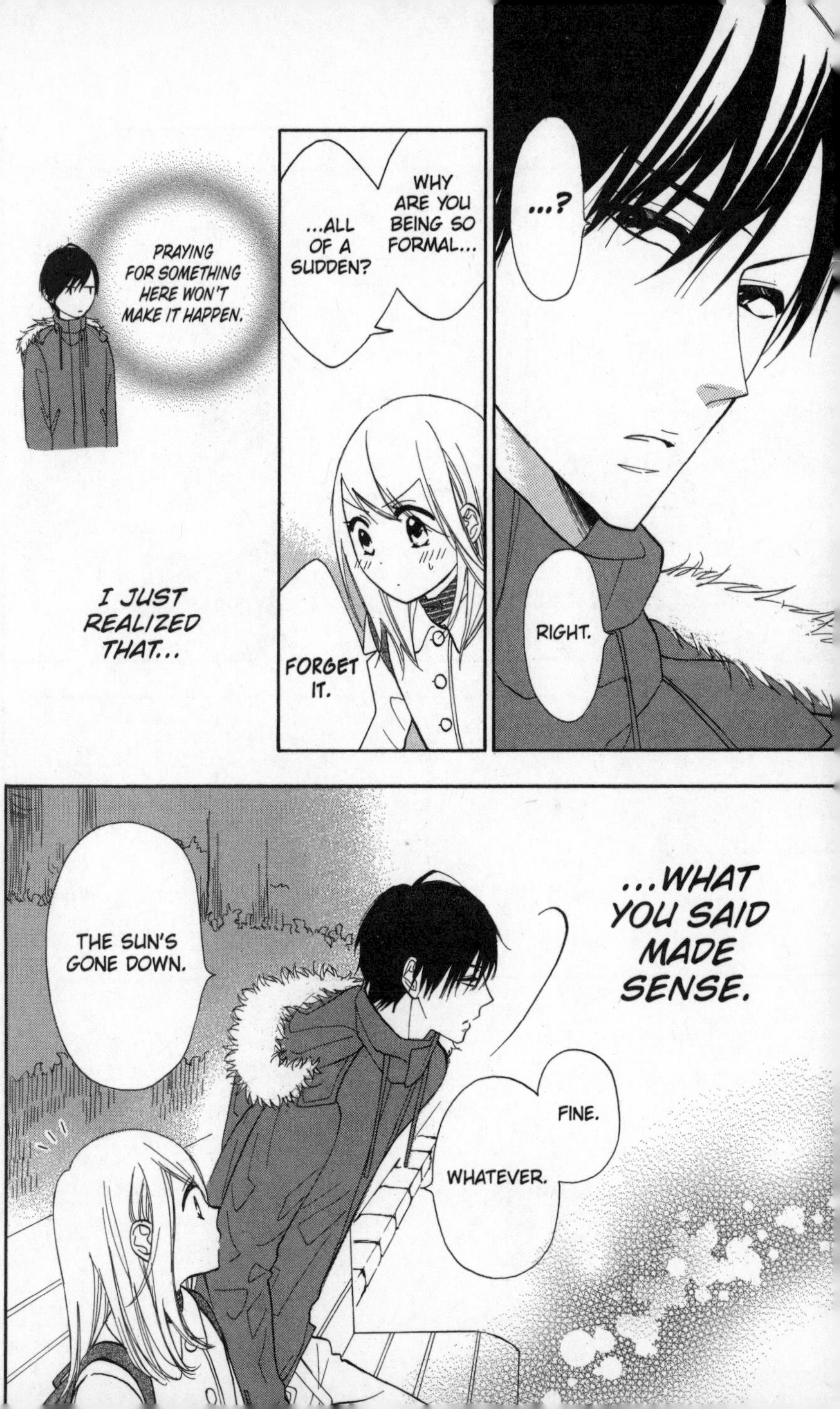
...?
RIGHT.
WHY ARE YOU BEING SO FORMAL...
...ALL OF A SUDDEN?
FORGET IT.
PRAYING FOR SOMETHING HERE WON'T MAKE IT HAPPEN.
I JUST REALIZED THAT...
...WHAT YOU SAID MADE SENSE.
FINE.
WHATEVER.
THE SUN'S GONE DOWN.

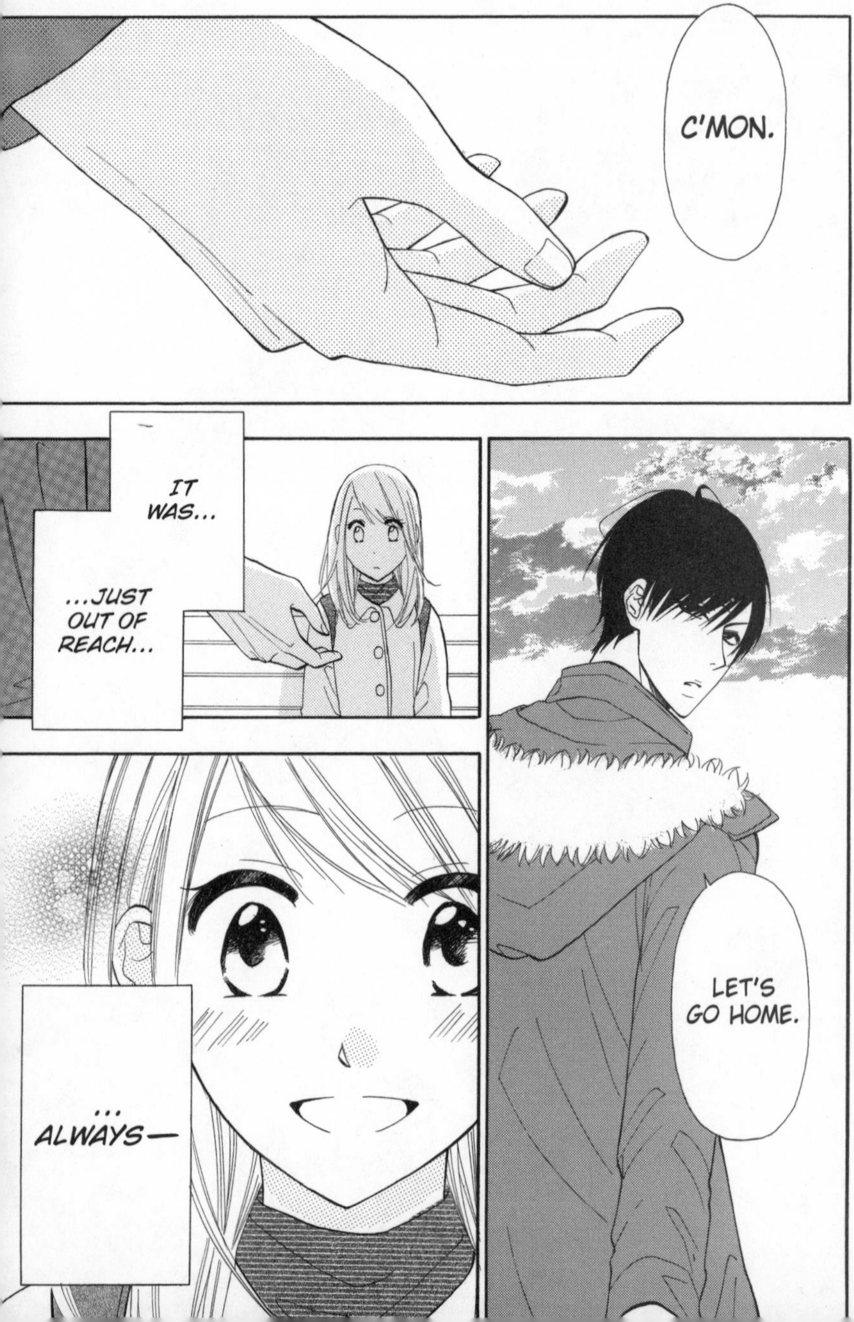
C'MON.
LET'S GO HOME.
IT WAS...
...JUST OUT OF REACH...
...ALWAYS—

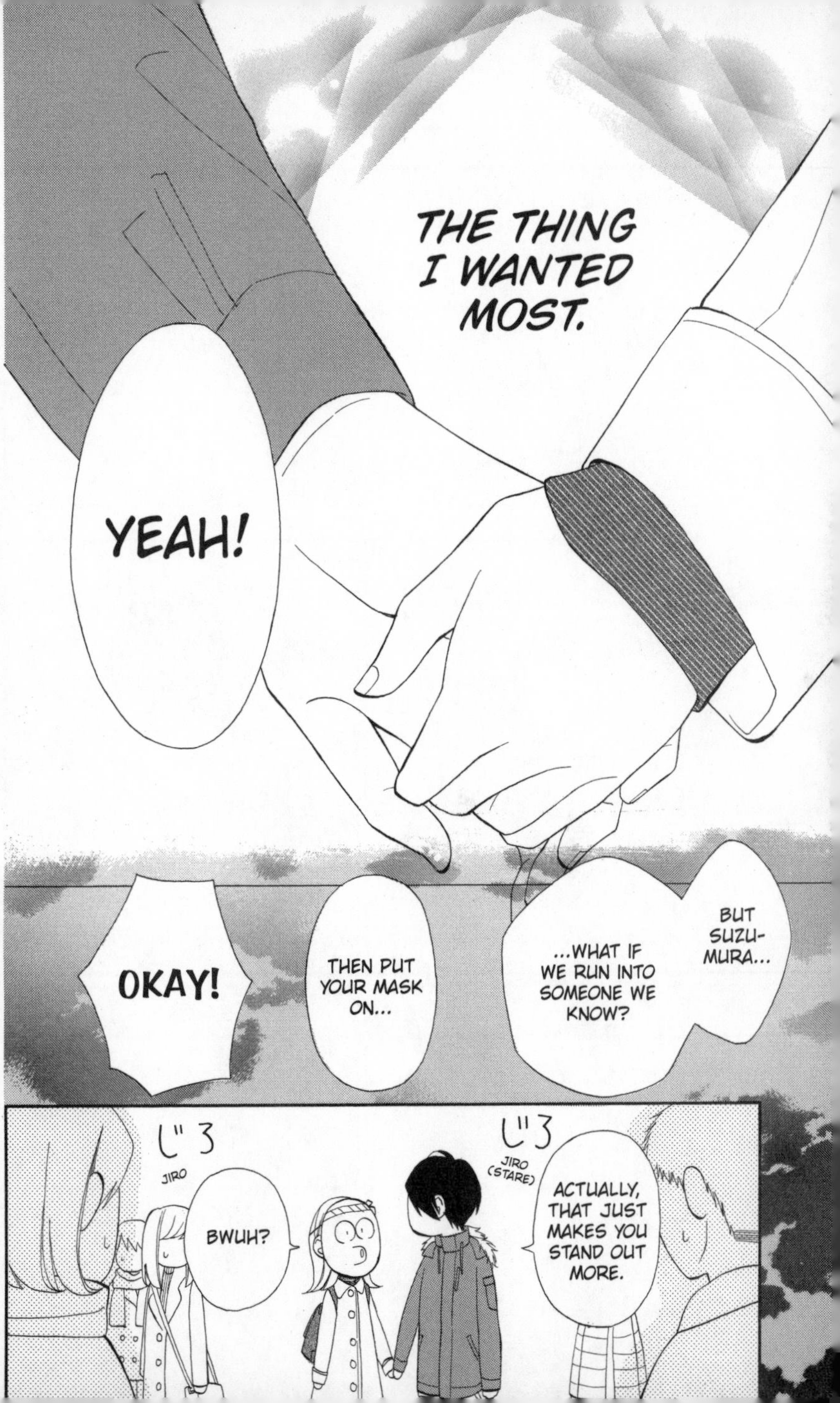
THE THING I WANTED MOST.
YEAH!
BUT SUZUMURA...
...WHAT IF WE RUN INTO SOMEONE WE KNOW?
THEN PUT YOUR MASK ON...
OKAY!
じろ
JIRO (STARE)
ACTUALLY, THAT JUST MAKES YOU STAND OUT MORE.
じろ
JIRO
BWUH?

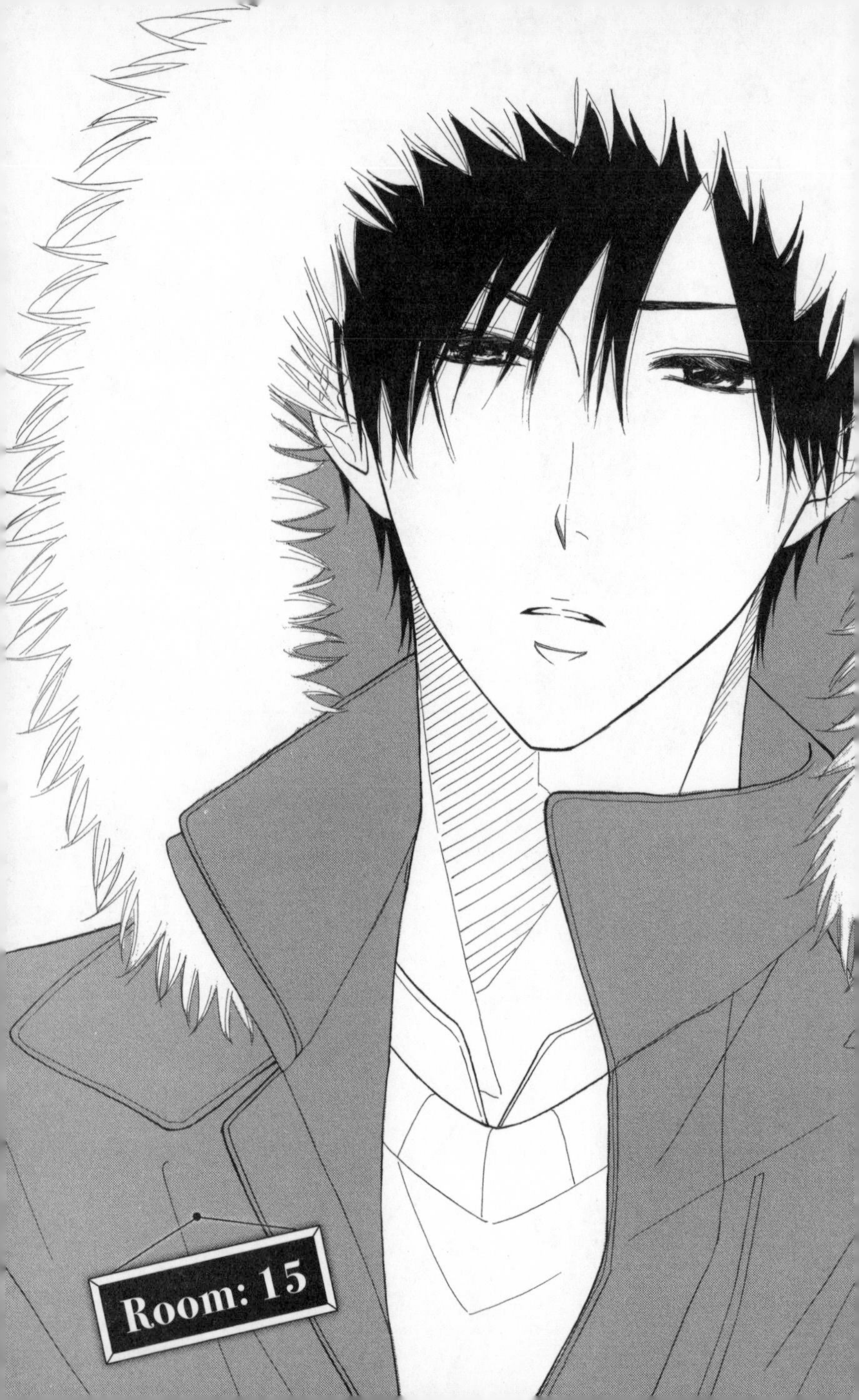
Room: 15

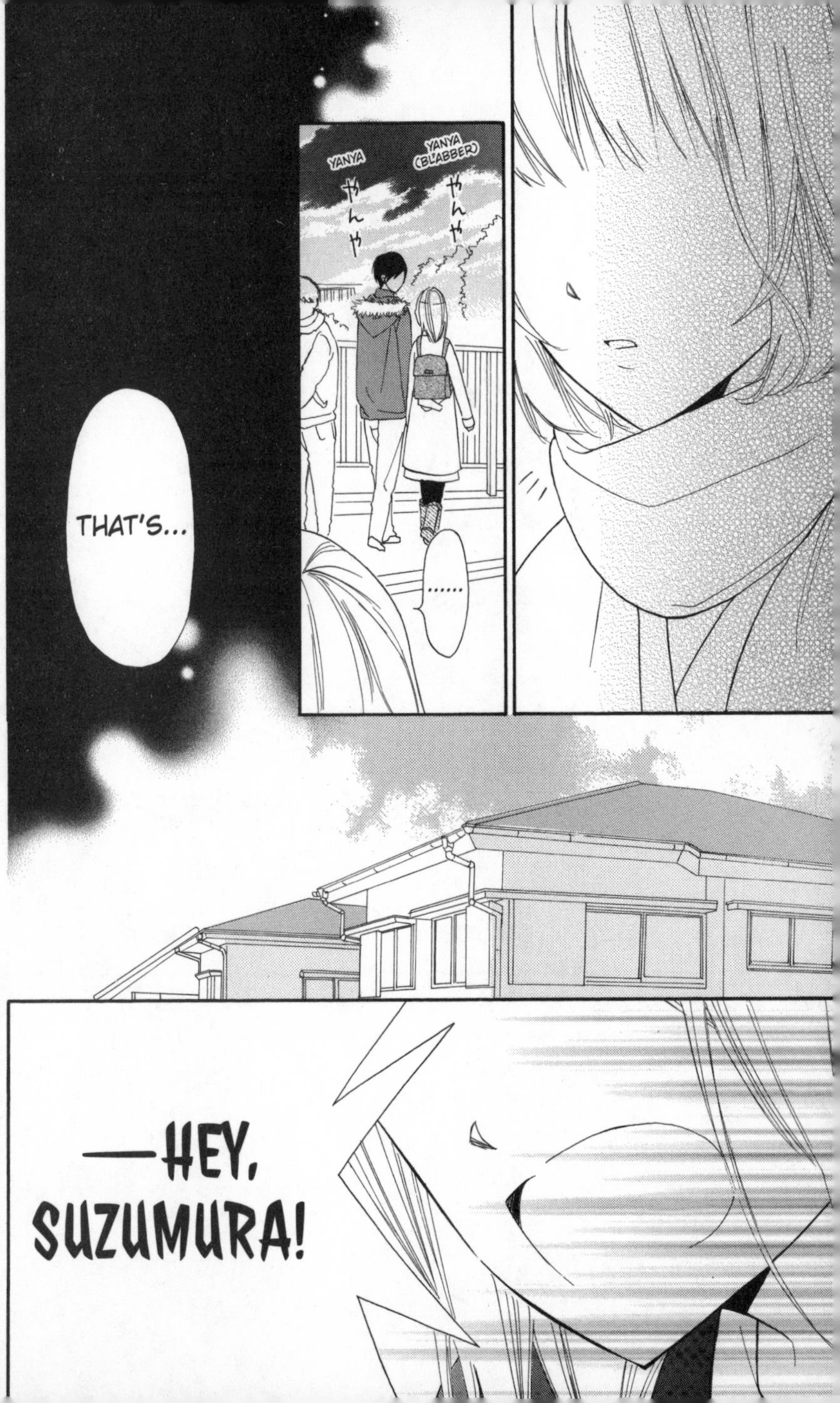
YANYA (BLABBER)
やんや
YANYA
やんや
......
THAT'S...
—HEY, SUZUMURA!

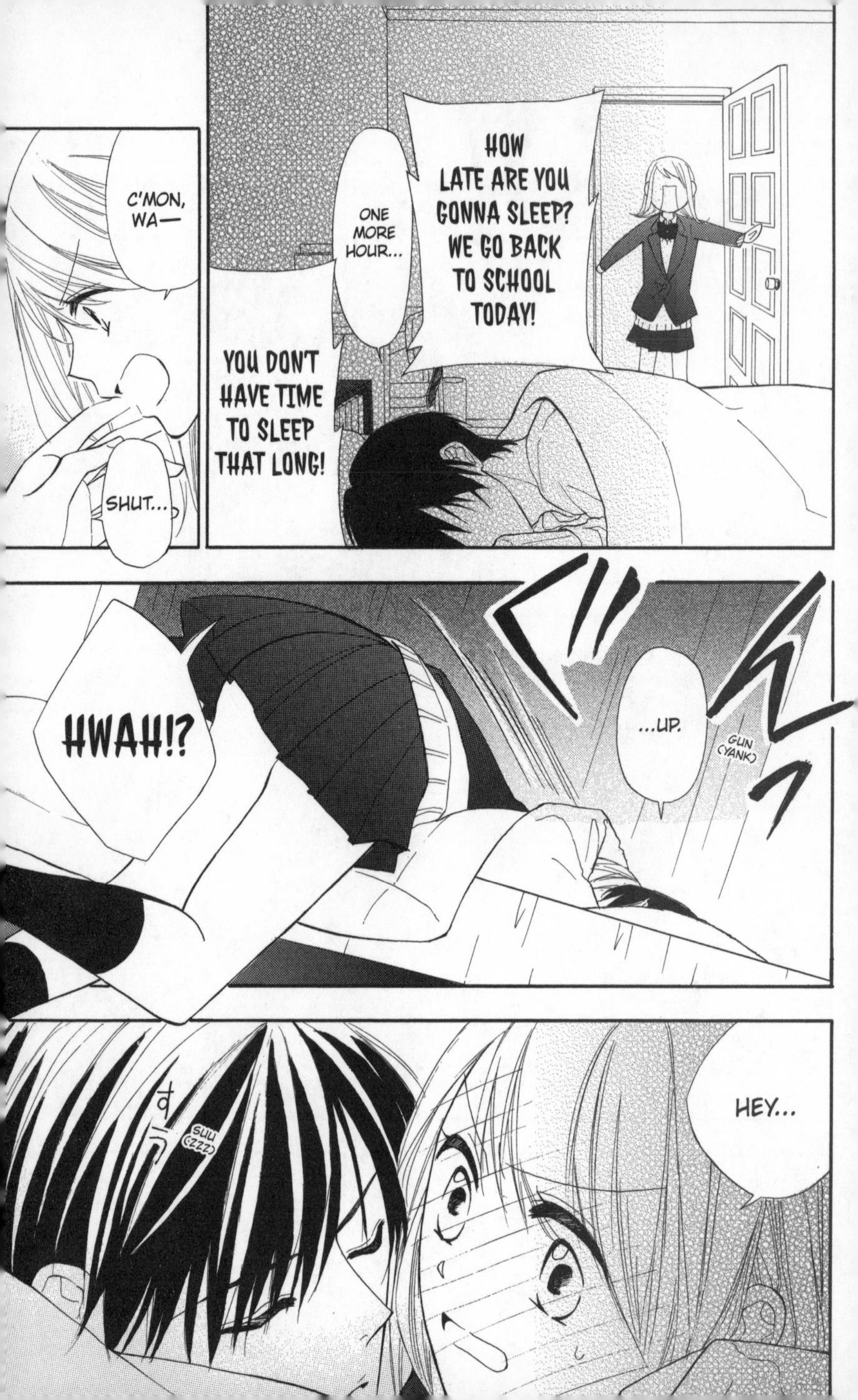
HOW LATE ARE YOU GONNA SLEEP? WE GO BACK TO SCHOOL TODAY!
ONE MORE HOUR...
YOU DON'T HAVE TIME TO SLEEP THAT LONG!
C'MON, WA—
SHUT...
...UP.
GUN (YANK)
HWAH!?
HEY...
SUU (ZZZ)

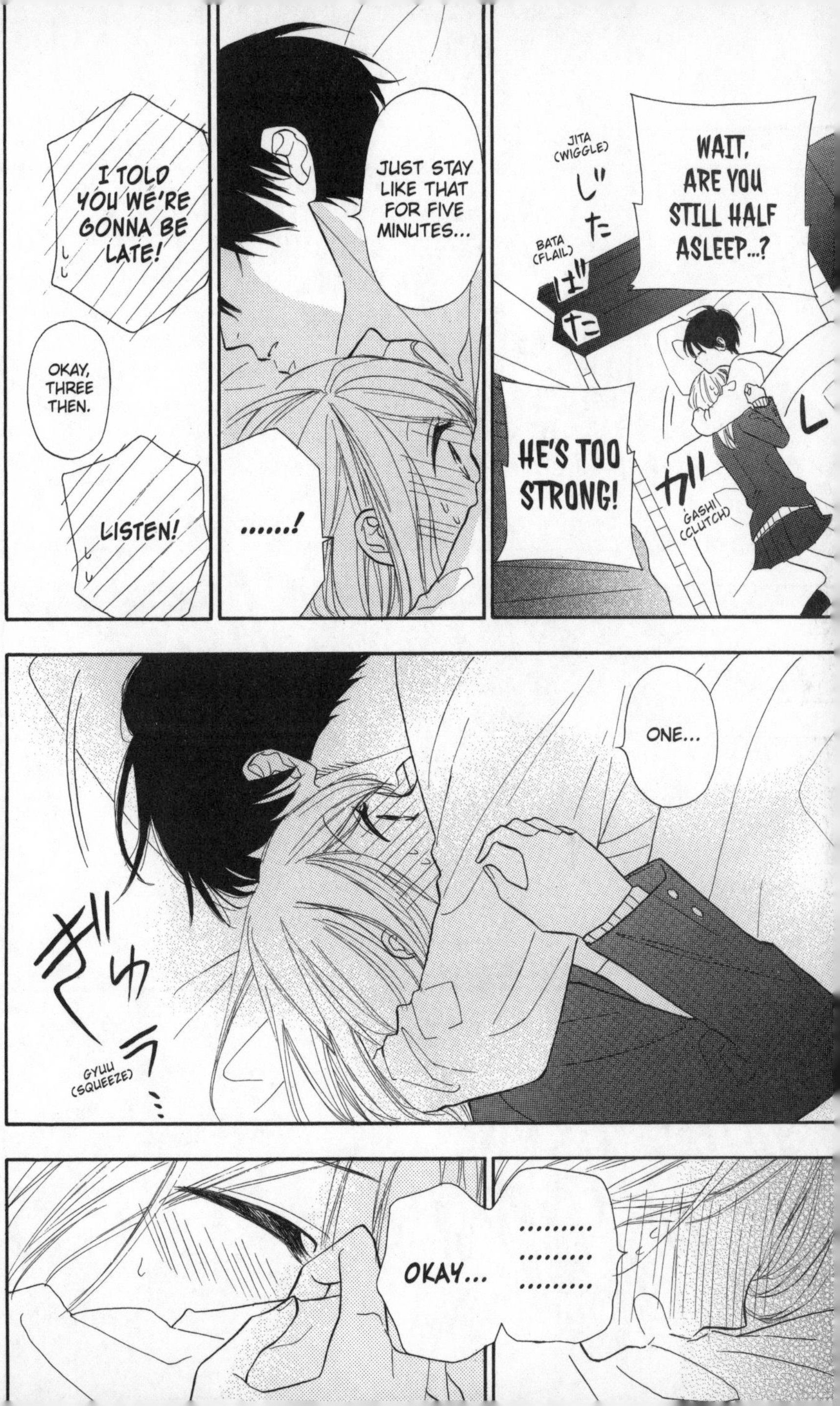
WAIT, ARE YOU STILL HALF ASLEEP...?
JITA (WIGGLE)
じた
BATA (FLAIL)
ばた
GASHI (CLUTCH)
ガシ
HE'S TOO STRONG!
JUST STAY LIKE THAT FOR FIVE MINUTES...
......!
I TOLD YOU WE'RE GONNA BE LATE!
OKAY, THREE THEN.
LISTEN!
ONE...
ぎゅう
GYUU (SQUEEZE)
....
....
....
OKAY...

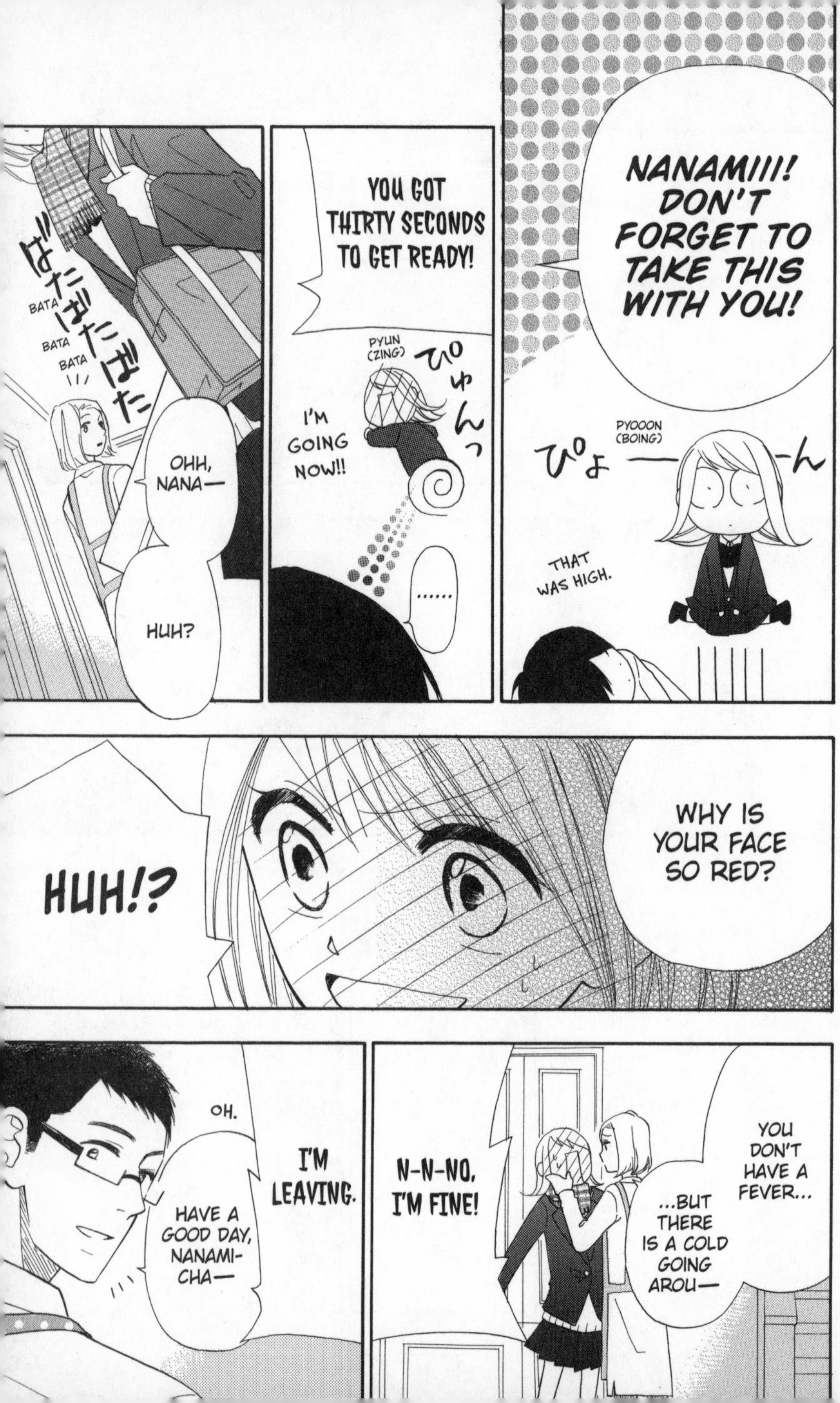
NANAMIII! DON'T FORGET TO TAKE THIS WITH YOU!
PYOOON (BOING)
ぴょ——ん
THAT WAS HIGH.
YOU GOT THIRTY SECONDS TO GET READY!
PYUN (ZING)
ぴゅんっ
I'M GOING NOW!!
......
ばたばたばた
BATA BATA BATA
OHH, NANA—
HUH?
WHY IS YOUR FACE SO RED?
HUH!?
YOU DON'T HAVE A FEVER...
...BUT THERE IS A COLD GOING AROU—
N-N-NO, I'M FINE!
I'M LEAVING.
OH.
HAVE A GOOD DAY, NANAMI-CHA—

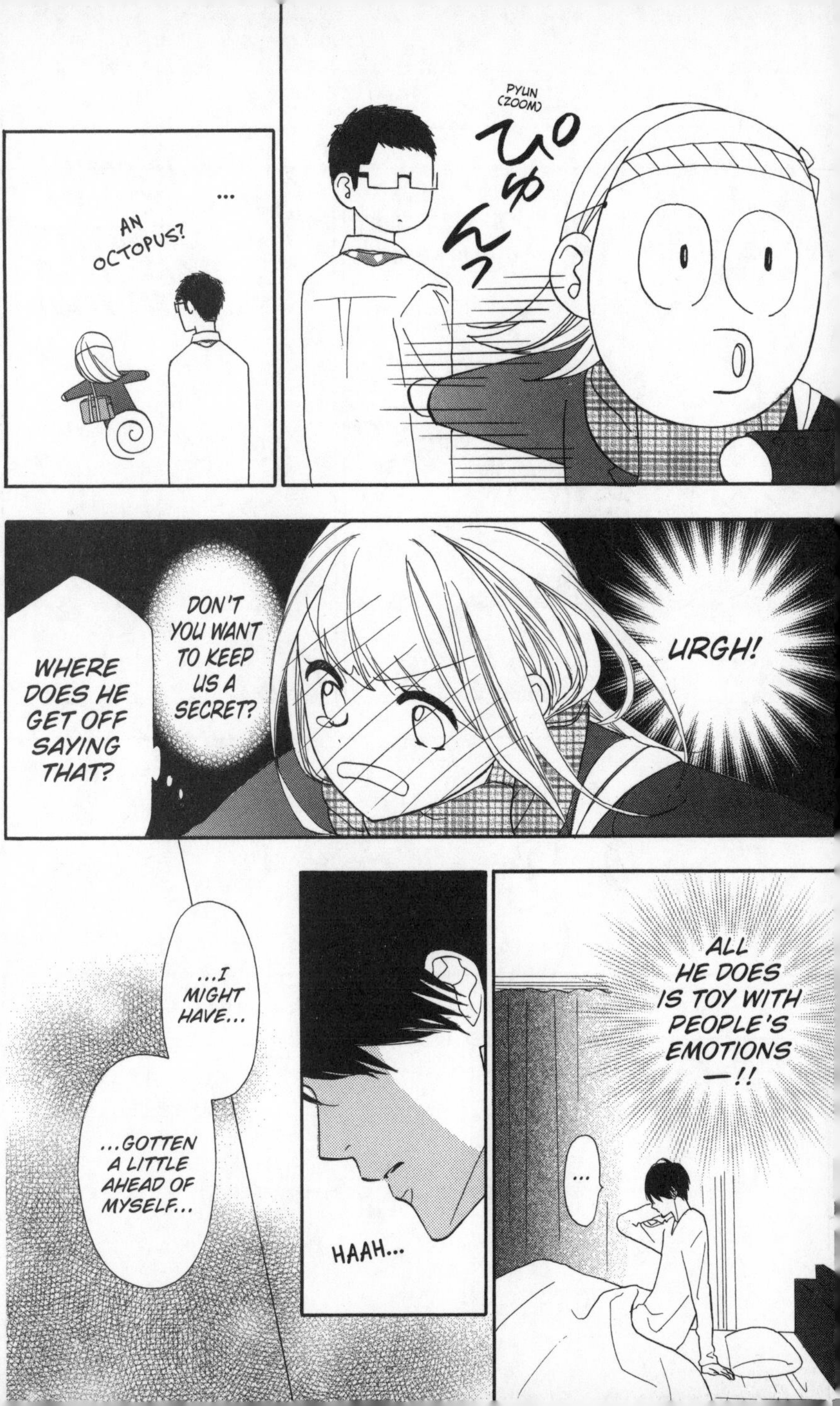
PYUN (ZOOM)
ぴゅん
...
AN OCTOPUS?
URGH!
DON'T YOU WANT TO KEEP US A SECRET?
WHERE DOES HE GET OFF SAYING THAT?
ALL HE DOES IS TOY WITH PEOPLE'S EMOTIONS—!!
...
HAAH...
...I MIGHT HAVE...
...GOTTEN A LITTLE AHEAD OF MYSELF...

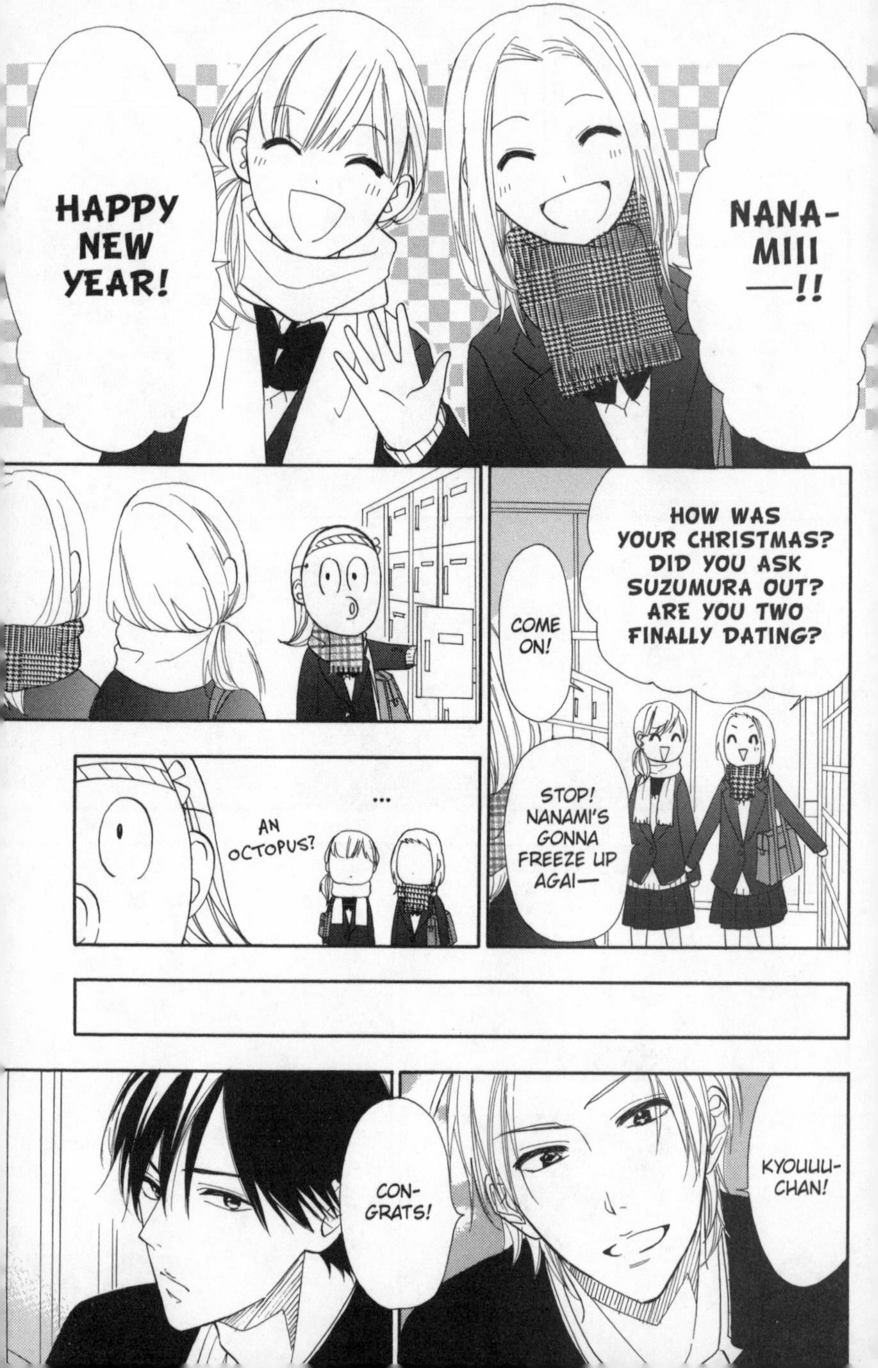
NANA-MIII —!!
HAPPY NEW YEAR!
HOW WAS YOUR CHRISTMAS? DID YOU ASK SUZUMURA OUT? ARE YOU TWO FINALLY DATING?
COME ON!
STOP! NANAMI'S GONNA FREEZE UP AGAI—
...
AN OCTOPUS?
KYOUUU-CHAN!
CON-GRATS!

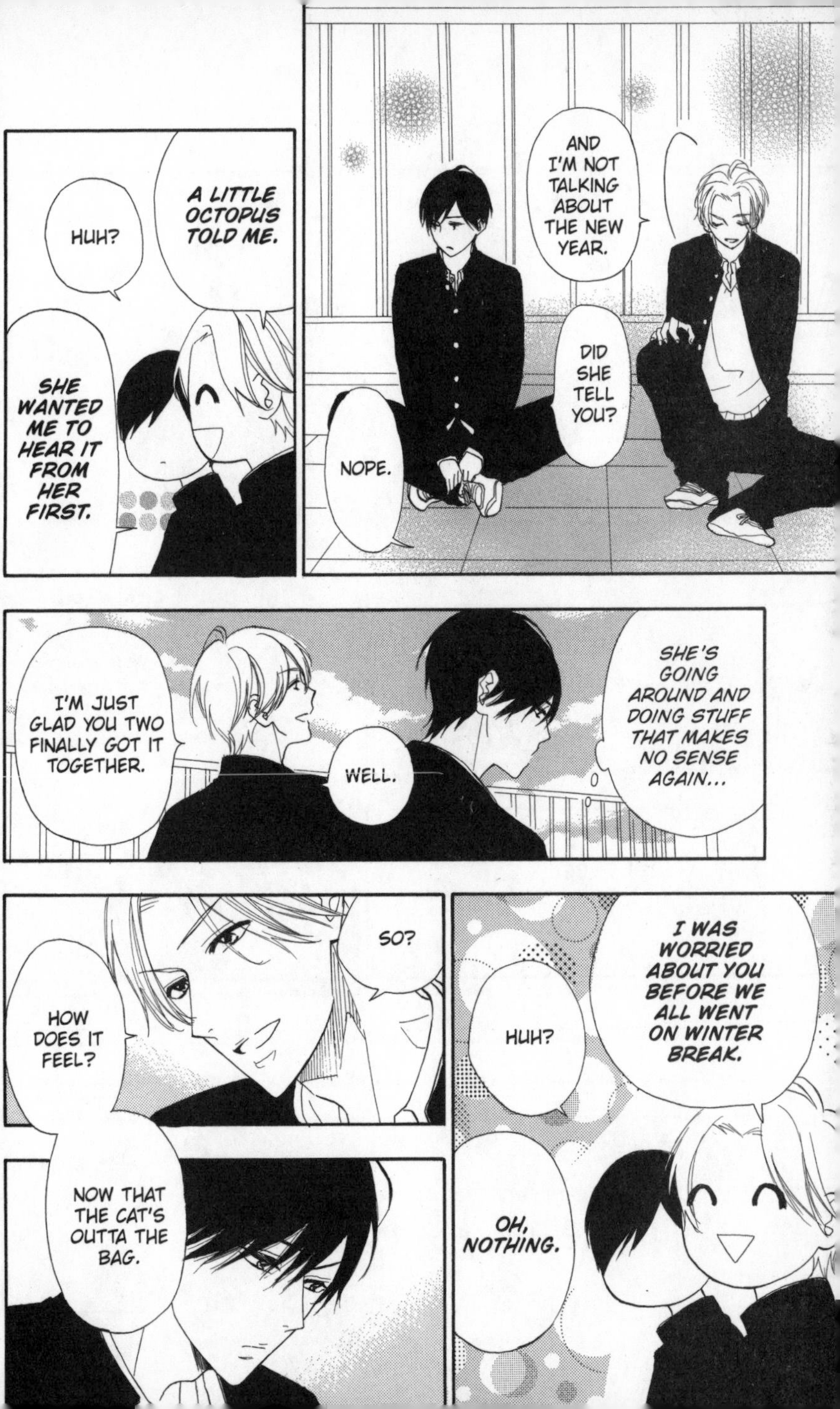
AND I'M NOT TALKING ABOUT THE NEW YEAR.
DID SHE TELL YOU?
NOPE.
A LITTLE OCTOPUS TOLD ME.
HUH?
SHE WANTED ME TO HEAR IT FROM HER FIRST.
SHE'S GOING AROUND AND DOING STUFF THAT MAKES NO SENSE AGAIN...
WELL.
I'M JUST GLAD YOU TWO FINALLY GOT IT TOGETHER.
I WAS WORRIED ABOUT YOU BEFORE WE ALL WENT ON WINTER BREAK.
HUH?
OH, NOTHING.
SO?
HOW DOES IT FEEL?
NOW THAT THE CAT'S OUTTA THE BAG.

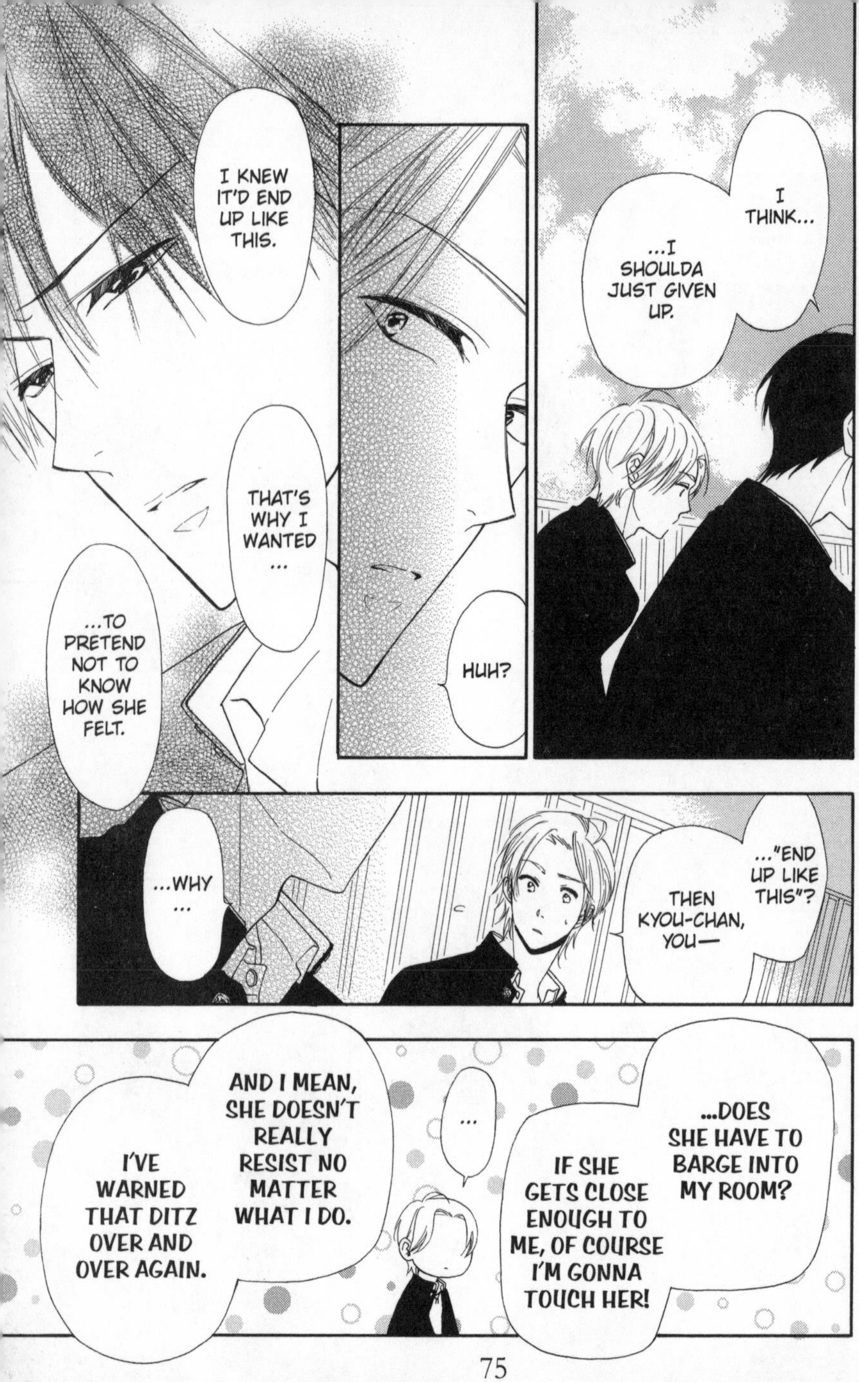
I THINK...
...I SHOULDA JUST GIVEN UP.
I KNEW IT'D END UP LIKE THIS.
HUH?
THAT'S WHY I WANTED...
...TO PRETEND NOT TO KNOW HOW SHE FELT.
..."END UP LIKE THIS"?
THEN KYOU-CHAN, YOU—
...WHY...
...DOES SHE HAVE TO BARGE INTO MY ROOM?
IF SHE GETS CLOSE ENOUGH TO ME, OF COURSE I'M GONNA TOUCH HER!
...
AND I MEAN, SHE DOESN'T REALLY RESIST NO MATTER WHAT I DO.
I'VE WARNED THAT DITZ OVER AND OVER AGAIN.

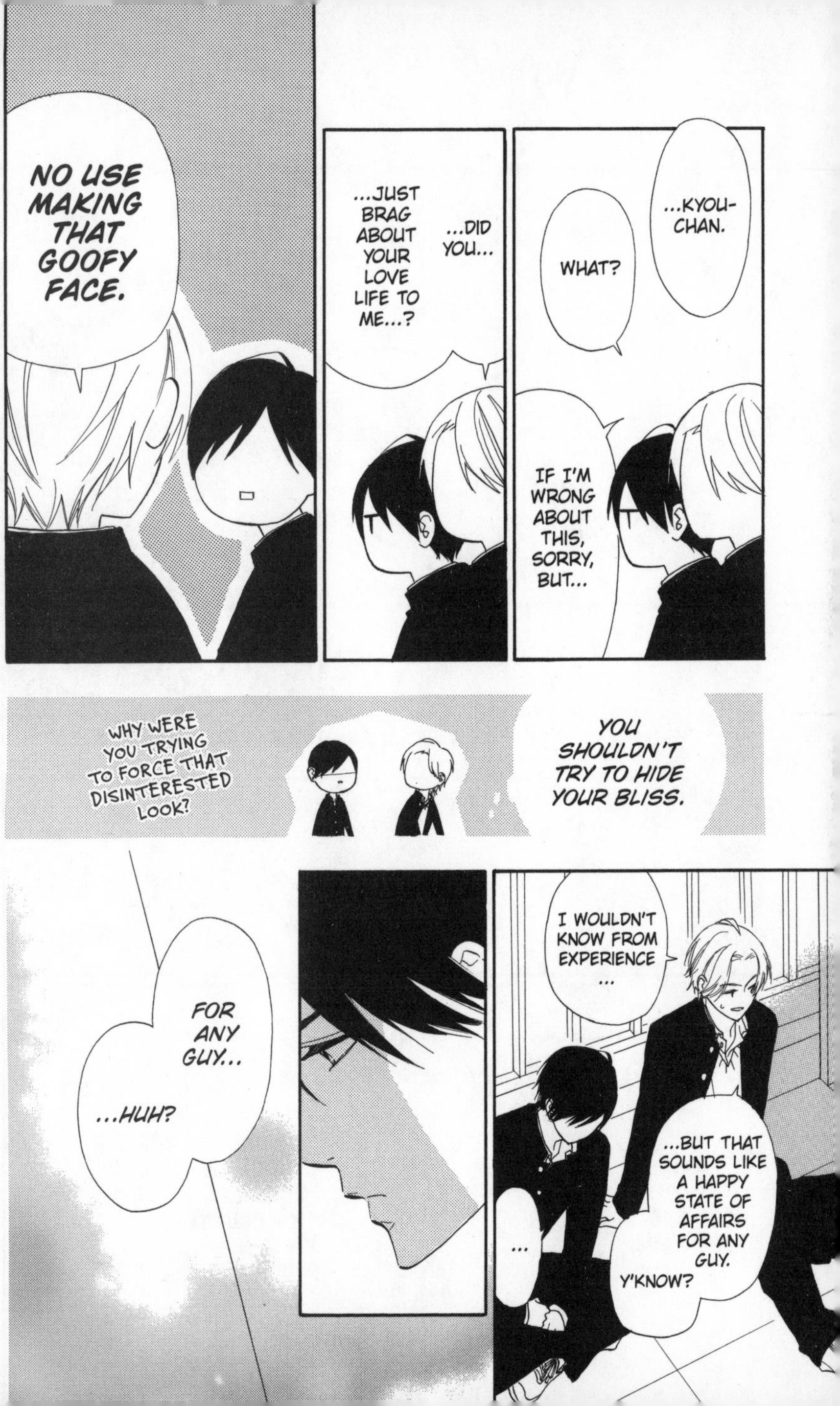
...KYOU-CHAN.
WHAT?
IF I'M WRONG ABOUT THIS, SORRY, BUT...
...DID YOU...
...JUST BRAG ABOUT YOUR LOVE LIFE TO ME...?
NO USE MAKING THAT GOOFY FACE.
YOU SHOULDN'T TRY TO HIDE YOUR BLISS.
WHY WERE YOU TRYING TO FORCE THAT DISINTERESTED LOOK?
I WOULDN'T KNOW FROM EXPERIENCE ...
...BUT THAT SOUNDS LIKE A HAPPY STATE OF AFFAIRS FOR ANY GUY.
Y'KNOW?
...
FOR ANY GUY...
...HUH?

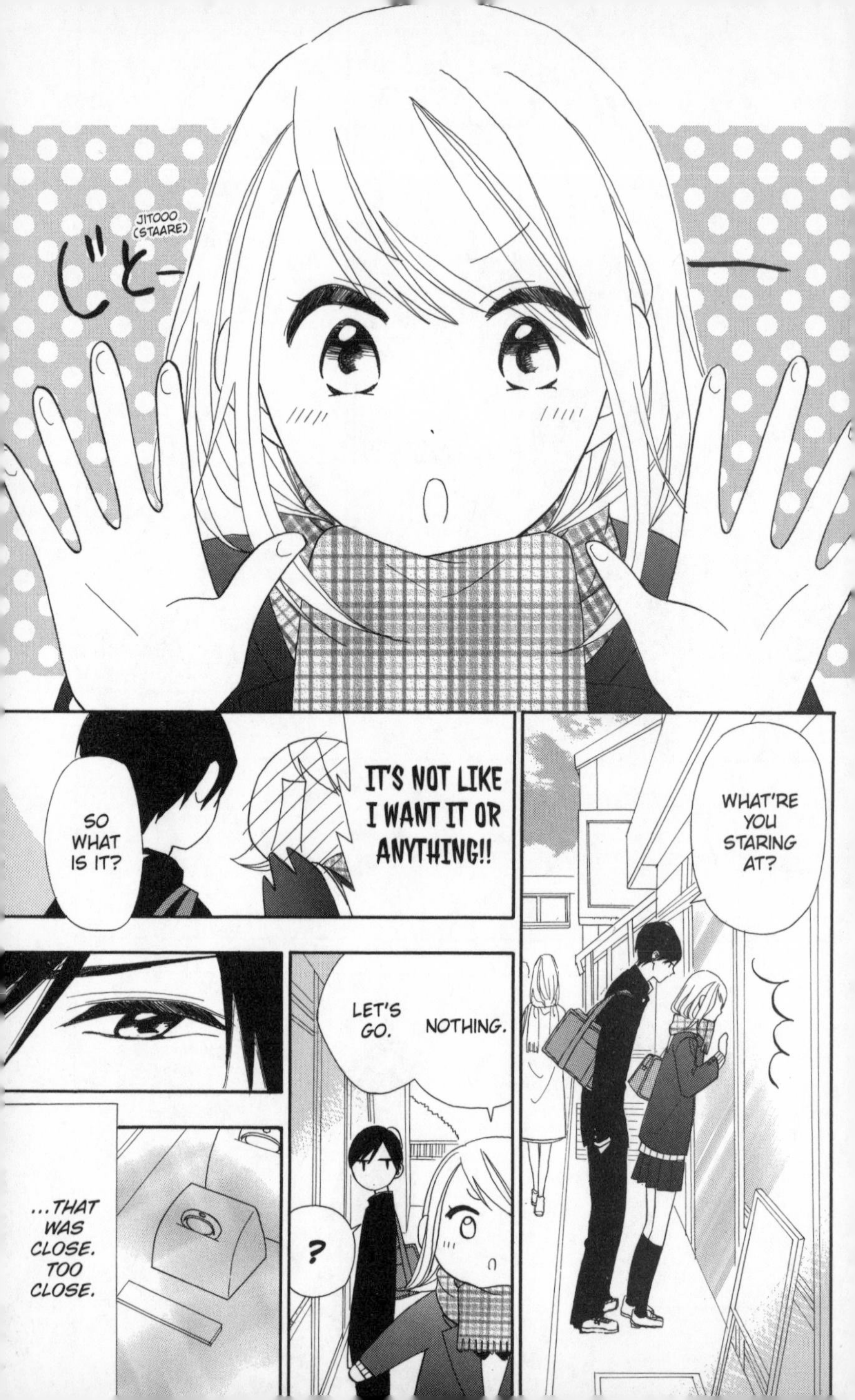
じとー
JITOOO (STAARE)
WHAT'RE YOU STARING AT?
IT'S NOT LIKE I WANT IT OR ANYTHING!!
SO WHAT IS IT?
NOTHING.
LET'S GO.
?
...THAT WAS CLOSE. TOO CLOSE.

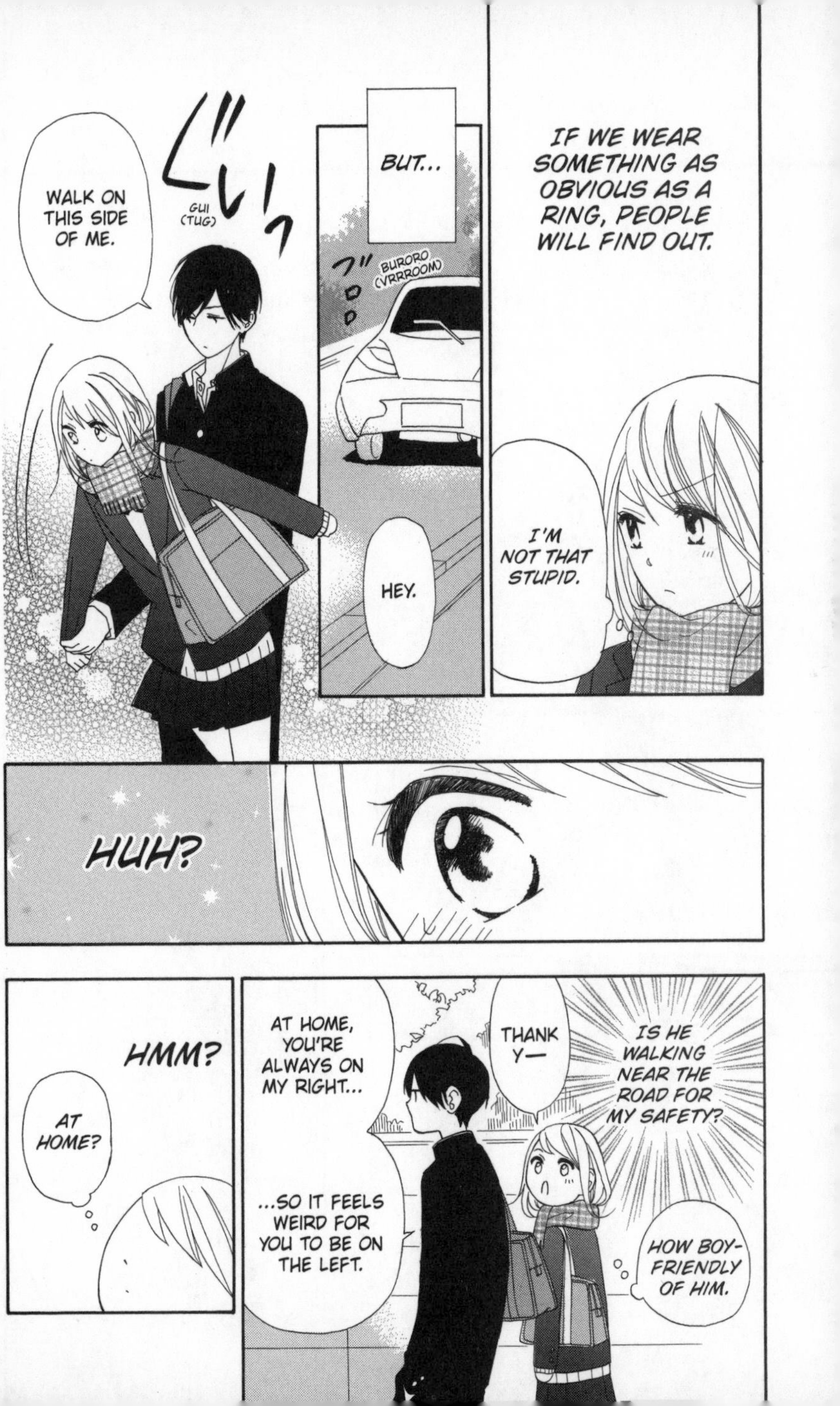
IF WE WEAR SOMETHING AS OBVIOUS AS A RING, PEOPLE WILL FIND OUT.
I'M NOT THAT STUPID.
BUT...
BURORO (VRRROOM)
HEY.
GUI (TUG)
WALK ON THIS SIDE OF ME.
HUH?
THANK Y—
IS HE WALKING NEAR THE ROAD FOR MY SAFETY?
HOW BOY-FRIENDLY OF HIM.
AT HOME, YOU'RE ALWAYS ON MY RIGHT...
...SO IT FEELS WEIRD FOR YOU TO BE ON THE LEFT.
HMM?
AT HOME?

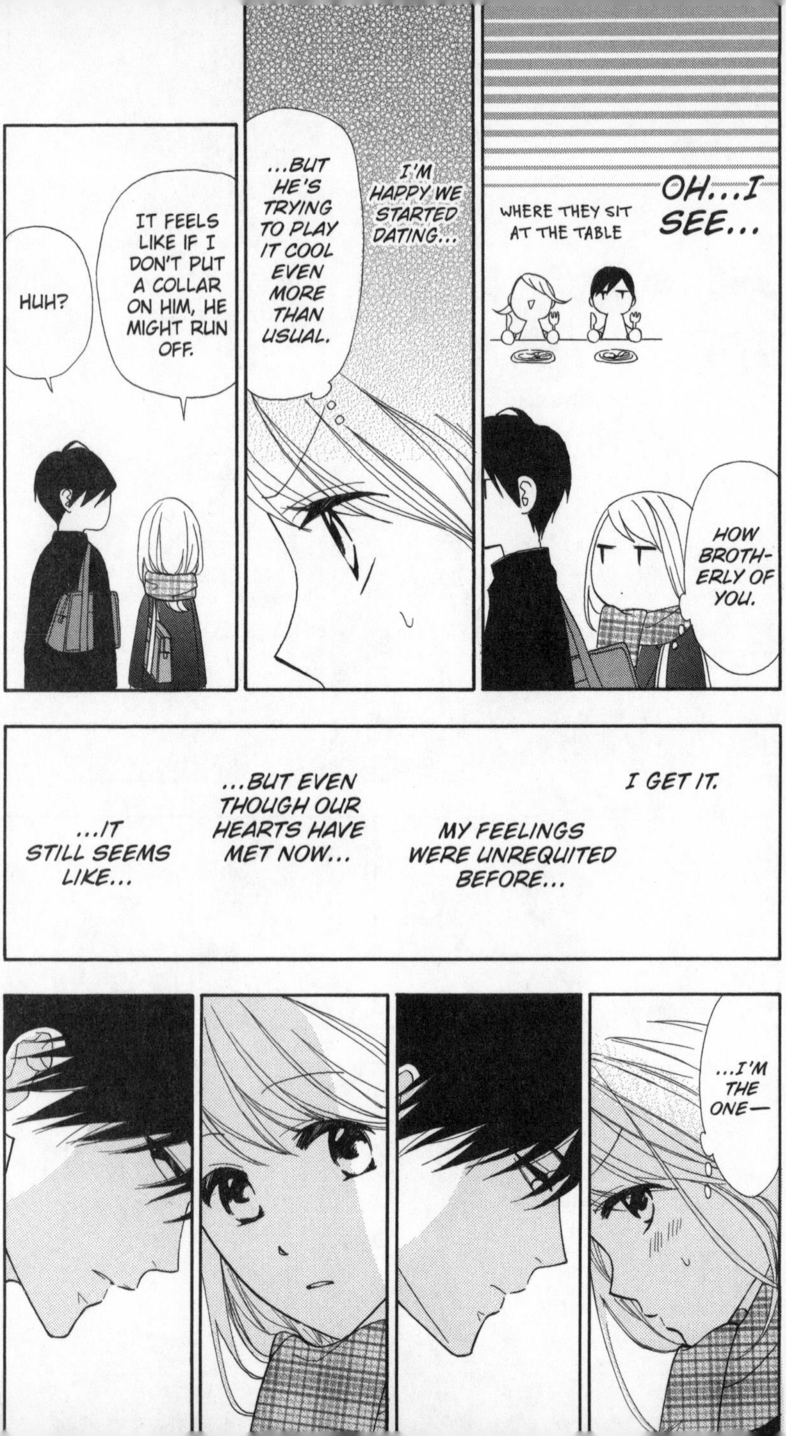
OH...I SEE...
WHERE THEY SIT AT THE TABLE
HOW BROTHERLY OF YOU.
I'M HAPPY WE STARTED DATING...
...BUT HE'S TRYING TO PLAY IT COOL EVEN MORE THAN USUAL.
IT FEELS LIKE IF I DON'T PUT A COLLAR ON HIM, HE MIGHT RUN OFF.
HUH?
I GET IT.
MY FEELINGS WERE UNREQUITED BEFORE...
...BUT EVEN THOUGH OUR HEARTS HAVE MET NOW...
...IT STILL SEEMS LIKE...
...I'M THE ONE—

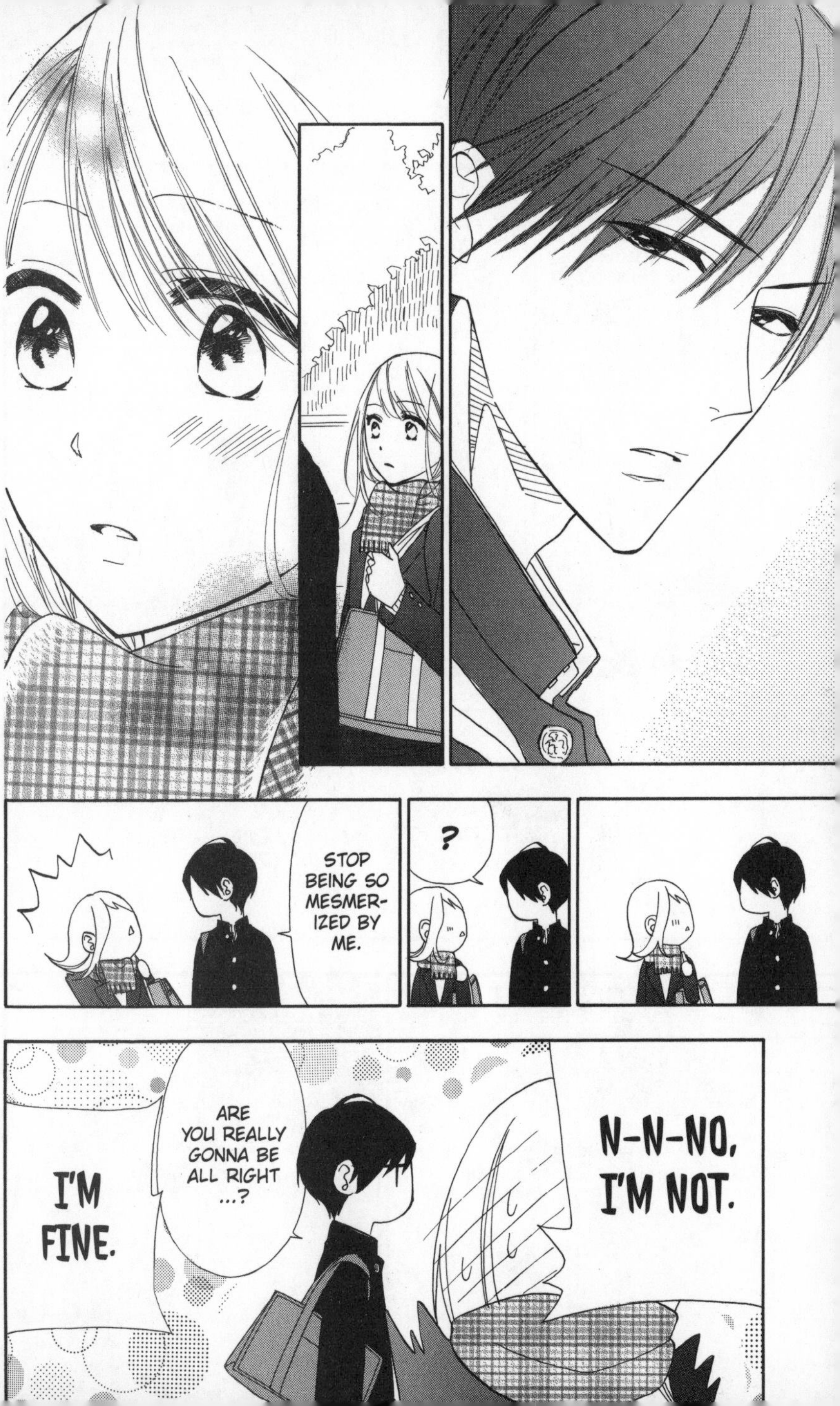
?
STOP BEING SO MESMER-IZED BY ME.
N-N-NO, I'M NOT.
ARE YOU REALLY GONNA BE ALL RIGHT ...?
I'M FINE.

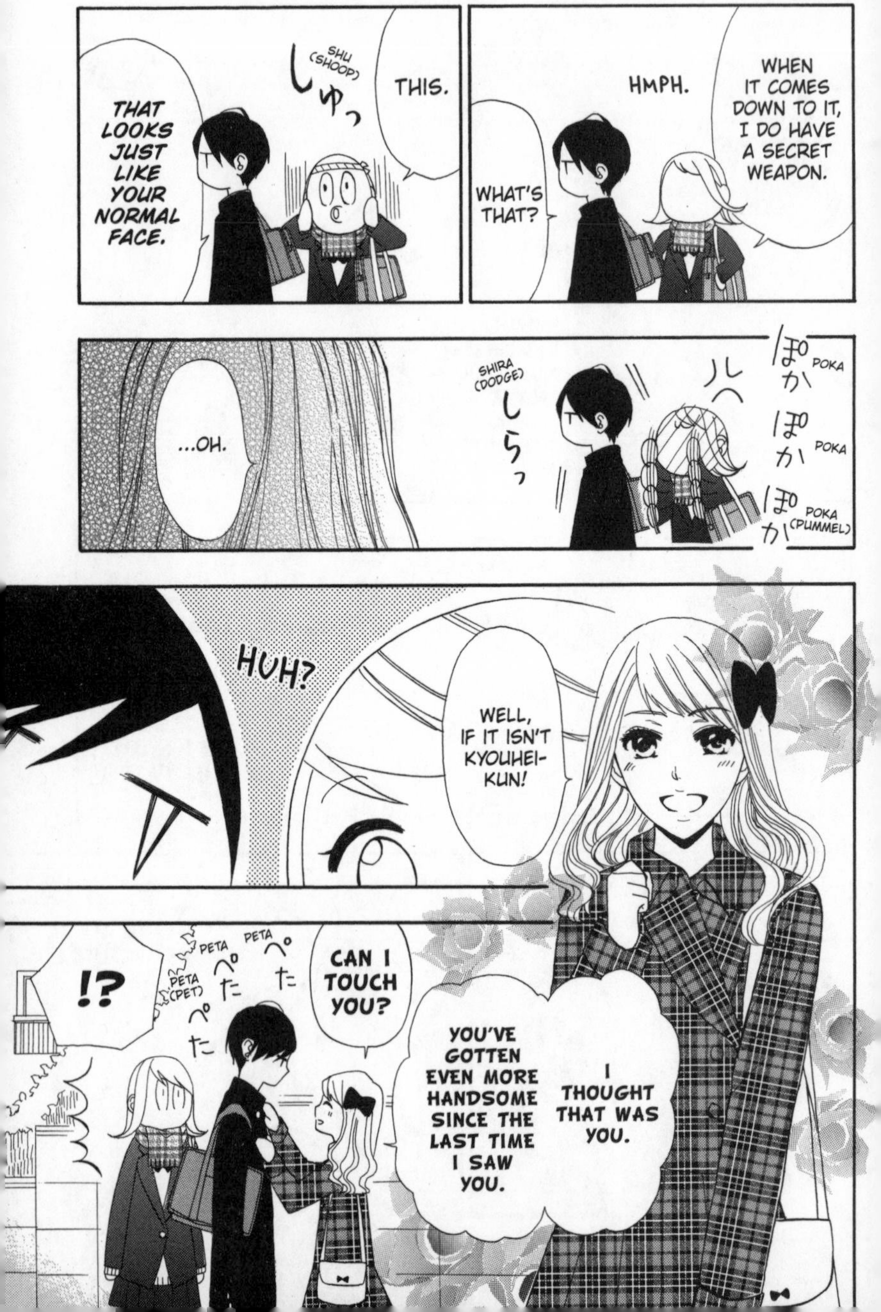
WHEN IT COMES DOWN TO IT, I DO HAVE A SECRET WEAPON.
HMPH.
WHAT'S THAT?
THIS.
しゅっ
SHU (SHOOP)
THAT LOOKS JUST LIKE YOUR NORMAL FACE.
ぽかぽかぽか
POKA
POKA
POKA (PUMMEL)
しらっ
SHIRA (DODGE)
...OH.
WELL, IF IT ISN'T KYOUHEI-KUN!
I THOUGHT THAT WAS YOU.
YOU'VE GOTTEN EVEN MORE HANDSOME SINCE THE LAST TIME I SAW YOU.
HUH?
CAN I TOUCH YOU?
ぺたぺたぺた
PETA
PETA
PETA (PET)
!?

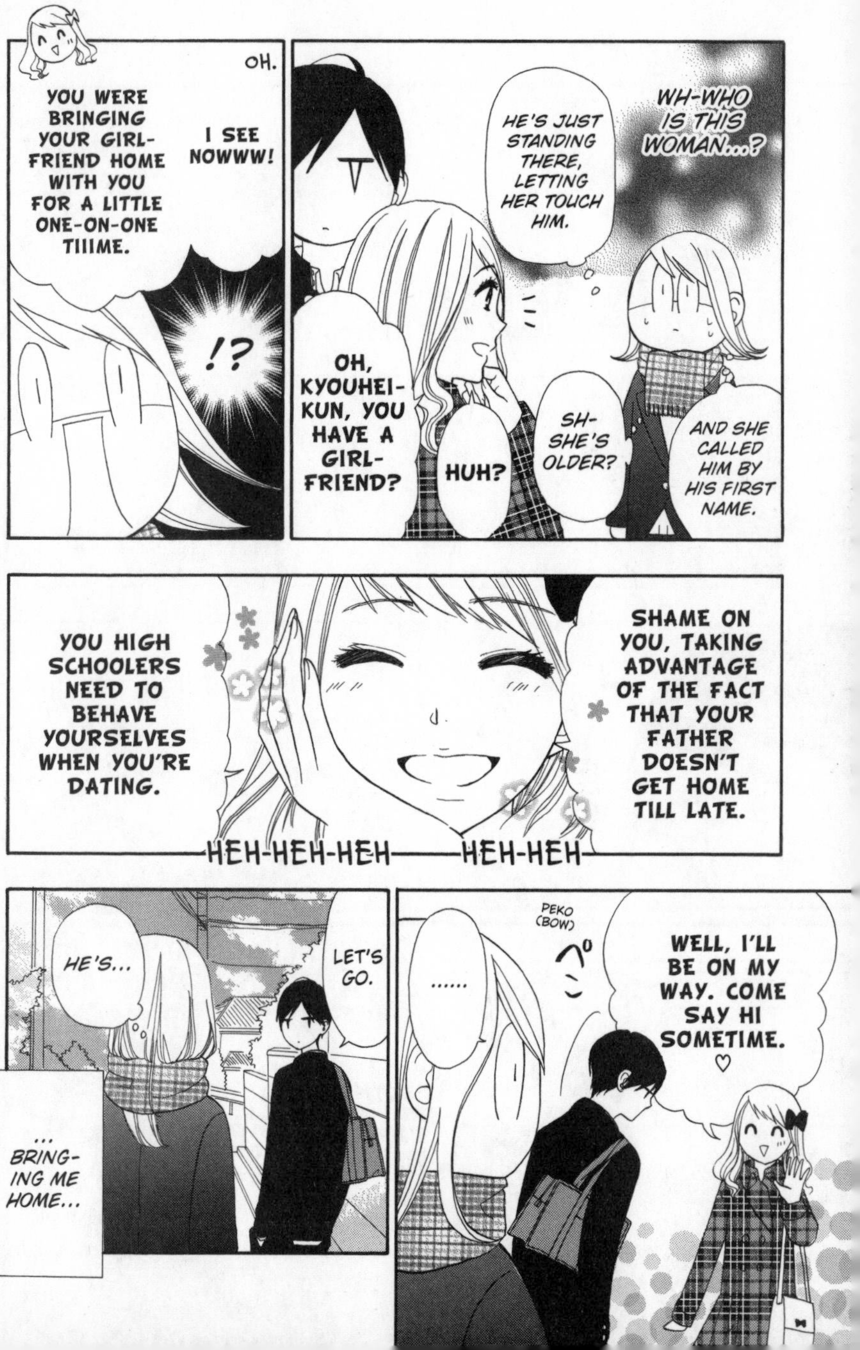
WH-WHO IS THIS WOMAN...?
HE'S JUST STANDING THERE, LETTING HER TOUCH HIM.
AND SHE CALLED HIM BY HIS FIRST NAME.
SH-SHE'S OLDER?
HUH?
OH, KYOUHEI-KUN, YOU HAVE A GIRL-FRIEND?
OH.
I SEE NOWWW!
YOU WERE BRINGING YOUR GIRL-FRIEND HOME WITH YOU FOR A LITTLE ONE-ON-ONE TIIIME.
!?
SHAME ON YOU, TAKING ADVANTAGE OF THE FACT THAT YOUR FATHER DOESN'T GET HOME TILL LATE.
YOU HIGH SCHOOLERS NEED TO BEHAVE YOURSELVES WHEN YOU'RE DATING.
HEH-HEH
HEH-HEH-HEH
WELL, I'LL BE ON MY WAY. COME SAY HI SOMETIME. ♡
PEKO (BOW)
......
LET'S GO.
HE'S...
...BRINGING ME HOME...

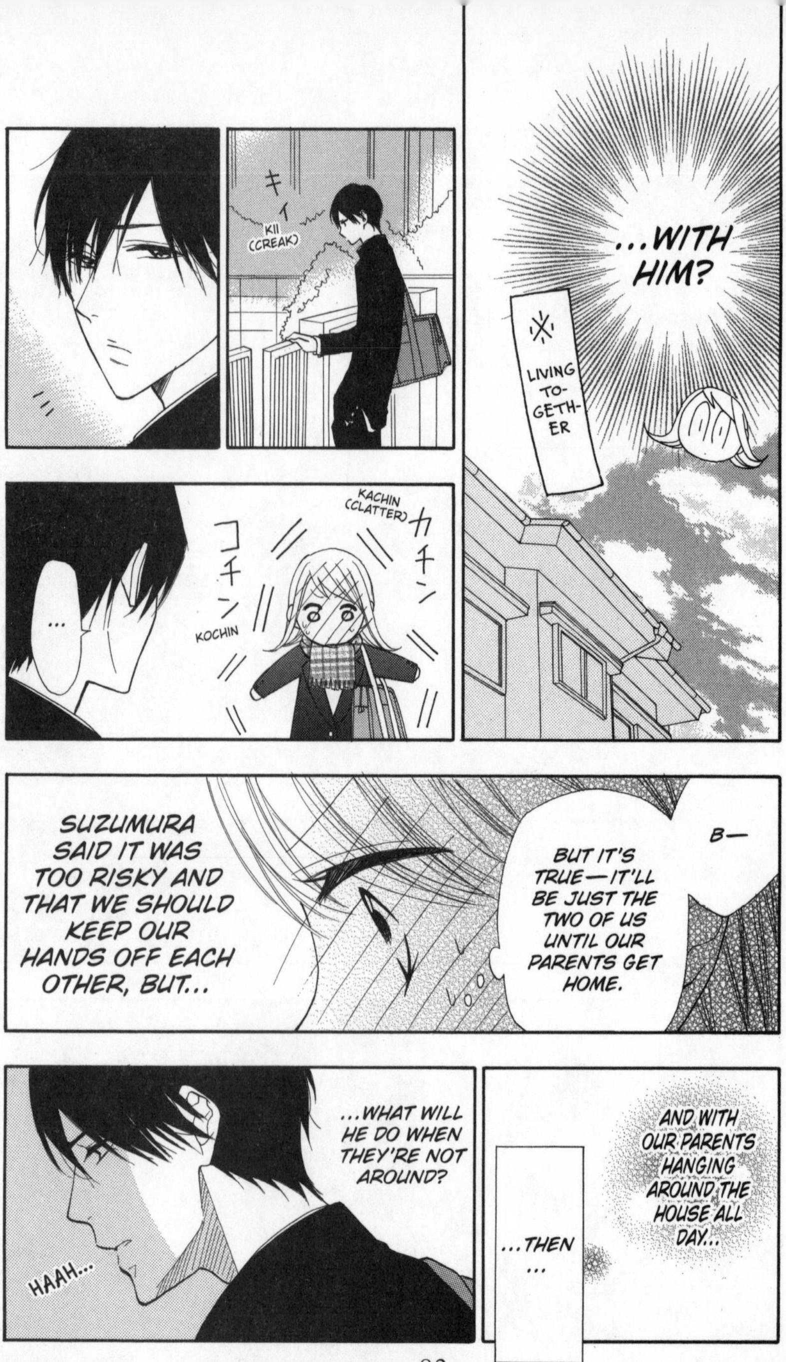
...WITH HIM?
※ LIVING TO-GETH-ER
キイ
KII (CREAK)
カチン
KACHIN (CLATTER)
コチン
KOCHIN
...
B—
BUT IT'S TRUE—IT'LL BE JUST THE TWO OF US UNTIL OUR PARENTS GET HOME.
SUZUMURA SAID IT WAS TOO RISKY AND THAT WE SHOULD KEEP OUR HANDS OFF EACH OTHER, BUT...
AND WITH OUR PARENTS HANGING AROUND THE HOUSE ALL DAY...
...THEN ...
...WHAT WILL HE DO WHEN THEY'RE NOT AROUND?
HAAH...

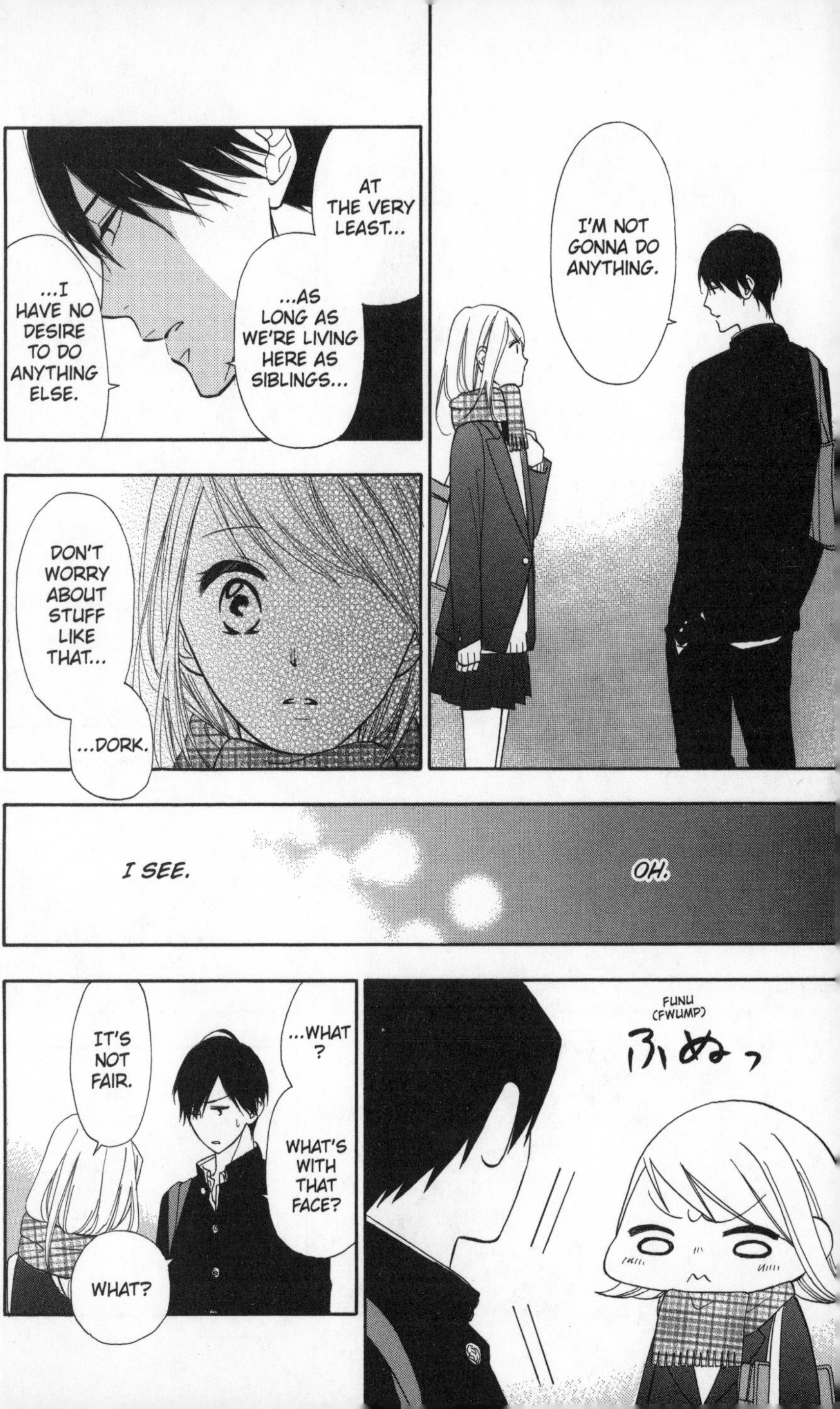
I'M NOT GONNA DO ANYTHING.
AT THE VERY LEAST...
...AS LONG AS WE'RE LIVING HERE AS SIBLINGS...
...I HAVE NO DESIRE TO DO ANYTHING ELSE.
DON'T WORRY ABOUT STUFF LIKE THAT...
...DORK.
OH.
I SEE.
FUNU (FWUMP)
ふぬっ
...WHAT?
WHAT'S WITH THAT FACE?
IT'S NOT FAIR.
WHAT?

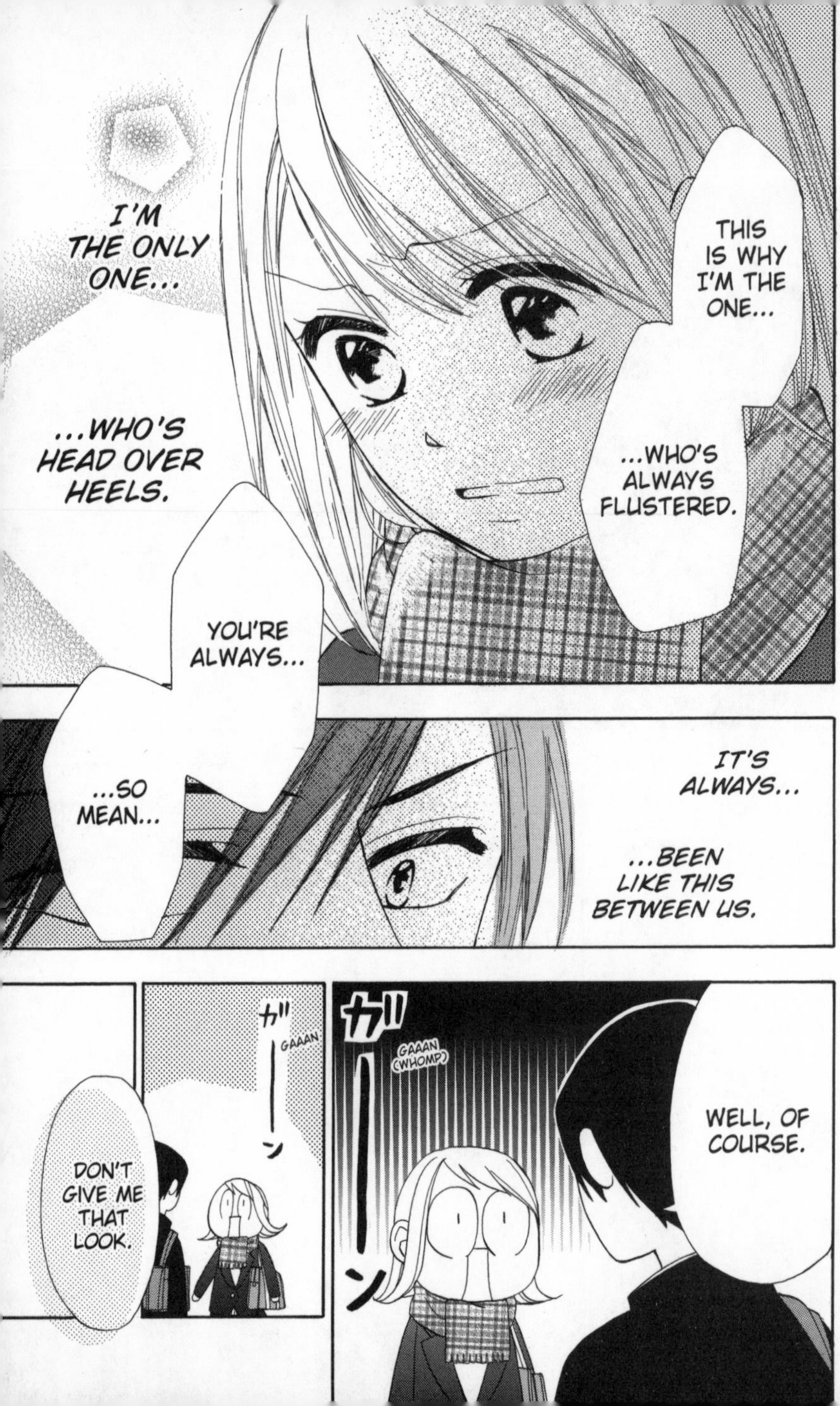
THIS IS WHY I'M THE ONE...
...WHO'S ALWAYS FLUSTERED.
I'M THE ONLY ONE...
...WHO'S HEAD OVER HEELS.
YOU'RE ALWAYS... ...SO MEAN...
IT'S ALWAYS...
...BEEN LIKE THIS BETWEEN US.
WELL, OF COURSE.
ガーン
GAAAN (WHOMP)
ガーン
GAAAN
DON'T GIVE ME THAT LOOK.

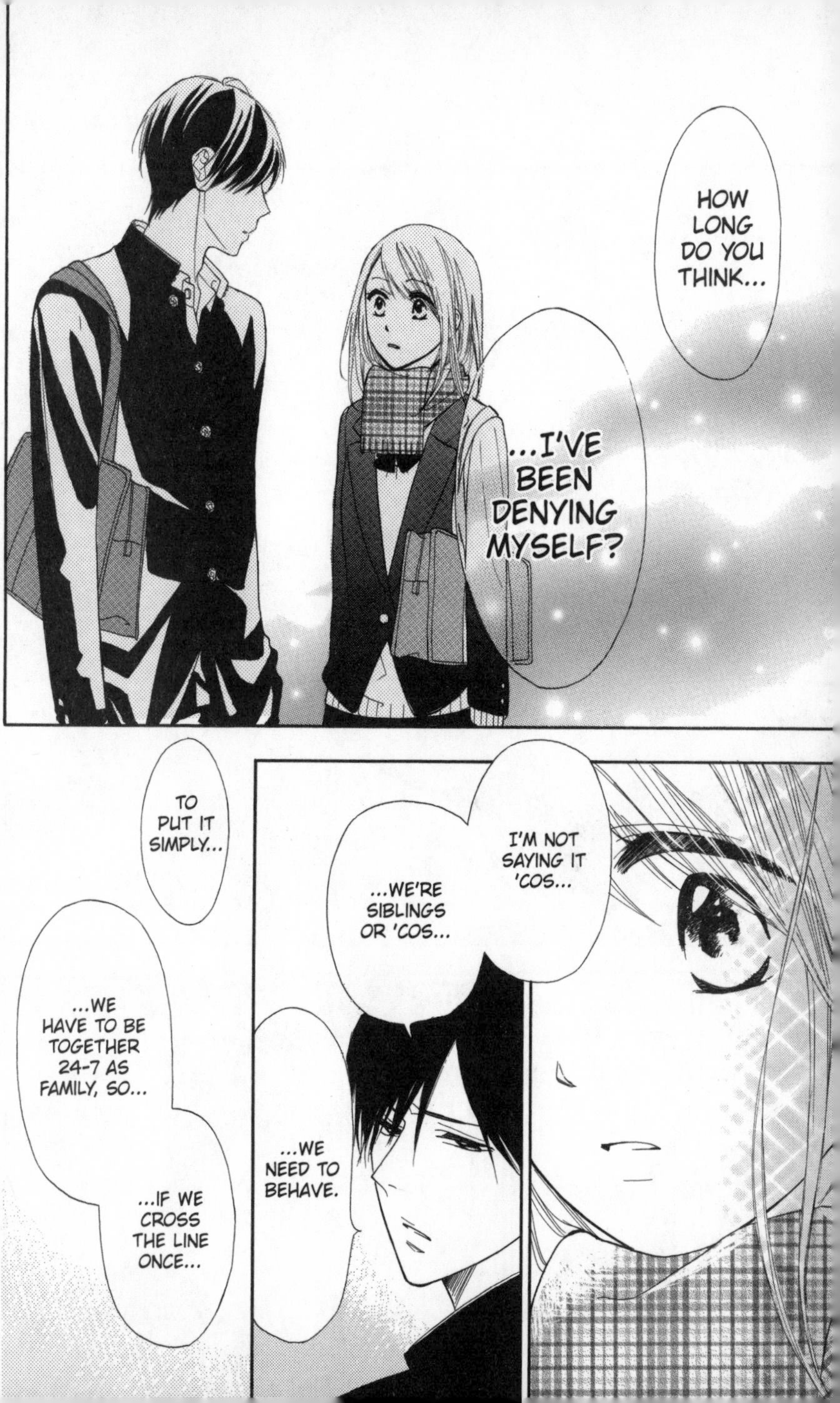
HOW LONG DO YOU THINK...
...I'VE BEEN DENYING MYSELF?
I'M NOT SAYING IT 'COS...
...WE'RE SIBLINGS OR 'COS...
...WE NEED TO BEHAVE.
TO PUT IT SIMPLY...
...WE HAVE TO BE TOGETHER 24-7 AS FAMILY, SO...
...IF WE CROSS THE LINE ONCE...

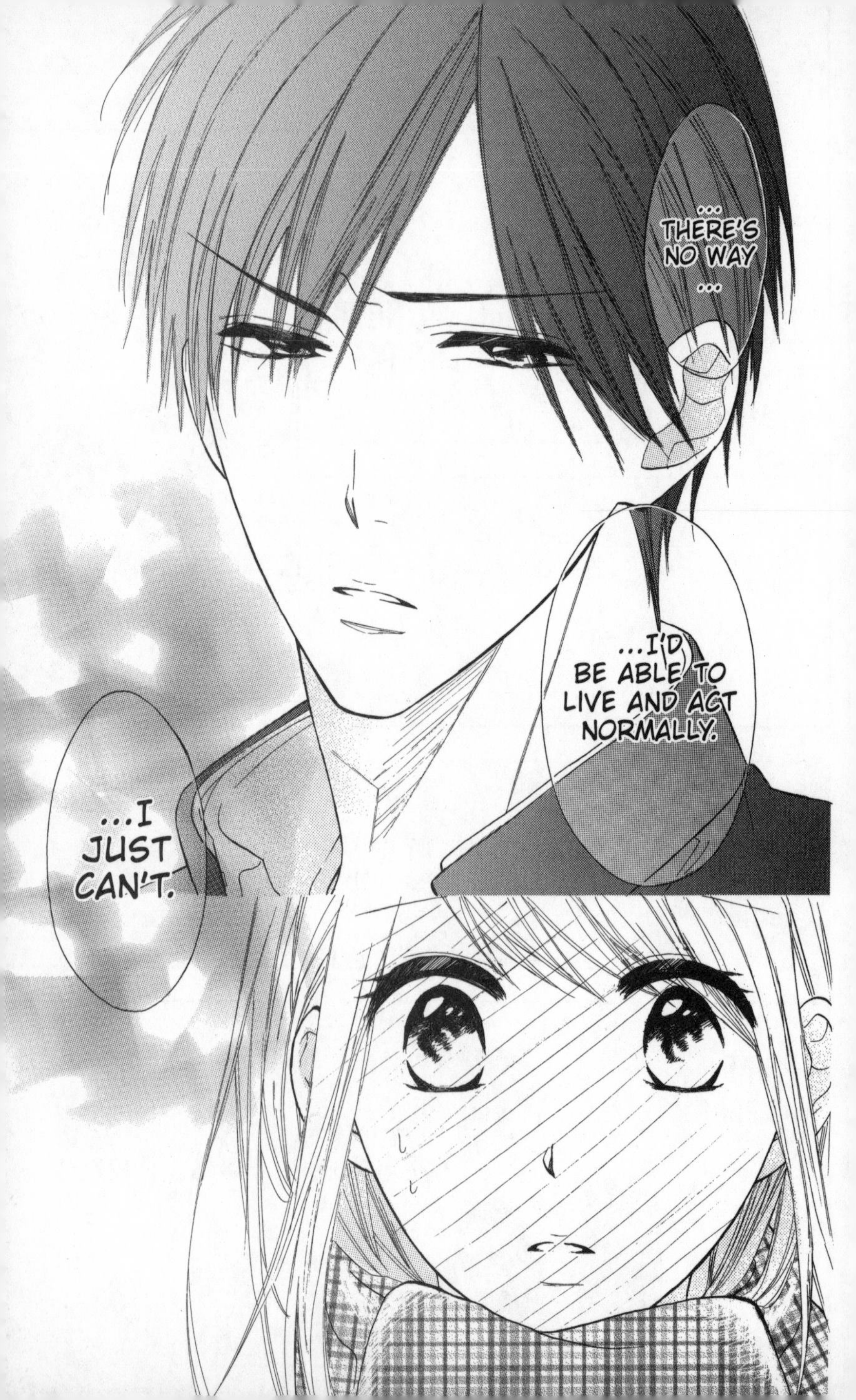
...THERE'S NO WAY ...
...I'D BE ABLE TO LIVE AND ACT NORMALLY.
...I JUST CAN'T.

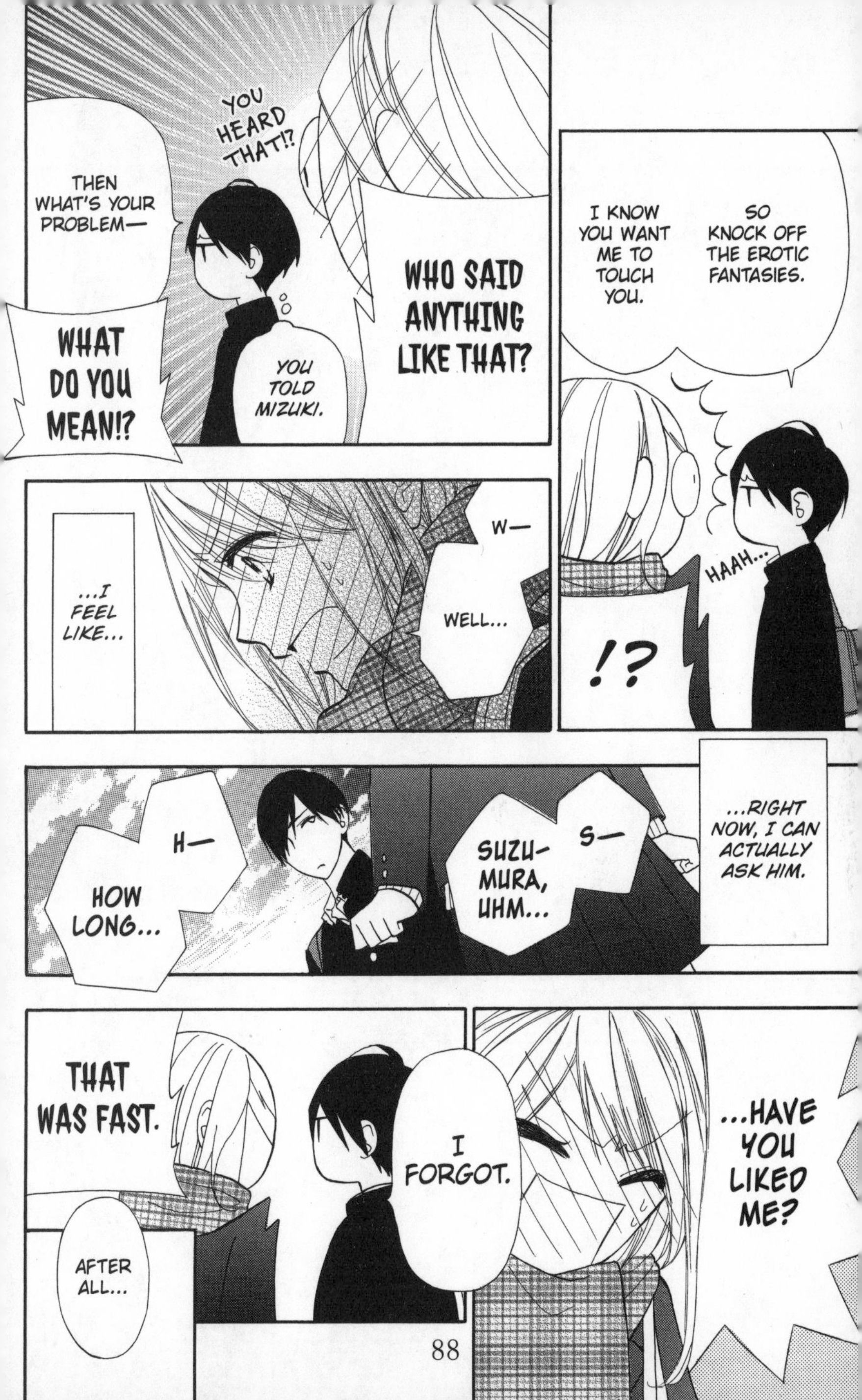
I KNOW YOU WANT ME TO TOUCH YOU.
SO KNOCK OFF THE EROTIC FANTASIES.
HAAH...
!?
WHO SAID ANYTHING LIKE THAT?
YOU HEARD THAT!?
YOU TOLD MIZUKI.
THEN WHAT'S YOUR PROBLEM—
WHAT DO YOU MEAN!?
W—
WELL...
...I FEEL LIKE...
...RIGHT NOW, I CAN ACTUALLY ASK HIM.
S—
SUZU-MURA, UHM...
H—
HOW LONG...
...HAVE YOU LIKED ME?
I FORGOT.
THAT WAS FAST.
AFTER ALL...

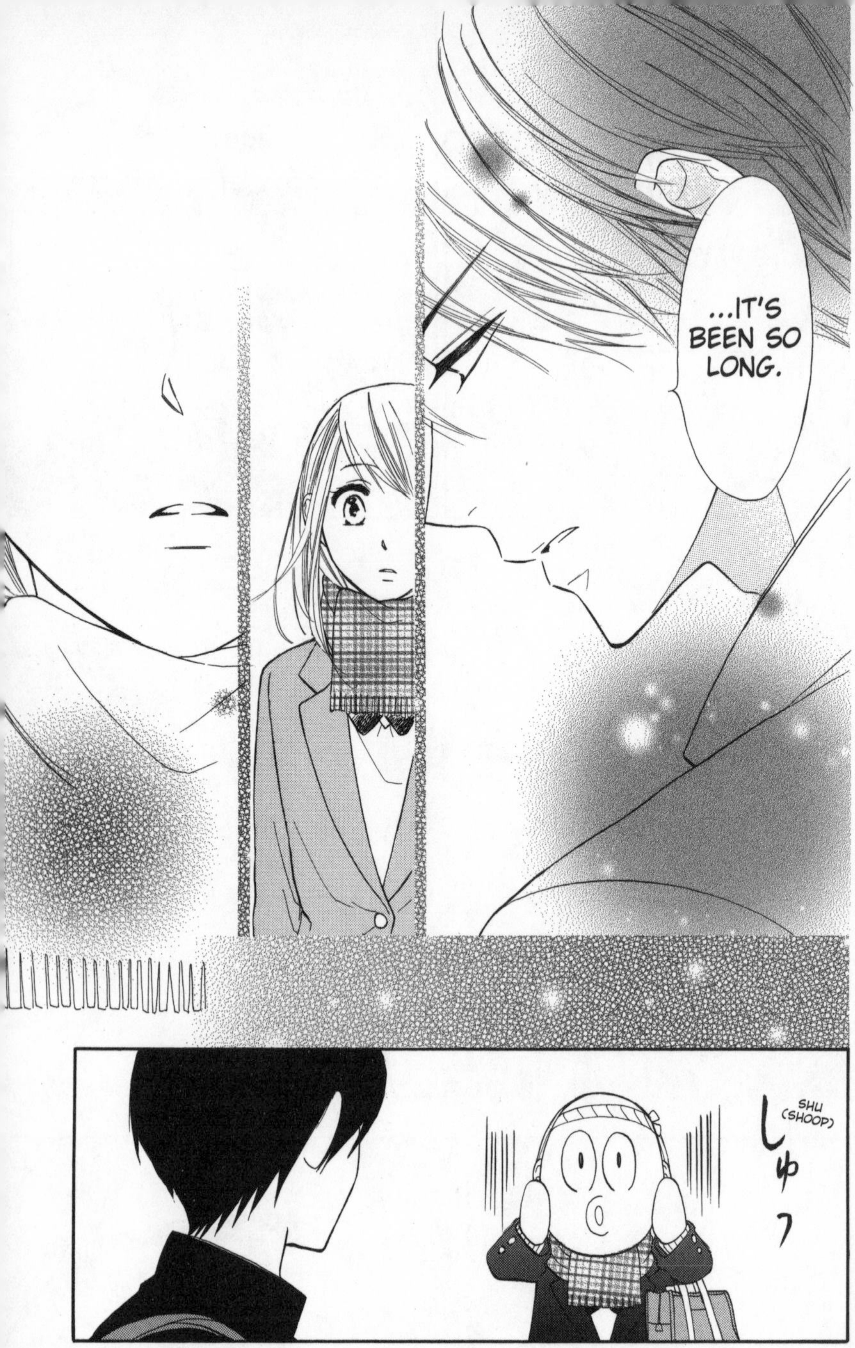
...IT'S BEEN SO LONG.
しゅっ
SHU (SHOOP)

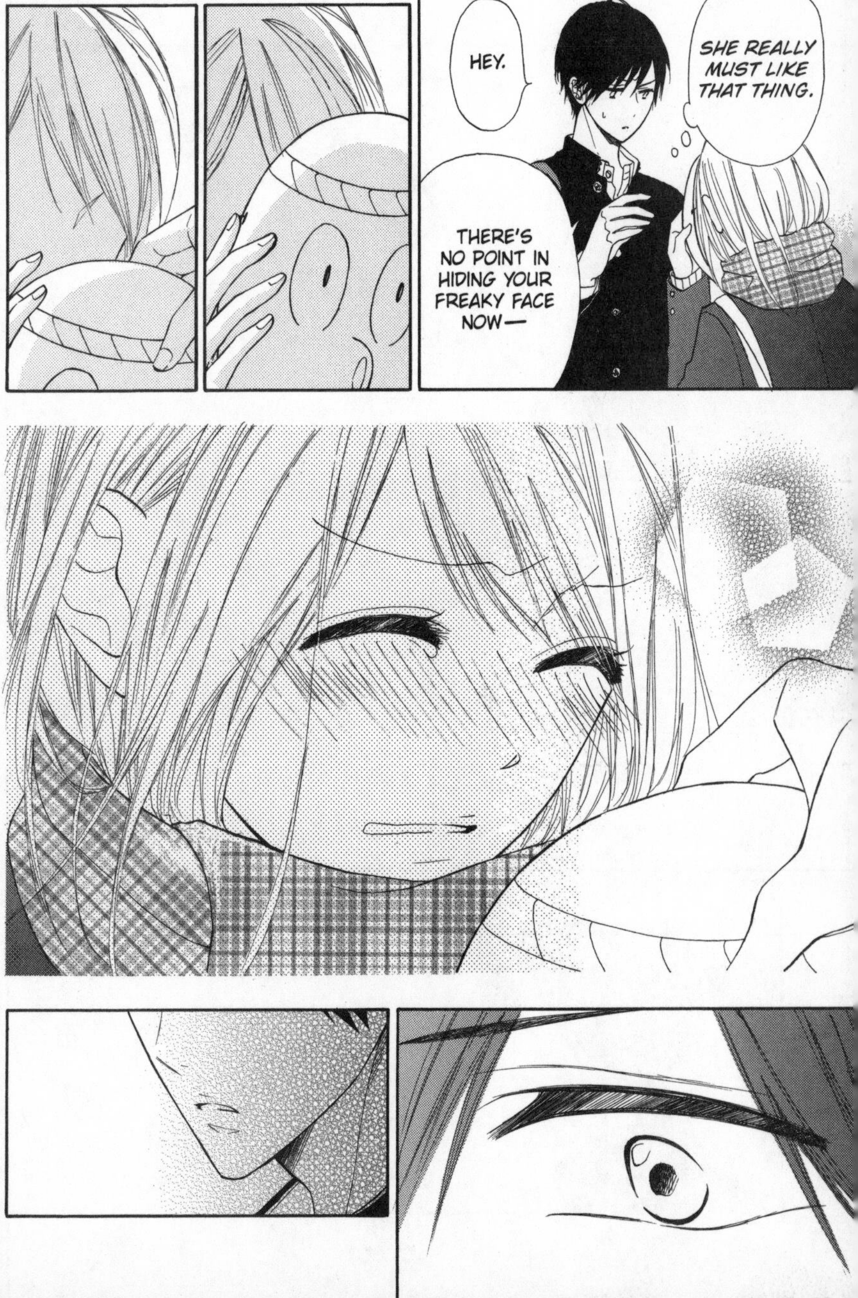
SHE REALLY MUST LIKE THAT THING.
HEY.
THERE'S NO POINT IN HIDING YOUR FREAKY FACE NOW—

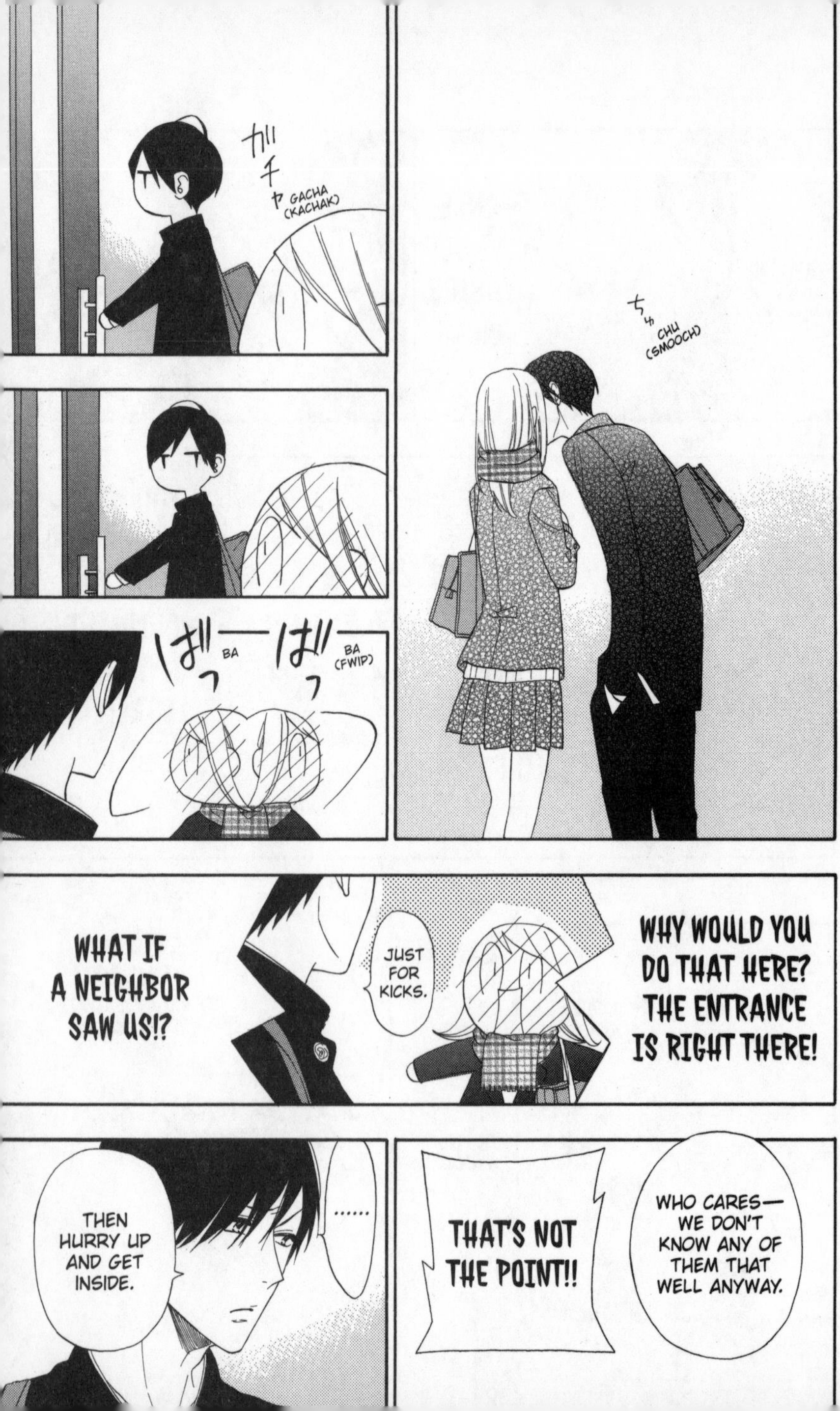
ちゅ
CHU (SMOOCH)
ガチャ
GACHA (KACHAK)
ばっ
BA
ばっ
BA (FWIP)
WHY WOULD YOU DO THAT HERE? THE ENTRANCE IS RIGHT THERE!
JUST FOR KICKS.
WHAT IF A NEIGHBOR SAW US!?
WHO CARES— WE DON'T KNOW ANY OF THEM THAT WELL ANYWAY.
THAT'S NOT THE POINT!!
......
THEN HURRY UP AND GET INSIDE.

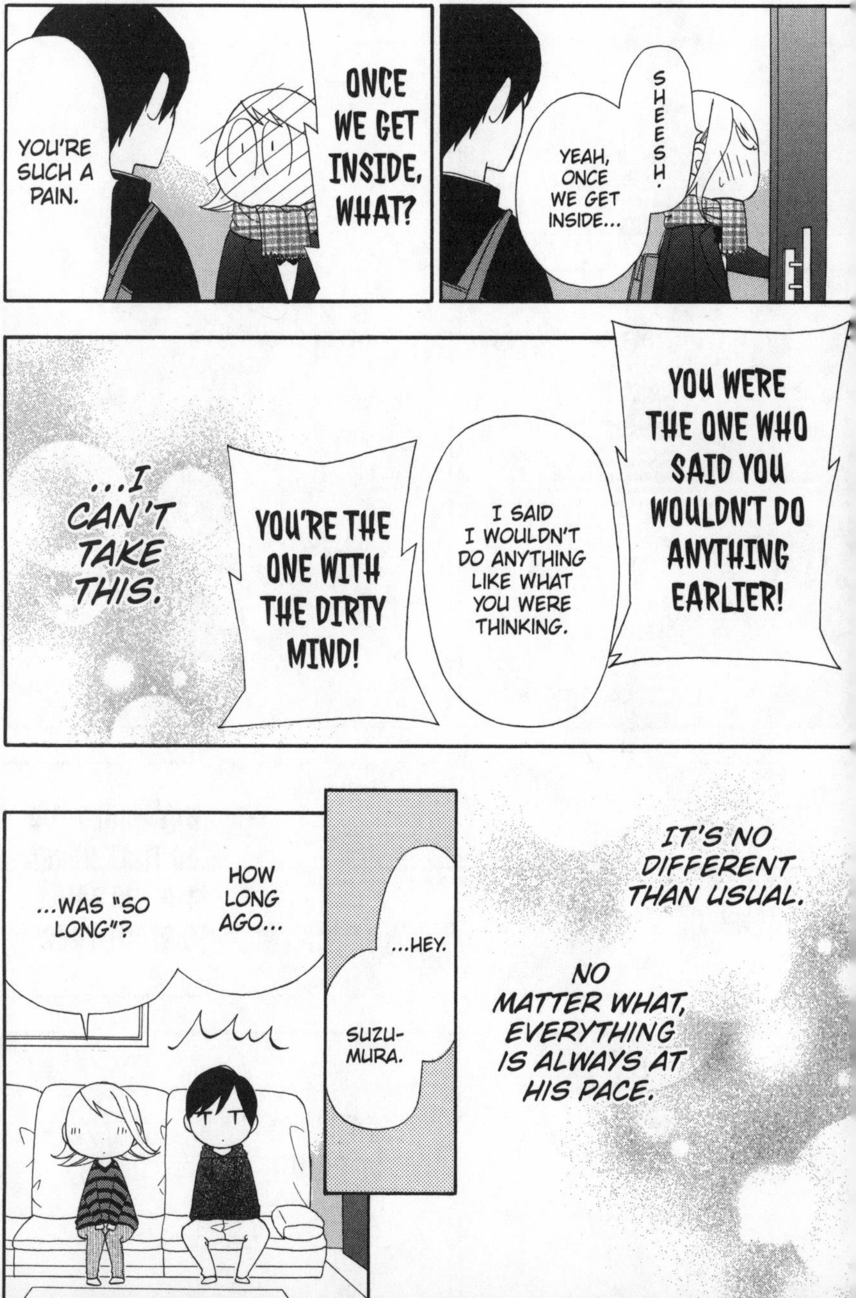
SHEESH.
YEAH, ONCE WE GET INSIDE...
ONCE WE GET INSIDE, WHAT?
YOU'RE SUCH A PAIN.
YOU WERE THE ONE WHO SAID YOU WOULDN'T DO ANYTHING EARLIER!
I SAID I WOULDN'T DO ANYTHING LIKE WHAT YOU WERE THINKING.
YOU'RE THE ONE WITH THE DIRTY MIND!
...I CAN'T TAKE THIS.
IT'S NO DIFFERENT THAN USUAL.
NO MATTER WHAT, EVERYTHING IS ALWAYS AT HIS PACE.
...HEY.
SUZU-MURA.
HOW LONG AGO...
...WAS "SO LONG"?

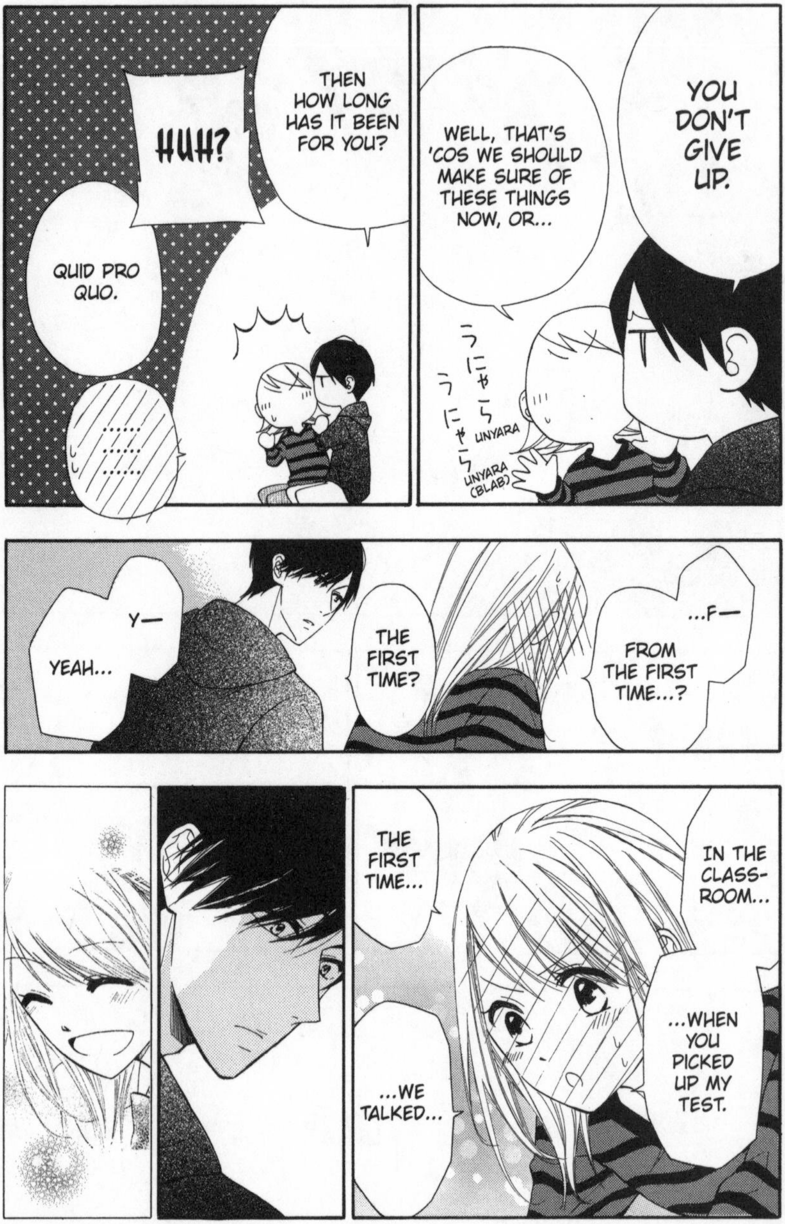
YOU DON'T GIVE UP.
WELL, THAT'S 'COS WE SHOULD MAKE SURE OF THESE THINGS NOW, OR...
うにゃら うにゃら
UNYARA UNYARA (BLAB)
THEN HOW LONG HAS IT BEEN FOR YOU?
HUH?
QUID PRO QUO.
......
...F— FROM THE FIRST TIME...?
THE FIRST TIME?
Y— YEAH...
IN THE CLASS-ROOM...
THE FIRST TIME...
...WHEN YOU PICKED UP MY TEST.
...WE TALKED...

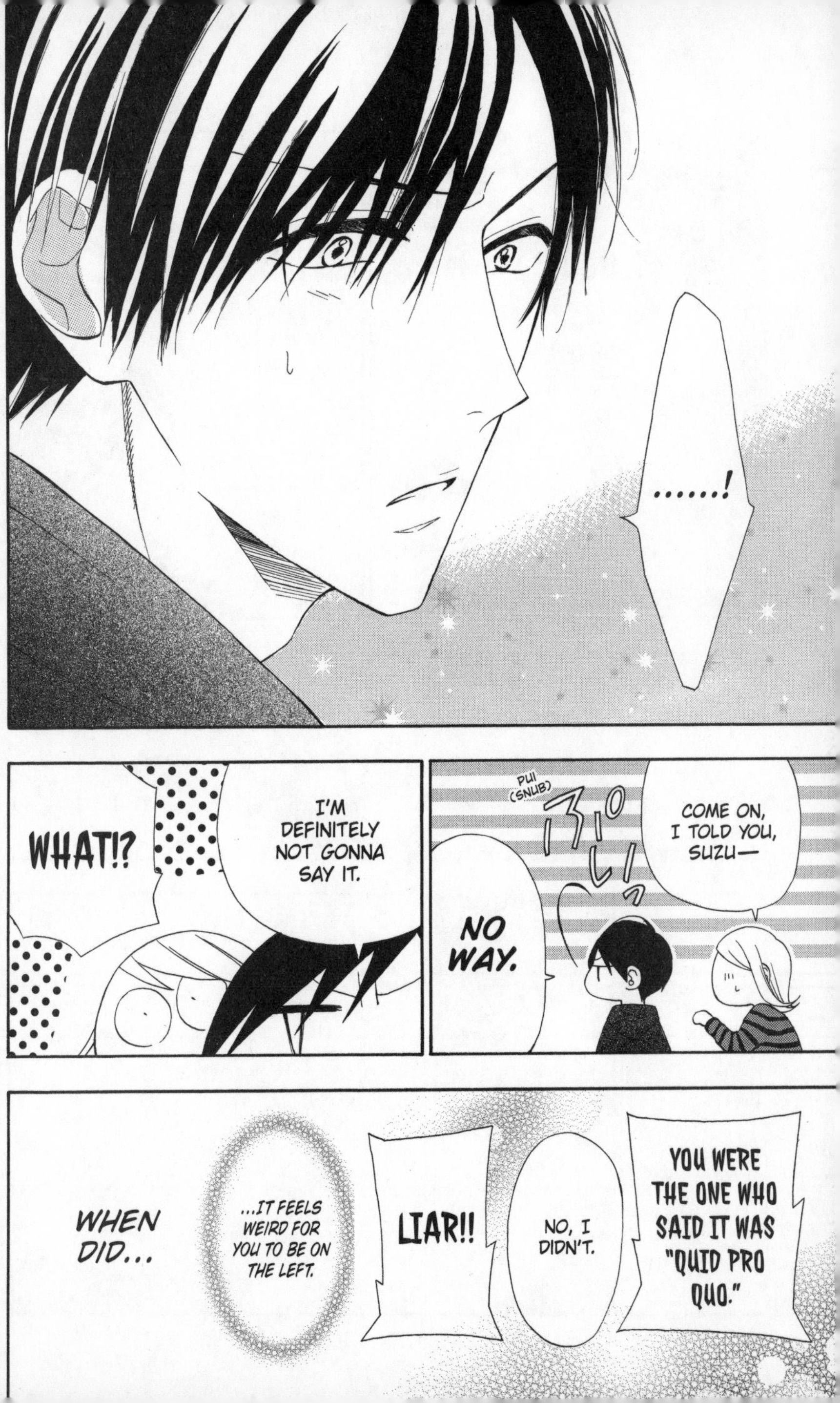
......!
COME ON, I TOLD YOU, SUZU—
PUI (SNUB)
NO WAY.
I'M DEFINITELY NOT GONNA SAY IT.
WHAT!?
YOU WERE THE ONE WHO SAID IT WAS "QUID PRO QUO."
NO, I DIDN'T.
LIAR!!
...IT FEELS WEIRD FOR YOU TO BE ON THE LEFT.
WHEN DID...

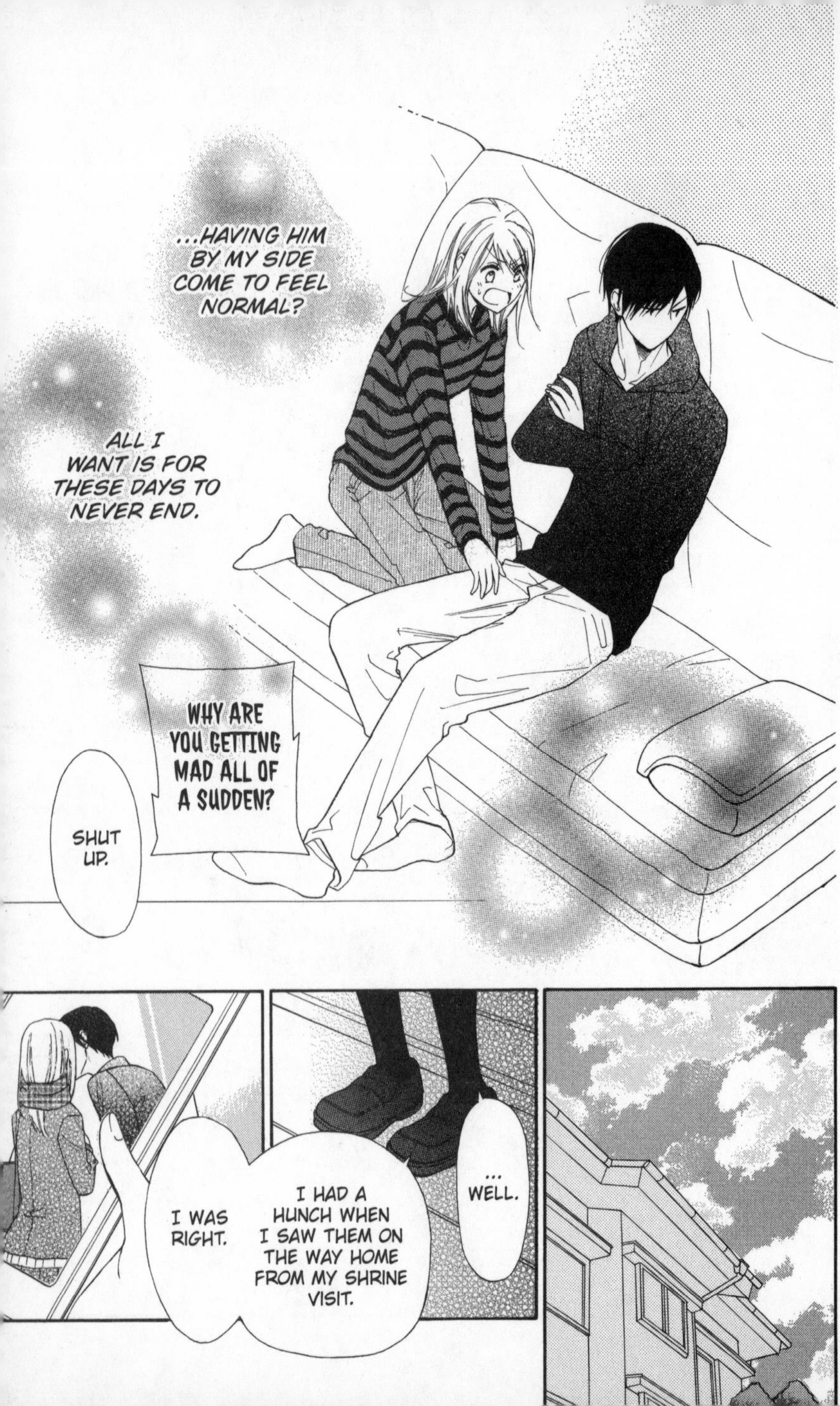
...HAVING HIM BY MY SIDE COME TO FEEL NORMAL?
ALL I WANT IS FOR THESE DAYS TO NEVER END.
WHY ARE YOU GETTING MAD ALL OF A SUDDEN?
SHUT UP.
...WELL.
I HAD A HUNCH WHEN I SAW THEM ON THE WAY HOME FROM MY SHRINE VISIT.
I WAS RIGHT.

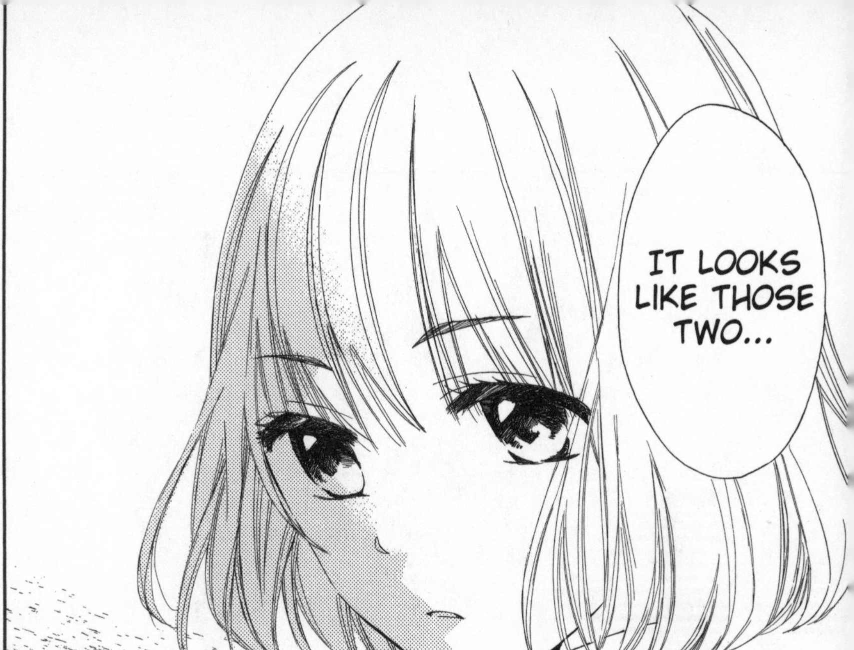
IT LOOKS LIKE THOSE TWO...
...ARE TOGETHER.

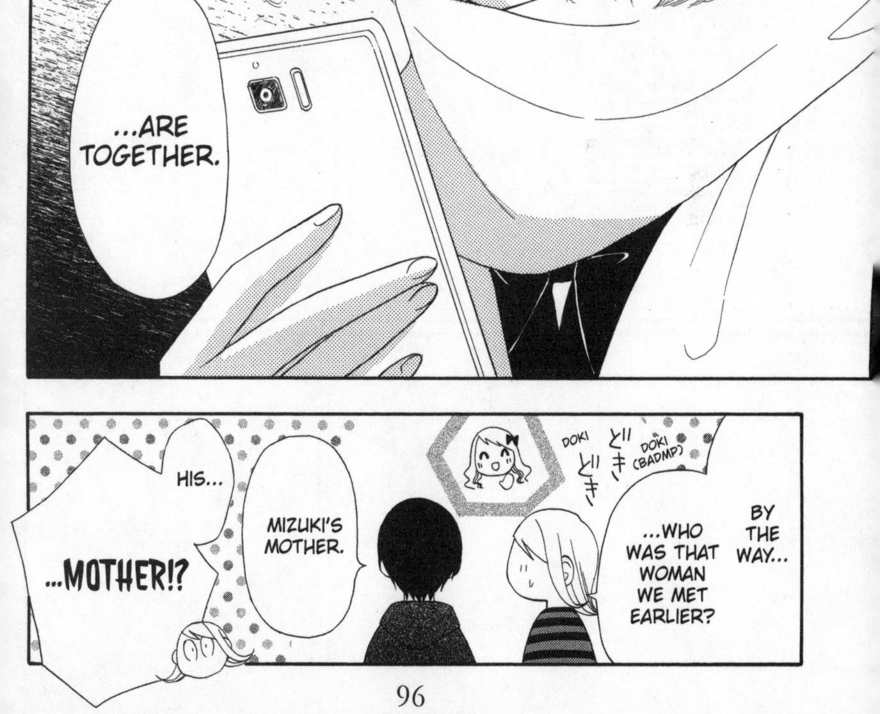
BY THE WAY...
...WHO WAS THAT WOMAN WE MET EARLIER?
DOKI
どき
DOKI (BADMP)
どき
MIZUKI'S MOTHER.
HIS...
...MOTHER!?

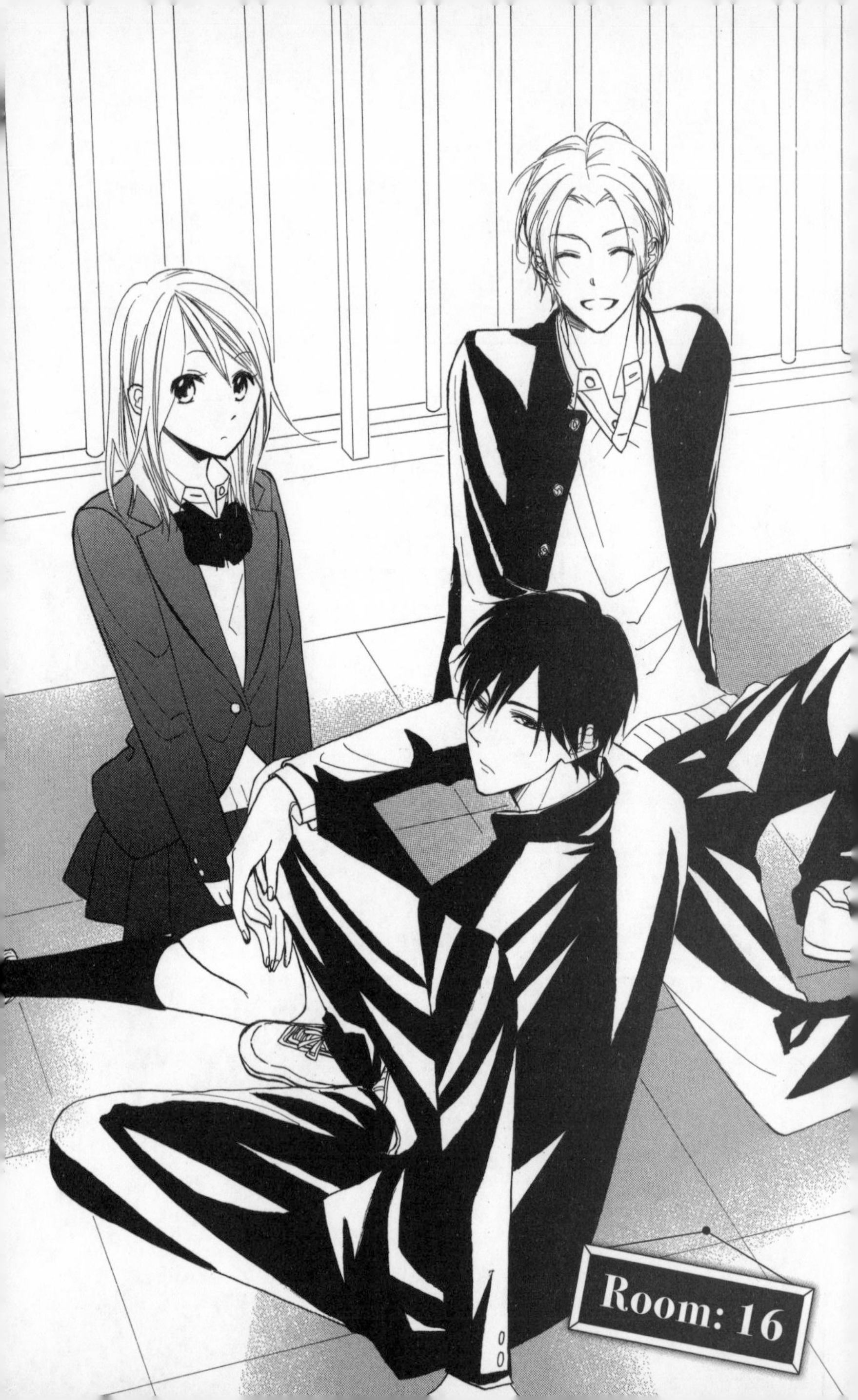
Room: 16

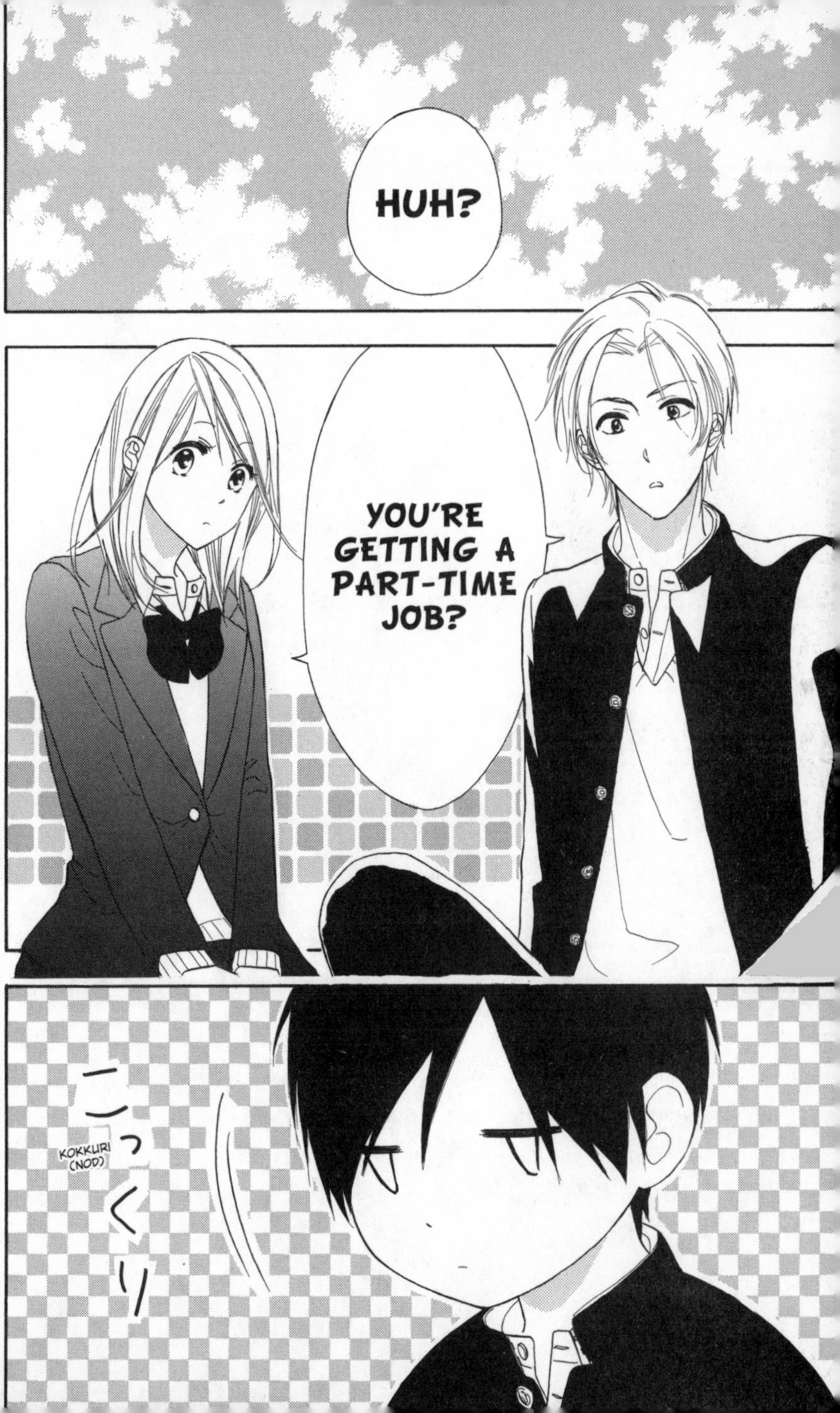
HUH?
YOU'RE GETTING A PART-TIME JOB?
KOKKURI (NOD)
こっくり

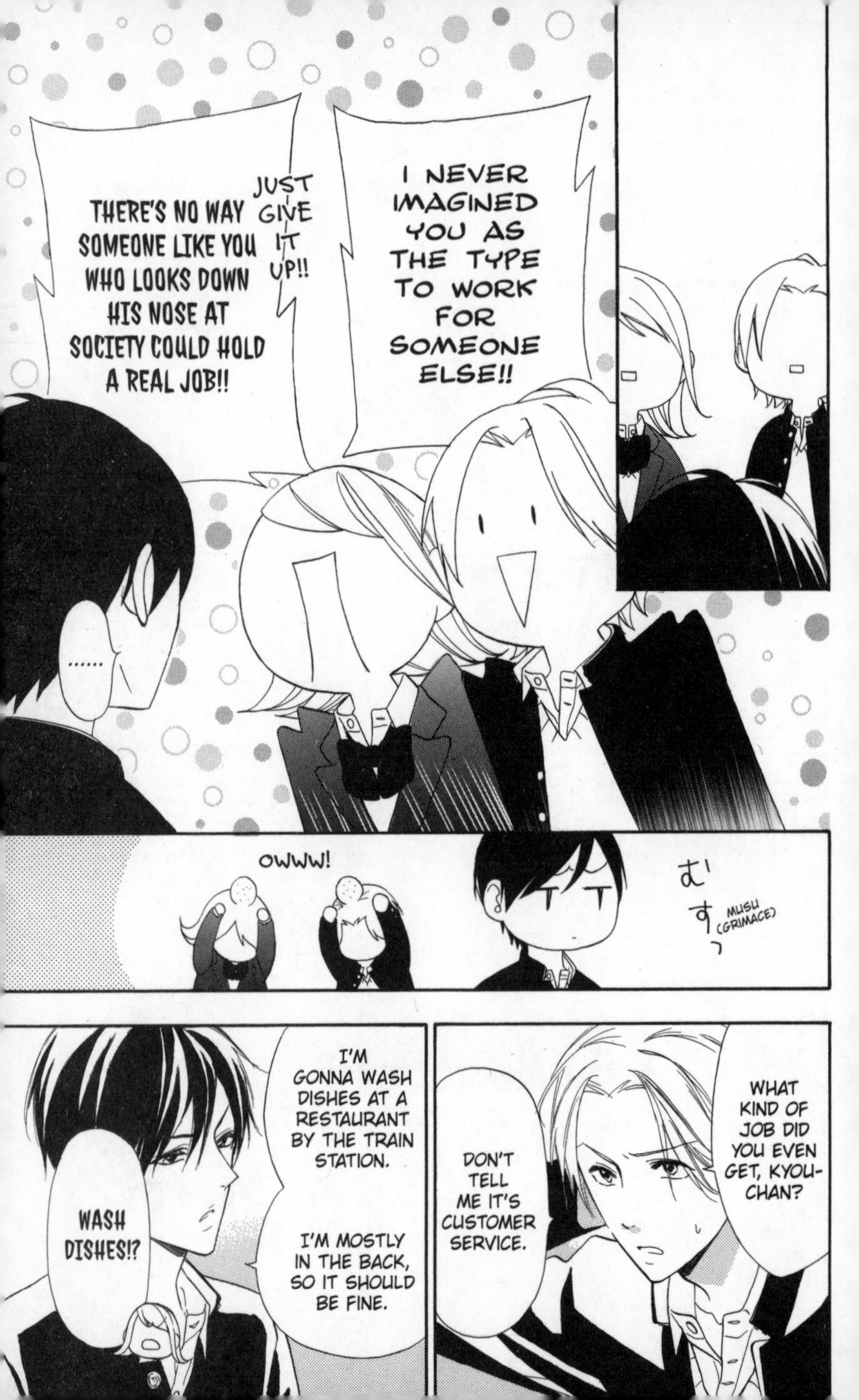
I NEVER IMAGINED YOU AS THE TYPE TO WORK FOR SOMEONE ELSE!!
JUST GIVE IT UP!!
THERE'S NO WAY SOMEONE LIKE YOU WHO LOOKS DOWN HIS NOSE AT SOCIETY COULD HOLD A REAL JOB!!
......
むす
MUSU (GRIMACE)
OWWW!
WHAT KIND OF JOB DID YOU EVEN GET, KYOU-CHAN?
DON'T TELL ME IT'S CUSTOMER SERVICE.
I'M GONNA WASH DISHES AT A RESTAURANT BY THE TRAIN STATION.
I'M MOSTLY IN THE BACK, SO IT SHOULD BE FINE.
WASH DISHES!?

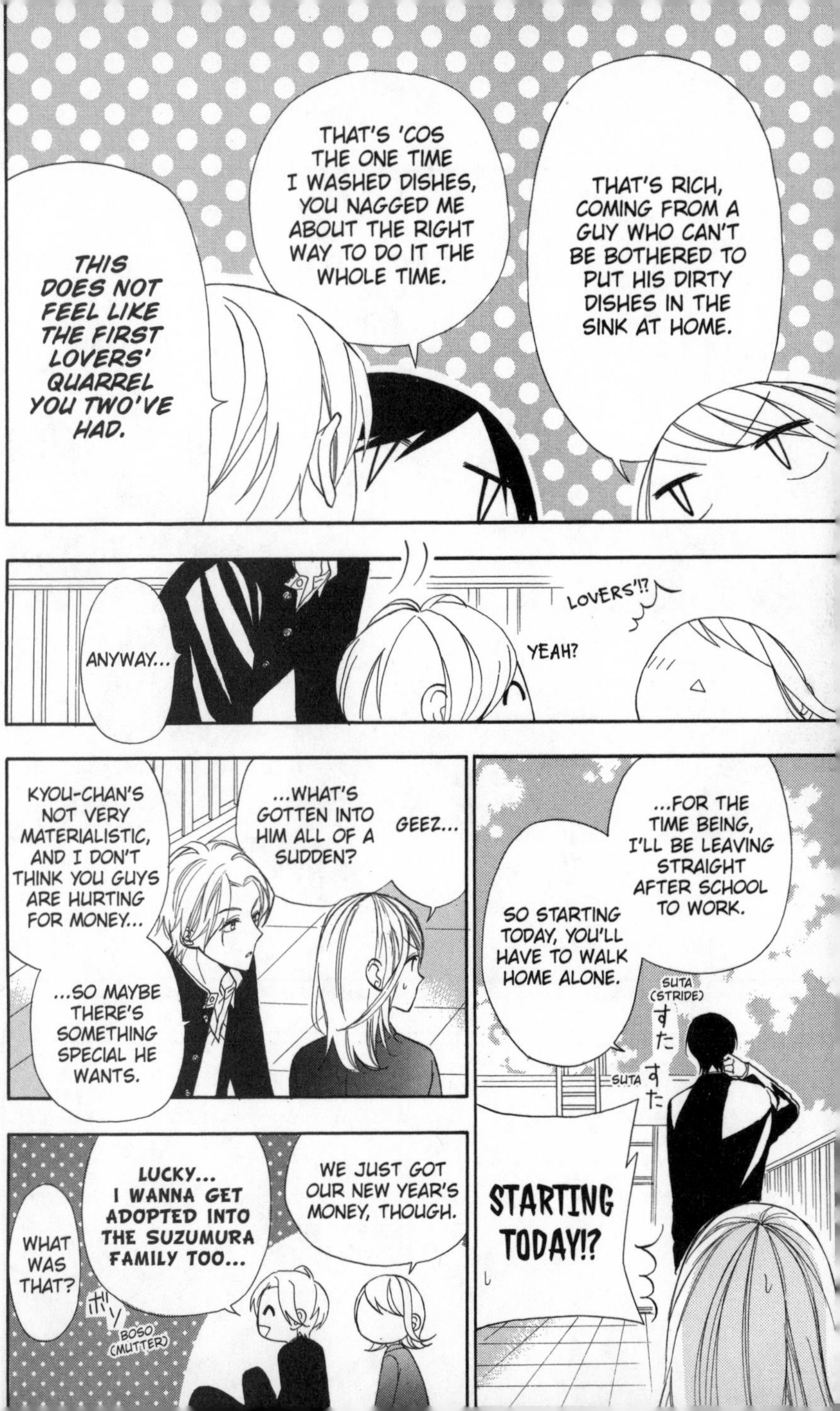
THAT'S RICH, COMING FROM A GUY WHO CAN'T BE BOTHERED TO PUT HIS DIRTY DISHES IN THE SINK AT HOME.
THAT'S 'COS THE ONE TIME I WASHED DISHES, YOU NAGGED ME ABOUT THE RIGHT WAY TO DO IT THE WHOLE TIME.
THIS DOES NOT FEEL LIKE THE FIRST LOVERS' QUARREL YOU TWO'VE HAD.
LOVERS'!?
YEAH?
ANYWAY...
...FOR THE TIME BEING, I'LL BE LEAVING STRAIGHT AFTER SCHOOL TO WORK.
SO STARTING TODAY, YOU'LL HAVE TO WALK HOME ALONE.
SUTA (STRIDE)
すた
すた
SUTA
STARTING TODAY!?
GEEZ...
...WHAT'S GOTTEN INTO HIM ALL OF A SUDDEN?
KYOU-CHAN'S NOT VERY MATERIALISTIC, AND I DON'T THINK YOU GUYS ARE HURTING FOR MONEY...
...SO MAYBE THERE'S SOMETHING SPECIAL HE WANTS.
WE JUST GOT OUR NEW YEAR'S MONEY, THOUGH.
LUCKY... I WANNA GET ADOPTED INTO THE SUZUMURA FAMILY TOO...
WHAT WAS THAT?
ボソ
BOSO (MUTTER)

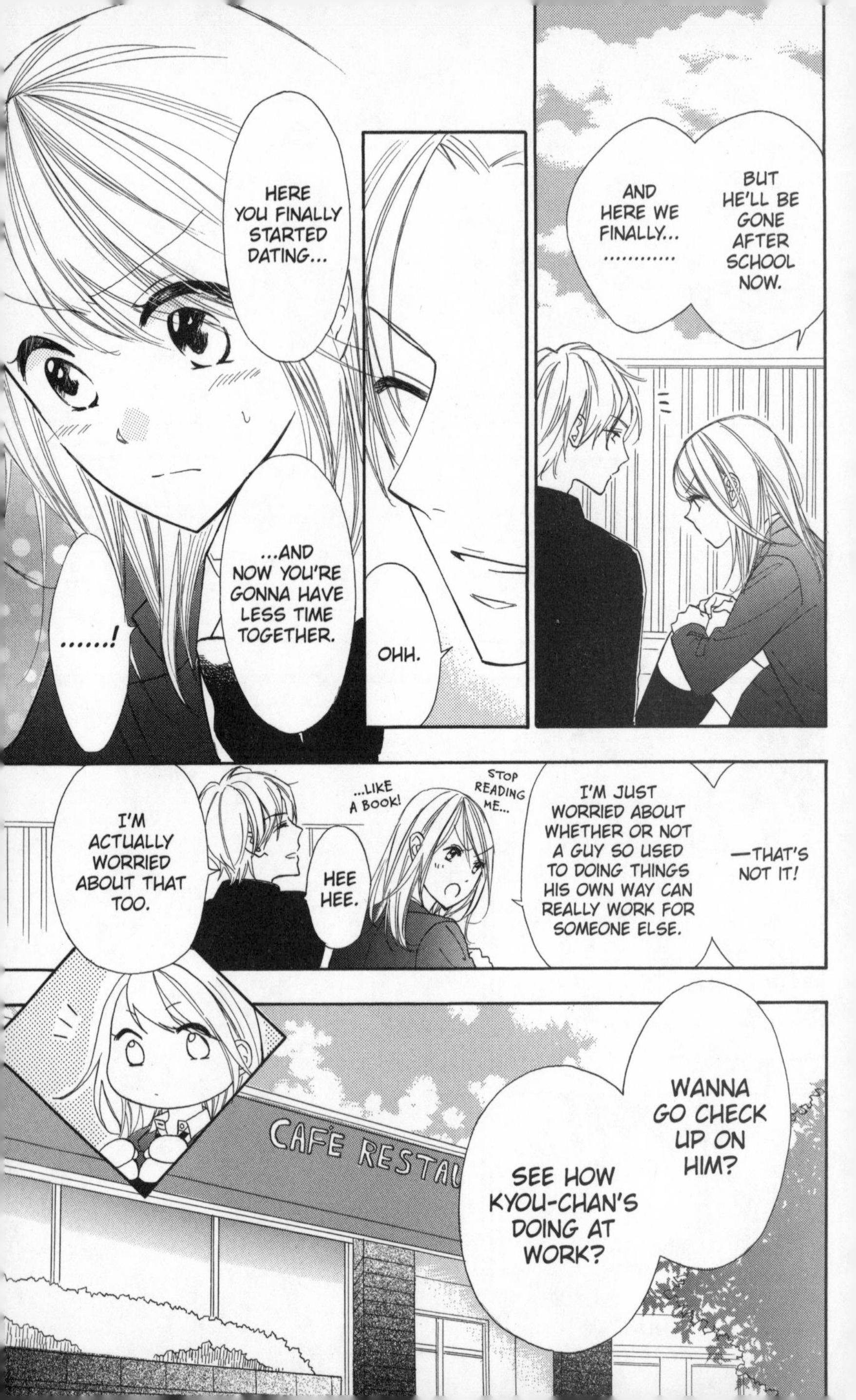

BUT HE'LL BE GONE AFTER SCHOOL NOW.
AND HERE WE FINALLY... ....
OHH.
HERE YOU FINALLY STARTED DATING...
...AND NOW YOU'RE GONNA HAVE LESS TIME TOGETHER.
......!
—THAT'S NOT IT!
I'M JUST WORRIED ABOUT WHETHER OR NOT A GUY SO USED TO DOING THINGS HIS OWN WAY CAN REALLY WORK FOR SOMEONE ELSE.
STOP READING ME...
...LIKE A BOOK!
HEE HEE.
I'M ACTUALLY WORRIED ABOUT THAT TOO.
WANNA GO CHECK UP ON HIM?
SEE HOW KYOU-CHAN'S DOING AT WORK?
CAFÉ RESTAU

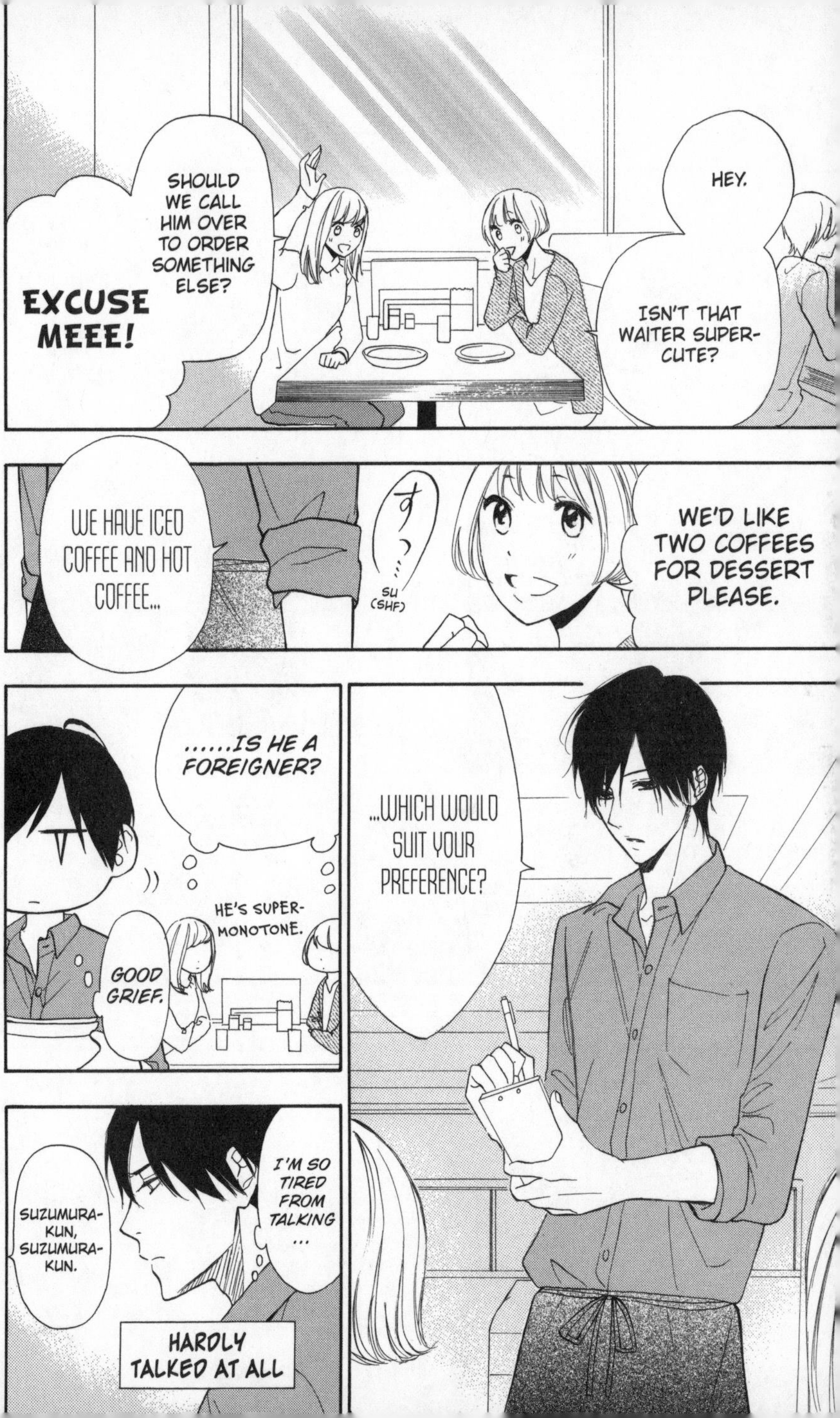
HEY.
ISN'T THAT WAITER SUPER-CUTE?
SHOULD WE CALL HIM OVER TO ORDER SOMETHING ELSE?
EXCUSE MEEE!
WE'D LIKE TWO COFFEES FOR DESSERT PLEASE.
すっ…
SU (SHF)
WE HAVE ICED COFFEE AND HOT COFFEE...
...WHICH WOULD SUIT YOUR PREFERENCE?
......IS HE A FOREIGNER?
HE'S SUPER-MONOTONE.
GOOD GRIEF.
I'M SO TIRED FROM TALKING...
SUZUMURA-KUN, SUZUMURA-KUN.
HARDLY TALKED AT ALL

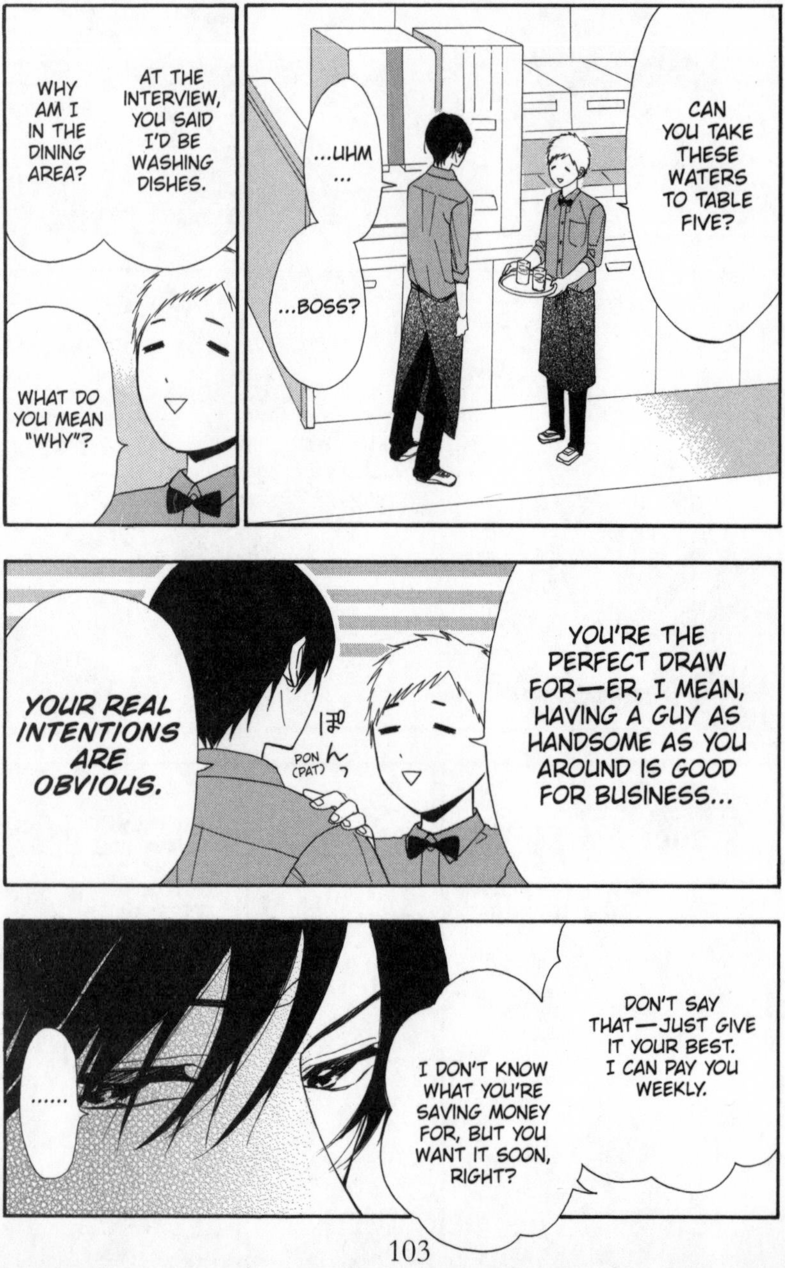
CAN YOU TAKE THESE WATERS TO TABLE FIVE?
...UHM ...
...BOSS?
AT THE INTERVIEW, YOU SAID I'D BE WASHING DISHES.
WHY AM I IN THE DINING AREA?
WHAT DO YOU MEAN "WHY"?
YOU'RE THE PERFECT DRAW FOR—ER, I MEAN, HAVING A GUY AS HANDSOME AS YOU AROUND IS GOOD FOR BUSINESS...
ぽんっ
PON (PAT)
YOUR REAL INTENTIONS ARE OBVIOUS.
DON'T SAY THAT—JUST GIVE IT YOUR BEST. I CAN PAY YOU WEEKLY.
I DON'T KNOW WHAT YOU'RE SAVING MONEY FOR, BUT YOU WANT IT SOON, RIGHT?
......

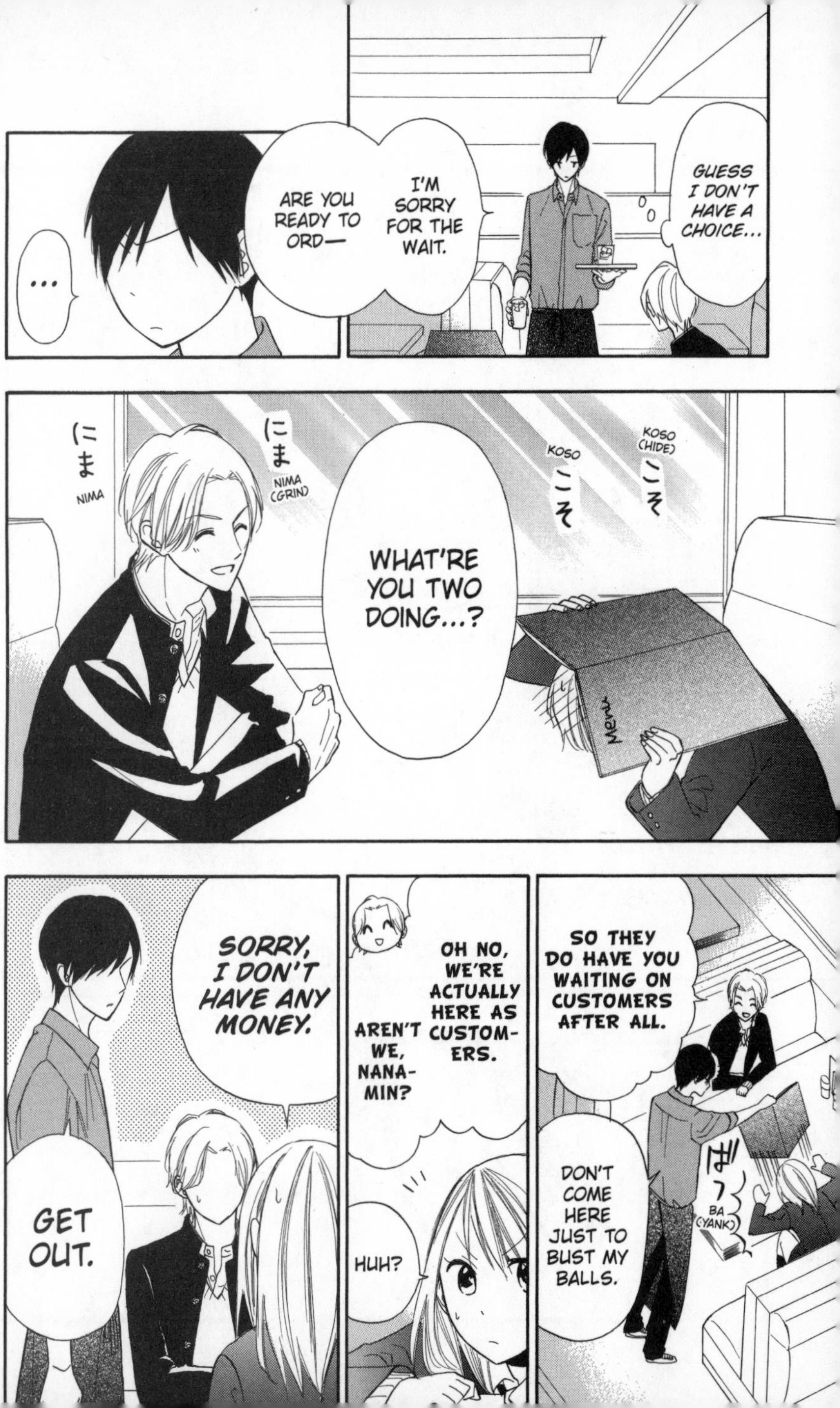
GUESS I DON'T HAVE A CHOICE...
I'M SORRY FOR THE WAIT.
ARE YOU READY TO ORD—
...
こそ
KOSO (HIDE)
こそ
KOSO
WHAT'RE YOU TWO DOING...?
にま
NIMA (GRIN)
にま
NIMA
SO THEY DO HAVE YOU WAITING ON CUSTOMERS AFTER ALL.
ぱっ
BA (YANK)
DON'T COME HERE JUST TO BUST MY BALLS.
OH NO, WE'RE ACTUALLY HERE AS CUSTOM-ERS.
AREN'T WE, NANA-MIN?
HUH?
SORRY, I DON'T HAVE ANY MONEY.
GET OUT.

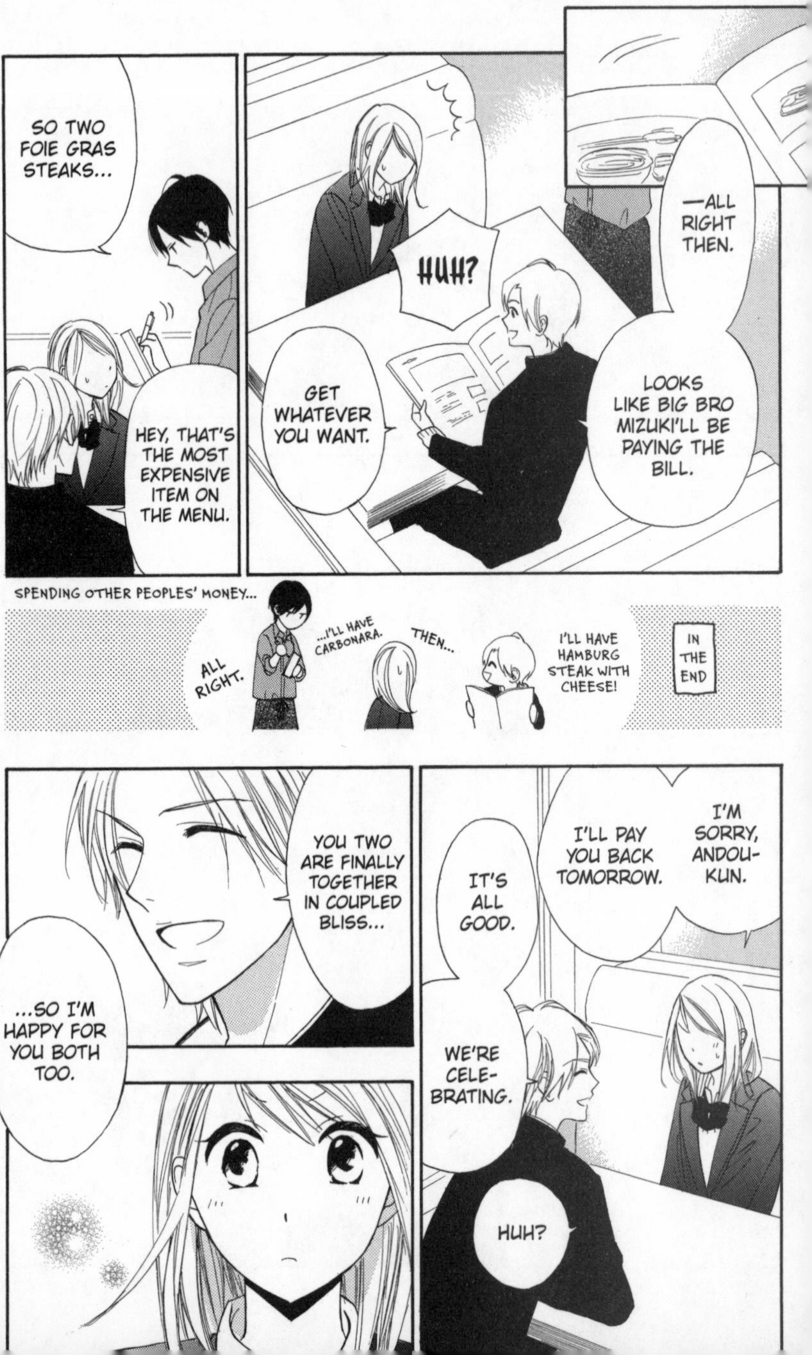
—ALL RIGHT THEN.
LOOKS LIKE BIG BRO MIZUKI'LL BE PAYING THE BILL.
HUH?
GET WHATEVER YOU WANT.
SO TWO FOIE GRAS STEAKS...
HEY, THAT'S THE MOST EXPENSIVE ITEM ON THE MENU.
SPENDING OTHER PEOPLES' MONEY...
IN THE END
I'LL HAVE HAMBURG STEAK WITH CHEESE!
THEN...
...I'LL HAVE CARBONARA.
ALL RIGHT.
I'M SORRY, ANDOU-KUN.
I'LL PAY YOU BACK TOMORROW.
IT'S ALL GOOD.
WE'RE CELE-BRATING.
HUH?
YOU TWO ARE FINALLY TOGETHER IN COUPLED BLISS...
...SO I'M HAPPY FOR YOU BOTH TOO.

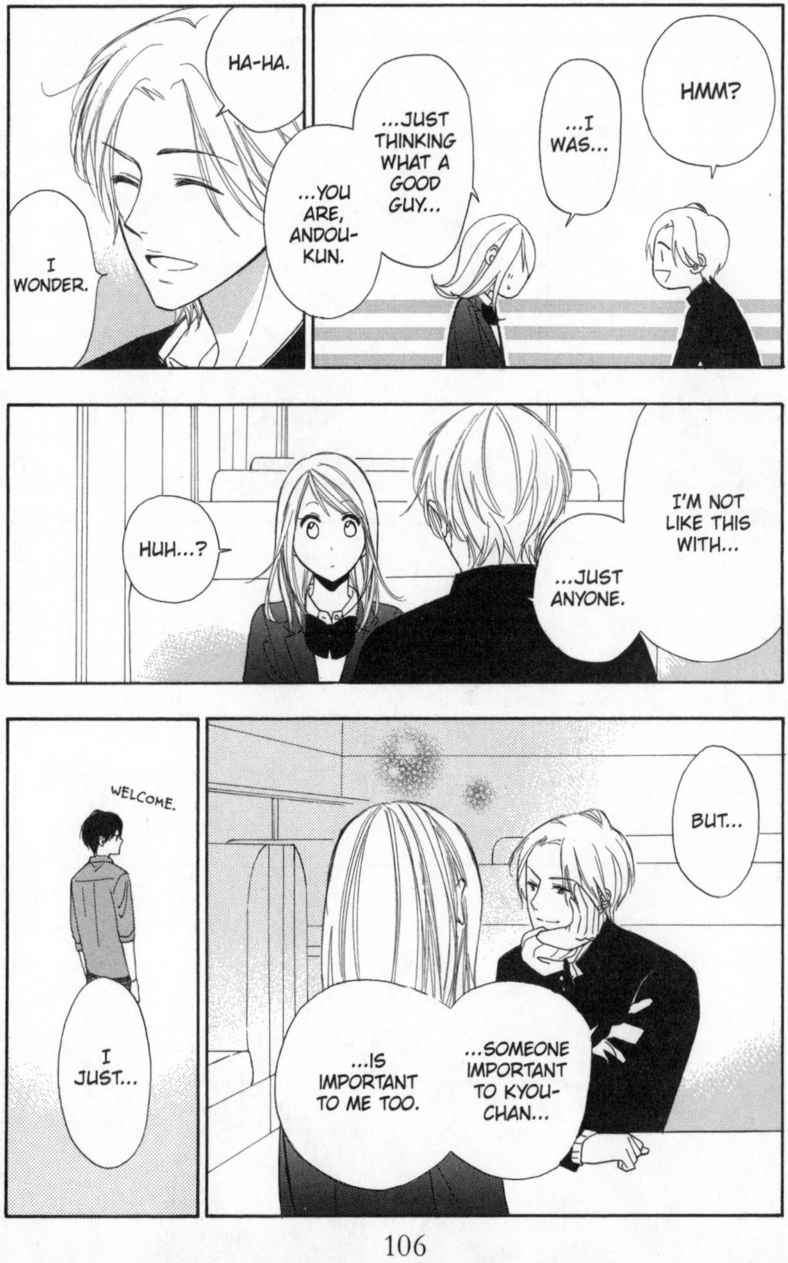
HMM?
...I WAS...
...JUST THINKING WHAT A GOOD GUY...
...YOU ARE, ANDOU-KUN.
HA-HA.
I WONDER.
I'M NOT LIKE THIS WITH...
...JUST ANYONE.
HUH...?
BUT...
...SOMEONE IMPORTANT TO KYOU-CHAN...
...IS IMPORTANT TO ME TOO.
WELCOME.
I JUST...

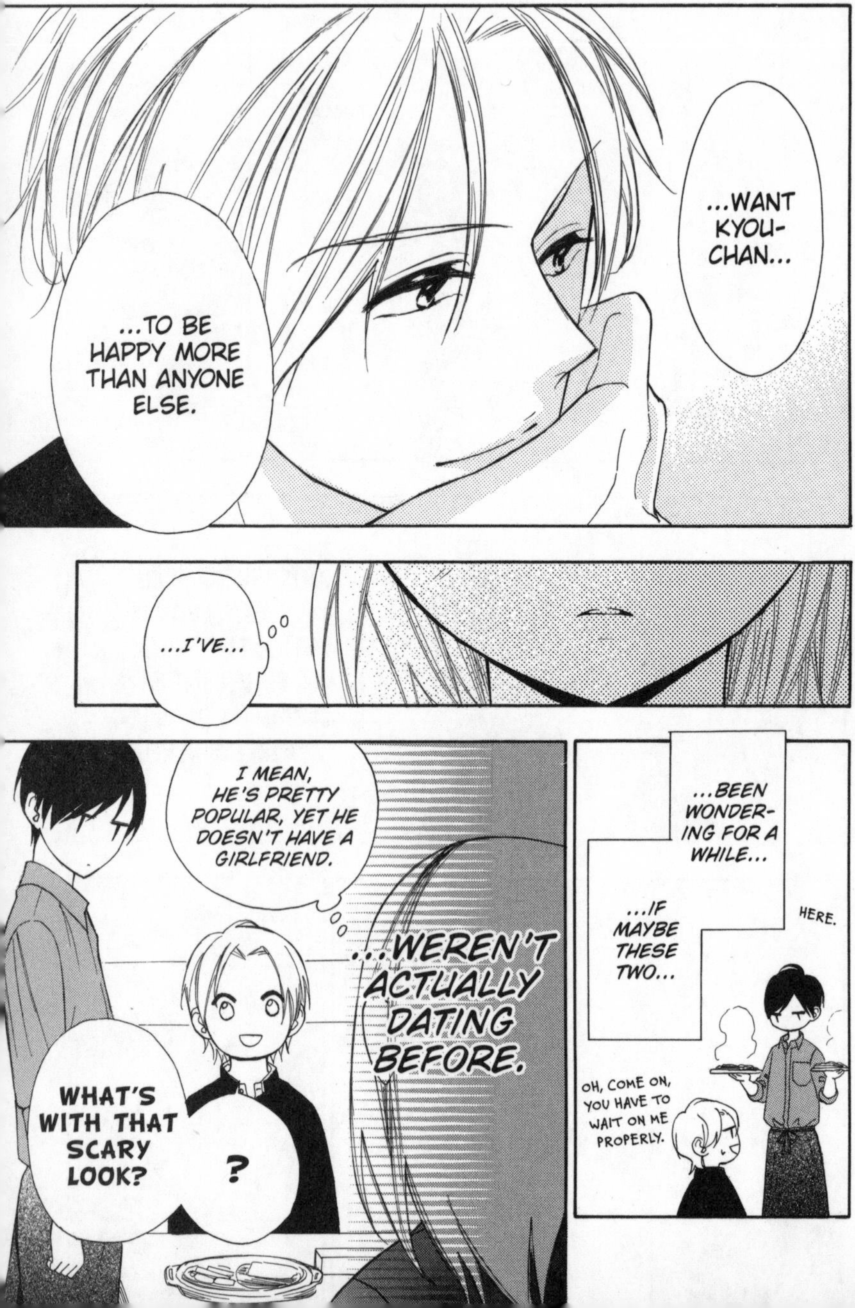
...WANT KYOU-CHAN...
...TO BE HAPPY MORE THAN ANYONE ELSE.
...I'VE...
...BEEN WONDER-ING FOR A WHILE...
...IF MAYBE THESE TWO...
HERE.
OH, COME ON, YOU HAVE TO WAIT ON ME PROPERLY.
I MEAN, HE'S PRETTY POPULAR, YET HE DOESN'T HAVE A GIRLFRIEND.
...WEREN'T ACTUALLY DATING BEFORE.
WHAT'S WITH THAT SCARY LOOK?
?

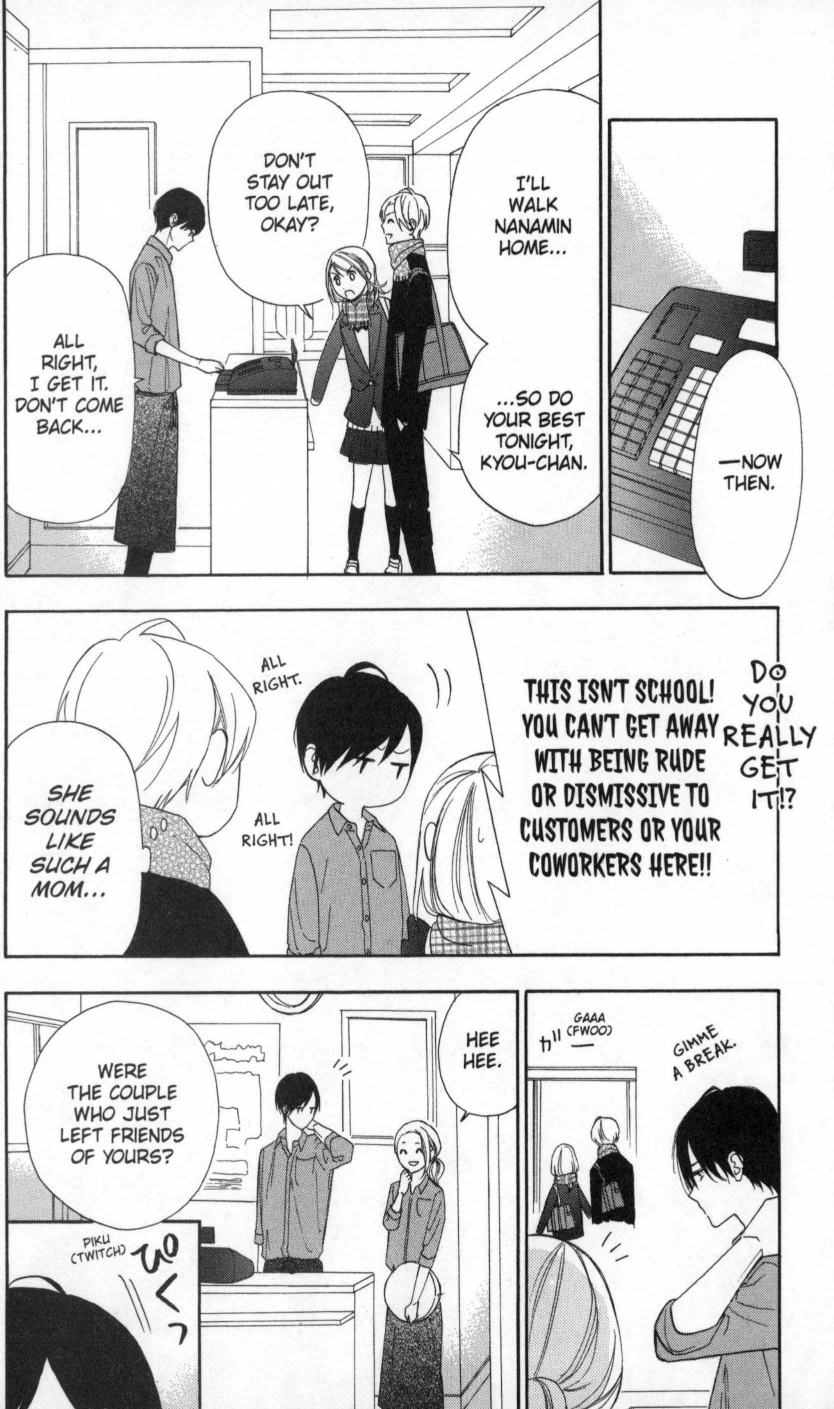
—NOW THEN.
I'LL WALK NANAMIN HOME...
...SO DO YOUR BEST TONIGHT, KYOU-CHAN.
DON'T STAY OUT TOO LATE, OKAY?
ALL RIGHT, I GET IT. DON'T COME BACK...
DO YOU REALLY GET IT!?
THIS ISN'T SCHOOL! YOU CAN'T GET AWAY WITH BEING RUDE OR DISMISSIVE TO CUSTOMERS OR YOUR COWORKERS HERE!!
ALL RIGHT.
ALL RIGHT!
SHE SOUNDS LIKE SUCH A MOM...
GIMME A BREAK.
GAAA (FWOO)
HEE HEE.
WERE THE COUPLE WHO JUST LEFT FRIENDS OF YOURS?
PIKU (TWITCH)

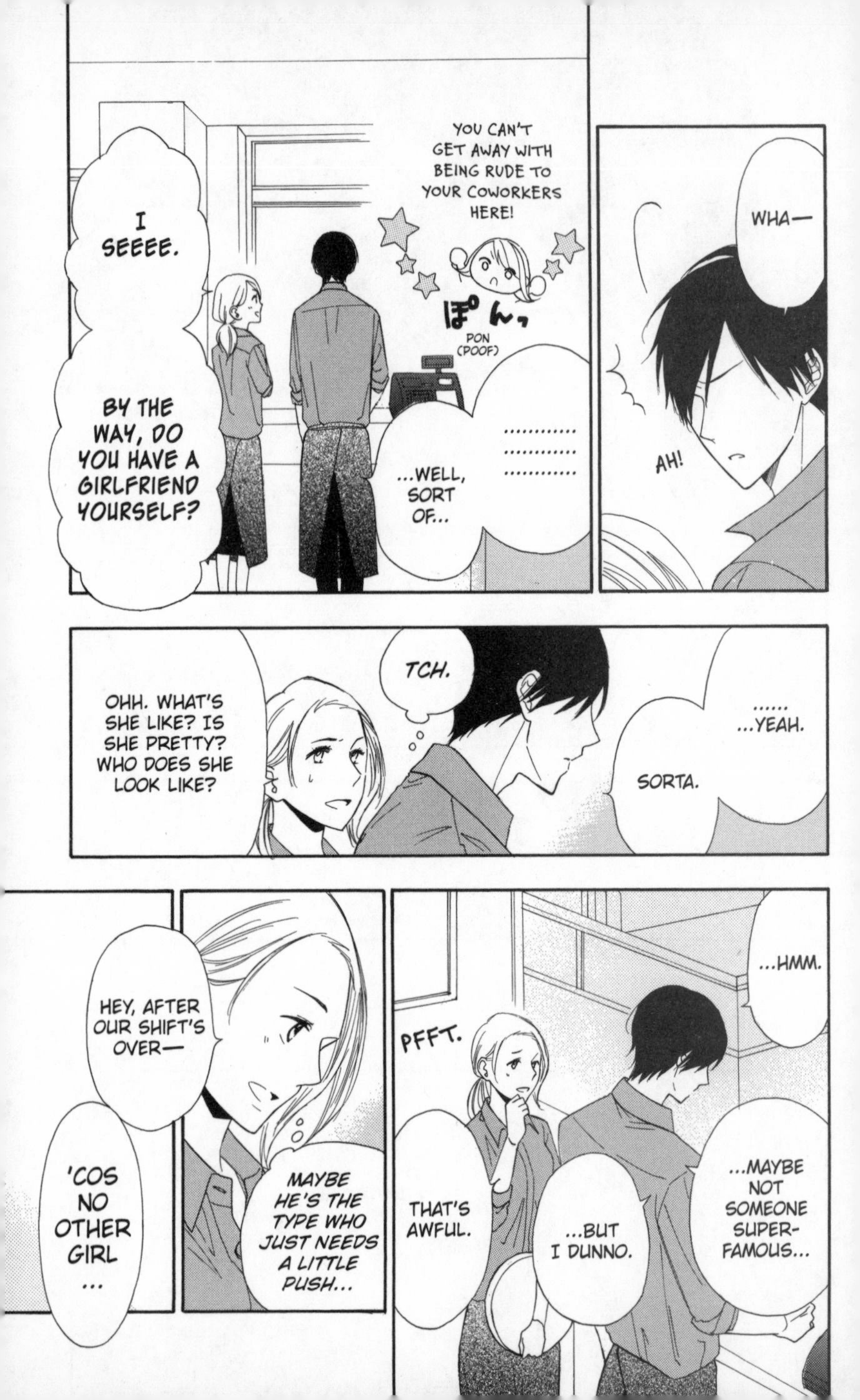
WHA—
AH!
YOU CAN'T GET AWAY WITH BEING RUDE TO YOUR COWORKERS HERE!
ぽんっ
PON (POOF)
....
...WELL, SORT OF...
I SEEEE.
BY THE WAY, DO YOU HAVE A GIRLFRIEND YOURSELF?
....YEAH.
SORTA.
TCH.
OHH. WHAT'S SHE LIKE? IS SHE PRETTY? WHO DOES SHE LOOK LIKE?
...HMM.
...MAYBE NOT SOMEONE SUPER-FAMOUS...
...BUT I DUNNO.
THAT'S AWFUL.
PFFT.
HEY, AFTER OUR SHIFT'S OVER—
MAYBE HE'S THE TYPE WHO JUST NEEDS A LITTLE PUSH...
'COS NO OTHER GIRL ...

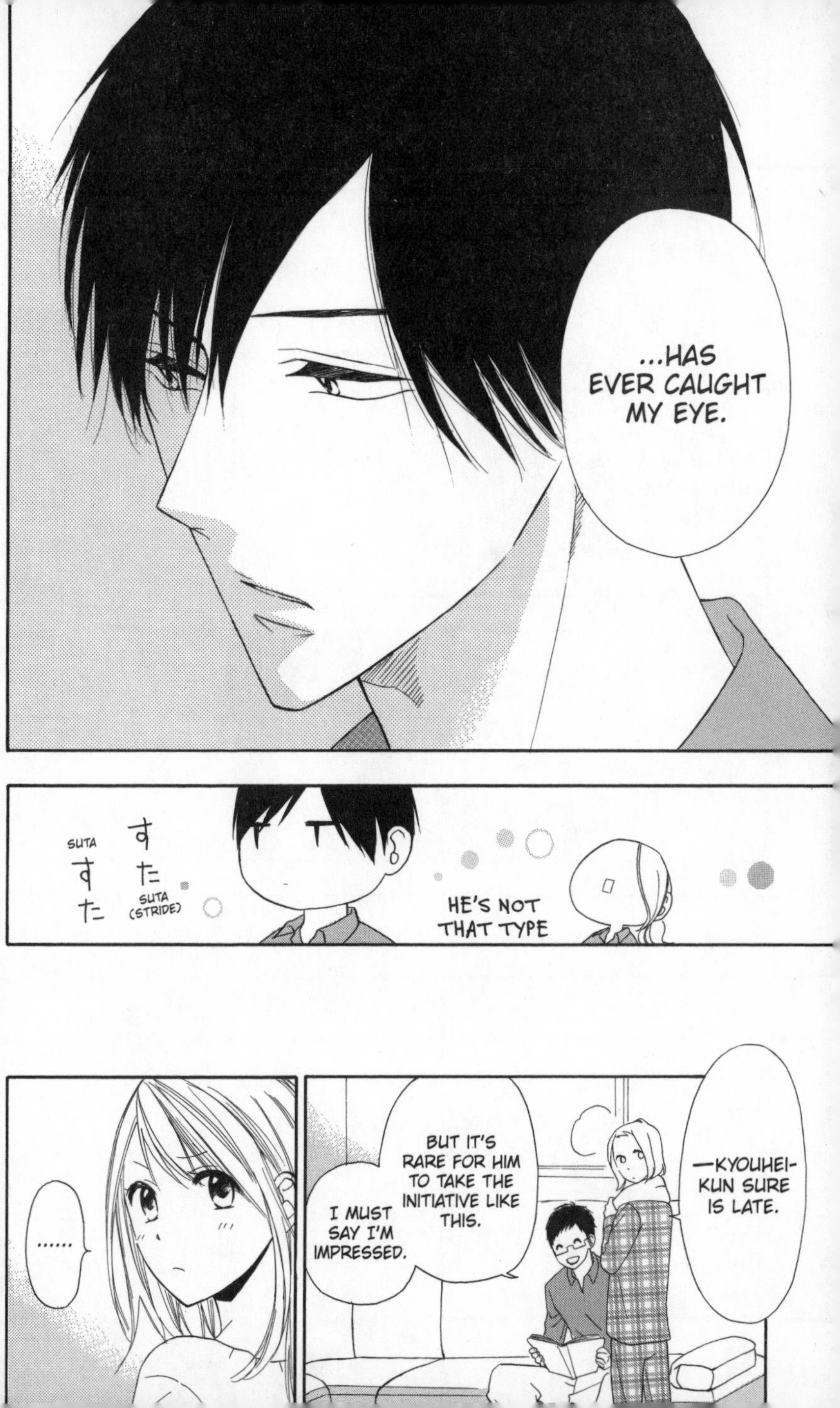
...HAS EVER CAUGHT MY EYE.
HE'S NOT THAT TYPE
すた
SUTA (STRIDE)
すた
SUTA
—KYOUHEI-KUN SURE IS LATE.
BUT IT'S RARE FOR HIM TO TAKE THE INITIATIVE LIKE THIS.
I MUST SAY I'M IMPRESSED.
......

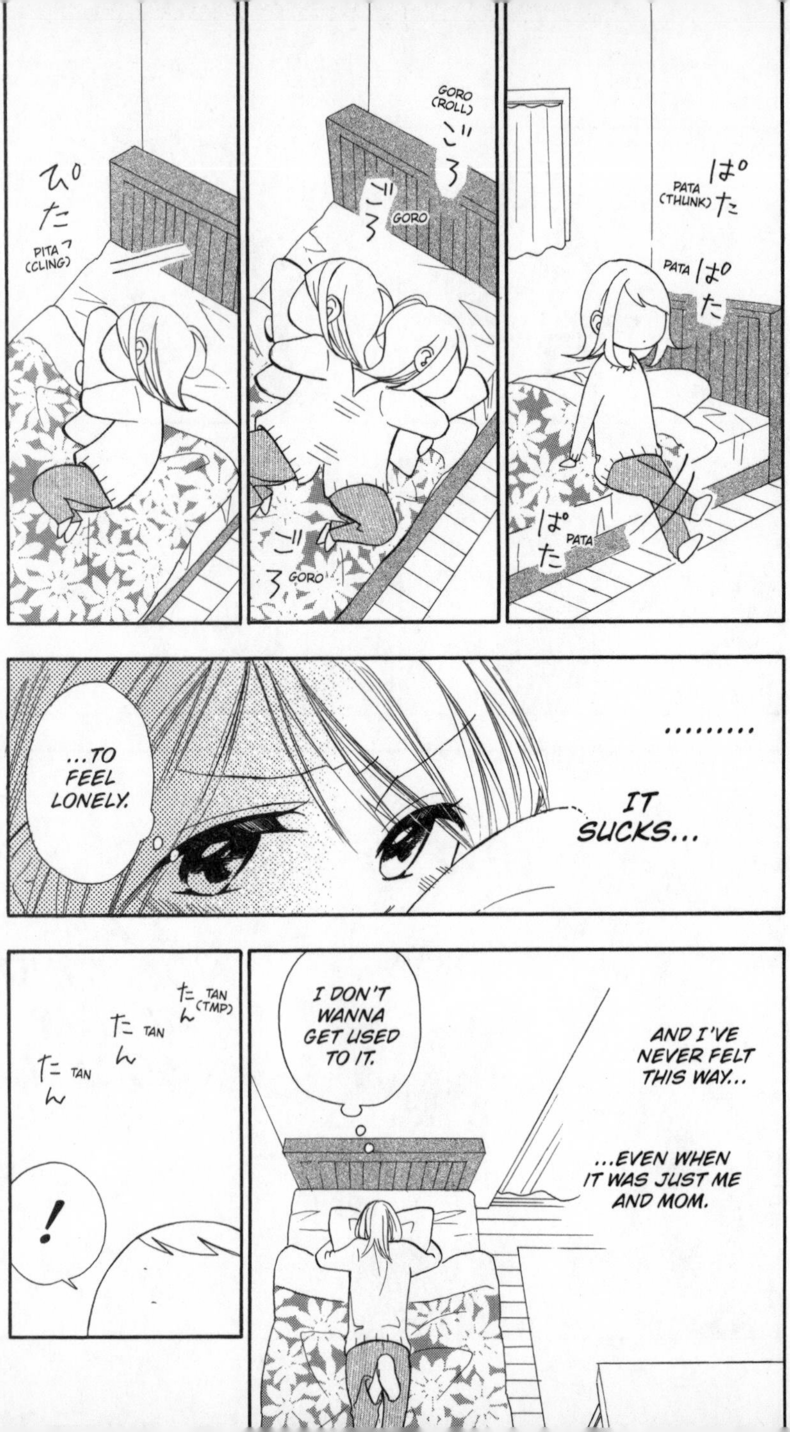
ぱた PATA (THUNK)
ぱた PATA
ぱた PATA
GORO (ROLL) ごろ
ごろ GORO
ごろ GORO
ぴた PITA (CLING)
....
IT SUCKS...
...TO FEEL LONELY.
AND I'VE NEVER FELT THIS WAY...
...EVEN WHEN IT WAS JUST ME AND MOM.
I DON'T WANNA GET USED TO IT.
たん TAN (TMP)
たん TAN
たん TAN
!

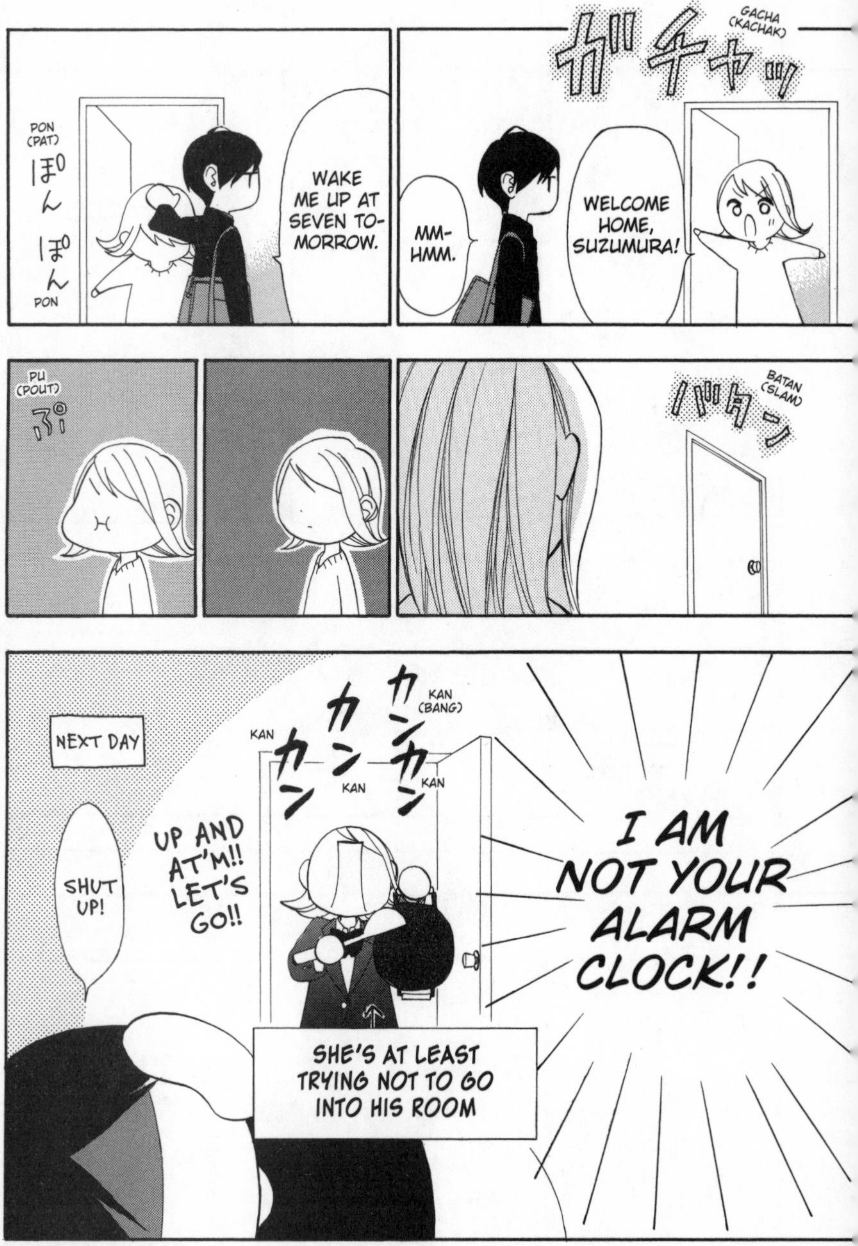
ガチャッ
GACHA (KACHAK)
WELCOME HOME, SUZUMURA!
MM-HMM.
WAKE ME UP AT SEVEN TO-MORROW.
PON (PAT)
ぽん ぽん
PON
バタン
BATAN (SLAM)
ぷ
PU (POUT)
カン カン カン カン
KAN (BANG)
KAN
KAN
KAN
I AM NOT YOUR ALARM CLOCK!!
UP AND AT'M!! LET'S GO!!
NEXT DAY
SHUT UP!
SHE'S AT LEAST TRYING NOT TO GO INTO HIS ROOM

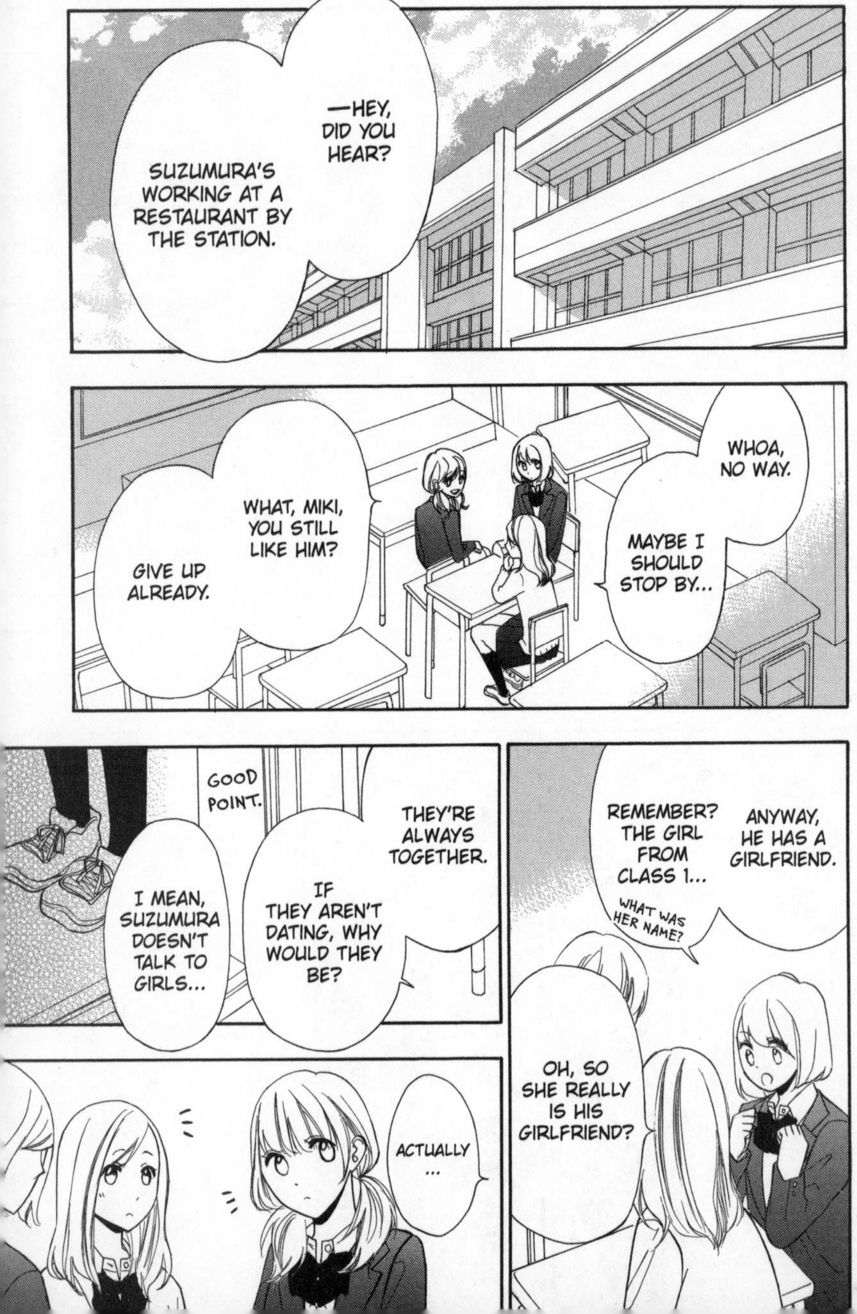
—HEY, DID YOU HEAR?
SUZUMURA'S WORKING AT A RESTAURANT BY THE STATION.
WHOA, NO WAY.
MAYBE I SHOULD STOP BY...
WHAT, MIKI, YOU STILL LIKE HIM?
GIVE UP ALREADY.
ANYWAY, HE HAS A GIRLFRIEND.
REMEMBER? THE GIRL FROM CLASS 1...
WHAT WAS HER NAME?
OH, SO SHE REALLY IS HIS GIRLFRIEND?
THEY'RE ALWAYS TOGETHER.
GOOD POINT.
IF THEY AREN'T DATING, WHY WOULD THEY BE?
I MEAN, SUZUMURA DOESN'T TALK TO GIRLS...
ACTUALLY...

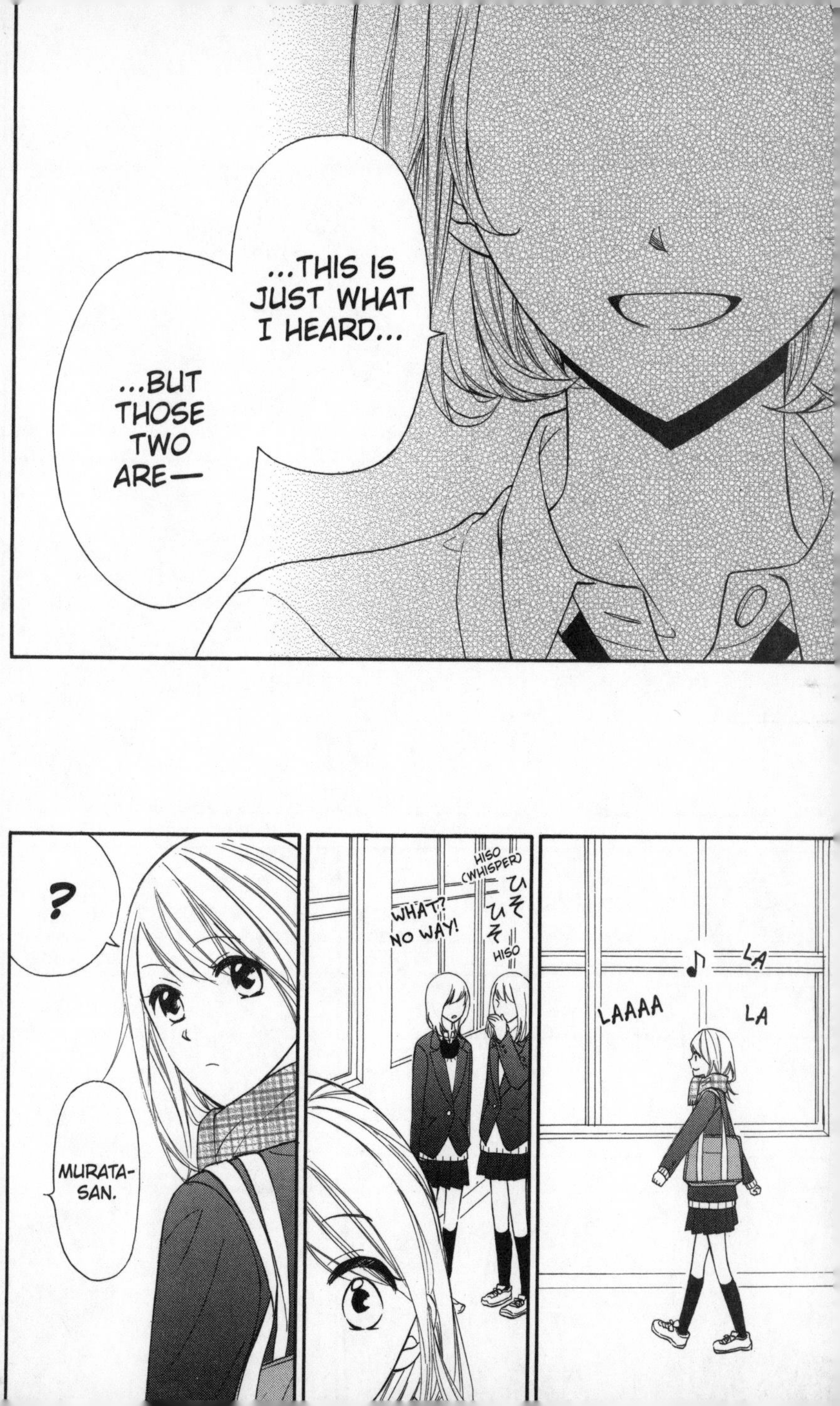
...THIS IS JUST WHAT I HEARD...
...BUT THOSE TWO ARE—
♪ LA
LAAAA
LA
HISO (WHISPER) ひそひそ HISO
WHAT? NO WAY!
?
MURATA-SAN.

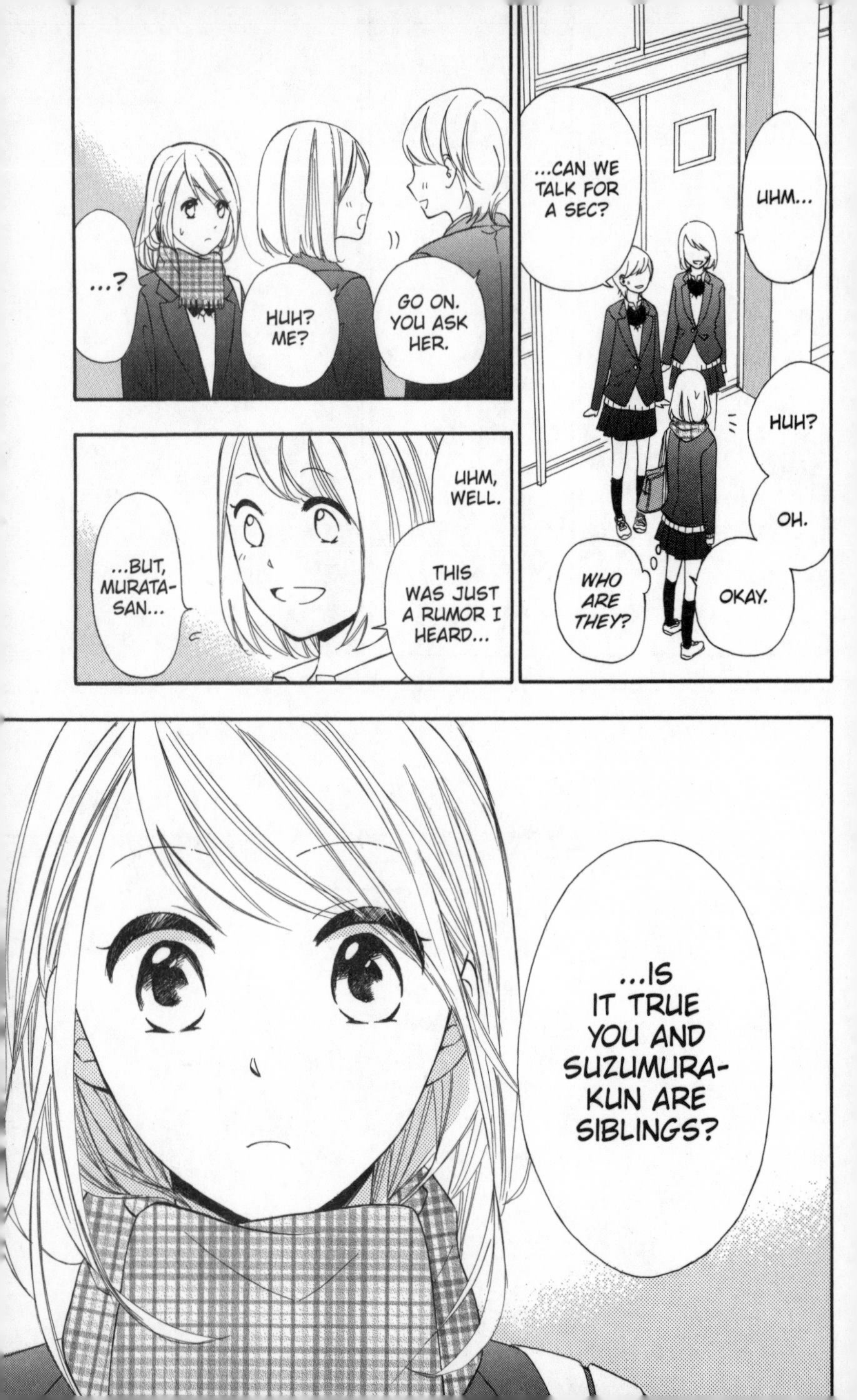
UHM...
...CAN WE TALK FOR A SEC?
HUH?
OH.
OKAY.
WHO ARE THEY?
GO ON. YOU ASK HER.
HUH? ME?
...?
UHM, WELL.
THIS WAS JUST A RUMOR I HEARD...
...BUT, MURATA-SAN...
...IS IT TRUE YOU AND SUZUMURA-KUN ARE SIBLINGS?

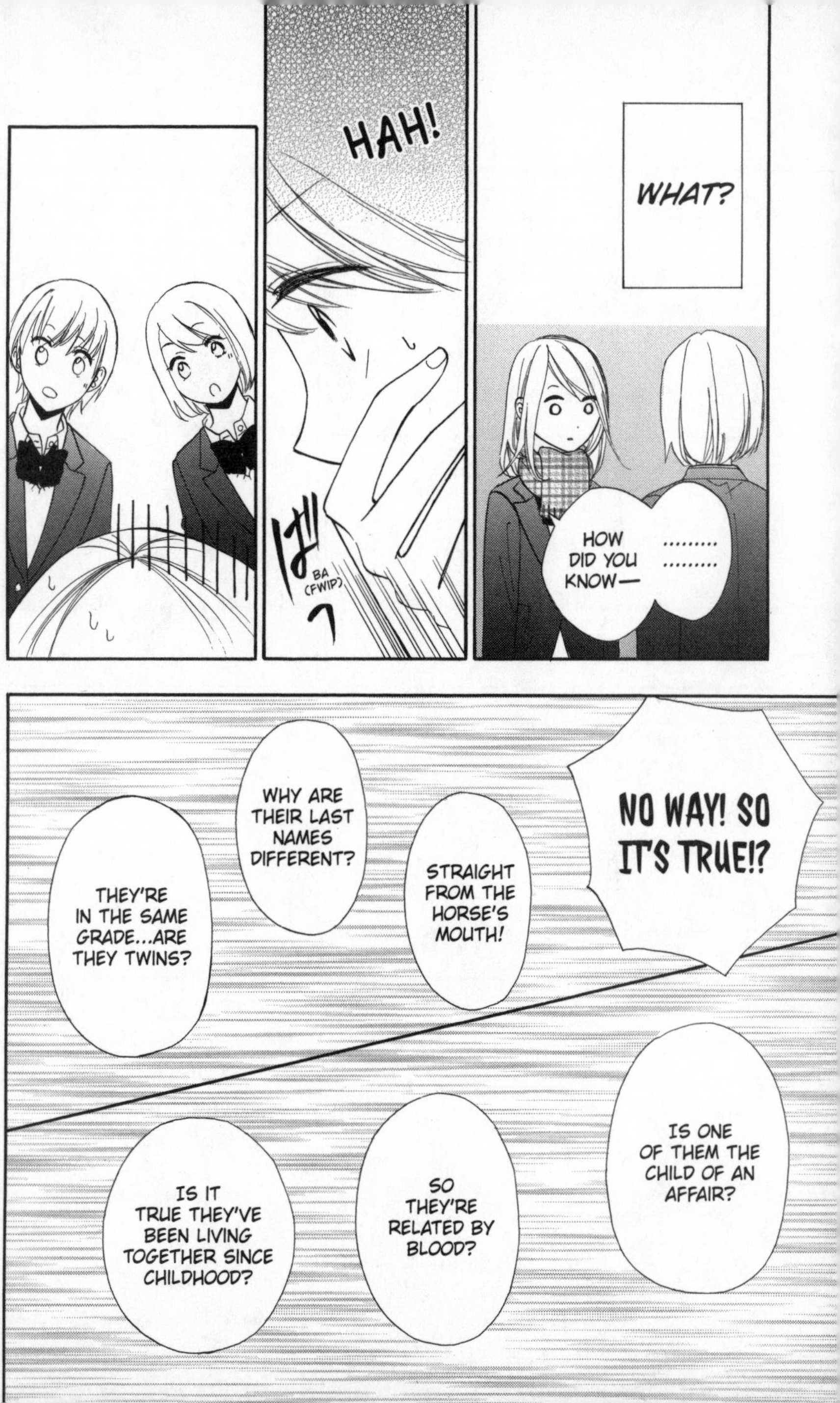
WHAT?
....
....
HOW DID YOU KNOW—
HAH!
ば
BA (FWIP)
NO WAY! SO IT'S TRUE!?
STRAIGHT FROM THE HORSE'S MOUTH!
WHY ARE THEIR LAST NAMES DIFFERENT?
THEY'RE IN THE SAME GRADE...ARE THEY TWINS?
IS ONE OF THEM THE CHILD OF AN AFFAIR?
SO THEY'RE RELATED BY BLOOD?
IS IT TRUE THEY'VE BEEN LIVING TOGETHER SINCE CHILDHOOD?

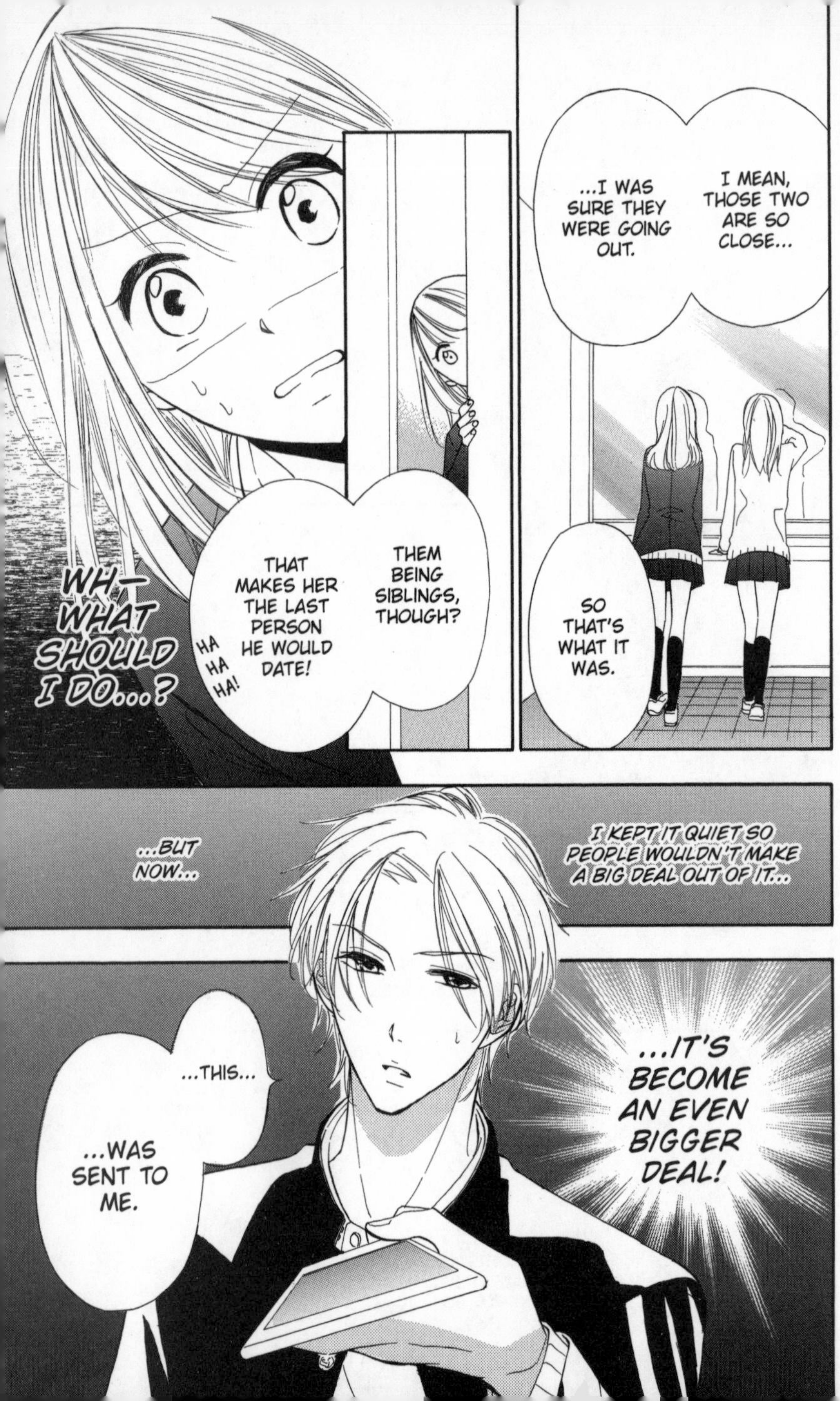
I MEAN, THOSE TWO ARE SO CLOSE...
...I WAS SURE THEY WERE GOING OUT.
SO THAT'S WHAT IT WAS.
THEM BEING SIBLINGS, THOUGH?
THAT MAKES HER THE LAST PERSON HE WOULD DATE!
HA HA HA!
WH— WHAT SHOULD I DO...?
I KEPT IT QUIET SO PEOPLE WOULDN'T MAKE A BIG DEAL OUT OF IT...
...BUT NOW...
...IT'S BECOME AN EVEN BIGGER DEAL!
...THIS...
...WAS SENT TO ME.

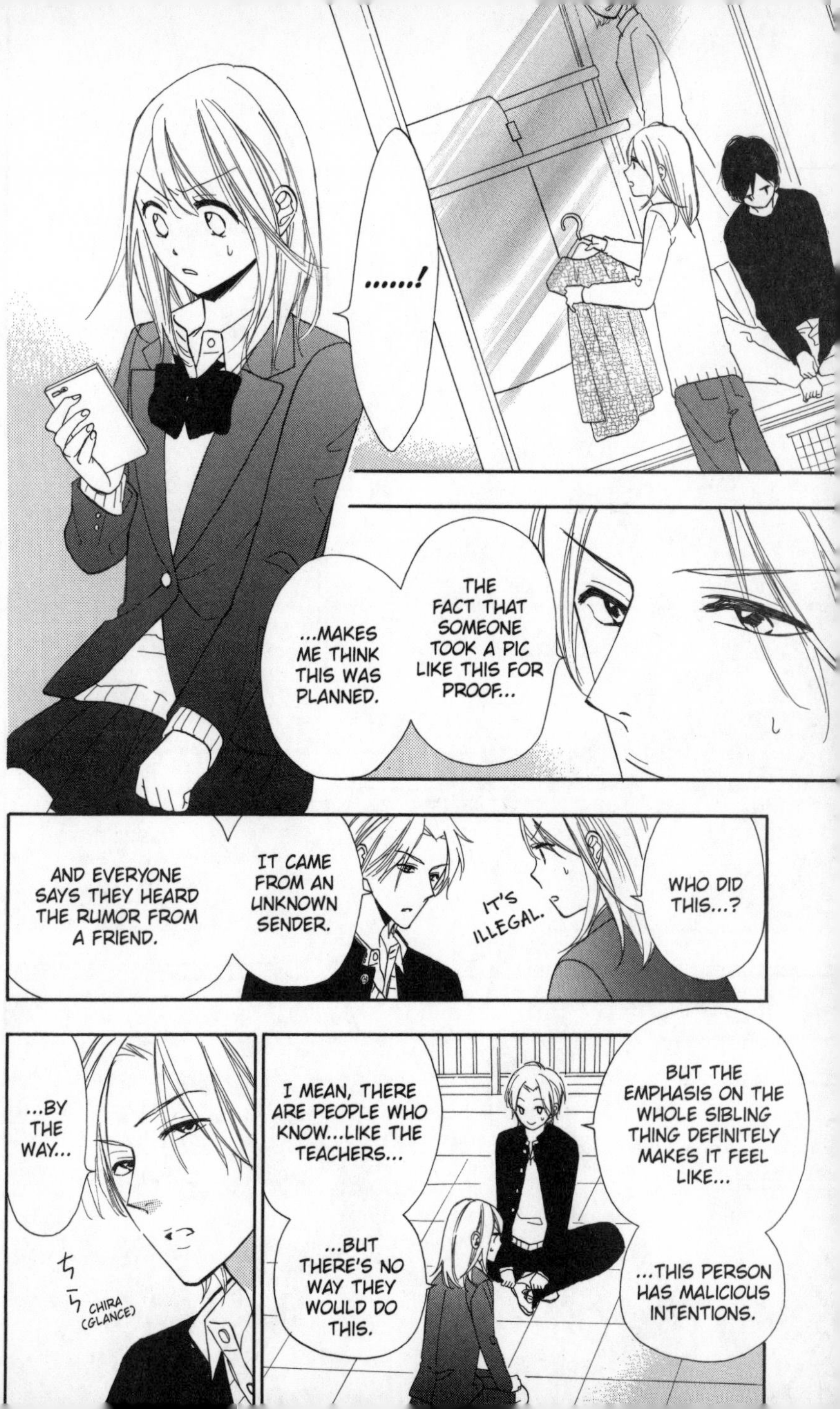

......!
THE FACT THAT SOMEONE TOOK A PIC LIKE THIS FOR PROOF...
...MAKES ME THINK THIS WAS PLANNED.
WHO DID THIS...?
IT'S ILLEGAL.
IT CAME FROM AN UNKNOWN SENDER.
AND EVERYONE SAYS THEY HEARD THE RUMOR FROM A FRIEND.
BUT THE EMPHASIS ON THE WHOLE SIBLING THING DEFINITELY MAKES IT FEEL LIKE...
...THIS PERSON HAS MALICIOUS INTENTIONS.
I MEAN, THERE ARE PEOPLE WHO KNOW...LIKE THE TEACHERS...
...BUT THERE'S NO WAY THEY WOULD DO THIS.
...BY THE WAY...
ちら
CHIRA (GLANCE)

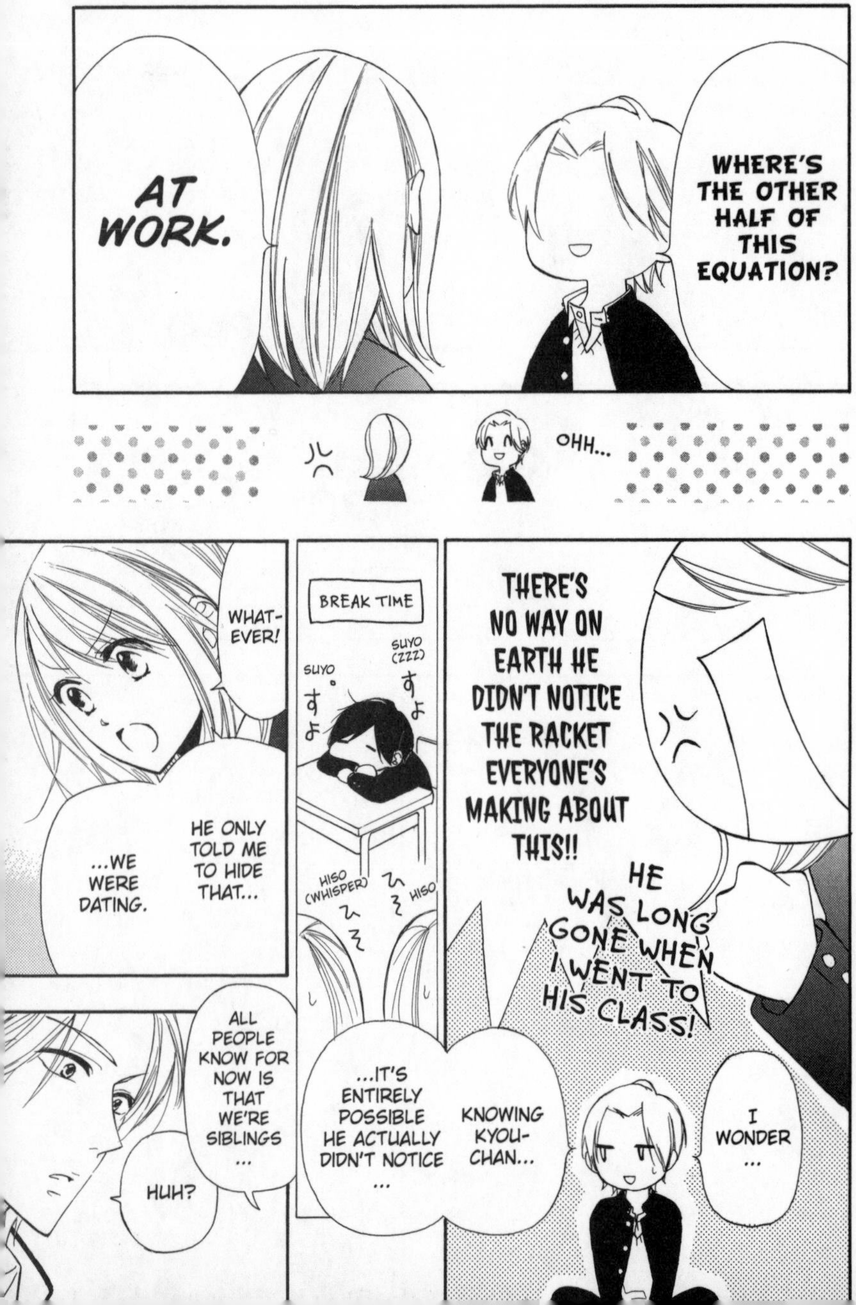
WHERE'S THE OTHER HALF OF THIS EQUATION?
AT WORK.
OHH...
THERE'S NO WAY ON EARTH HE DIDN'T NOTICE THE RACKET EVERYONE'S MAKING ABOUT THIS!!
HE WAS LONG GONE WHEN I WENT TO HIS CLASS!
I WONDER...
KNOWING KYOU-CHAN...
...IT'S ENTIRELY POSSIBLE HE ACTUALLY DIDN'T NOTICE...
BREAK TIME
SUYO (ZZZ) すよ
SUYO すよ
HISO ひそ
HISO (WHISPER) ひそ
WHAT-EVER!
HE ONLY TOLD ME TO HIDE THAT...
...WE WERE DATING.
ALL PEOPLE KNOW FOR NOW IS THAT WE'RE SIBLINGS...
HUH?

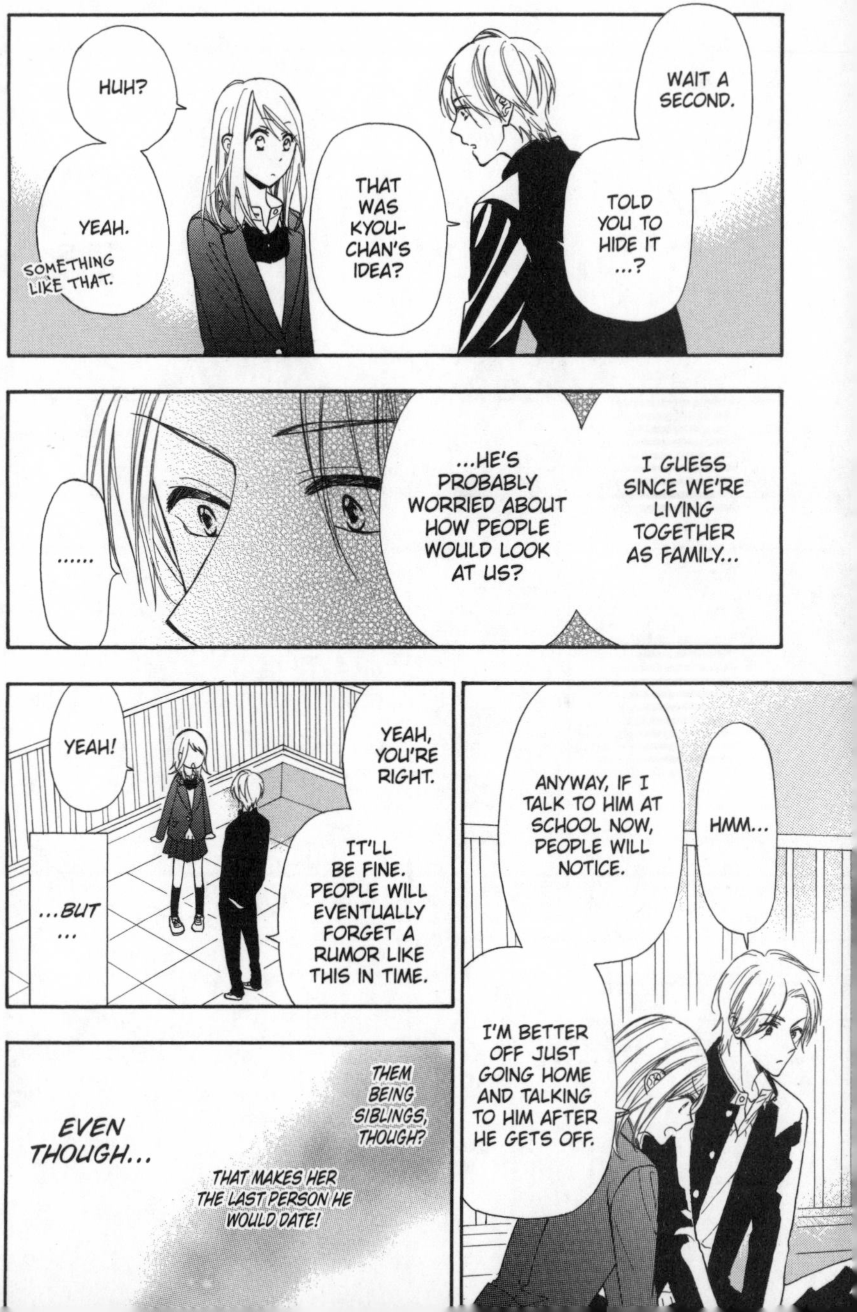
WAIT A SECOND.
TOLD YOU TO HIDE IT ...?
THAT WAS KYOU-CHAN'S IDEA?
HUH?
YEAH.
SOMETHING LIKE THAT.
I GUESS SINCE WE'RE LIVING TOGETHER AS FAMILY...
...HE'S PROBABLY WORRIED ABOUT HOW PEOPLE WOULD LOOK AT US?
......
HMM...
ANYWAY, IF I TALK TO HIM AT SCHOOL NOW, PEOPLE WILL NOTICE.
I'M BETTER OFF JUST GOING HOME AND TALKING TO HIM AFTER HE GETS OFF.
YEAH, YOU'RE RIGHT.
IT'LL BE FINE. PEOPLE WILL EVENTUALLY FORGET A RUMOR LIKE THIS IN TIME.
YEAH!
...BUT ...
THEM BEING SIBLINGS, THOUGH?
THAT MAKES HER THE LAST PERSON HE WOULD DATE!
EVEN THOUGH...

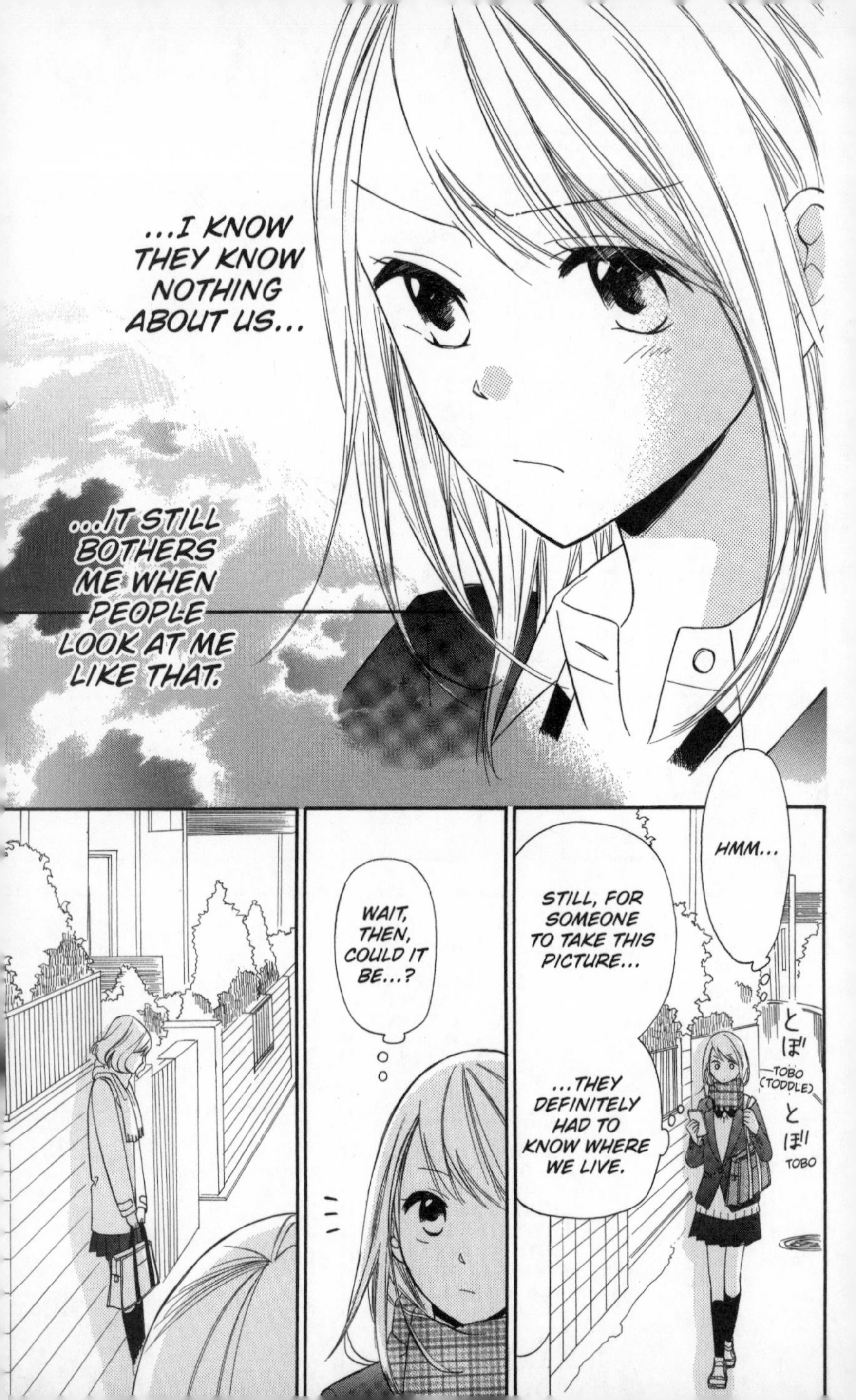
...I KNOW THEY KNOW NOTHING ABOUT US...
...IT STILL BOTHERS ME WHEN PEOPLE LOOK AT ME LIKE THAT.
HMM...
STILL, FOR SOMEONE TO TAKE THIS PICTURE...
...THEY DEFINITELY HAD TO KNOW WHERE WE LIVE.
とぼ
TOBO (TODDLE)
とぼ
TOBO
WAIT, THEN, COULD IT BE...?

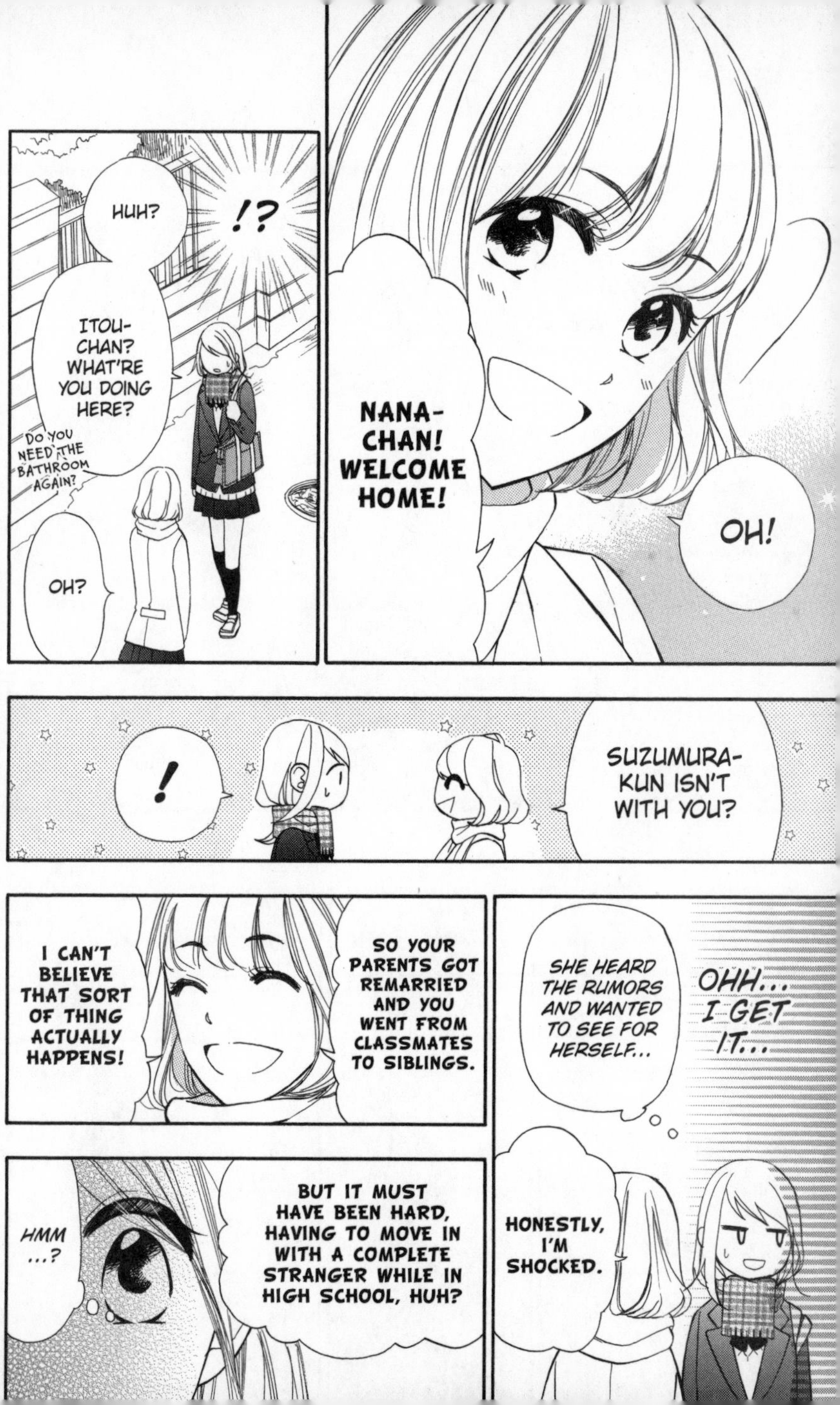
OH!
NANA-CHAN! WELCOME HOME!
!?
HUH?
ITOU-CHAN? WHAT'RE YOU DOING HERE?
DO YOU NEED THE BATHROOM AGAIN?
OH?
SUZUMURA-KUN ISN'T WITH YOU?
!
OHH... I GET IT...
SHE HEARD THE RUMORS AND WANTED TO SEE FOR HERSELF...
HONESTLY, I'M SHOCKED.
SO YOUR PARENTS GOT REMARRIED AND YOU WENT FROM CLASSMATES TO SIBLINGS.
I CAN'T BELIEVE THAT SORT OF THING ACTUALLY HAPPENS!
BUT IT MUST HAVE BEEN HARD, HAVING TO MOVE IN WITH A COMPLETE STRANGER WHILE IN HIGH SCHOOL, HUH?
HMM ...?

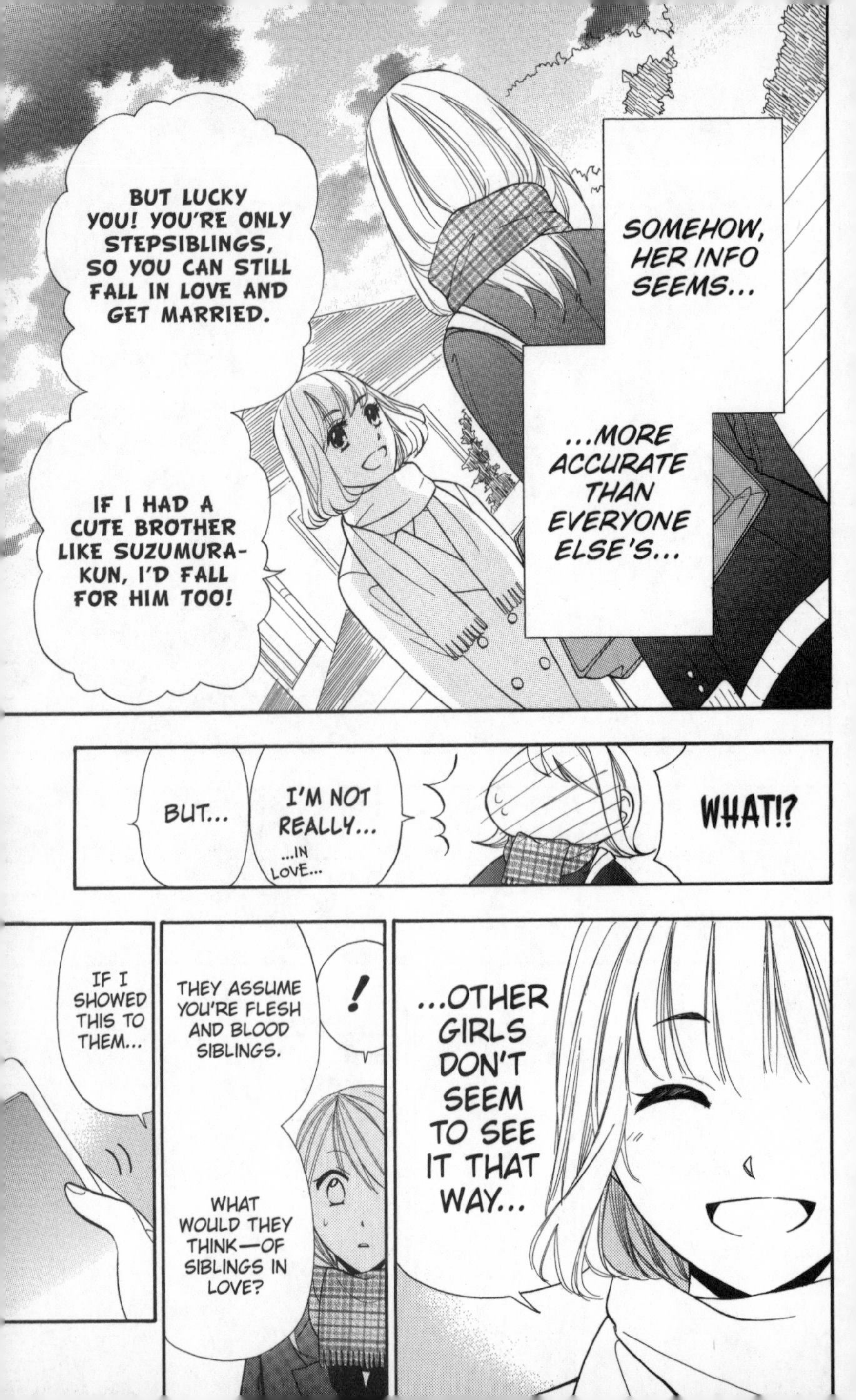
SOMEHOW, HER INFO SEEMS...
...MORE ACCURATE THAN EVERYONE ELSE'S...
BUT LUCKY YOU! YOU'RE ONLY STEPSIBLINGS, SO YOU CAN STILL FALL IN LOVE AND GET MARRIED.
IF I HAD A CUTE BROTHER LIKE SUZUMURA-KUN, I'D FALL FOR HIM TOO!
WHAT!?
I'M NOT REALLY...
...IN LOVE...
BUT...
...OTHER GIRLS DON'T SEEM TO SEE IT THAT WAY...
!
THEY ASSUME YOU'RE FLESH AND BLOOD SIBLINGS.
WHAT WOULD THEY THINK—OF SIBLINGS IN LOVE?
IF I SHOWED THIS TO THEM...

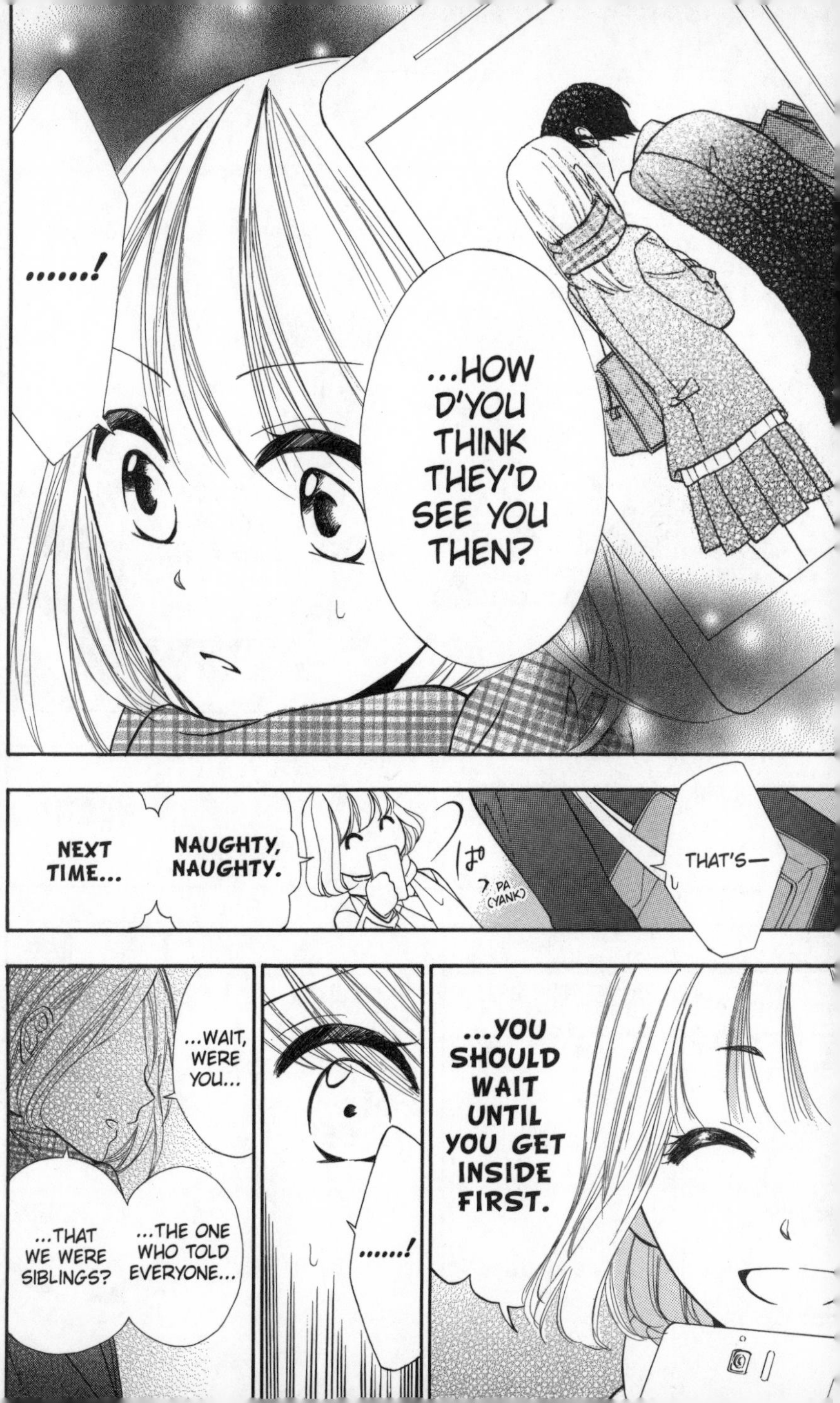
...HOW D'YOU THINK THEY'D SEE YOU THEN?
......!
THAT'S—
PA (YANK)
NAUGHTY, NAUGHTY.
NEXT TIME...
...YOU SHOULD WAIT UNTIL YOU GET INSIDE FIRST.
......!
...WAIT, WERE YOU...
...THE ONE WHO TOLD EVERYONE...
...THAT WE WERE SIBLINGS?

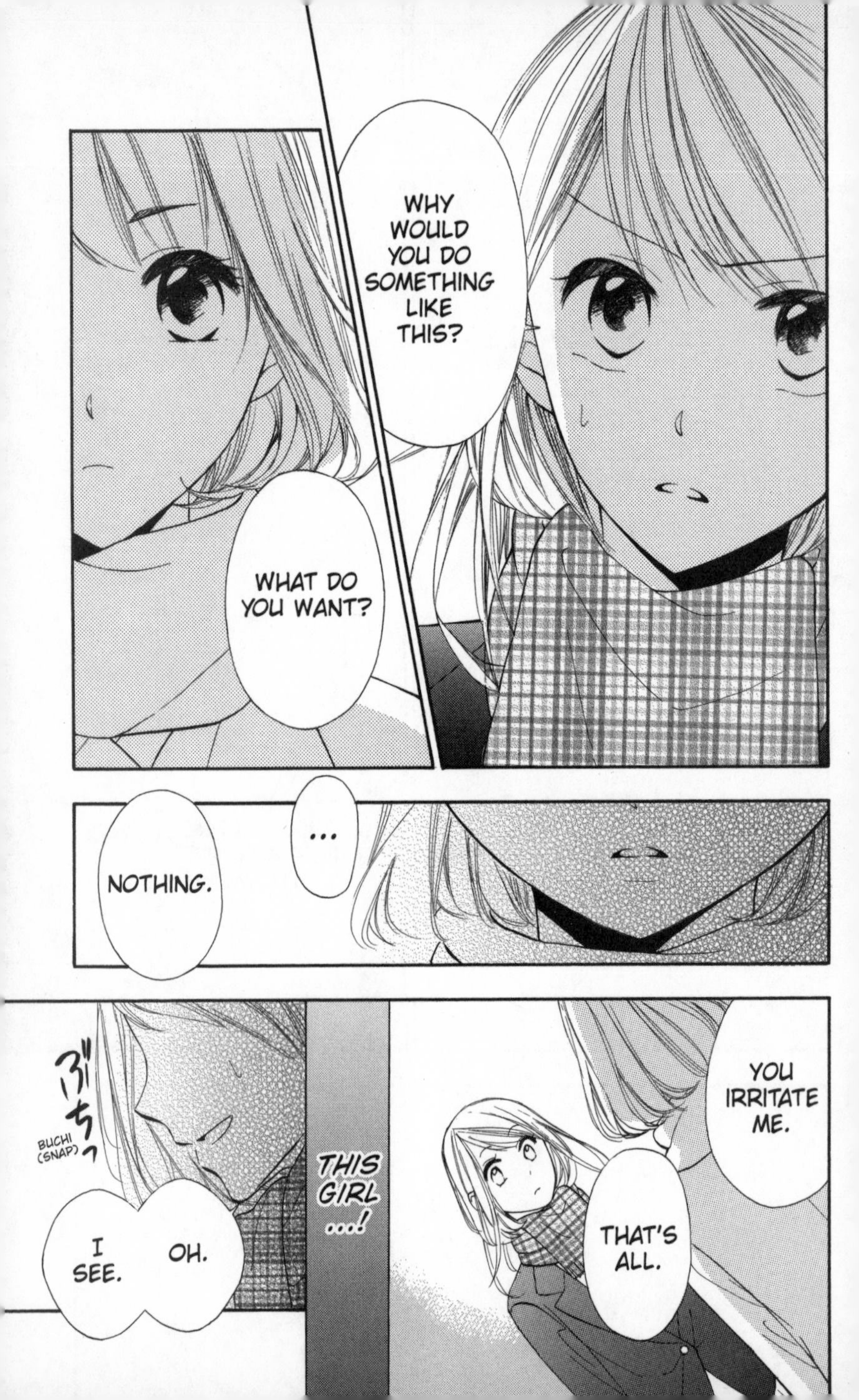
WHY WOULD YOU DO SOMETHING LIKE THIS?
WHAT DO YOU WANT?
...
NOTHING.
YOU IRRITATE ME.
THAT'S ALL.
THIS GIRL...!
ぶちっ
BUCHI (SNAP)
OH.
I SEE.

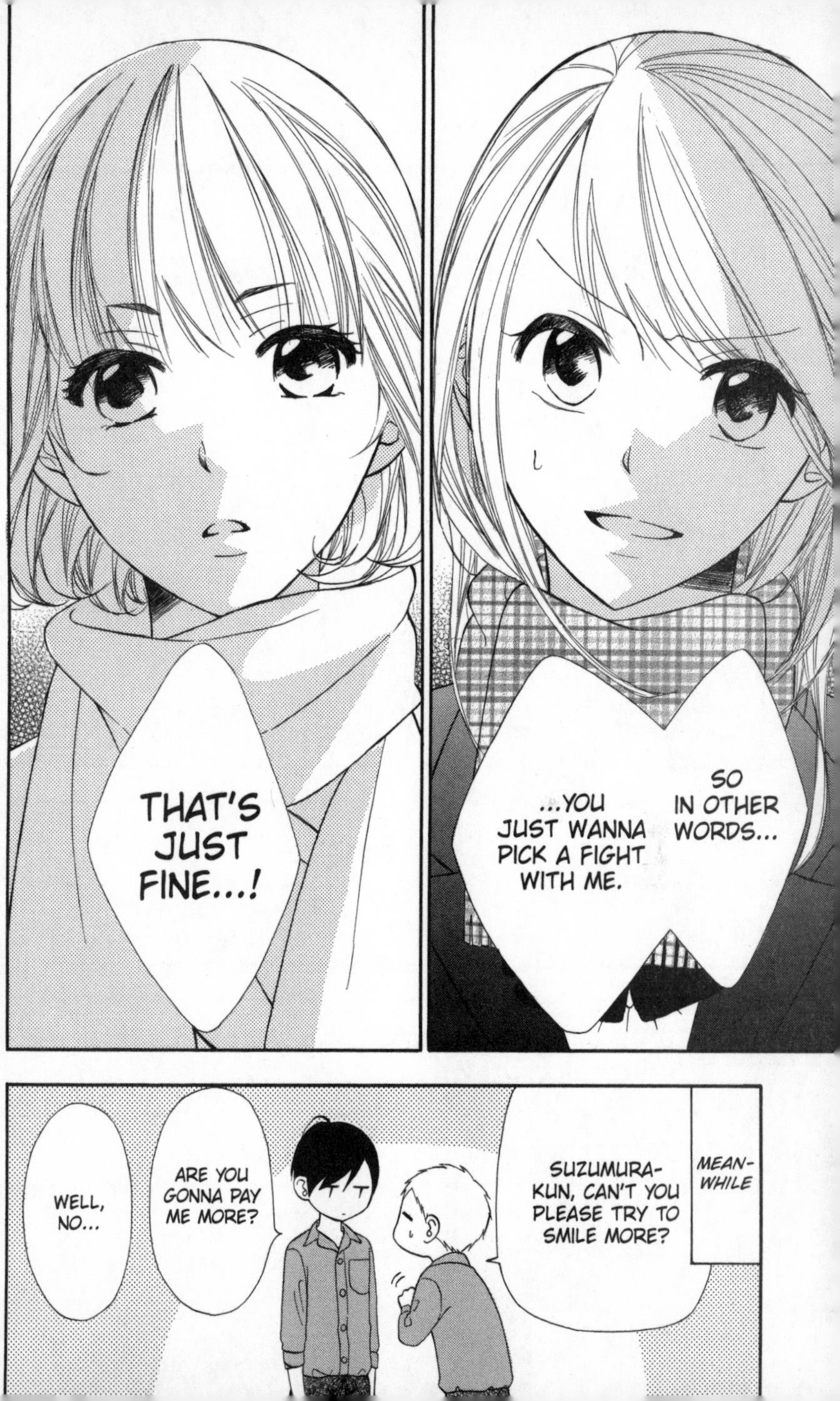
SO IN OTHER WORDS...
...YOU JUST WANNA PICK A FIGHT WITH ME.
THAT'S JUST FINE...!
MEAN-WHILE
SUZUMURA-KUN, CAN'T YOU PLEASE TRY TO SMILE MORE?
ARE YOU GONNA PAY ME MORE?
WELL, NO...

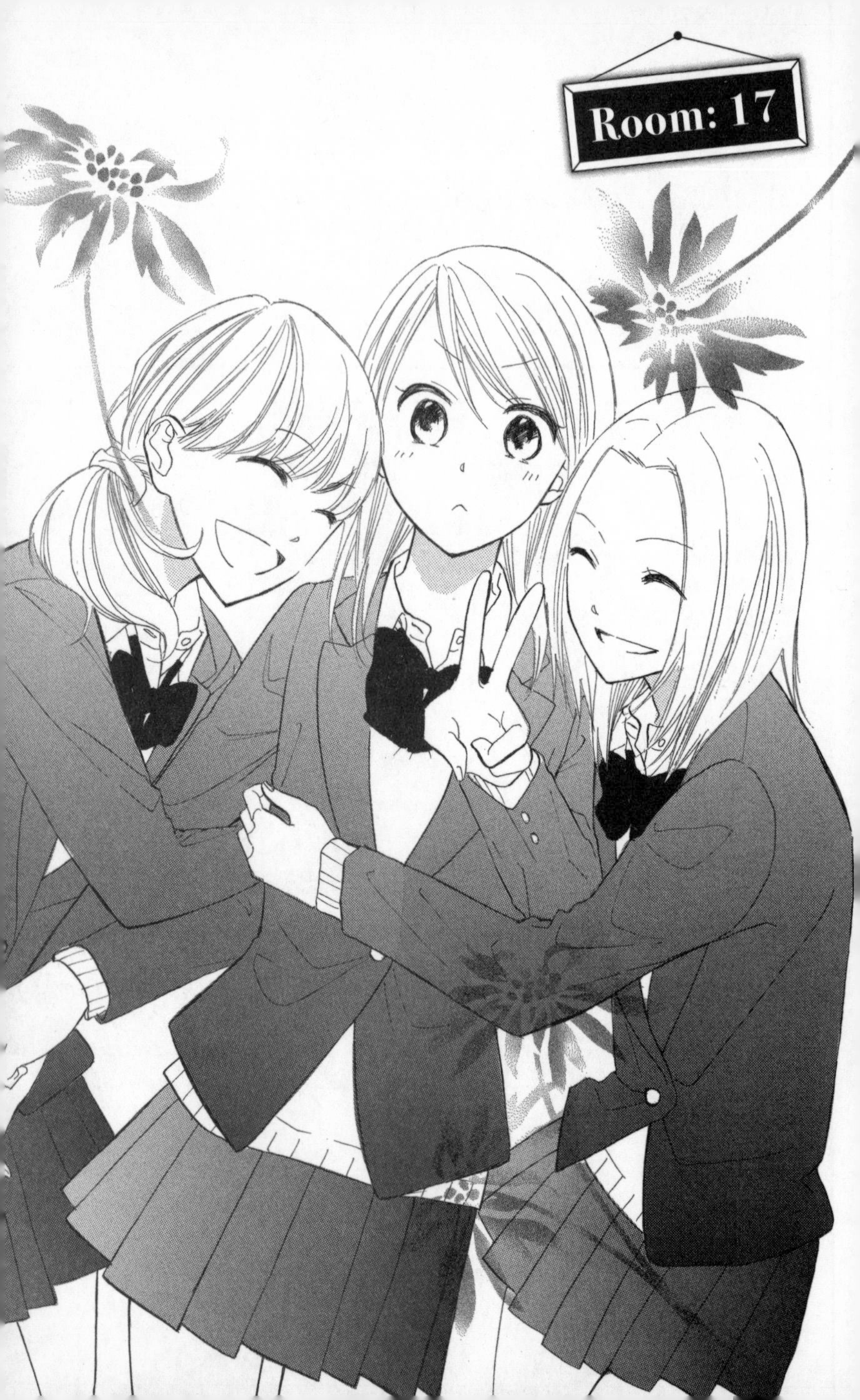
Room: 17

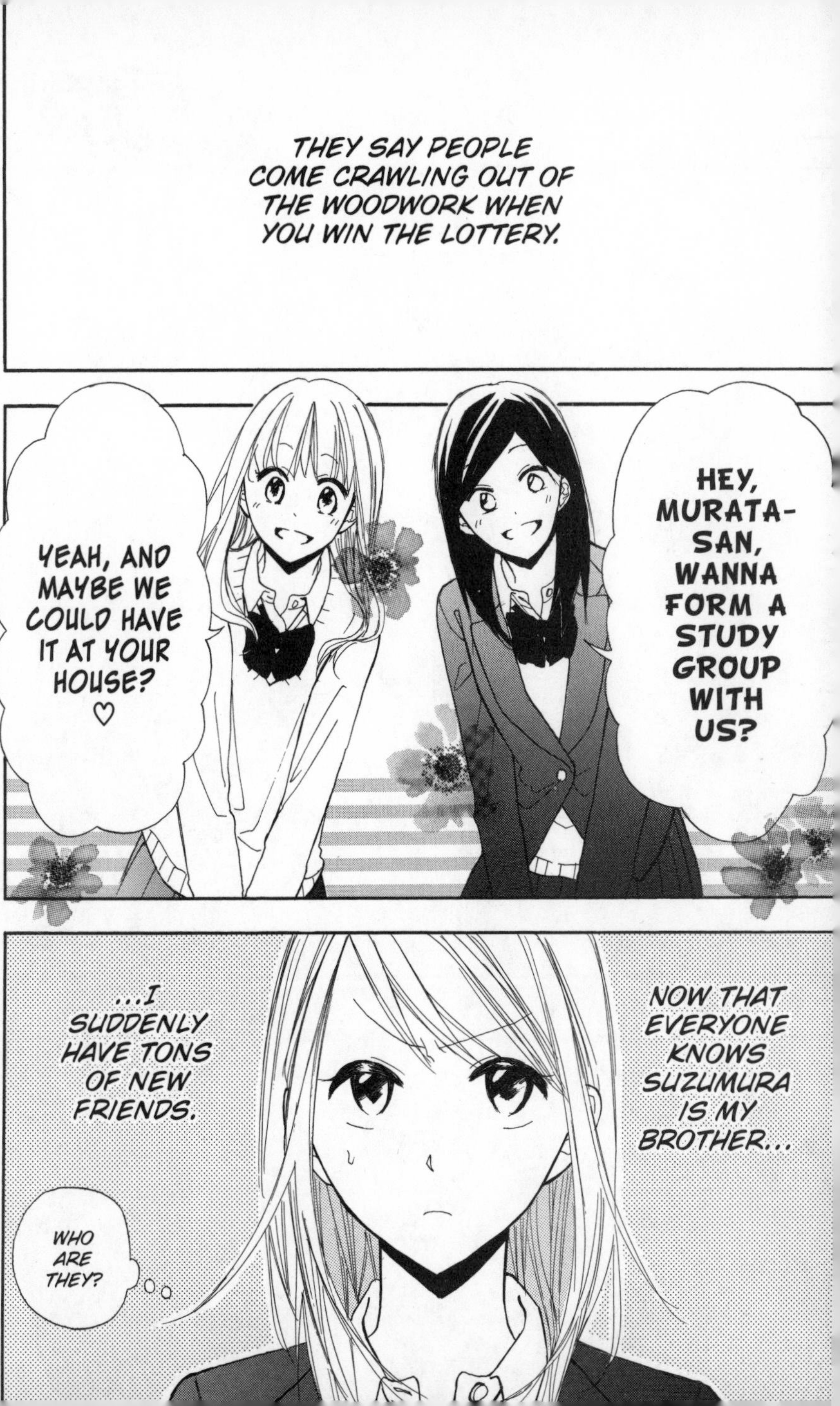
THEY SAY PEOPLE COME CRAWLING OUT OF THE WOODWORK WHEN YOU WIN THE LOTTERY.
HEY, MURATA-SAN, WANNA FORM A STUDY GROUP WITH US?
YEAH, AND MAYBE WE COULD HAVE IT AT YOUR HOUSE? ♡
NOW THAT EVERYONE KNOWS SUZUMURA IS MY BROTHER...
...I SUDDENLY HAVE TONS OF NEW FRIENDS.
WHO ARE THEY?

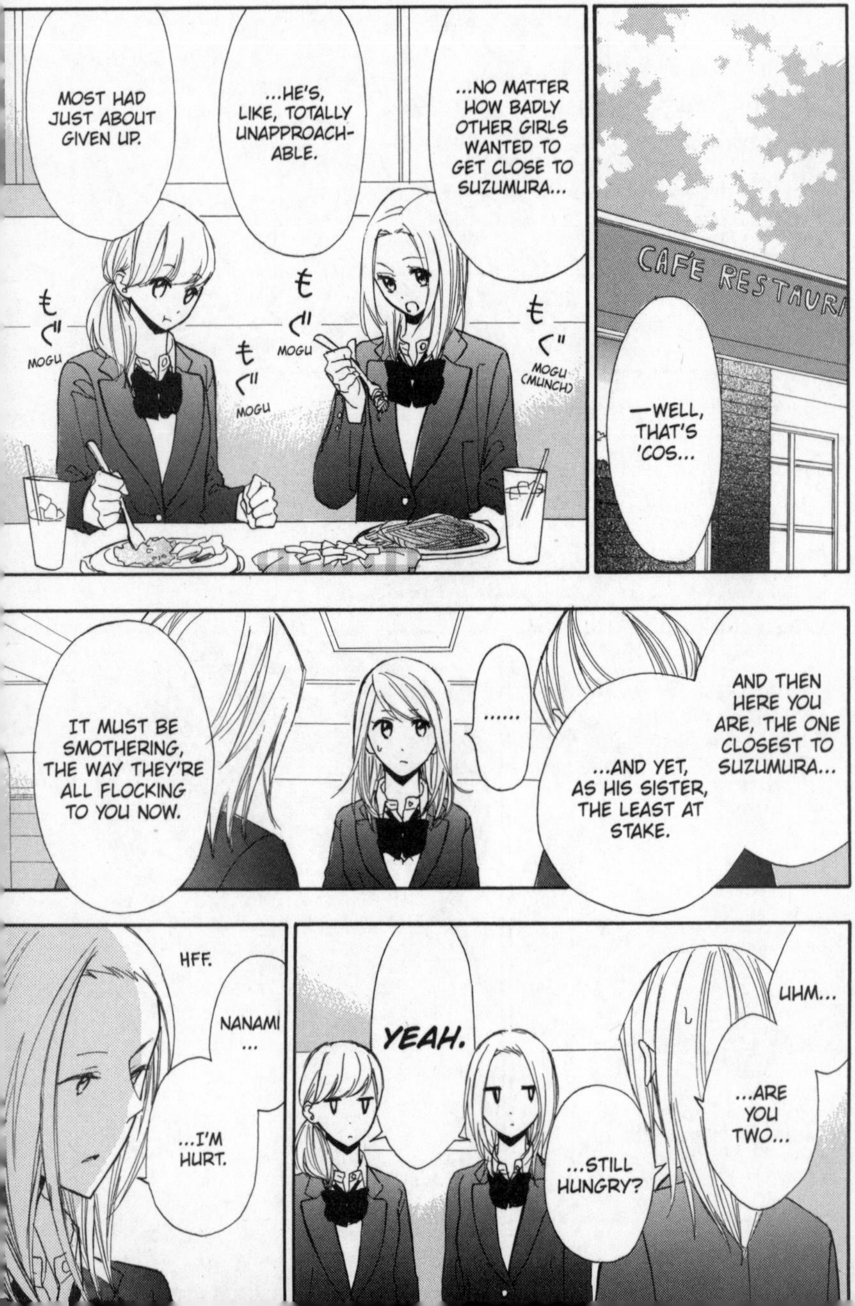
—WELL, THAT'S 'COS...
...NO MATTER HOW BADLY OTHER GIRLS WANTED TO GET CLOSE TO SUZUMURA...
もぐ MOGU (MUNCH)
...HE'S, LIKE, TOTALLY UNAPPROACHABLE.
もぐ MOGU
もぐ MOGU
MOST HAD JUST ABOUT GIVEN UP.
もぐ MOGU
AND THEN HERE YOU ARE, THE ONE CLOSEST TO SUZUMURA...
...AND YET, AS HIS SISTER, THE LEAST AT STAKE.
......
IT MUST BE SMOTHERING, THE WAY THEY'RE ALL FLOCKING TO YOU NOW.
UHM...
...ARE YOU TWO...
...STILL HUNGRY?
YEAH.
HFF.
NANAMI...
...I'M HURT.

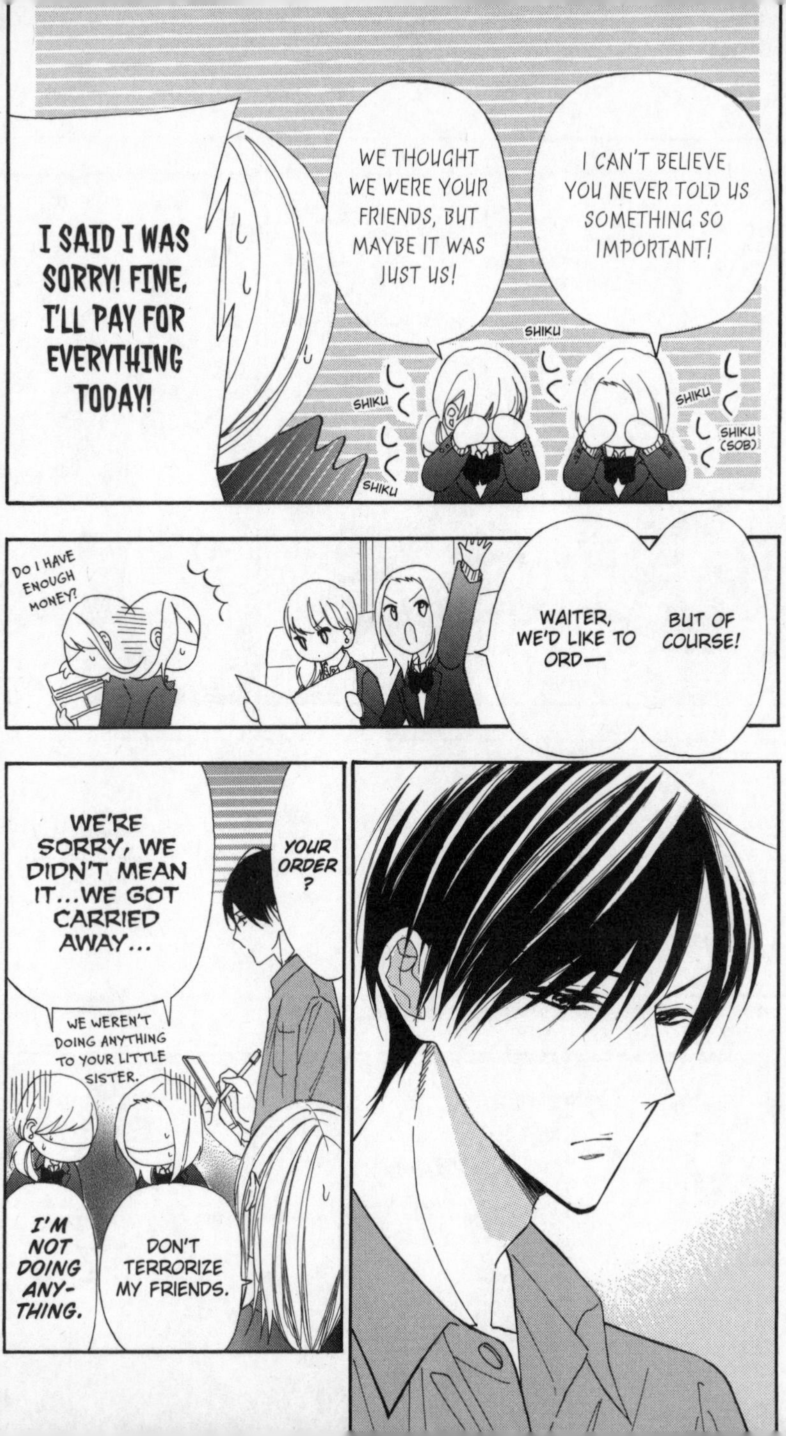
I CAN'T BELIEVE YOU NEVER TOLD US SOMETHING SO IMPORTANT!
WE THOUGHT WE WERE YOUR FRIENDS, BUT MAYBE IT WAS JUST US!
SHIKU
SHIKU
SHIKU (SOB)
SHIKU
SHIKU
I SAID I WAS SORRY! FINE, I'LL PAY FOR EVERYTHING TODAY!
BUT OF COURSE!
WAITER, WE'D LIKE TO ORD—
DO I HAVE ENOUGH MONEY?
YOUR ORDER?
WE'RE SORRY, WE DIDN'T MEAN IT...WE GOT CARRIED AWAY...
WE WEREN'T DOING ANYTHING TO YOUR LITTLE SISTER.
DON'T TERRORIZE MY FRIENDS.
I'M NOT DOING ANY-THING.

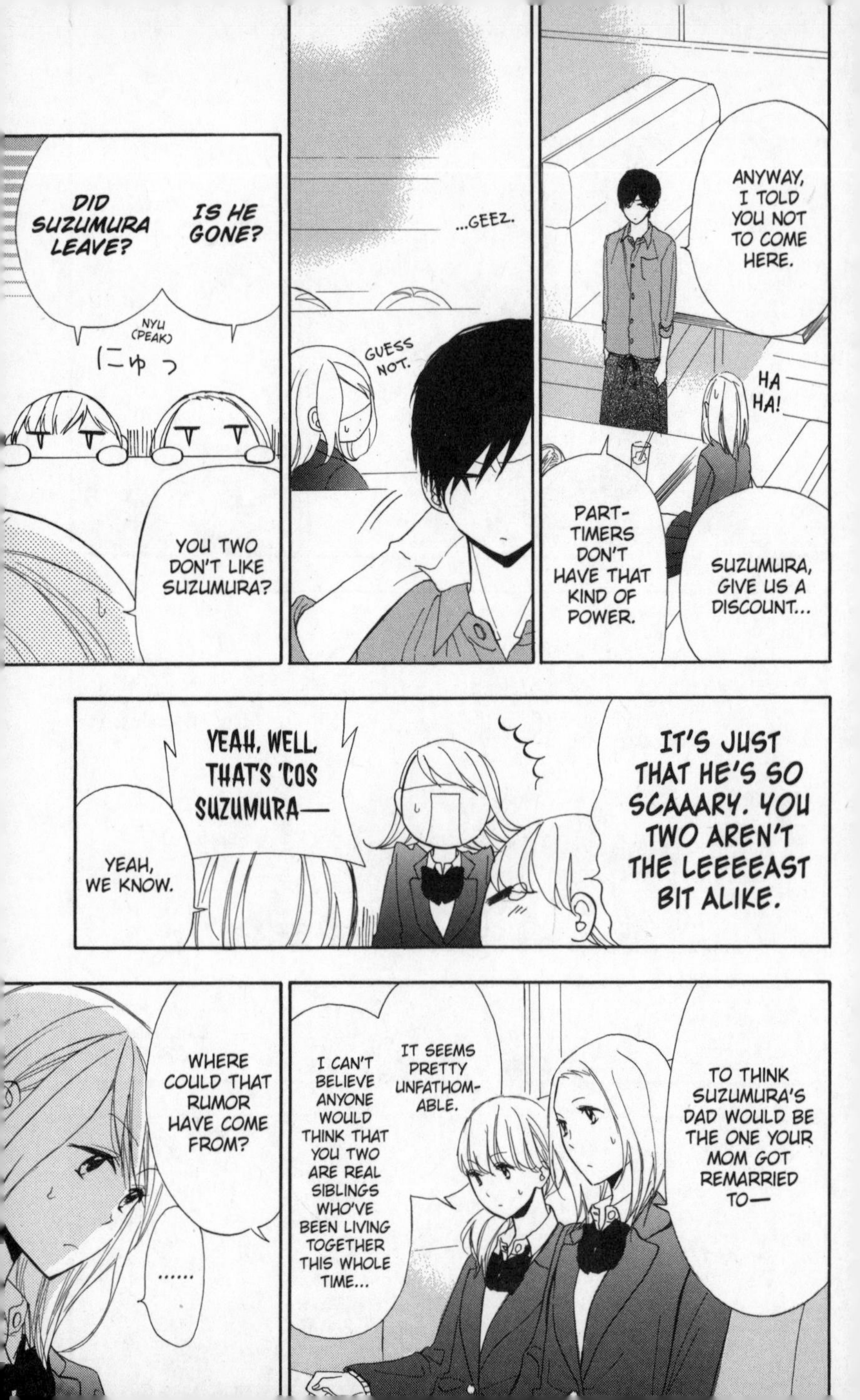
ANYWAY, I TOLD YOU NOT TO COME HERE.
HA HA!
SUZUMURA, GIVE US A DISCOUNT...
PART-TIMERS DON'T HAVE THAT KIND OF POWER.
...GEEZ.
GUESS NOT.
IS HE GONE?
DID SUZUMURA LEAVE?
NYU (PEAK)
にゅっ
YOU TWO DON'T LIKE SUZUMURA?
IT'S JUST THAT HE'S SO SCAAARY. YOU TWO AREN'T THE LEEEEAST BIT ALIKE.
YEAH, WELL, THAT'S 'COS SUZUMURA—
YEAH, WE KNOW.
TO THINK SUZUMURA'S DAD WOULD BE THE ONE YOUR MOM GOT REMARRIED TO—
IT SEEMS PRETTY UNFATHOM-ABLE.
I CAN'T BELIEVE ANYONE WOULD THINK THAT YOU TWO ARE REAL SIBLINGS WHO'VE BEEN LIVING TOGETHER THIS WHOLE TIME...
WHERE COULD THAT RUMOR HAVE COME FROM?
......

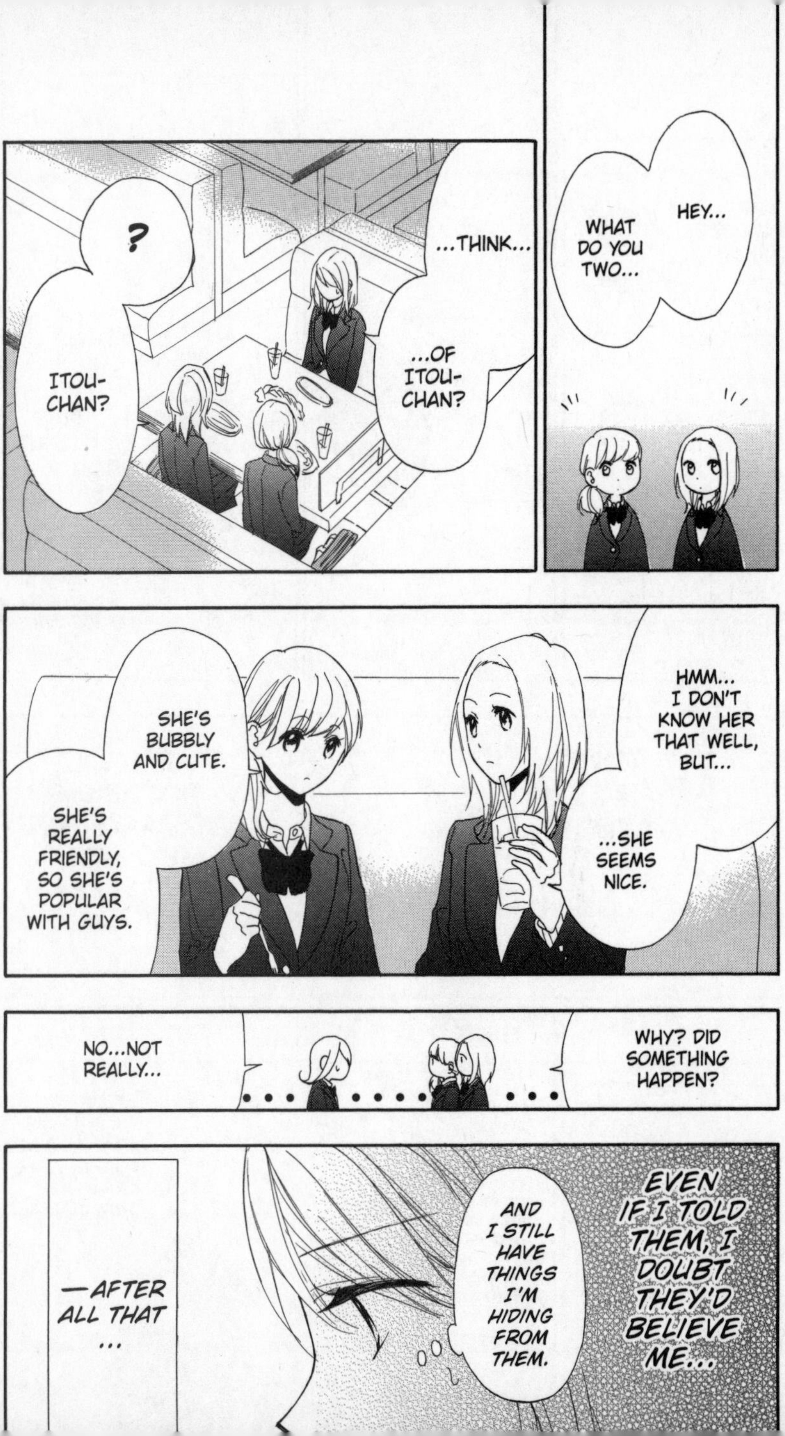
HEY... WHAT DO YOU TWO...
...THINK...
...OF ITOU-CHAN?
?
ITOU-CHAN?
HMM... I DON'T KNOW HER THAT WELL, BUT...
...SHE SEEMS NICE.
SHE'S BUBBLY AND CUTE.
SHE'S REALLY FRIENDLY, SO SHE'S POPULAR WITH GUYS.
WHY? DID SOMETHING HAPPEN?
...
....
...
NO...NOT REALLY...
EVEN IF I TOLD THEM, I DOUBT THEY'D BELIEVE ME...
AND I STILL HAVE THINGS I'M HIDING FROM THEM.
—AFTER ALL THAT...

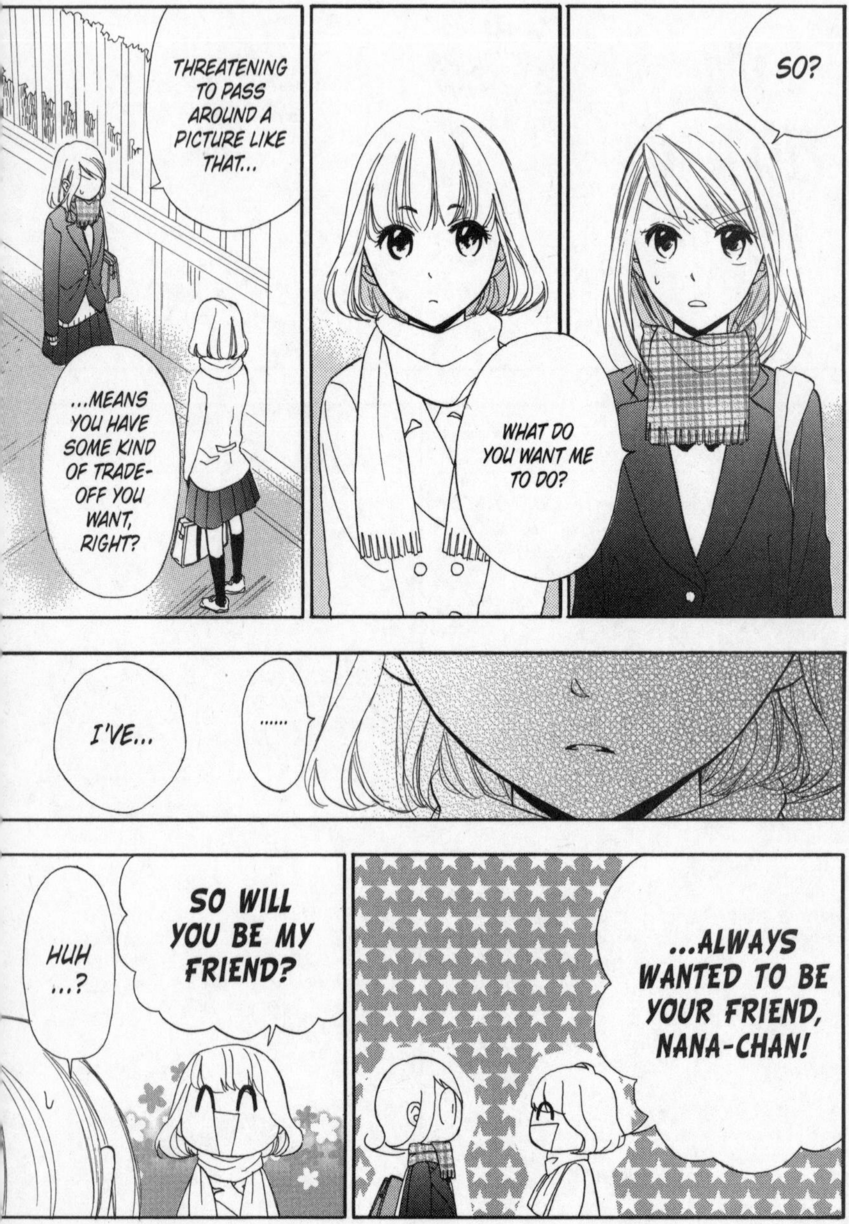
SO?
WHAT DO YOU WANT ME TO DO?
THREATENING TO PASS AROUND A PICTURE LIKE THAT...
...MEANS YOU HAVE SOME KIND OF TRADE-OFF YOU WANT, RIGHT?
......
I'VE...
...ALWAYS WANTED TO BE YOUR FRIEND, NANA-CHAN!
SO WILL YOU BE MY FRIEND?
HUH ...?

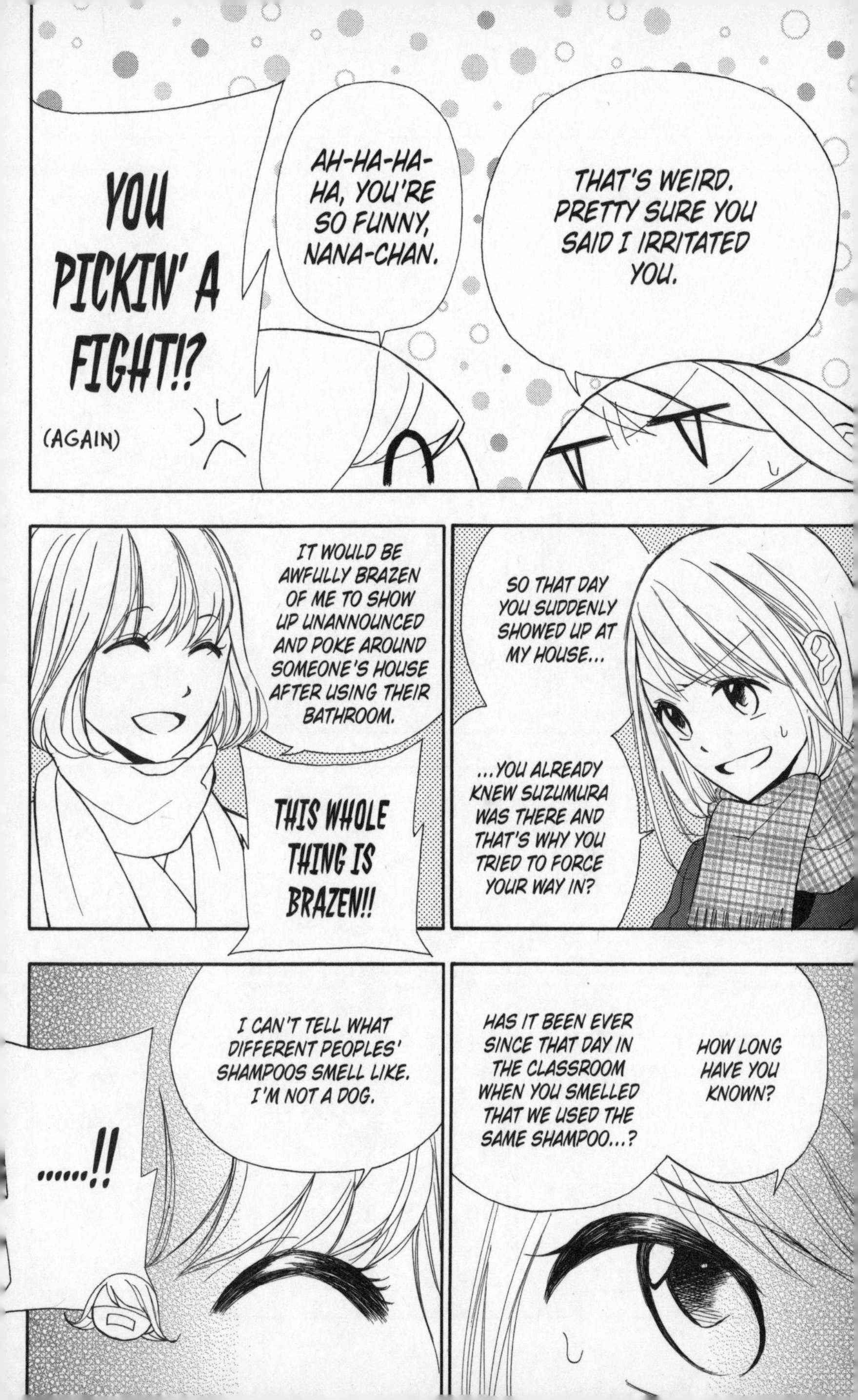
THAT'S WEIRD. PRETTY SURE YOU SAID I IRRITATED YOU.
AH-HA-HA-HA, YOU'RE SO FUNNY, NANA-CHAN.
YOU PICKIN' A FIGHT!?
(AGAIN)
SO THAT DAY YOU SUDDENLY SHOWED UP AT MY HOUSE...
...YOU ALREADY KNEW SUZUMURA WAS THERE AND THAT'S WHY YOU TRIED TO FORCE YOUR WAY IN?
IT WOULD BE AWFULLY BRAZEN OF ME TO SHOW UP UNANNOUNCED AND POKE AROUND SOMEONE'S HOUSE AFTER USING THEIR BATHROOM.
THIS WHOLE THING IS BRAZEN!!
HOW LONG HAVE YOU KNOWN?
HAS IT BEEN EVER SINCE THAT DAY IN THE CLASSROOM WHEN YOU SMELLED THAT WE USED THE SAME SHAMPOO...?
I CAN'T TELL WHAT DIFFERENT PEOPLES' SHAMPOOS SMELL LIKE. I'M NOT A DOG.
......!!

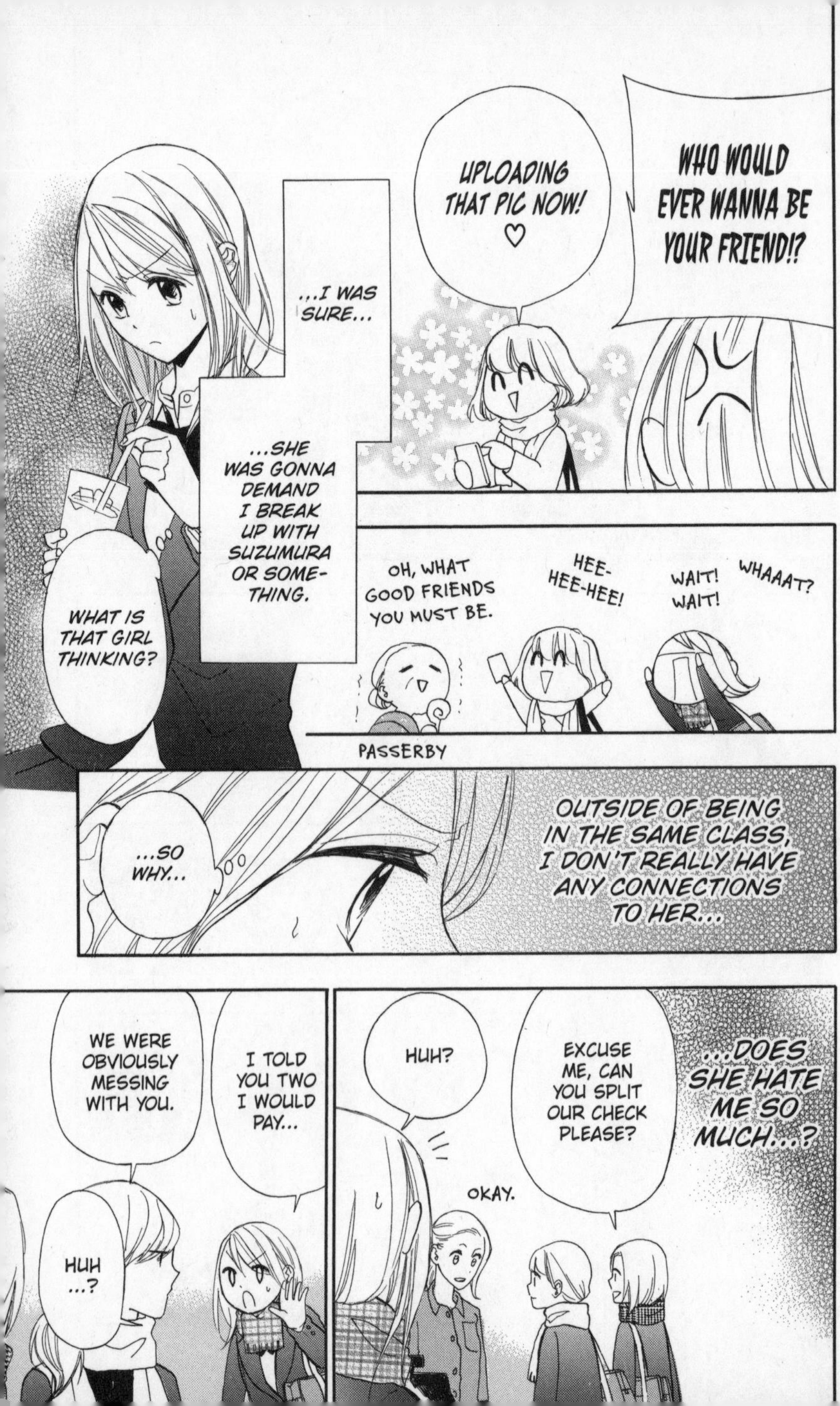
WHO WOULD EVER WANNA BE YOUR FRIEND!?
UPLOADING THAT PIC NOW! ♡
WHAAAT?
WAIT! WAIT!
HEE-HEE-HEE!
OH, WHAT GOOD FRIENDS YOU MUST BE.
PASSERBY
...I WAS SURE...
...SHE WAS GONNA DEMAND I BREAK UP WITH SUZUMURA OR SOME-THING.
WHAT IS THAT GIRL THINKING?
OUTSIDE OF BEING IN THE SAME CLASS, I DON'T REALLY HAVE ANY CONNECTIONS TO HER...
...SO WHY...
...DOES SHE HATE ME SO MUCH...?
EXCUSE ME, CAN YOU SPLIT OUR CHECK PLEASE?
HUH?
OKAY.
I TOLD YOU TWO I WOULD PAY...
WE WERE OBVIOUSLY MESSING WITH YOU.
HUH ...?

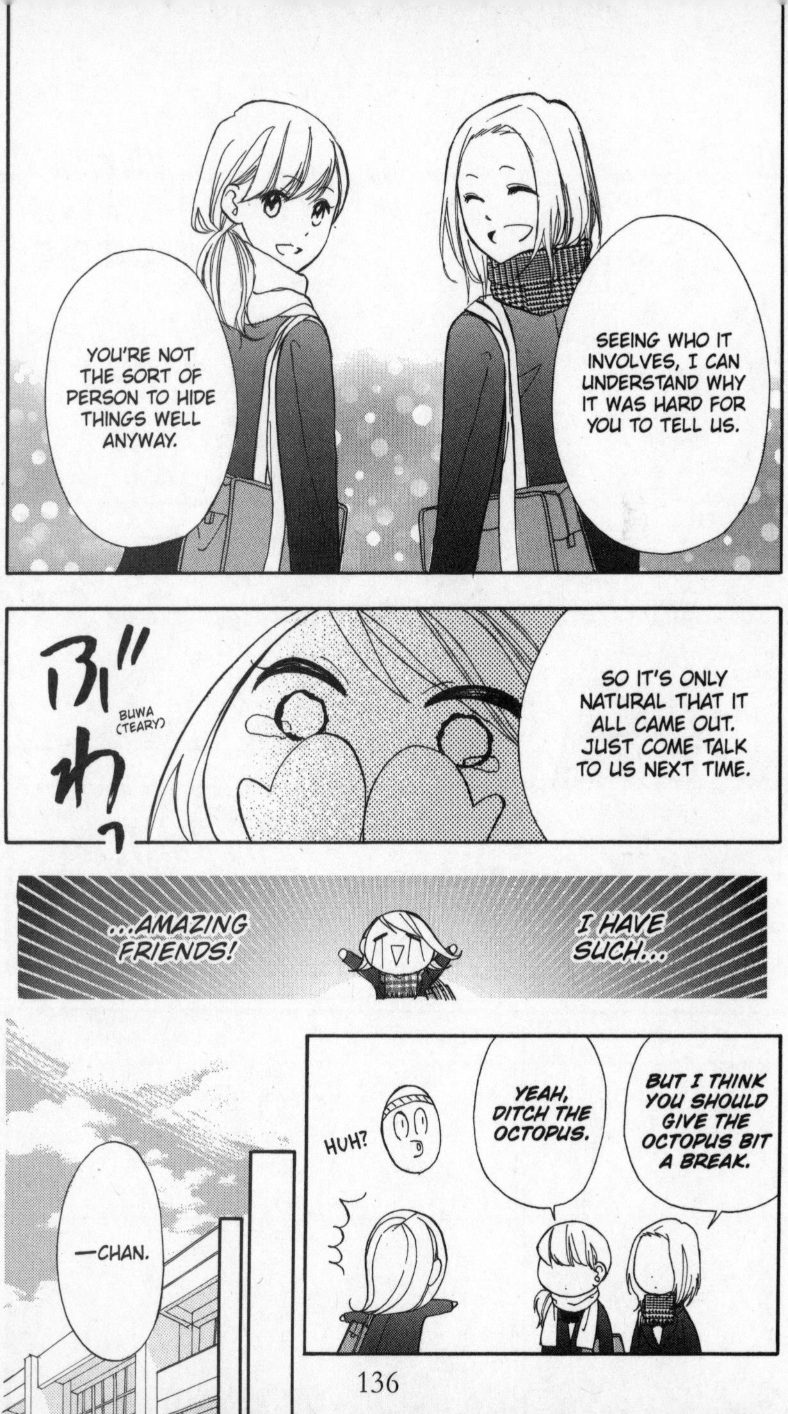
SEEING WHO IT INVOLVES, I CAN UNDERSTAND WHY IT WAS HARD FOR YOU TO TELL US.
YOU'RE NOT THE SORT OF PERSON TO HIDE THINGS WELL ANYWAY.
SO IT'S ONLY NATURAL THAT IT ALL CAME OUT. JUST COME TALK TO US NEXT TIME.
ぶわっ
BUWA (TEARY)
I HAVE SUCH...
...AMAZING FRIENDS!
BUT I THINK YOU SHOULD GIVE THE OCTOPUS BIT A BREAK.
YEAH, DITCH THE OCTOPUS.
HUH?
—CHAN.

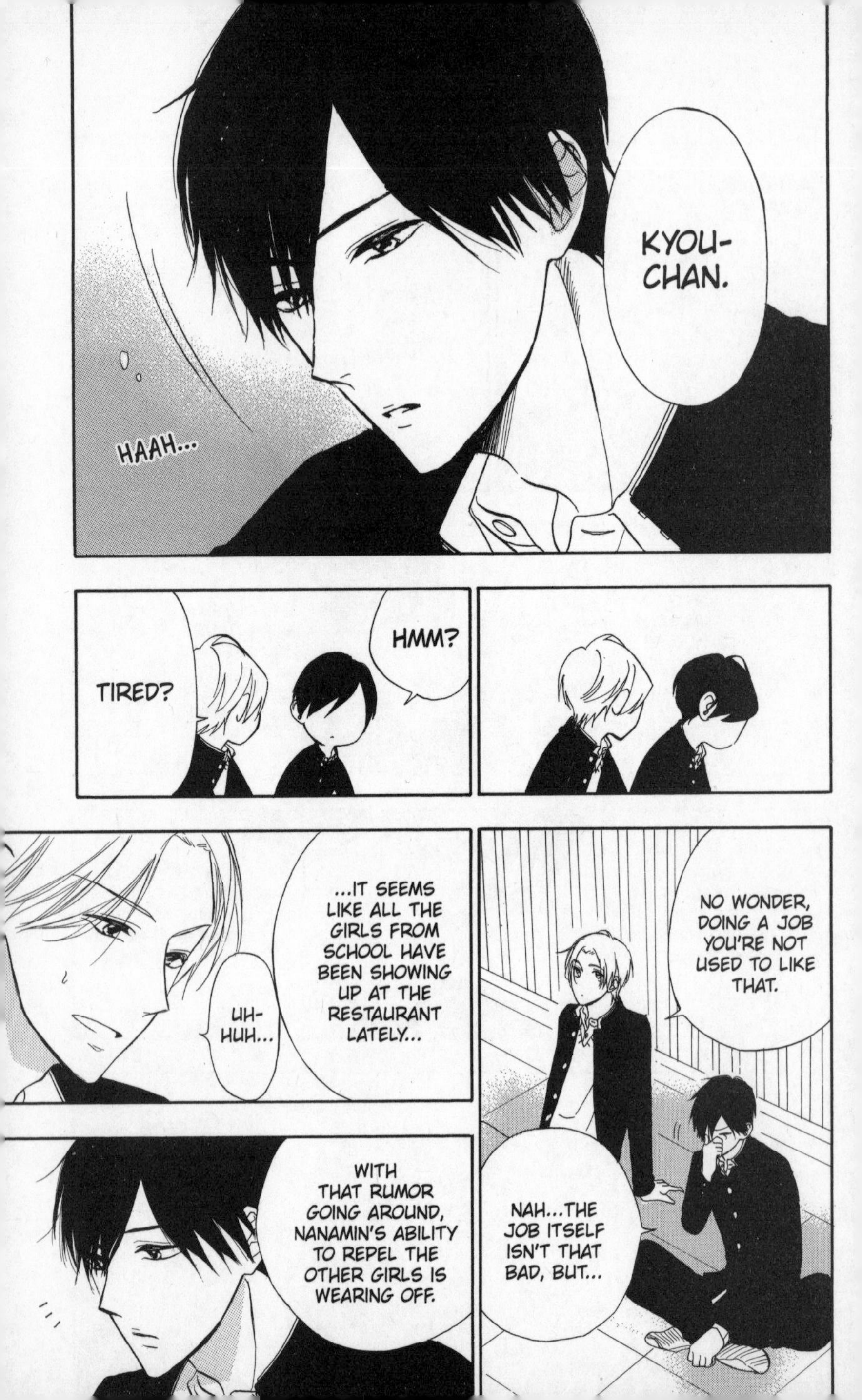
KYOU-CHAN.
HAAH...
HMM?
TIRED?
NO WONDER, DOING A JOB YOU'RE NOT USED TO LIKE THAT.
NAH...THE JOB ITSELF ISN'T THAT BAD, BUT...
...IT SEEMS LIKE ALL THE GIRLS FROM SCHOOL HAVE BEEN SHOWING UP AT THE RESTAURANT LATELY...
UH-HUH...
WITH THAT RUMOR GOING AROUND, NANAMIN'S ABILITY TO REPEL THE OTHER GIRLS IS WEARING OFF.

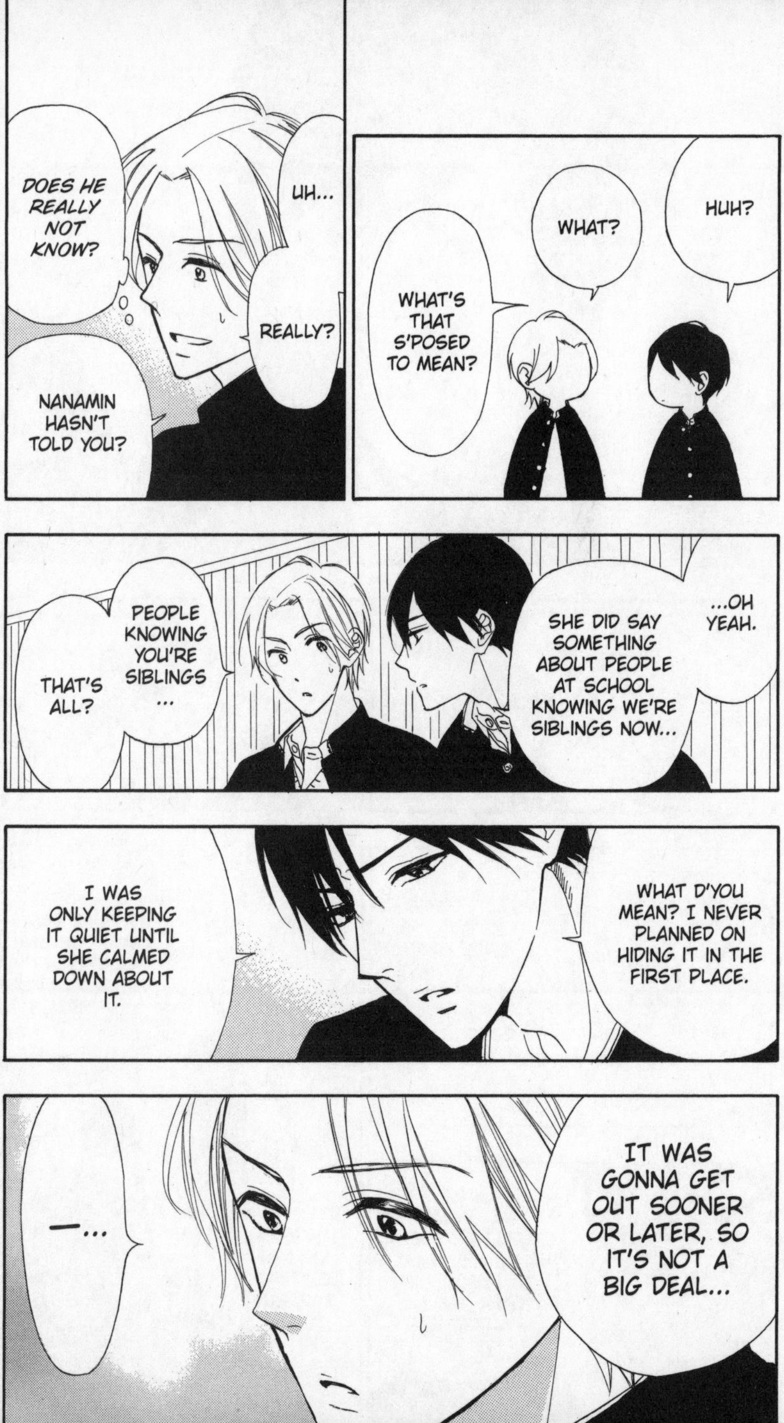
HUH?
WHAT?
WHAT'S THAT S'POSED TO MEAN?
UH...
REALLY?
DOES HE REALLY NOT KNOW?
NANAMIN HASN'T TOLD YOU?
...OH YEAH.
SHE DID SAY SOMETHING ABOUT PEOPLE AT SCHOOL KNOWING WE'RE SIBLINGS NOW...
PEOPLE KNOWING YOU'RE SIBLINGS ...
THAT'S ALL?
WHAT D'YOU MEAN? I NEVER PLANNED ON HIDING IT IN THE FIRST PLACE.
I WAS ONLY KEEPING IT QUIET UNTIL SHE CALMED DOWN ABOUT IT.
IT WAS GONNA GET OUT SOONER OR LATER, SO IT'S NOT A BIG DEAL...
—...

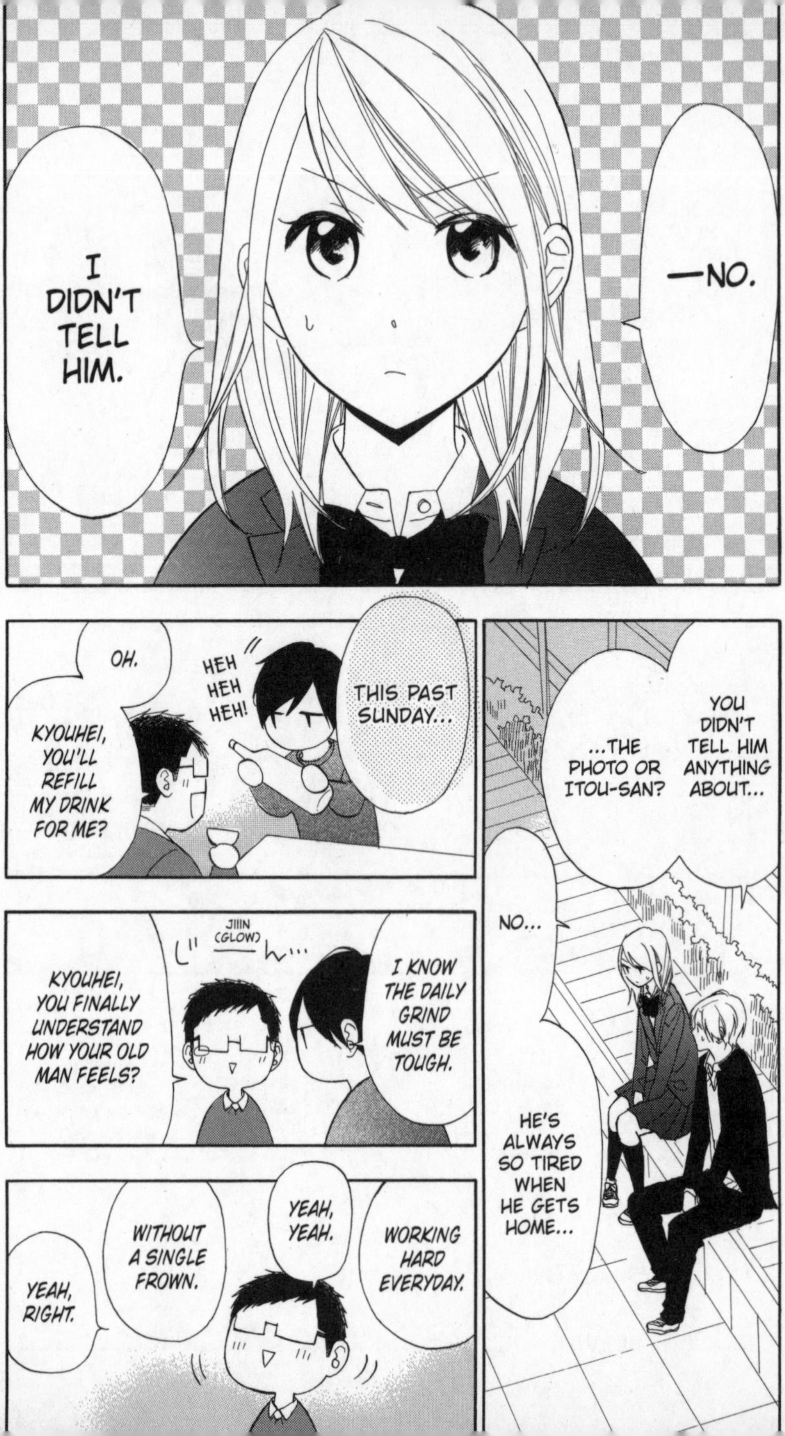
—NO.
I DIDN'T TELL HIM.
YOU DIDN'T TELL HIM ANYTHING ABOUT...
...THE PHOTO OR ITOU-SAN?
NO...
HE'S ALWAYS SO TIRED WHEN HE GETS HOME...
THIS PAST SUNDAY...
HEH HEH HEH!
OH.
KYOUHEI, YOU'LL REFILL MY DRINK FOR ME?
I KNOW THE DAILY GRIND MUST BE TOUGH.
JIIN (GLOW)
KYOUHEI, YOU FINALLY UNDERSTAND HOW YOUR OLD MAN FEELS?
WORKING HARD EVERYDAY.
YEAH, YEAH.
WITHOUT A SINGLE FROWN.
YEAH, RIGHT.

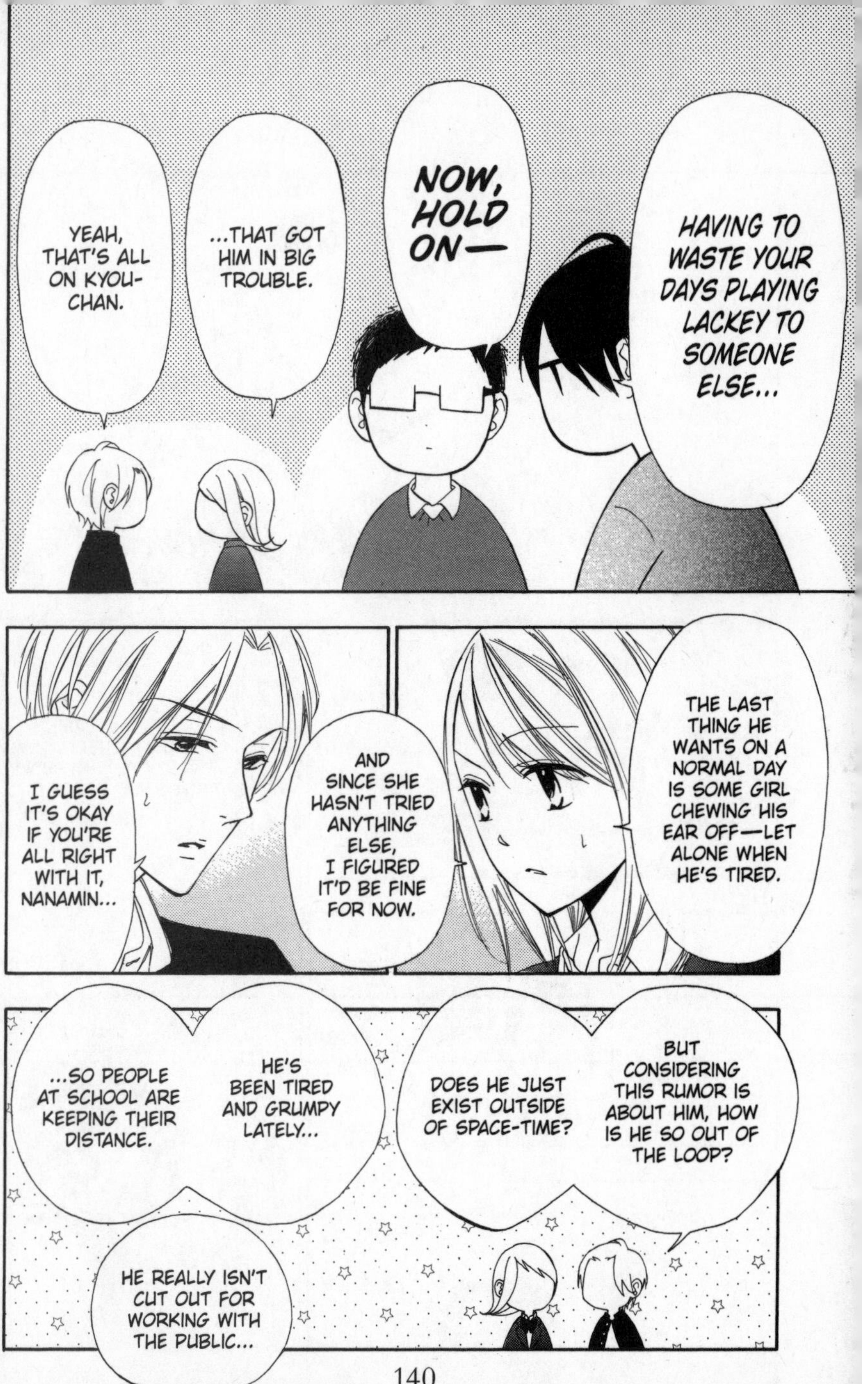
HAVING TO WASTE YOUR DAYS PLAYING LACKEY TO SOMEONE ELSE...
NOW, HOLD ON—
...THAT GOT HIM IN BIG TROUBLE.
YEAH, THAT'S ALL ON KYOU-CHAN.
THE LAST THING HE WANTS ON A NORMAL DAY IS SOME GIRL CHEWING HIS EAR OFF—LET ALONE WHEN HE'S TIRED.
AND SINCE SHE HASN'T TRIED ANYTHING ELSE, I FIGURED IT'D BE FINE FOR NOW.
I GUESS IT'S OKAY IF YOU'RE ALL RIGHT WITH IT, NANAMIN...
BUT CONSIDERING THIS RUMOR IS ABOUT HIM, HOW IS HE SO OUT OF THE LOOP?
DOES HE JUST EXIST OUTSIDE OF SPACE-TIME?
HE'S BEEN TIRED AND GRUMPY LATELY...
...SO PEOPLE AT SCHOOL ARE KEEPING THEIR DISTANCE.
HE REALLY ISN'T CUT OUT FOR WORKING WITH THE PUBLIC...

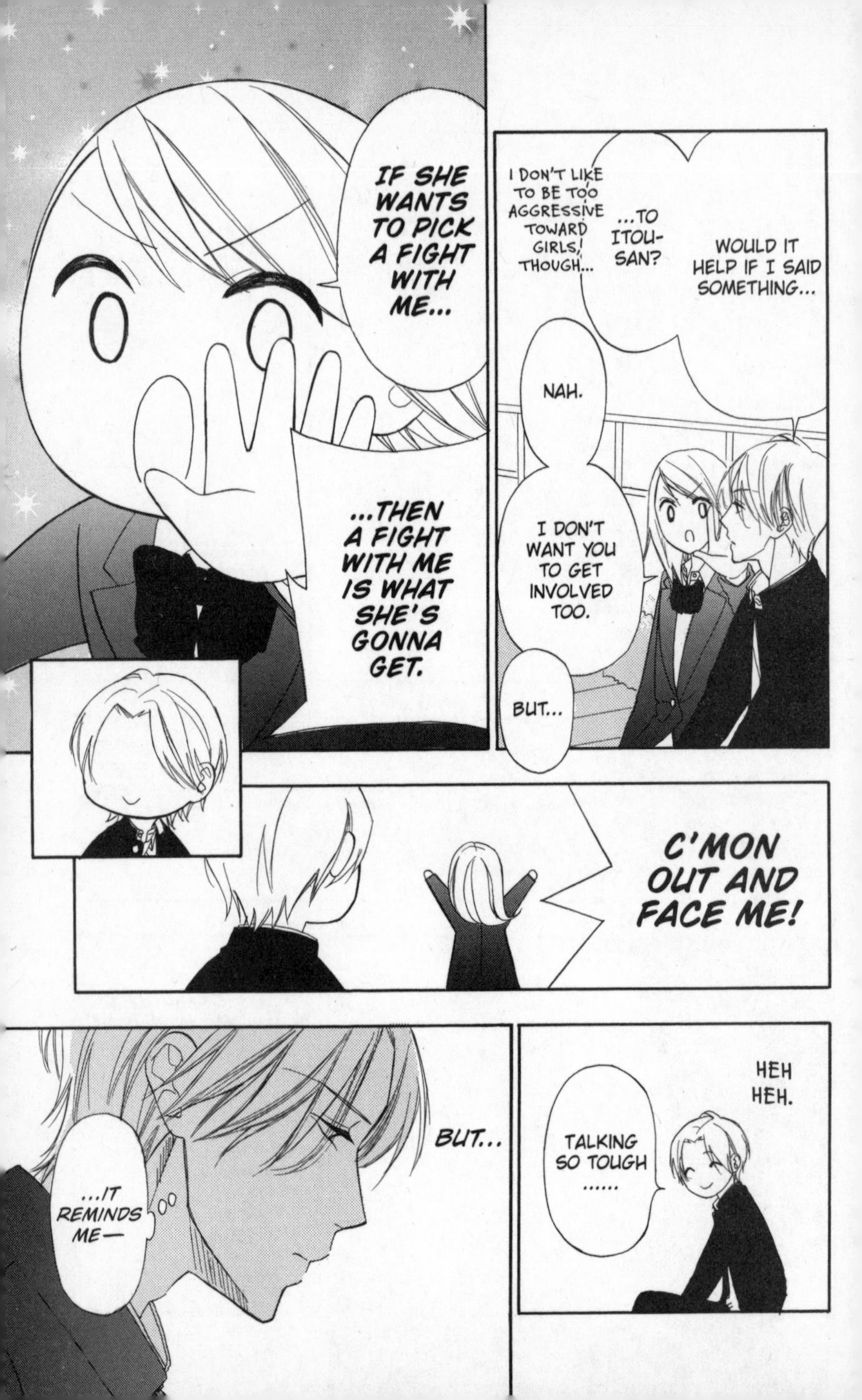
WOULD IT HELP IF I SAID SOMETHING...
...TO ITOU-SAN?
I DON'T LIKE TO BE TOO AGGRESSIVE TOWARD GIRLS, THOUGH...
NAH.
I DON'T WANT YOU TO GET INVOLVED TOO.
BUT...
IF SHE WANTS TO PICK A FIGHT WITH ME...
...THEN A FIGHT WITH ME IS WHAT SHE'S GONNA GET.
C'MON OUT AND FACE ME!
HEH HEH.
TALKING SO TOUGH......
BUT...
...IT REMINDS ME—

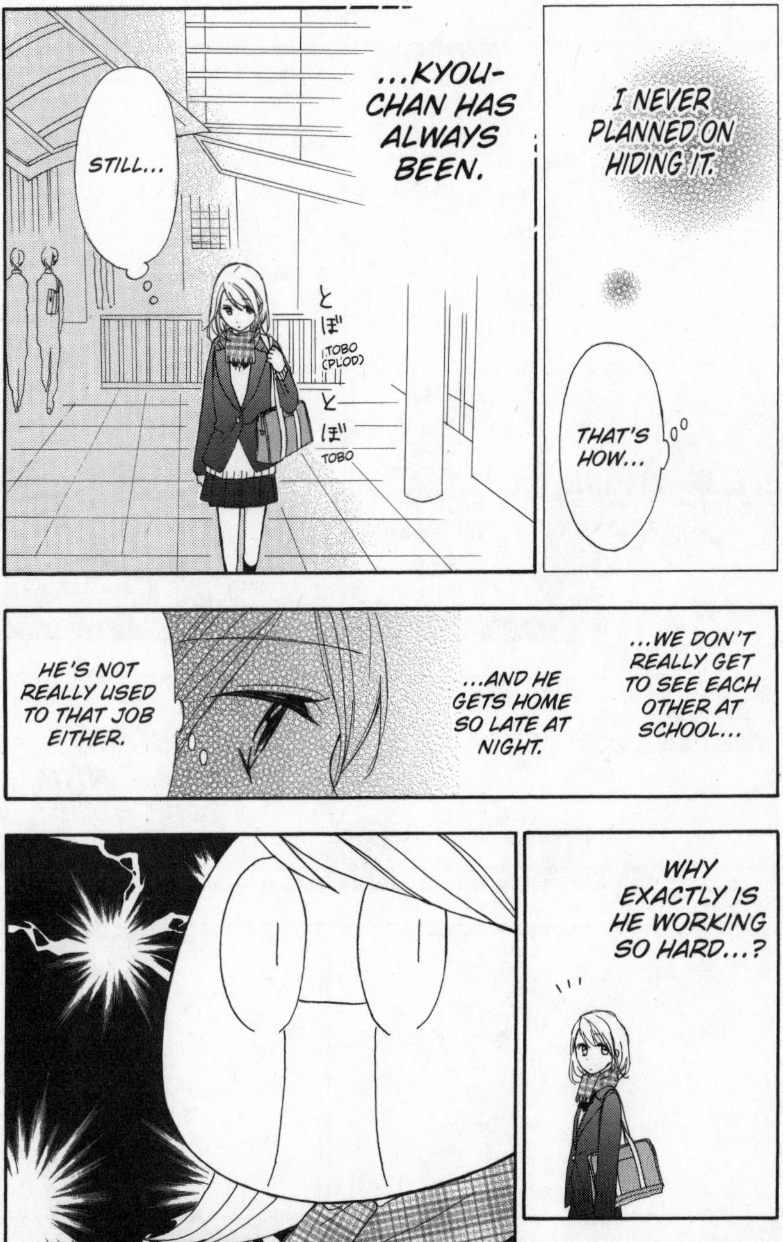
I NEVER PLANNED ON HIDING IT.
THAT'S HOW...
...KYOU-CHAN HAS ALWAYS BEEN.
STILL...
とぼ
TOBO (PLOD)
とぼ
TOBO
...WE DON'T REALLY GET TO SEE EACH OTHER AT SCHOOL...
...AND HE GETS HOME SO LATE AT NIGHT.
HE'S NOT REALLY USED TO THAT JOB EITHER.
WHY EXACTLY IS HE WORKING SO HARD...?

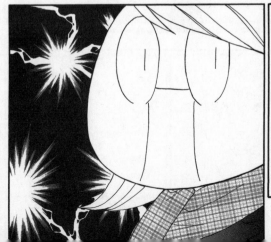

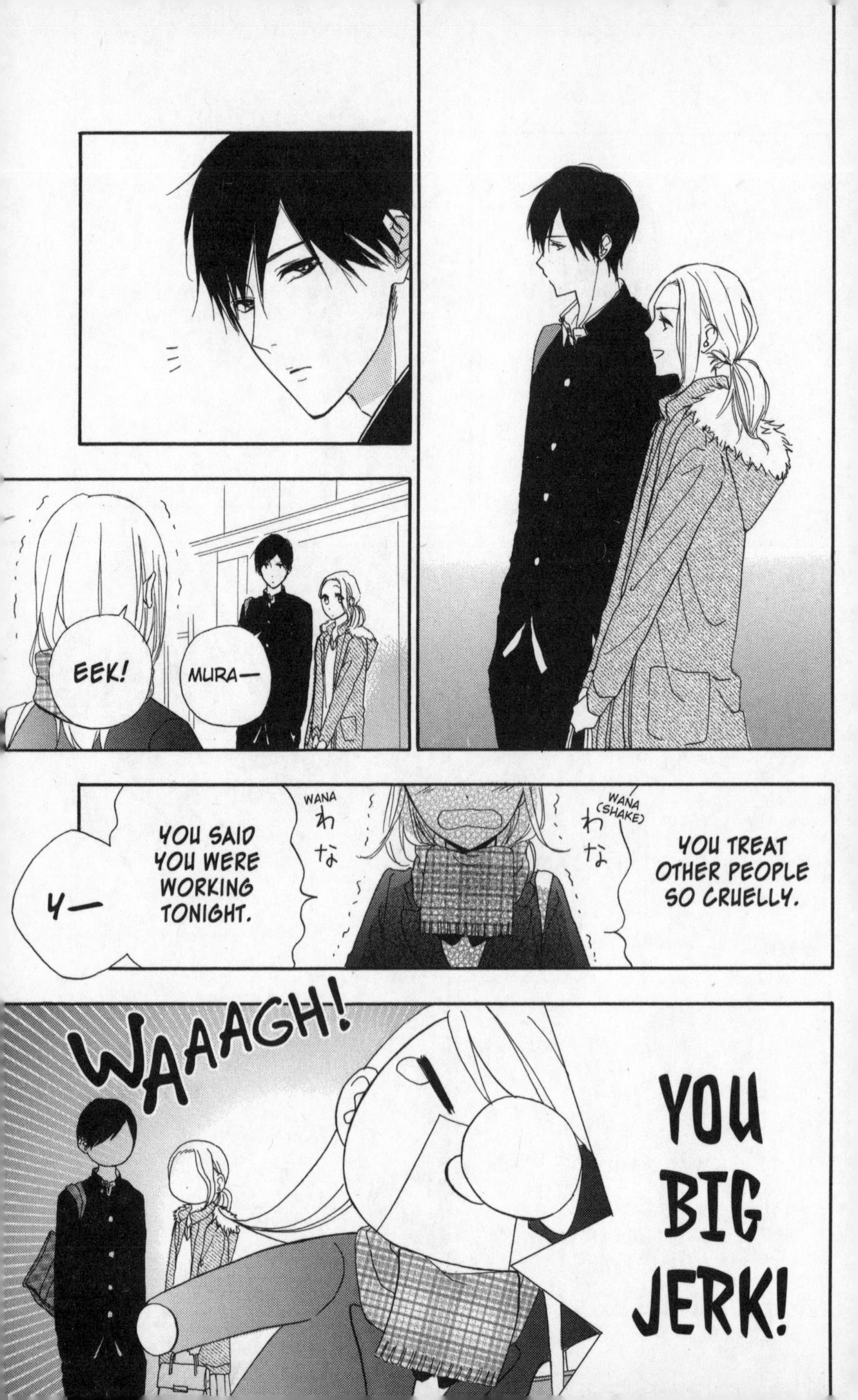
MURA—
EEK!
YOU TREAT OTHER PEOPLE SO CRUELLY.
WANA (SHAKE)
わな
WANA
わな
YOU SAID YOU WERE WORKING TONIGHT.
Y—
YOU BIG JERK!
WAAAGH!

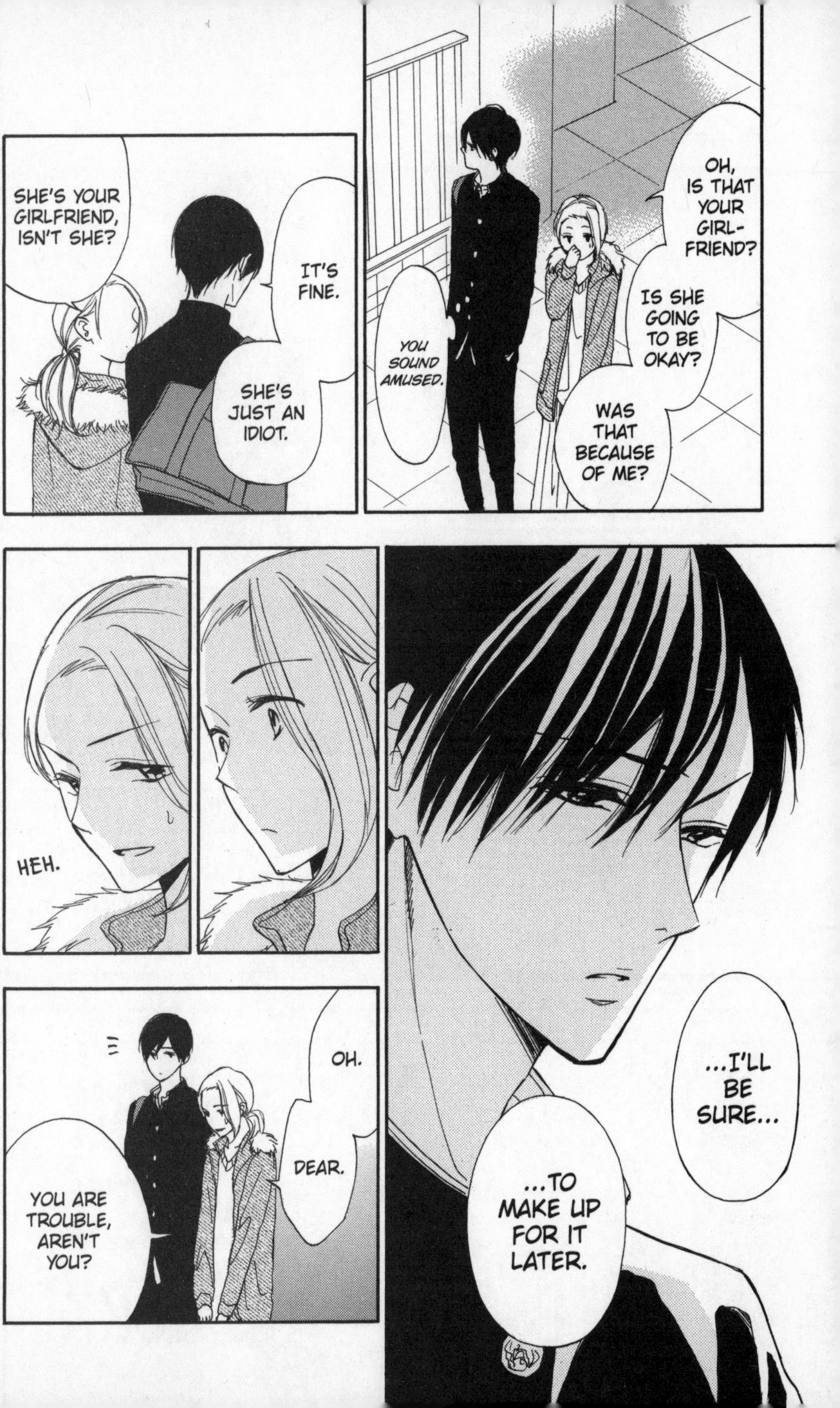
OH, IS THAT YOUR GIRL-FRIEND?
IS SHE GOING TO BE OKAY?
WAS THAT BECAUSE OF ME?
YOU SOUND AMUSED.
IT'S FINE.
SHE'S JUST AN IDIOT.
SHE'S YOUR GIRLFRIEND, ISN'T SHE?
...I'LL BE SURE...
...TO MAKE UP FOR IT LATER.
HEH.
OH.
DEAR.
YOU ARE TROUBLE, AREN'T YOU?

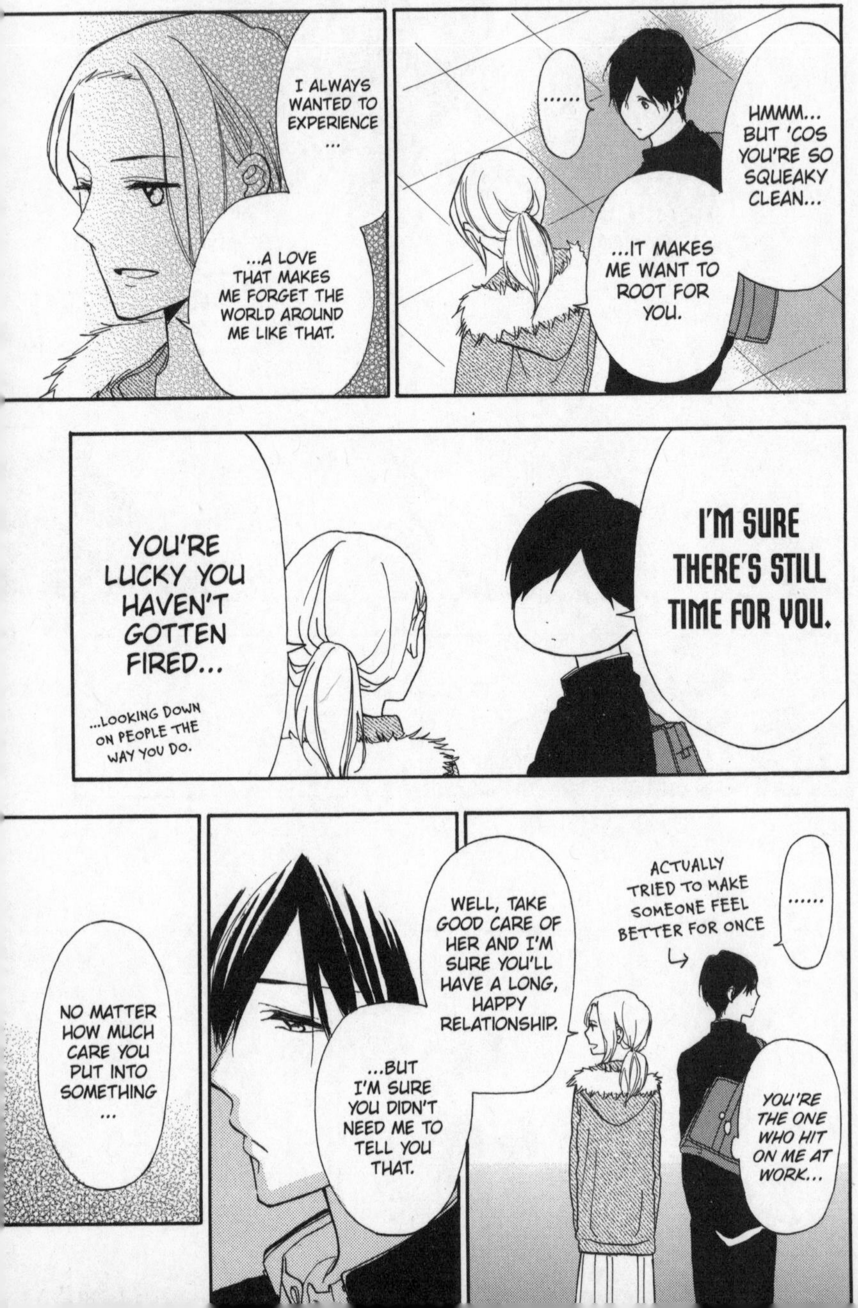
HMMM... BUT 'COS YOU'RE SO SQUEAKY CLEAN...
......
...IT MAKES ME WANT TO ROOT FOR YOU.
I ALWAYS WANTED TO EXPERIENCE ...
...A LOVE THAT MAKES ME FORGET THE WORLD AROUND ME LIKE THAT.
I'M SURE THERE'S STILL TIME FOR YOU.
YOU'RE LUCKY YOU HAVEN'T GOTTEN FIRED...
...LOOKING DOWN ON PEOPLE THE WAY YOU DO.
......
ACTUALLY TRIED TO MAKE SOMEONE FEEL BETTER FOR ONCE
WELL, TAKE GOOD CARE OF HER AND I'M SURE YOU'LL HAVE A LONG, HAPPY RELATIONSHIP.
YOU'RE THE ONE WHO HIT ON ME AT WORK...
...BUT I'M SURE YOU DIDN'T NEED ME TO TELL YOU THAT.
NO MATTER HOW MUCH CARE YOU PUT INTO SOMETHING ...

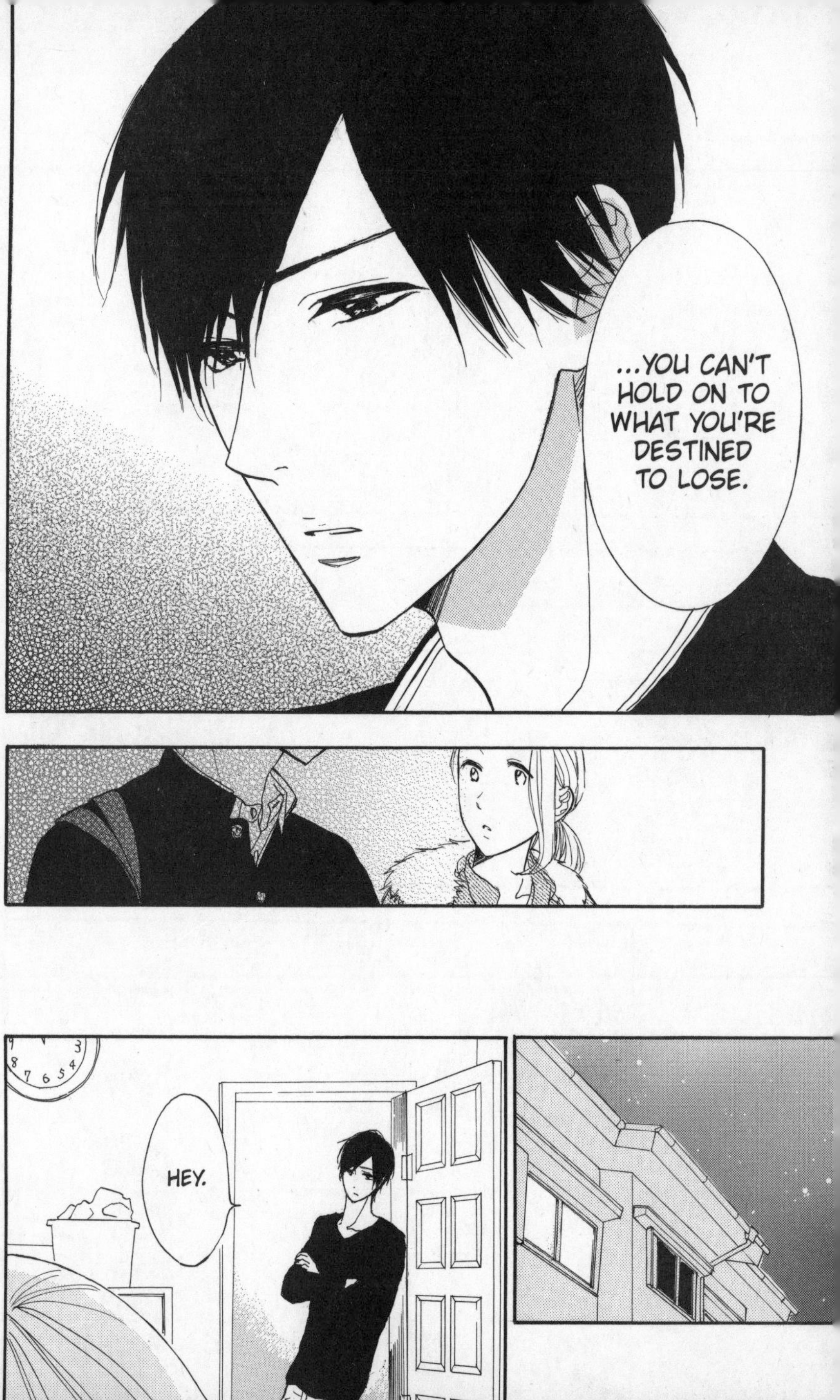
...YOU CAN'T HOLD ON TO WHAT YOU'RE DESTINED TO LOSE.
HEY.

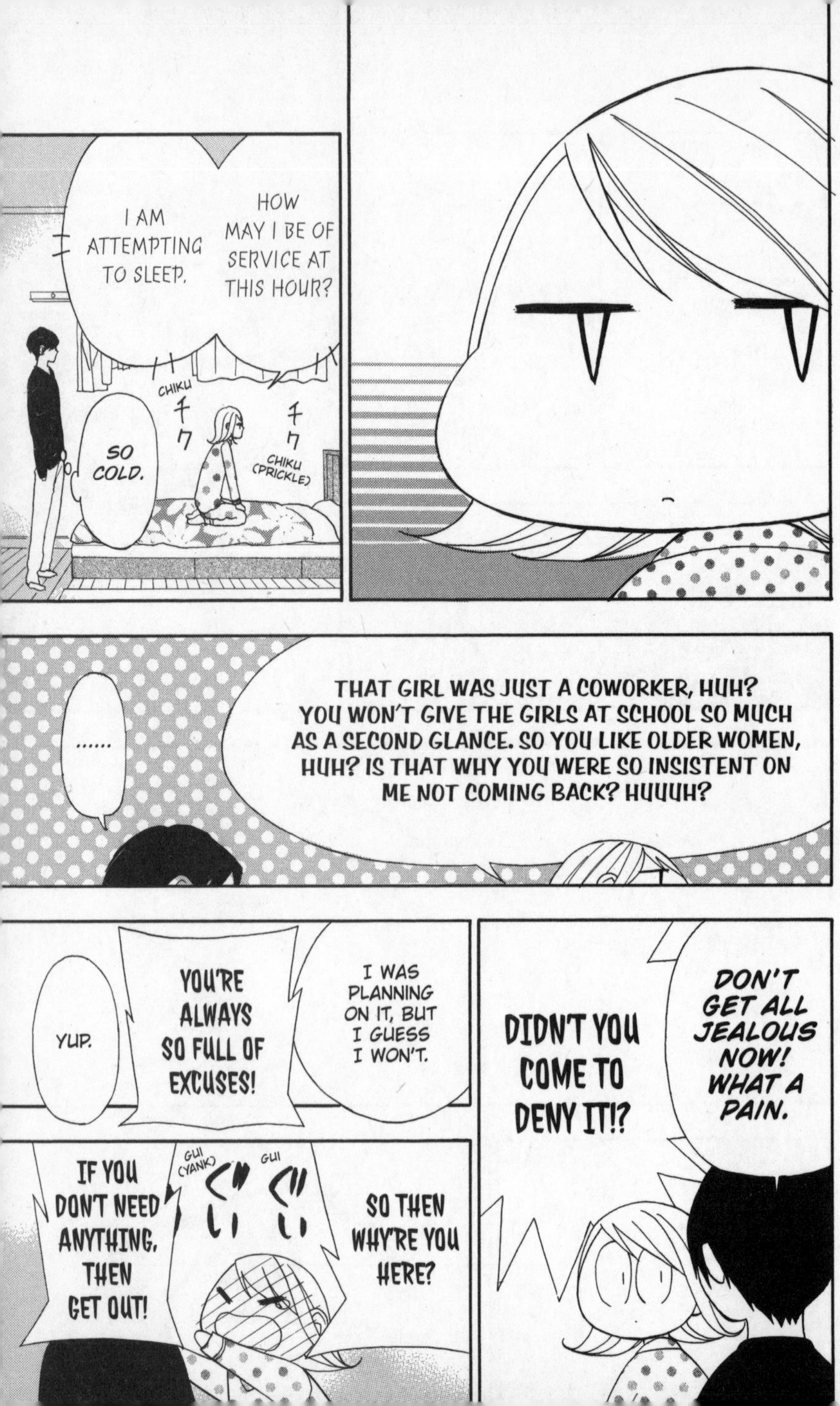
HOW MAY I BE OF SERVICE AT THIS HOUR?
I AM ATTEMPTING TO SLEEP.
チク CHIKU (PRICKLE)
チク CHIKU
SO COLD.
THAT GIRL WAS JUST A COWORKER, HUH? YOU WON'T GIVE THE GIRLS AT SCHOOL SO MUCH AS A SECOND GLANCE. SO YOU LIKE OLDER WOMEN, HUH? IS THAT WHY YOU WERE SO INSISTENT ON ME NOT COMING BACK? HUUUH?
......
DON'T GET ALL JEALOUS NOW! WHAT A PAIN.
DIDN'T YOU COME TO DENY IT!?
I WAS PLANNING ON IT, BUT I GUESS I WON'T.
YOU'RE ALWAYS SO FULL OF EXCUSES!
YUP.
SO THEN WHY'RE YOU HERE?
ぐい GUI
ぐい GUI (YANK)
IF YOU DON'T NEED ANYTHING, THEN GET OUT!

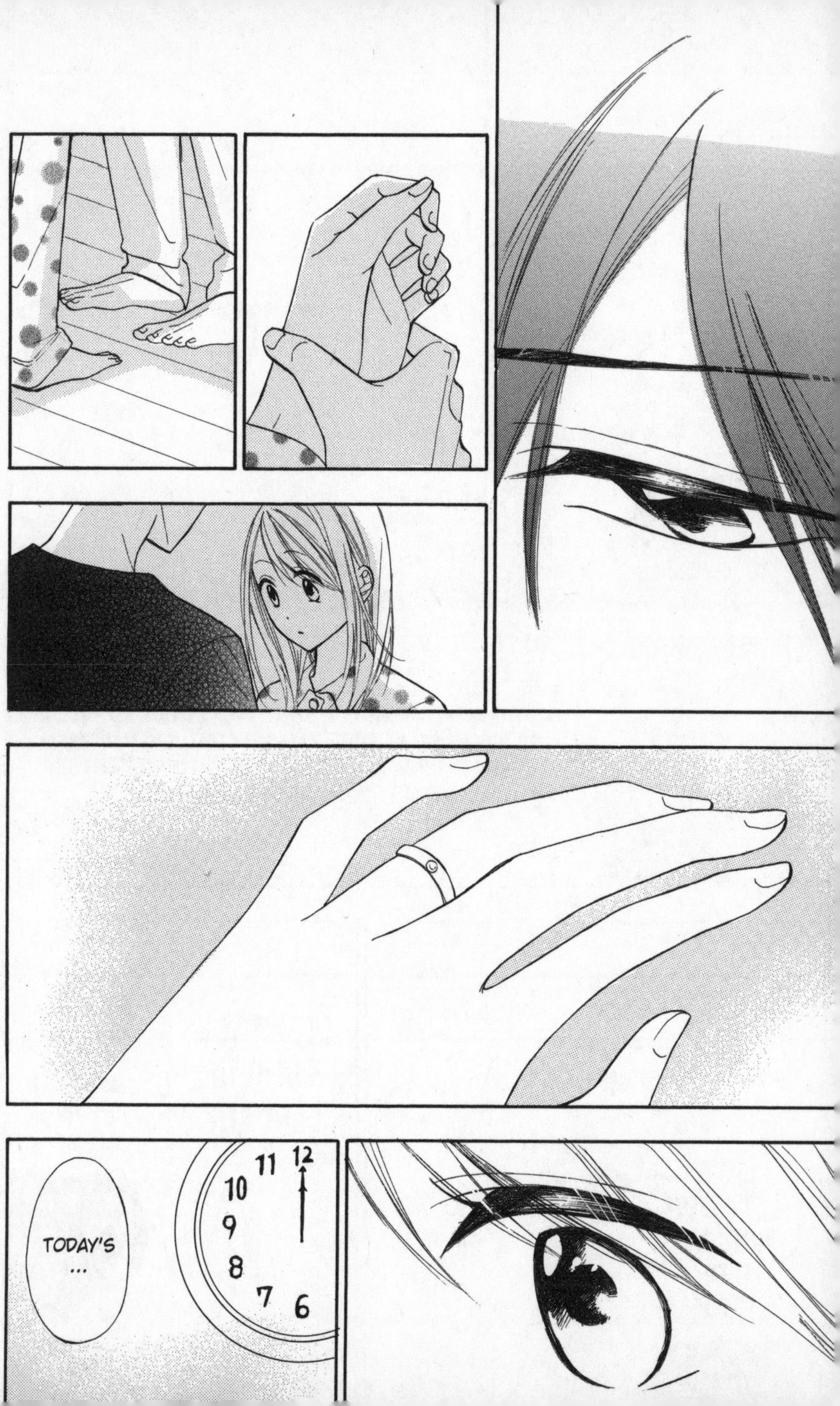
TODAY'S
...

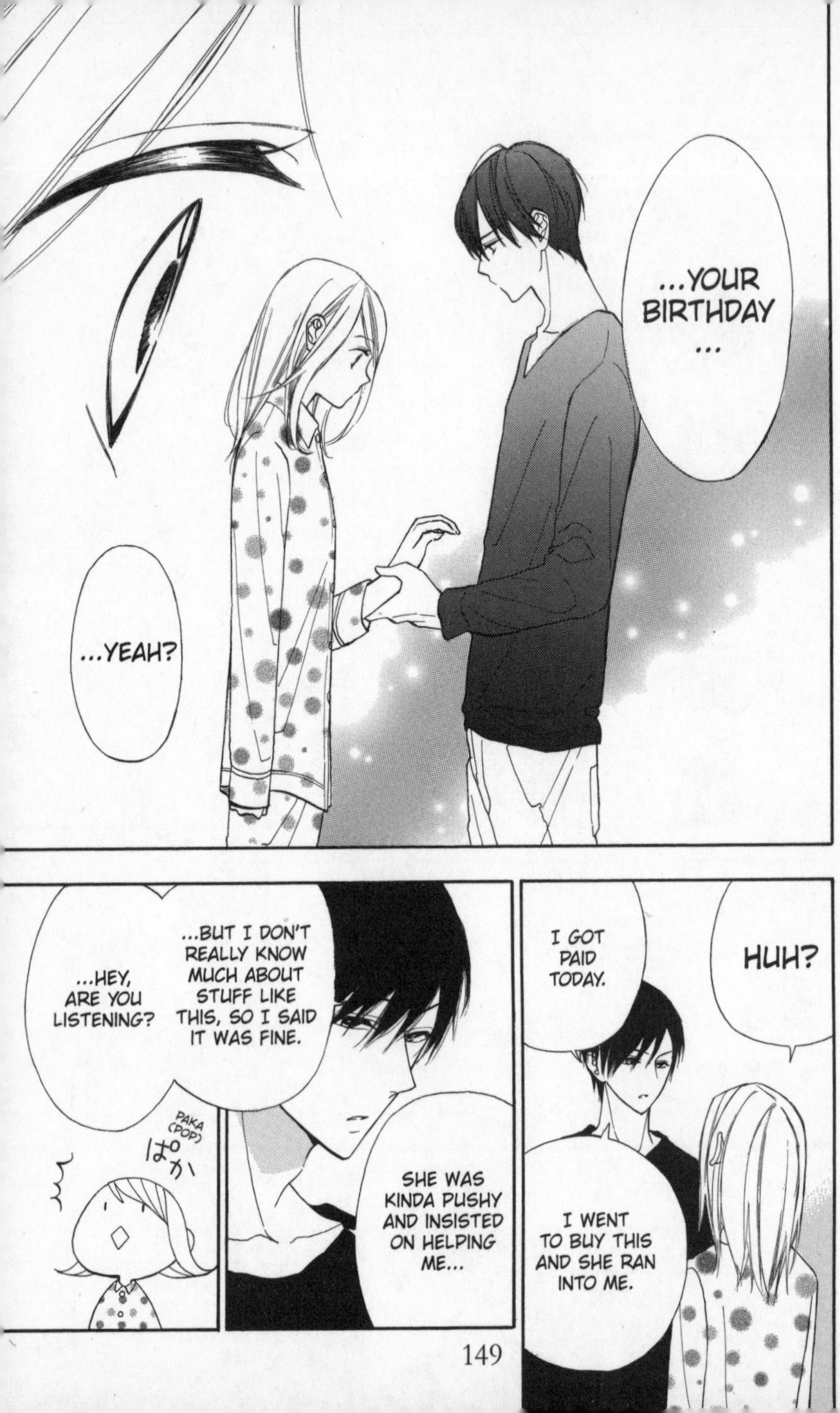
...YOUR BIRTHDAY ...
...YEAH?
HUH?
I GOT PAID TODAY.
I WENT TO BUY THIS AND SHE RAN INTO ME.
SHE WAS KINDA PUSHY AND INSISTED ON HELPING ME...
...BUT I DON'T REALLY KNOW MUCH ABOUT STUFF LIKE THIS, SO I SAID IT WAS FINE.
...HEY, ARE YOU LISTENING?
PAKA (POP)
ぱか

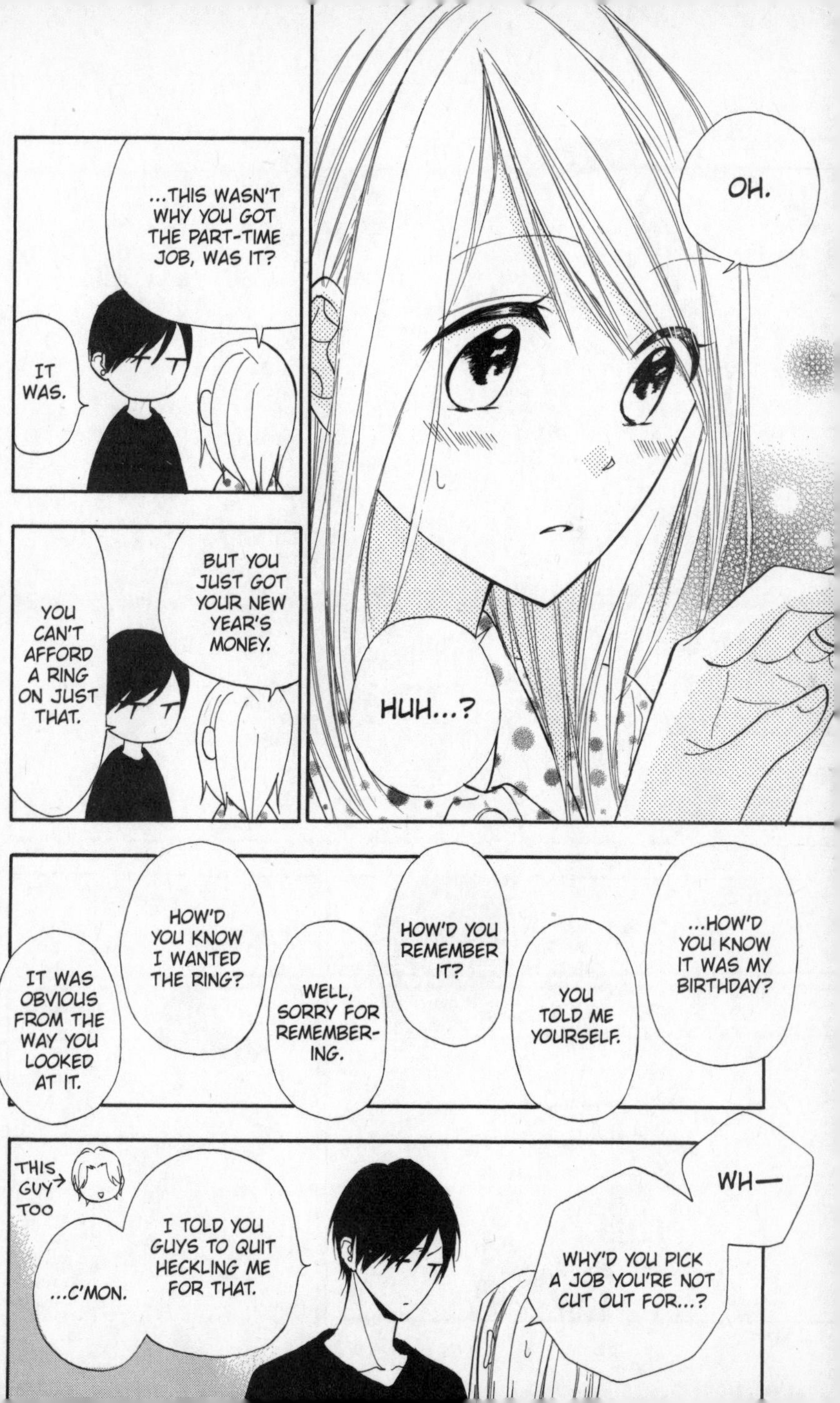
OH.
HUH...?
...THIS WASN'T WHY YOU GOT THE PART-TIME JOB, WAS IT?
IT WAS.
BUT YOU JUST GOT YOUR NEW YEAR'S MONEY.
YOU CAN'T AFFORD A RING ON JUST THAT.
...HOW'D YOU KNOW IT WAS MY BIRTHDAY?
YOU TOLD ME YOURSELF.
HOW'D YOU REMEMBER IT?
WELL, SORRY FOR REMEMBER-ING.
HOW'D YOU KNOW I WANTED THE RING?
IT WAS OBVIOUS FROM THE WAY YOU LOOKED AT IT.
WH—
WHY'D YOU PICK A JOB YOU'RE NOT CUT OUT FOR...?
I TOLD YOU GUYS TO QUIT HECKLING ME FOR THAT.
...C'MON.
THIS GUY TOO

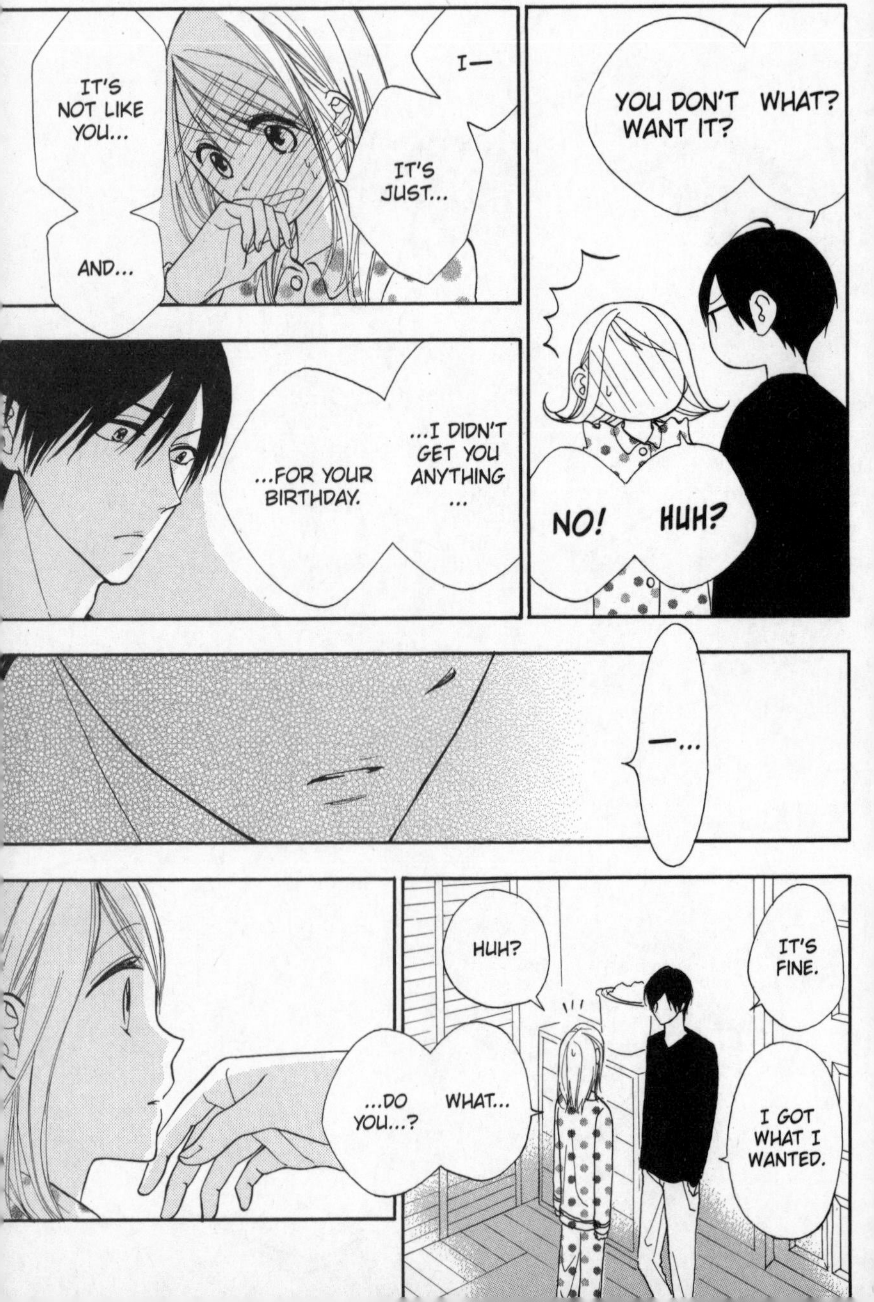
WHAT?
YOU DON'T WANT IT?
HUH?
NO!
I—
IT'S JUST...
IT'S NOT LIKE YOU...
AND...
...I DIDN'T GET YOU ANYTHING ...
...FOR YOUR BIRTHDAY.
—...
IT'S FINE.
HUH?
I GOT WHAT I WANTED.
WHAT...
...DO YOU...?

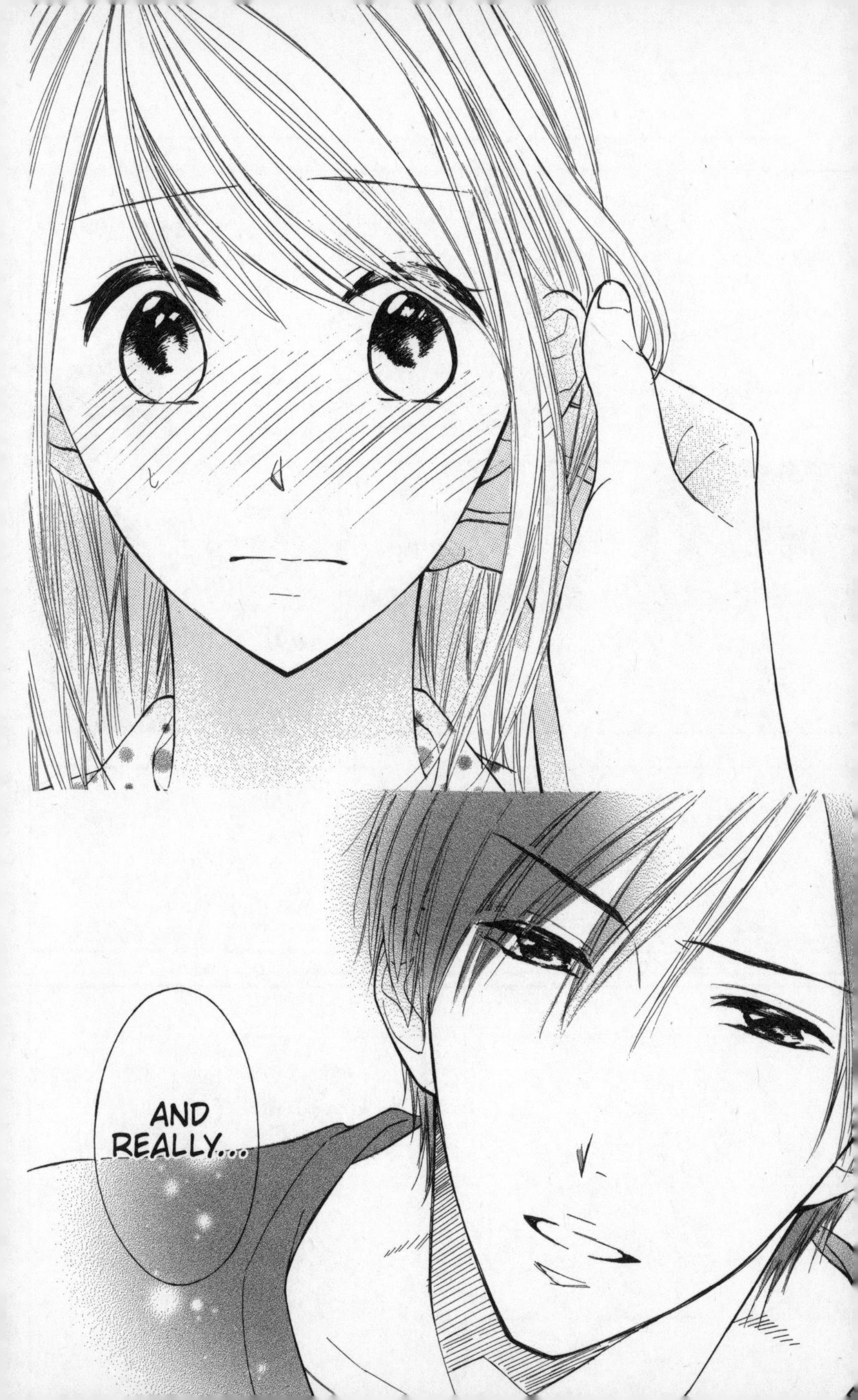
AND REALLY...

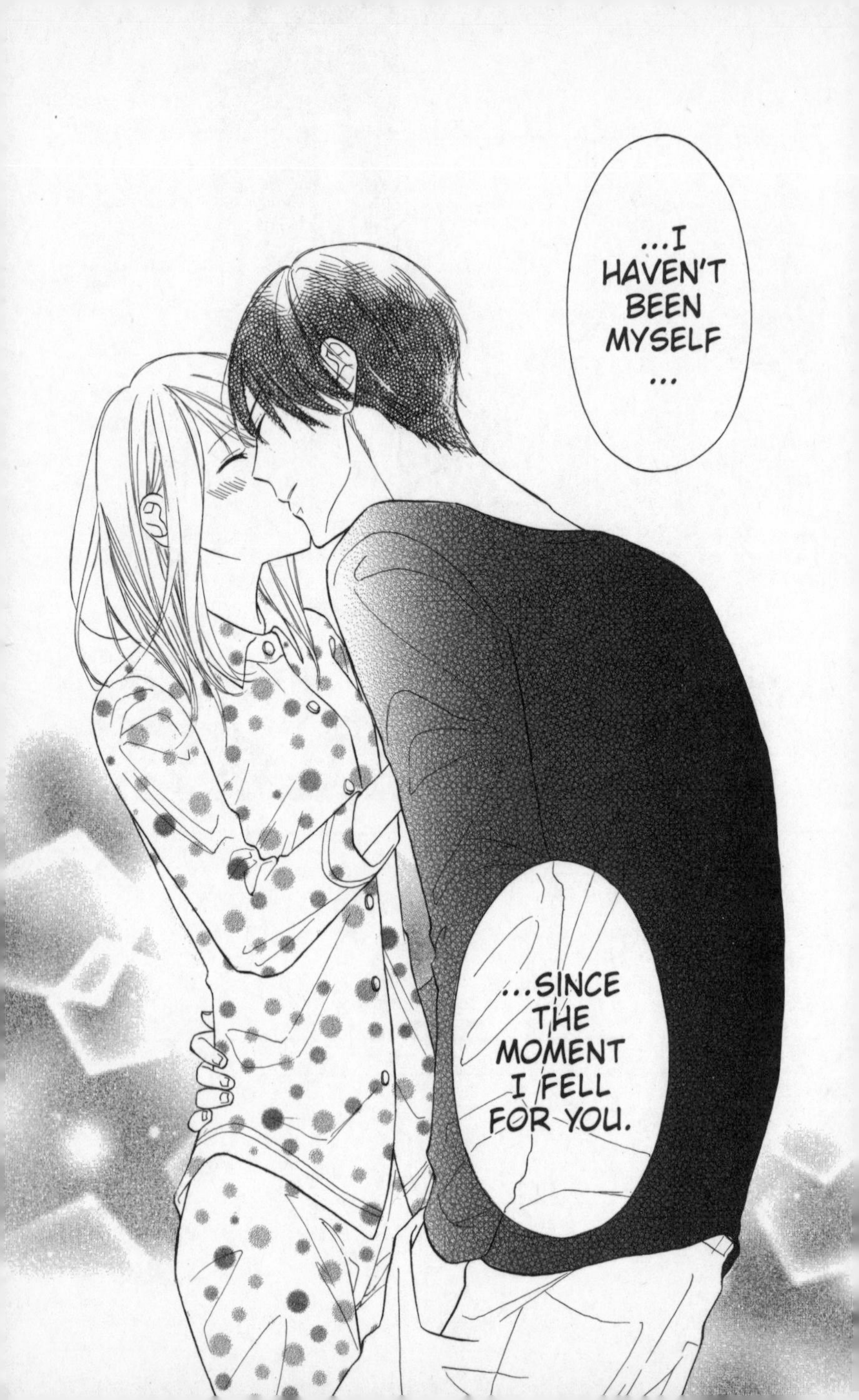
...I HAVEN'T BEEN MYSELF ...
...SINCE THE MOMENT I FELL FOR YOU.

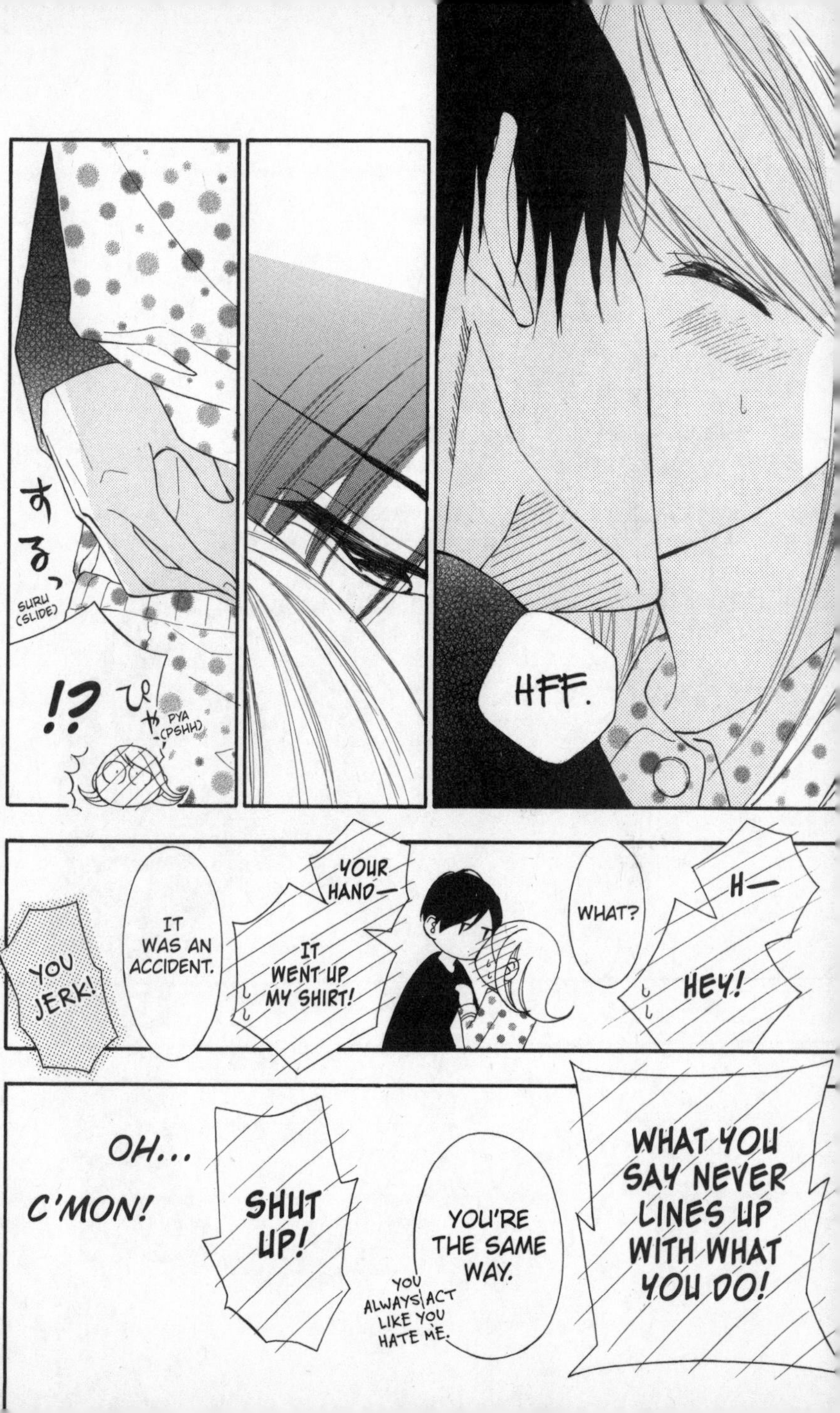

HFF.
するっ
SURU (SLIDE)
ぴゃ
PYA (PSHH)
!?
H—
HEY!
WHAT?
YOUR HAND—
IT WENT UP MY SHIRT!
IT WAS AN ACCIDENT.
YOU JERK!
WHAT YOU SAY NEVER LINES UP WITH WHAT YOU DO!
YOU'RE THE SAME WAY.
YOU ALWAYS ACT LIKE YOU HATE ME.
SHUT UP!
OH... C'MON!

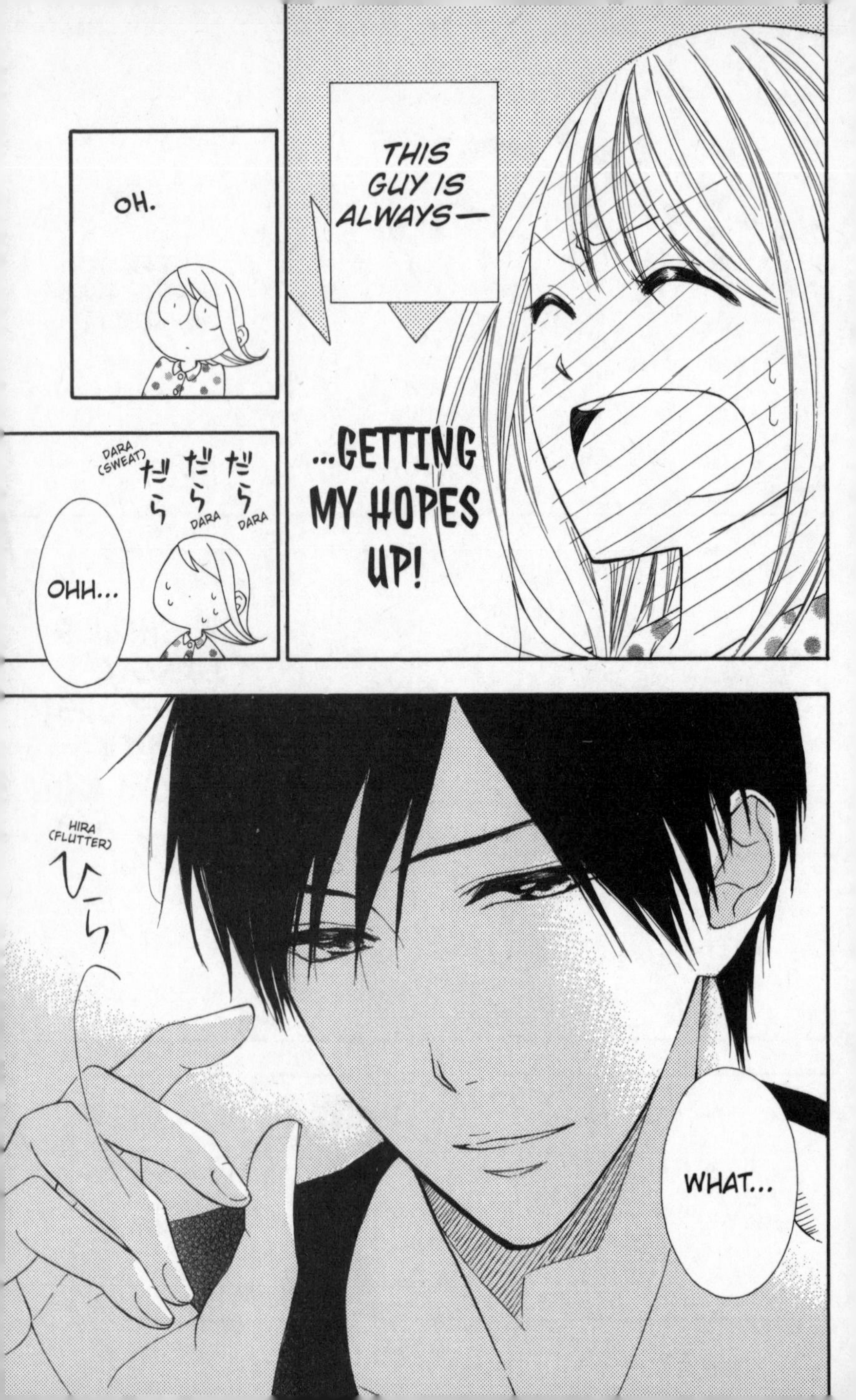
THIS GUY IS ALWAYS—
...GETTING MY HOPES UP!
OH.
DARA (SWEAT)
だらだらだら
DARA DARA
OHH...
WHAT...
HIRA (FLUTTER)
ひら

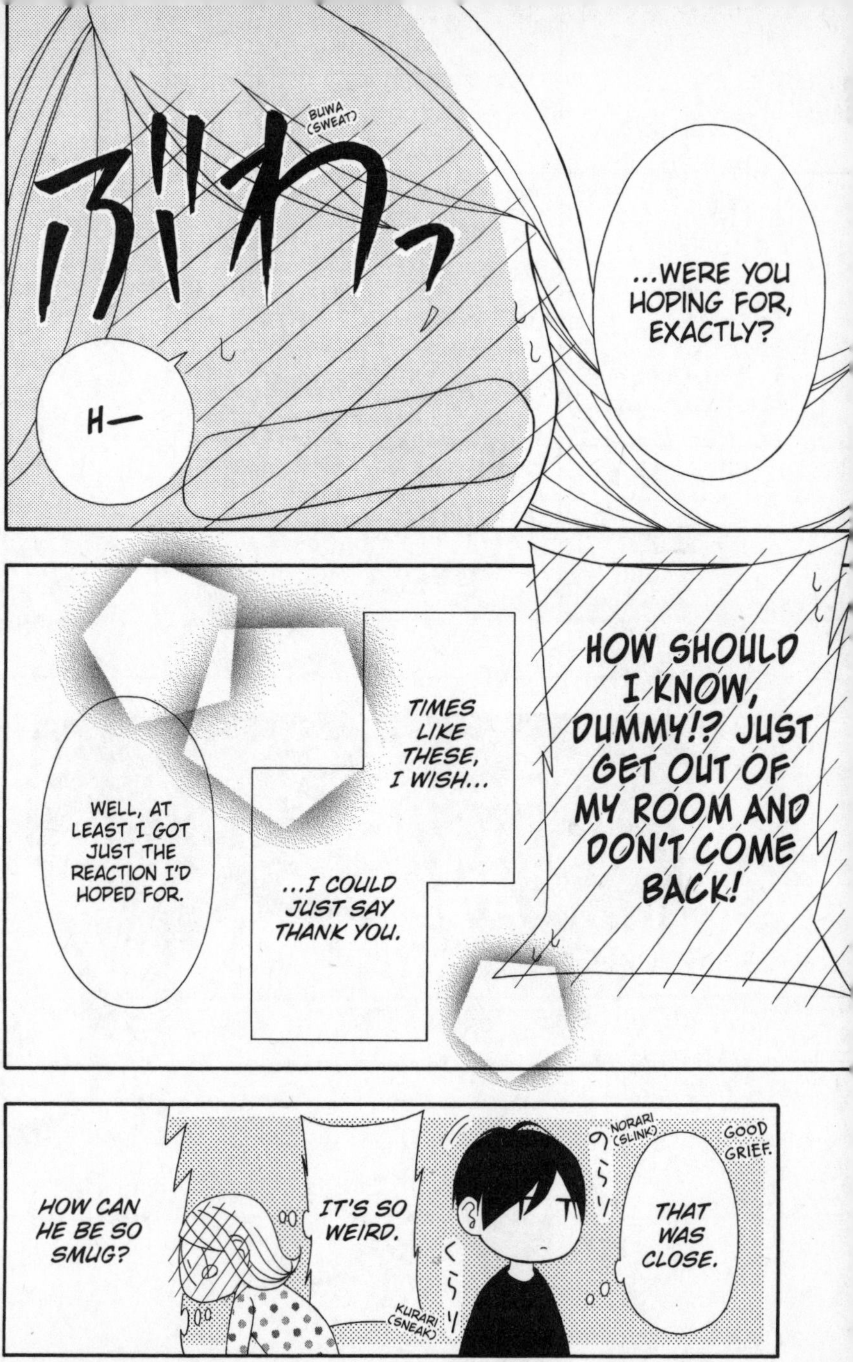
...WERE YOU HOPING FOR, EXACTLY?
BUWA (SWEAT)
H—
HOW SHOULD I KNOW, DUMMY!? JUST GET OUT OF MY ROOM AND DON'T COME BACK!
TIMES LIKE THESE, I WISH...
...I COULD JUST SAY THANK YOU.
WELL, AT LEAST I GOT JUST THE REACTION I'D HOPED FOR.
GOOD GRIEF.
NORARI (SLINK)
THAT WAS CLOSE.
KURARI (SNEAK)
IT'S SO WEIRD.
HOW CAN HE BE SO SMUG?

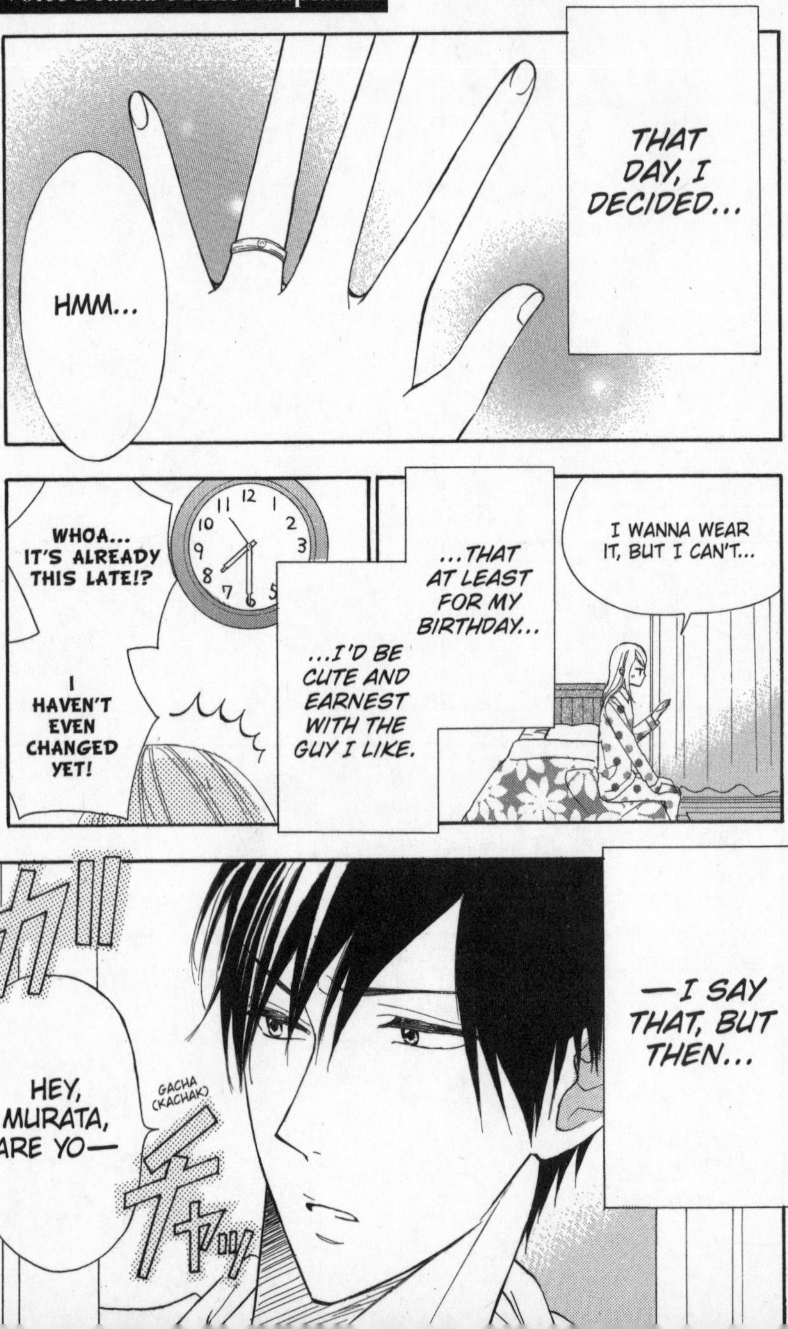
THAT DAY, I DECIDED...
HMM...
I WANNA WEAR IT, BUT I CAN'T...
...THAT AT LEAST FOR MY BIRTHDAY...
...I'D BE CUTE AND EARNEST WITH THE GUY I LIKE.
WHOA... IT'S ALREADY THIS LATE!?
I HAVEN'T EVEN CHANGED YET!
—I SAY THAT, BUT THEN...
HEY, MURATA, ARE YO—
GACHA (KACHAK)

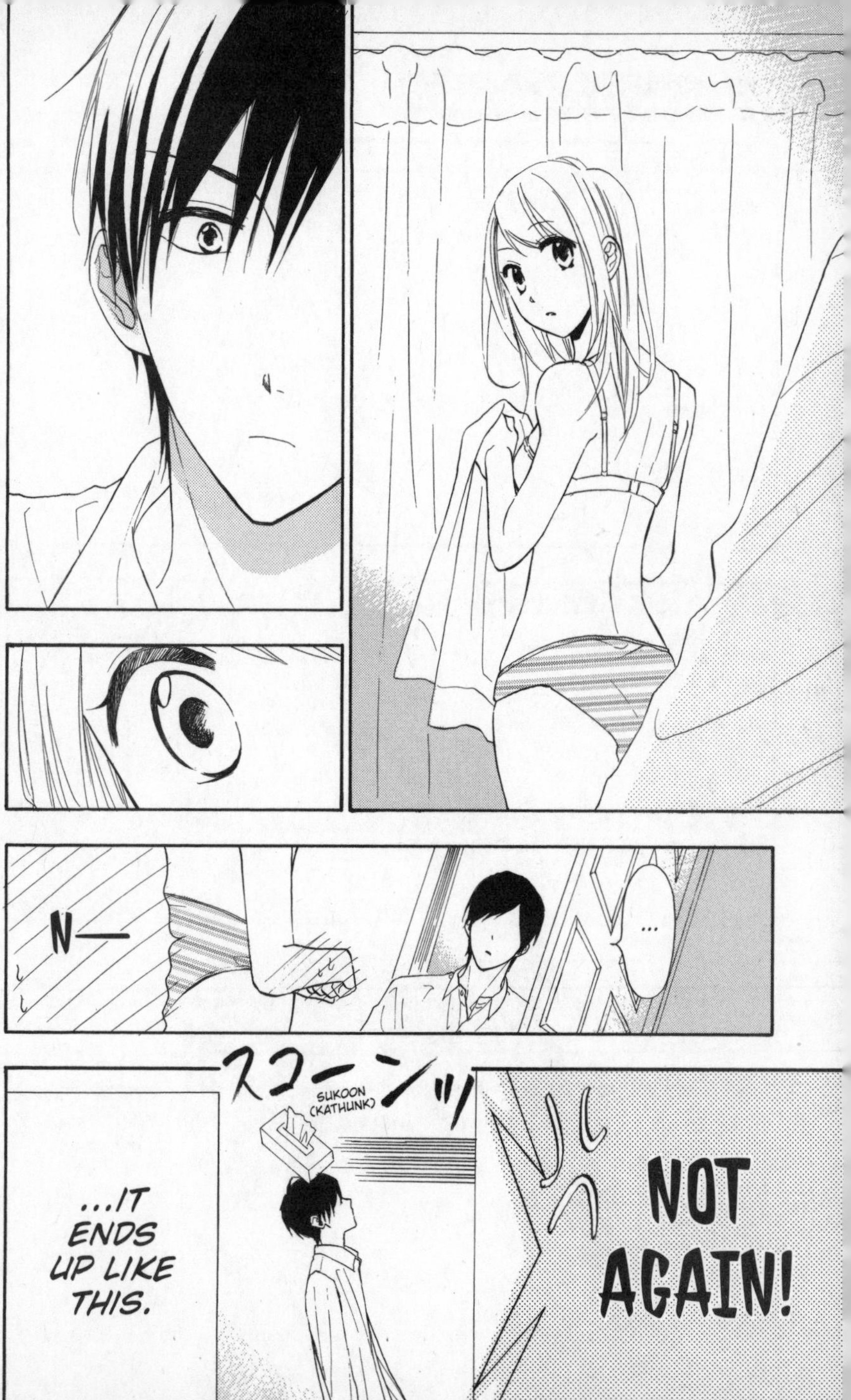
...
N—
スコーンッ
SUKOON (KATHUNK)
NOT AGAIN!
...IT ENDS UP LIKE THIS.

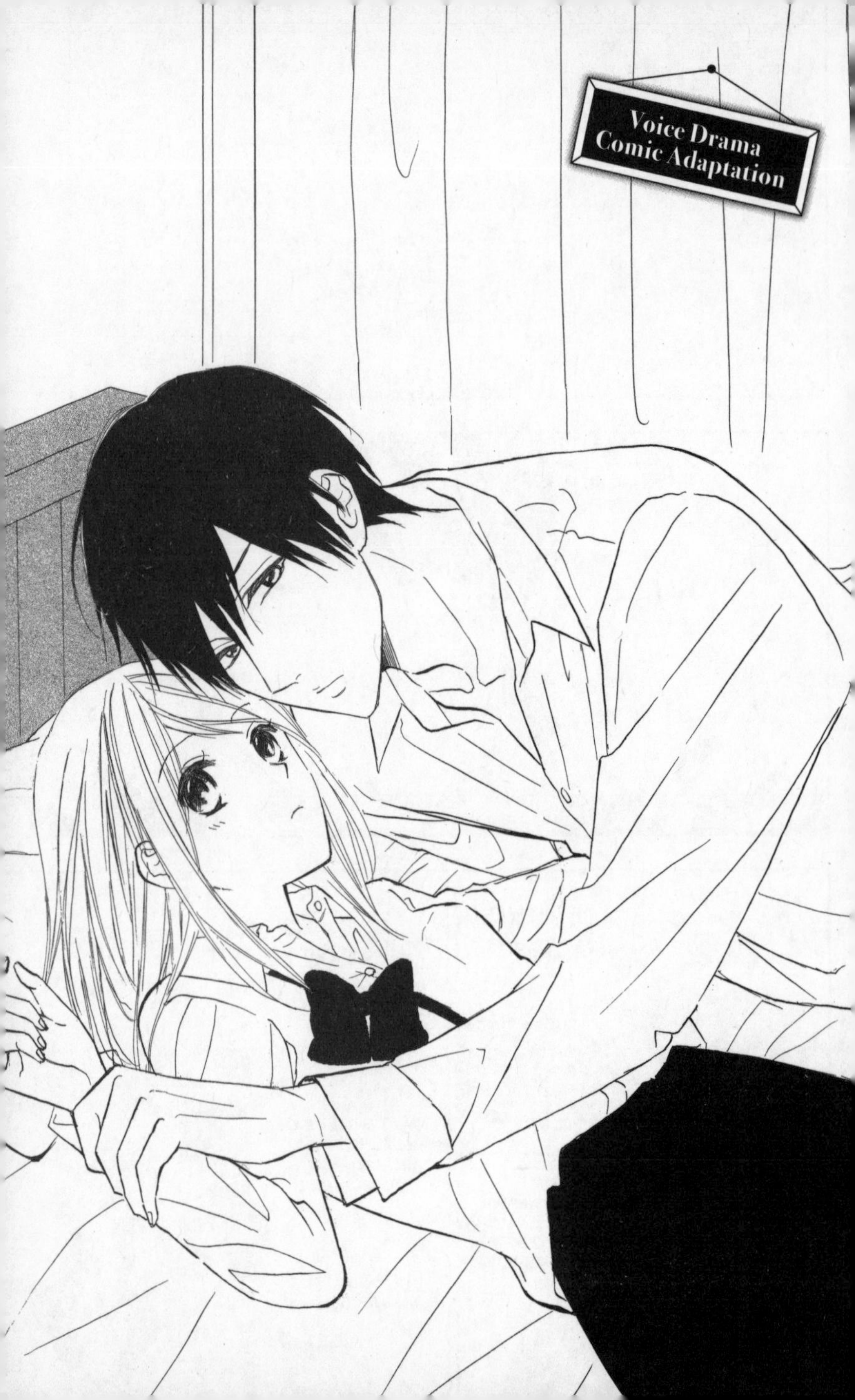
Voice Drama
Comic Adaptation

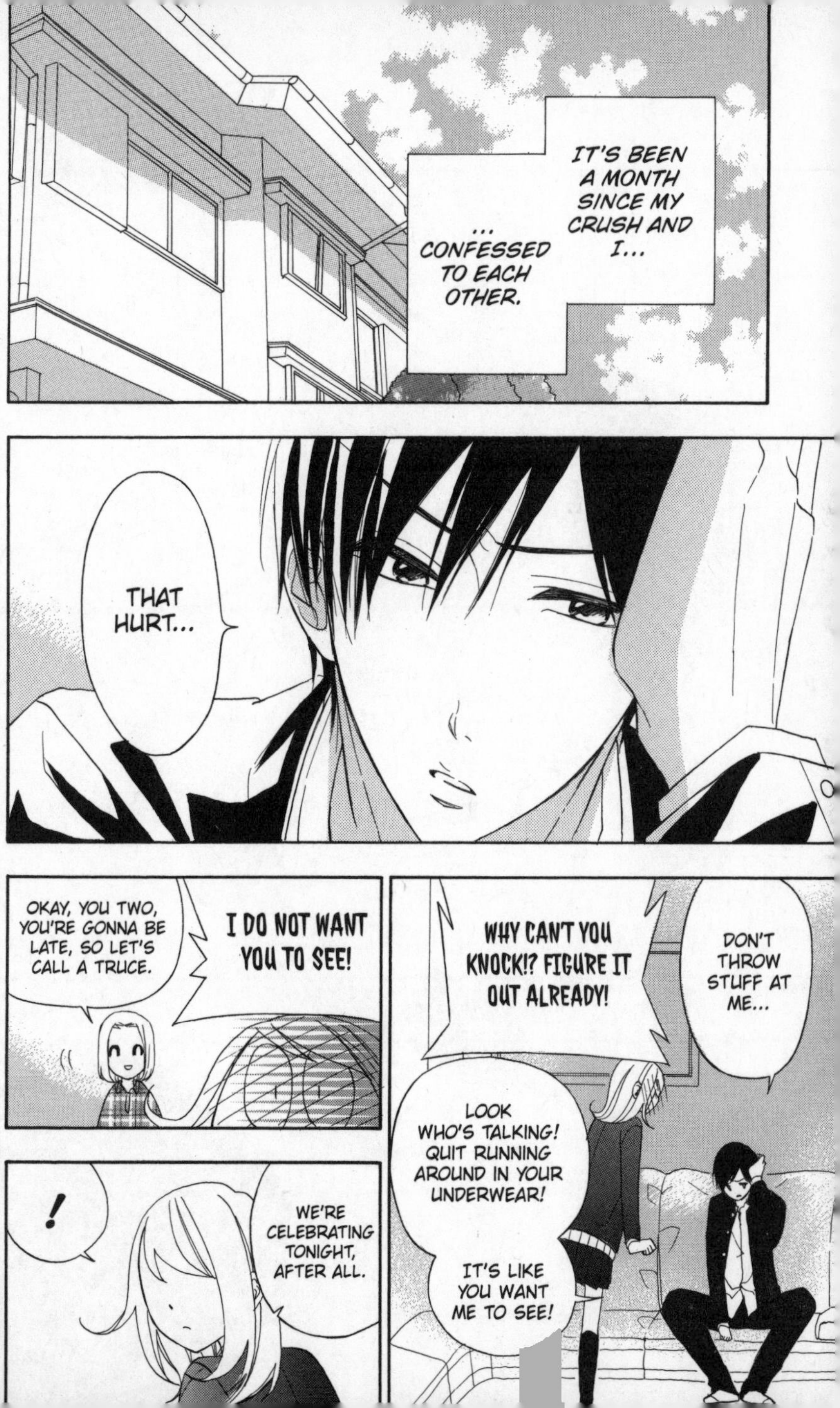
IT'S BEEN A MONTH SINCE MY CRUSH AND I...
...CONFESSED TO EACH OTHER.
THAT HURT...
DON'T THROW STUFF AT ME...
WHY CAN'T YOU KNOCK!? FIGURE IT OUT ALREADY!
LOOK WHO'S TALKING! QUIT RUNNING AROUND IN YOUR UNDERWEAR!
IT'S LIKE YOU WANT ME TO SEE!
I DO NOT WANT YOU TO SEE!
OKAY, YOU TWO, YOU'RE GONNA BE LATE, SO LET'S CALL A TRUCE.
WE'RE CELEBRATING TONIGHT, AFTER ALL.
!

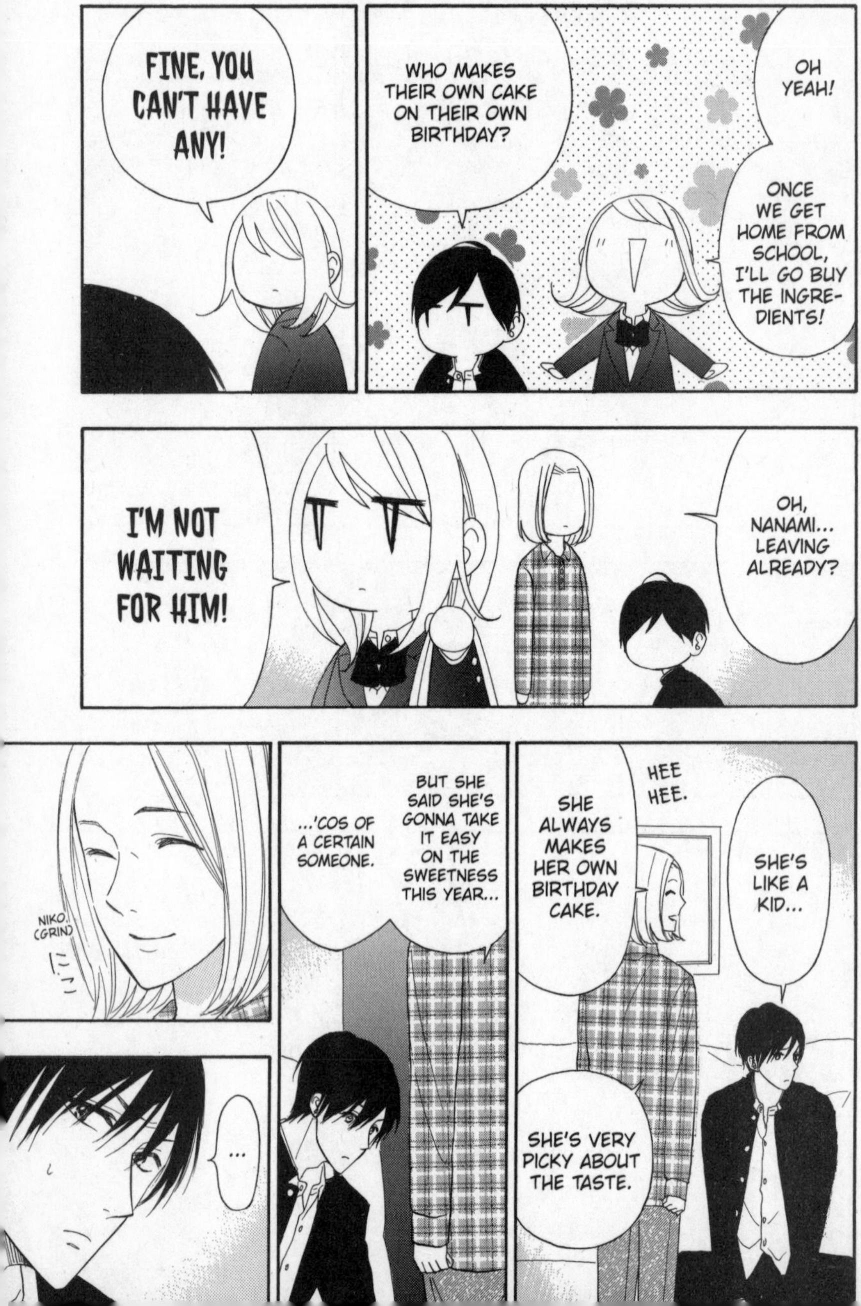
OH YEAH!
ONCE WE GET HOME FROM SCHOOL, I'LL GO BUY THE INGREDIENTS!
WHO MAKES THEIR OWN CAKE ON THEIR OWN BIRTHDAY?
FINE, YOU CAN'T HAVE ANY!
OH, NANAMI... LEAVING ALREADY?
I'M NOT WAITING FOR HIM!
SHE'S LIKE A KID...
HEE HEE.
SHE ALWAYS MAKES HER OWN BIRTHDAY CAKE.
SHE'S VERY PICKY ABOUT THE TASTE.
BUT SHE SAID SHE'S GONNA TAKE IT EASY ON THE SWEETNESS THIS YEAR...
...'COS OF A CERTAIN SOMEONE.
NIKO (GRIN)
...

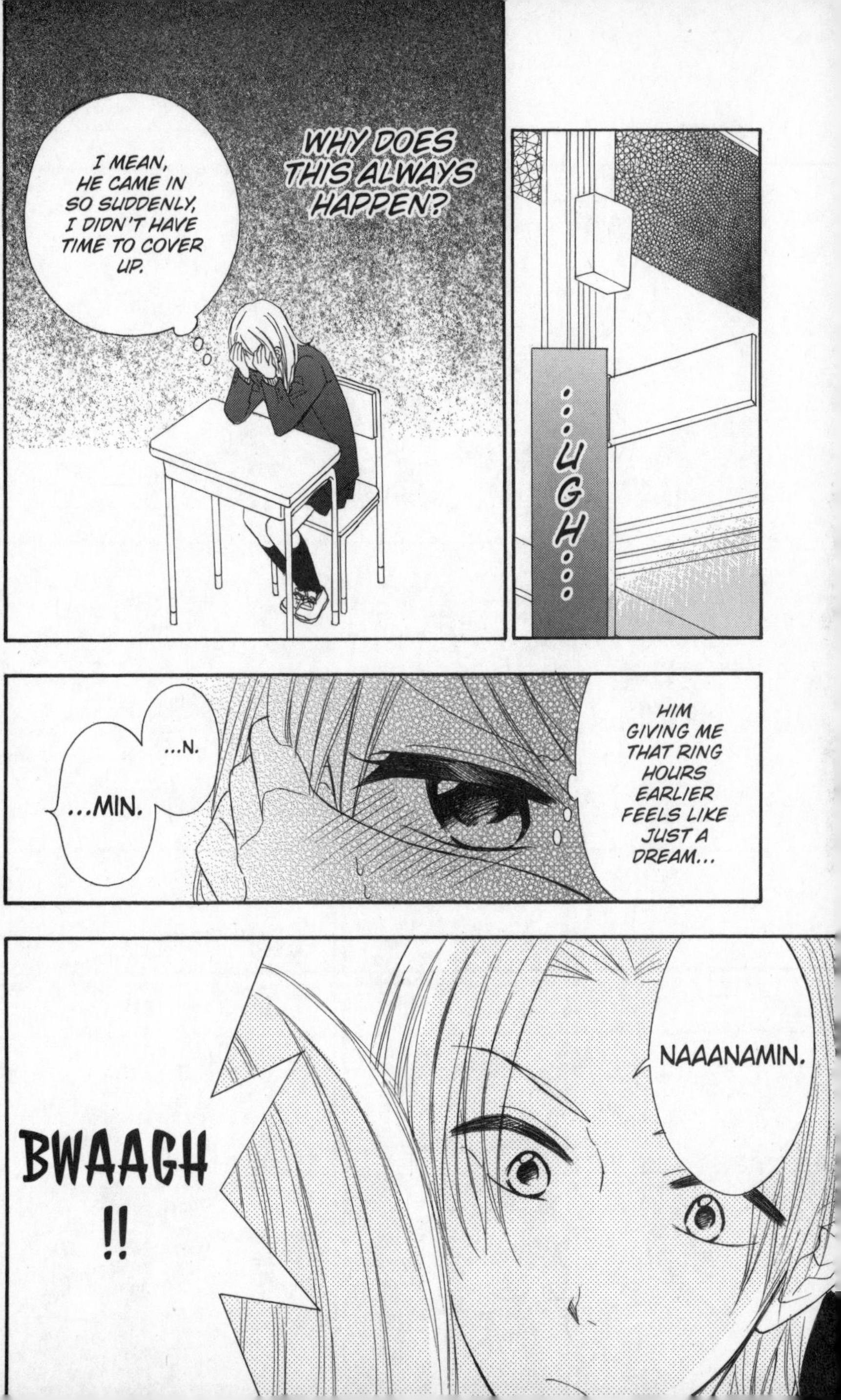
...UGH...
WHY DOES THIS ALWAYS HAPPEN?
I MEAN, HE CAME IN SO SUDDENLY, I DIDN'T HAVE TIME TO COVER UP.
HIM GIVING ME THAT RING HOURS EARLIER FEELS LIKE JUST A DREAM...
...N.
...MIN.
NAAANAMIN.
BWAAGH !!

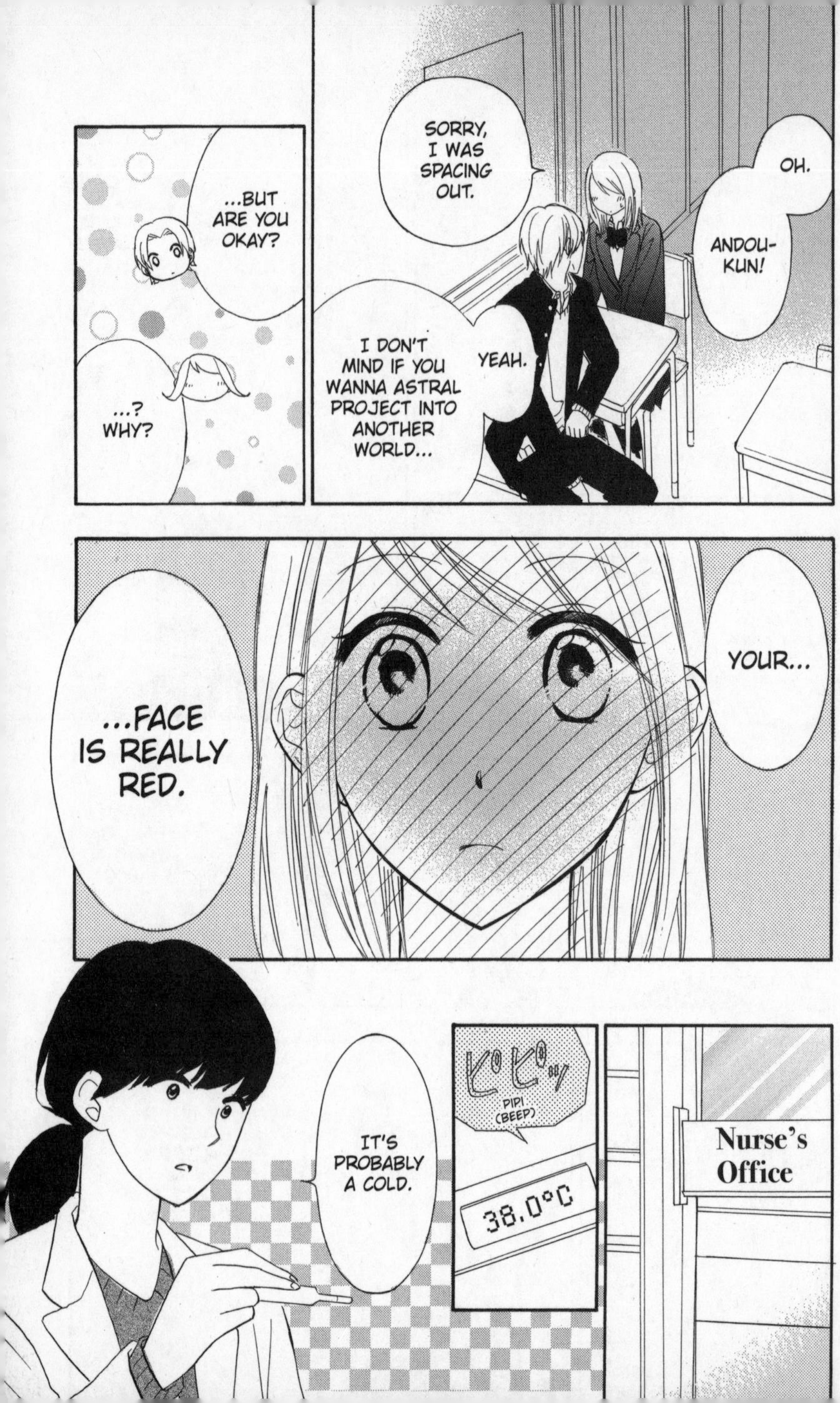
OH.
ANDOU-KUN!
SORRY, I WAS SPACING OUT.
YEAH.
I DON'T MIND IF YOU WANNA ASTRAL PROJECT INTO ANOTHER WORLD...
...BUT ARE YOU OKAY?
...? WHY?
YOUR...
...FACE IS REALLY RED.
Nurse's Office
ピピッ
PIPI (BEEP)
38.0°C
IT'S PROBABLY A COLD.

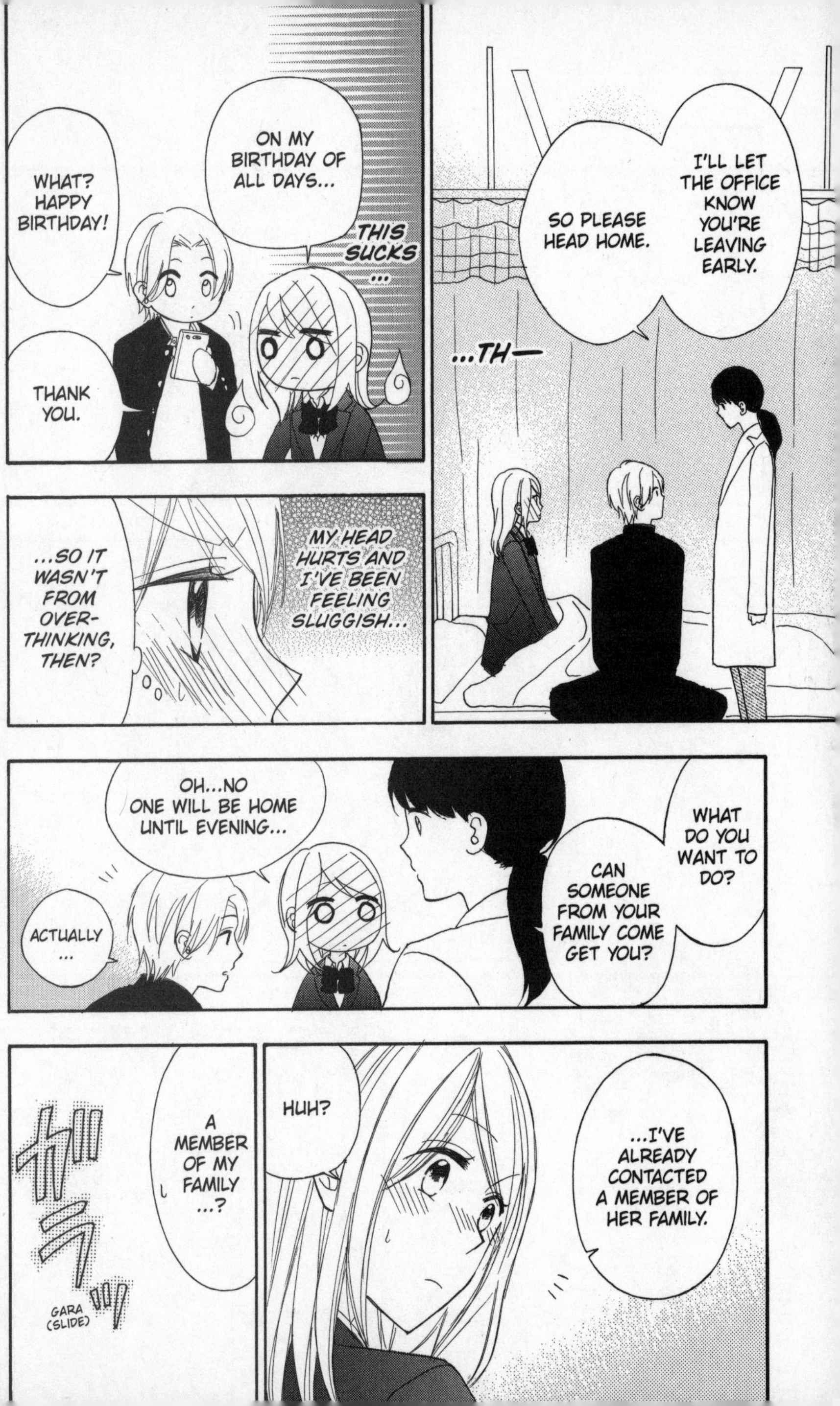
I'LL LET THE OFFICE KNOW YOU'RE LEAVING EARLY.
SO PLEASE HEAD HOME.
...TH—
ON MY BIRTHDAY OF ALL DAYS...
THIS SUCKS...
WHAT? HAPPY BIRTHDAY!
THANK YOU.
MY HEAD HURTS AND I'VE BEEN FEELING SLUGGISH...
...SO IT WASN'T FROM OVER-THINKING, THEN?
WHAT DO YOU WANT TO DO?
CAN SOMEONE FROM YOUR FAMILY COME GET YOU?
OH...NO ONE WILL BE HOME UNTIL EVENING...
ACTUALLY...
...I'VE ALREADY CONTACTED A MEMBER OF HER FAMILY.
HUH?
A MEMBER OF MY FAMILY...?
GARA (SLIDE)

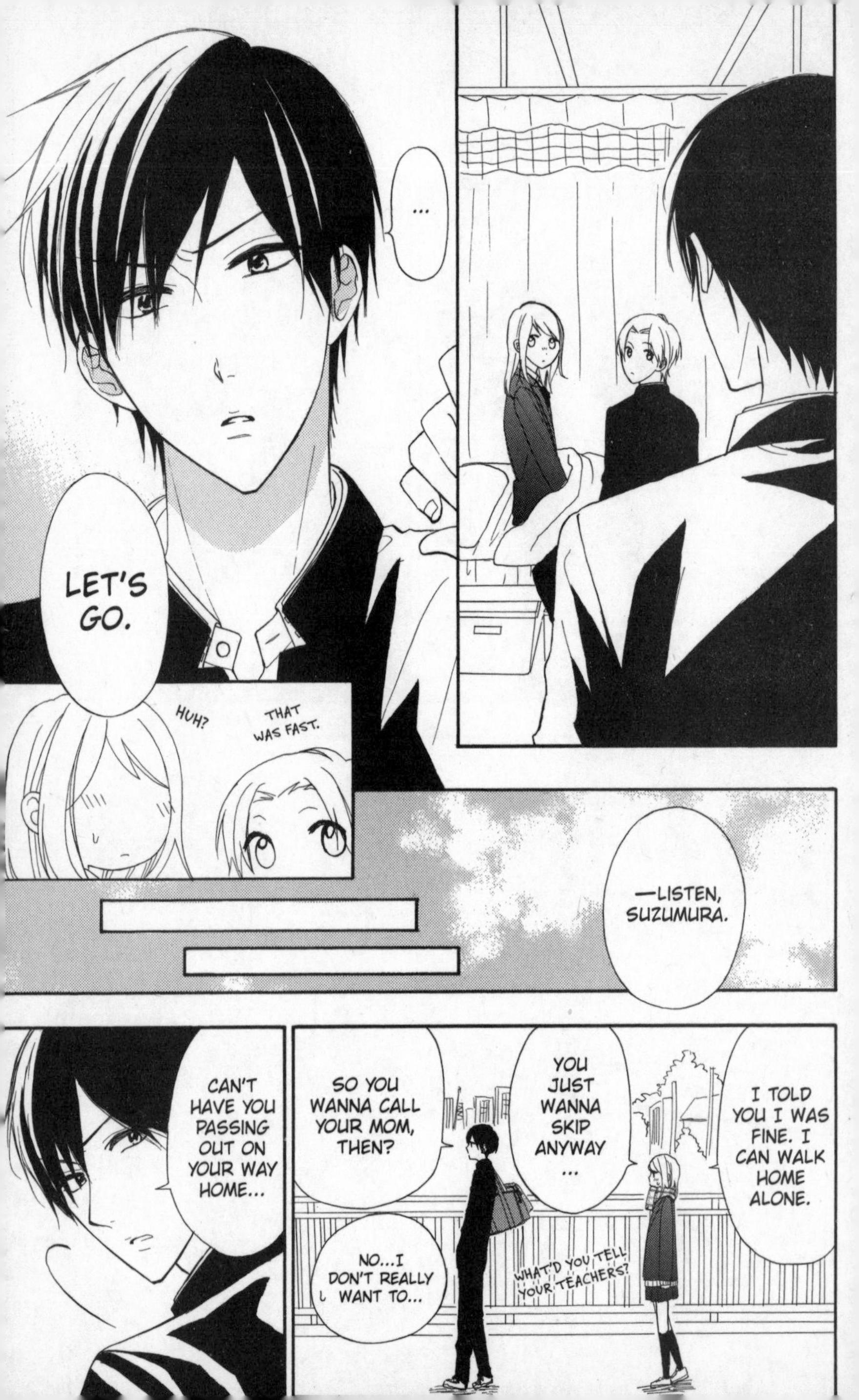
...
LET'S GO.
THAT WAS FAST.
HUH?
—LISTEN, SUZUMURA.
I TOLD YOU I WAS FINE. I CAN WALK HOME ALONE.
YOU JUST WANNA SKIP ANYWAY ...
SO YOU WANNA CALL YOUR MOM, THEN?
WHAT'D YOU TELL YOUR TEACHERS?
NO...I DON'T REALLY WANT TO...
CAN'T HAVE YOU PASSING OUT ON YOUR WAY HOME...

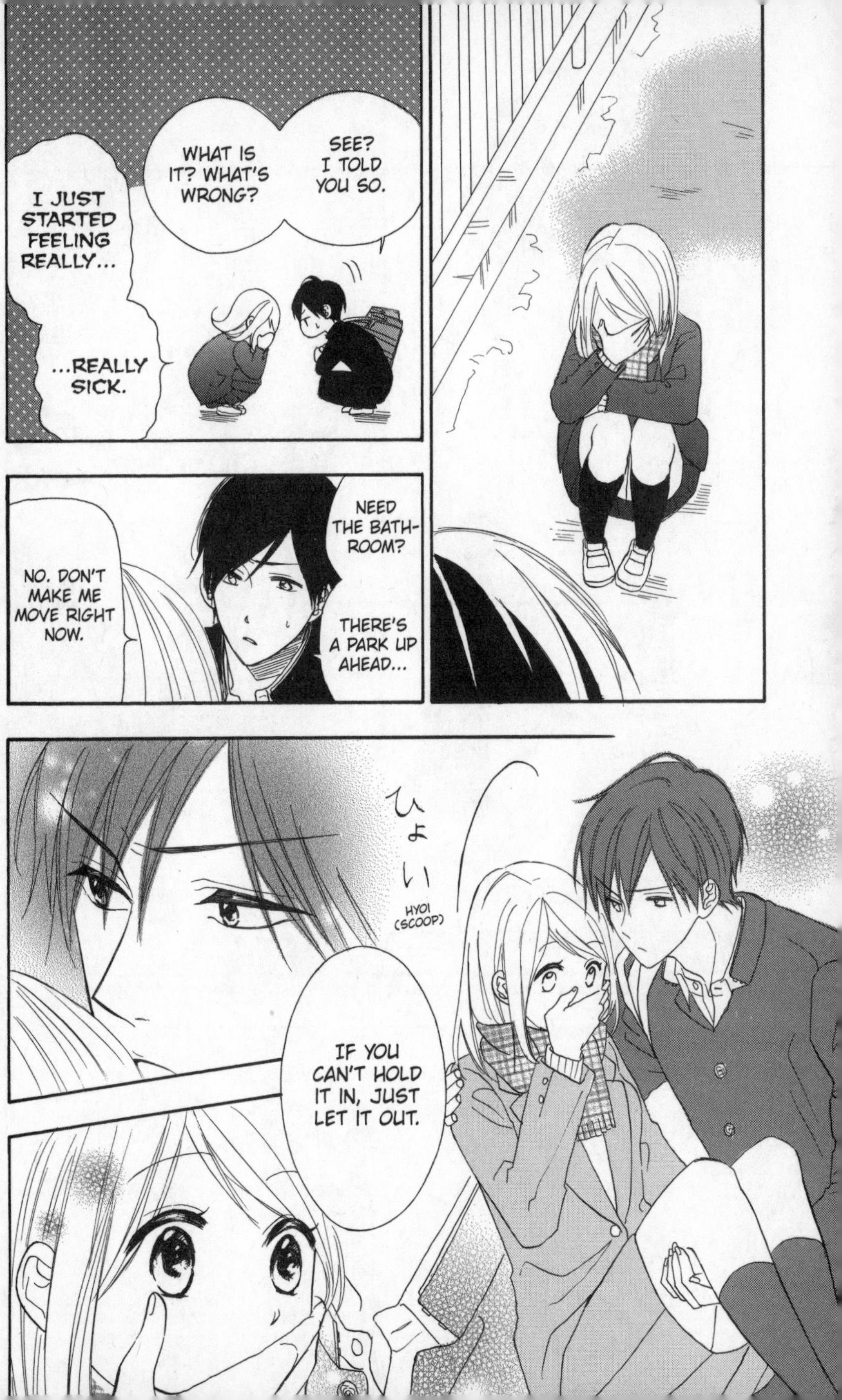
SEE? I TOLD YOU SO.
WHAT IS IT? WHAT'S WRONG?
I JUST STARTED FEELING REALLY...
...REALLY SICK.
NEED THE BATH-ROOM?
THERE'S A PARK UP AHEAD...
NO. DON'T MAKE ME MOVE RIGHT NOW.
ひょい
HYOI (SCOOP)
IF YOU CAN'T HOLD IT IN, JUST LET IT OUT.

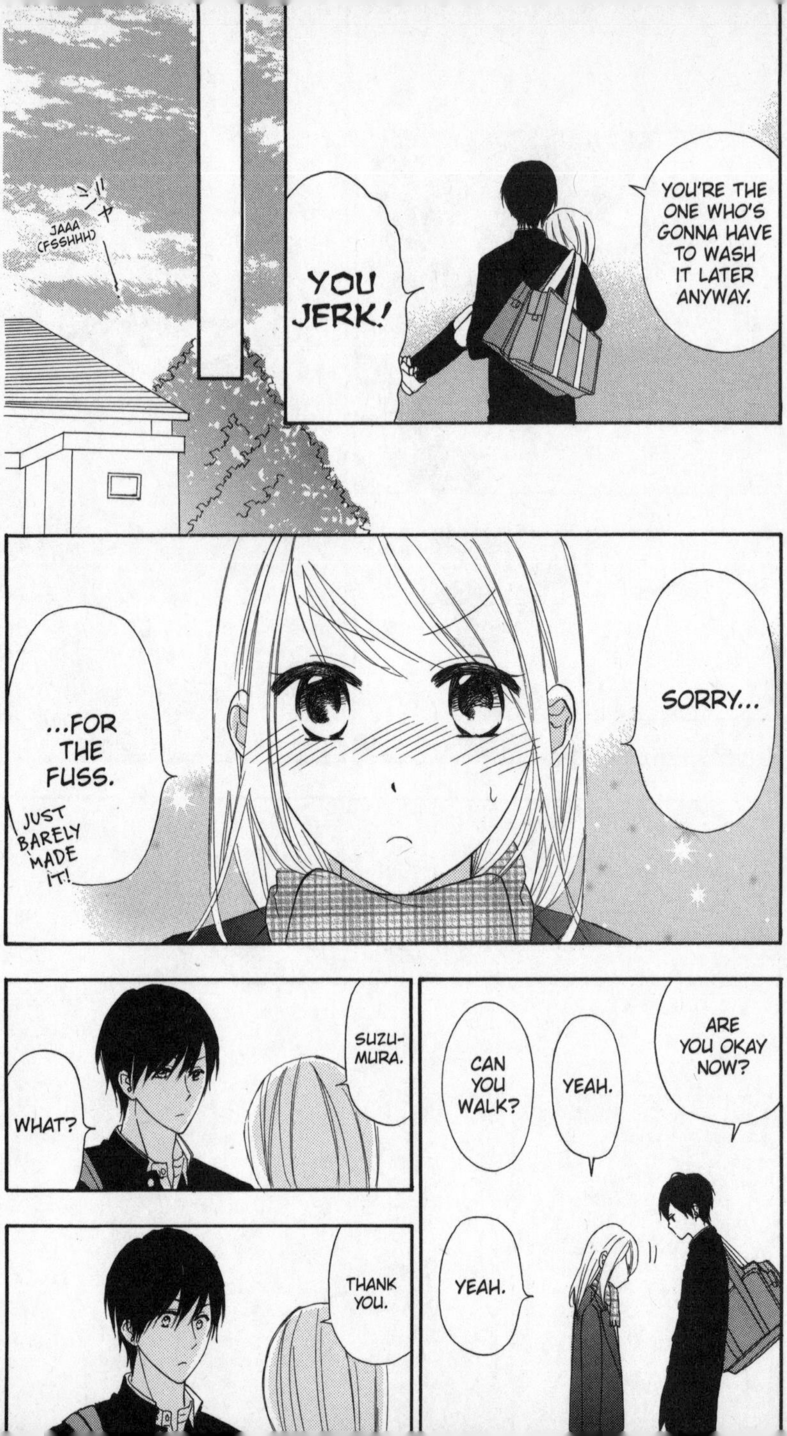
YOU'RE THE ONE WHO'S GONNA HAVE TO WASH IT LATER ANYWAY.
YOU JERK!
ジャー
JAAA (FSSHHH)
SORRY...
...FOR THE FUSS.
JUST BARELY MADE IT!
ARE YOU OKAY NOW?
YEAH.
CAN YOU WALK?
YEAH.
SUZU-MURA.
WHAT?
THANK YOU.

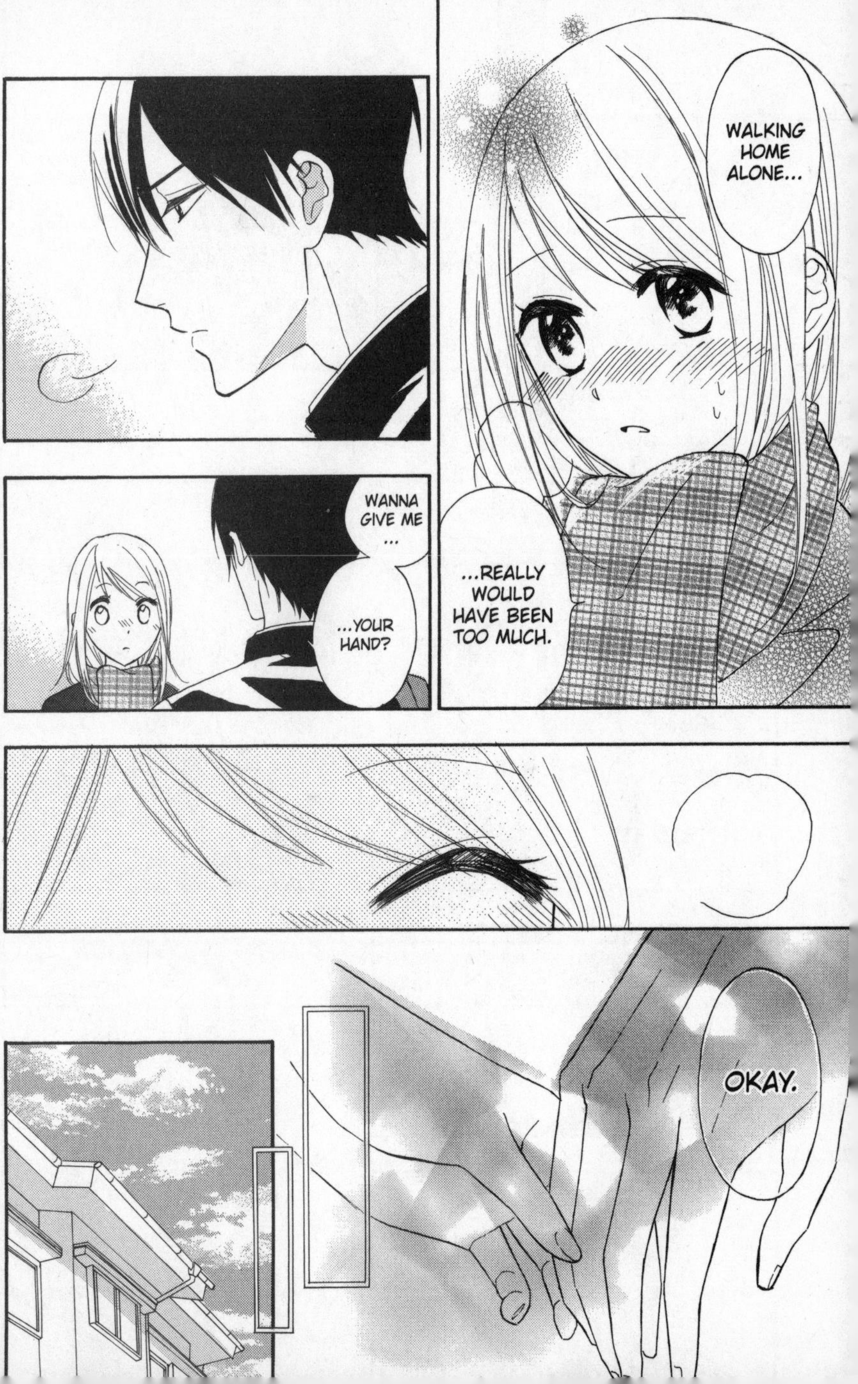
WALKING HOME ALONE...
...REALLY WOULD HAVE BEEN TOO MUCH.
WANNA GIVE ME ...
...YOUR HAND?
OKAY.

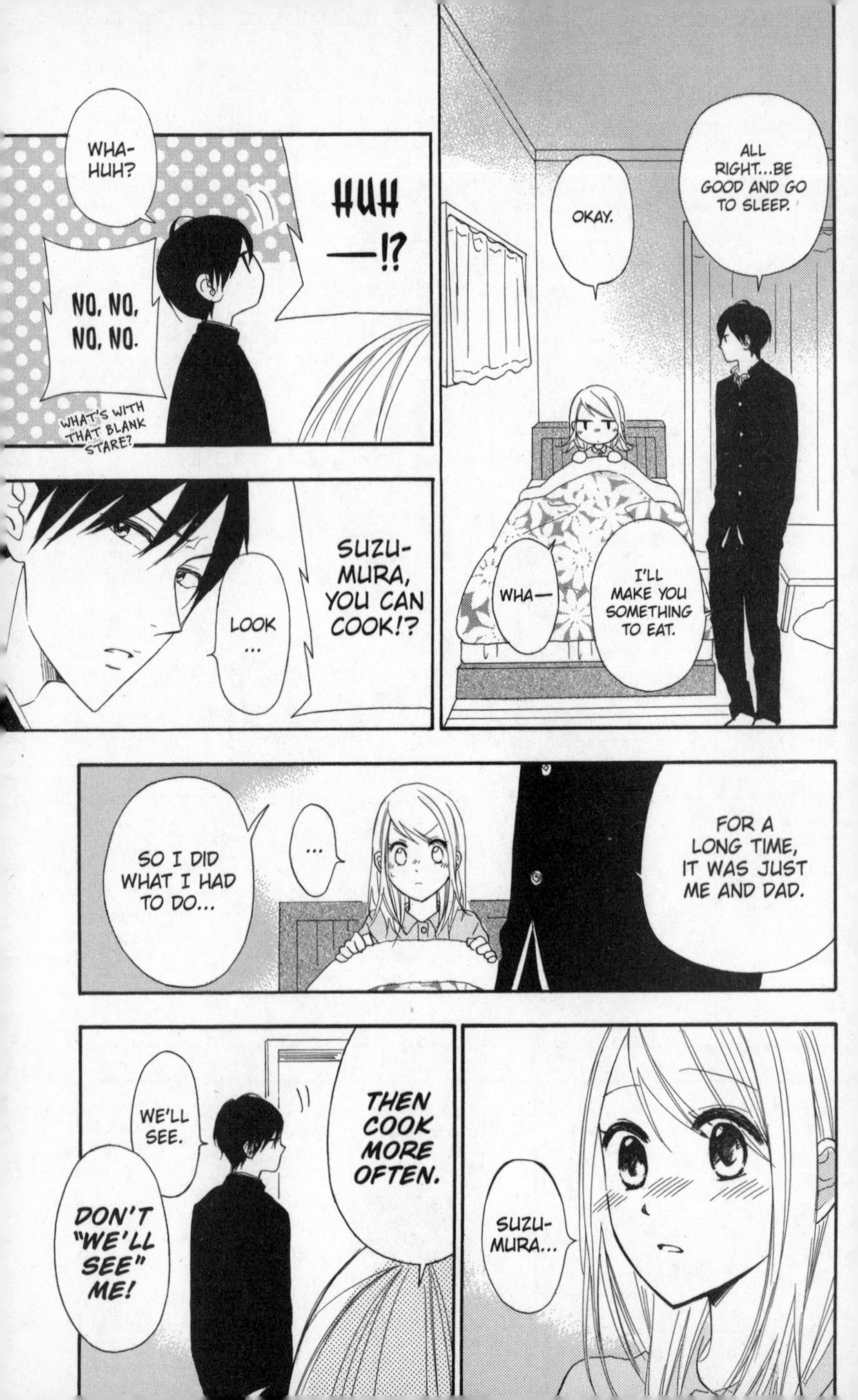
ALL RIGHT...BE GOOD AND GO TO SLEEP.
OKAY.
I'LL MAKE YOU SOMETHING TO EAT.
WHA—
HUH—!?
WHA-HUH?
NO, NO, NO, NO.
WHAT'S WITH THAT BLANK STARE?
SUZUMURA, YOU CAN COOK!?
LOOK...
FOR A LONG TIME, IT WAS JUST ME AND DAD.
...
SO I DID WHAT I HAD TO DO...
SUZUMURA...
THEN COOK MORE OFTEN.
WE'LL SEE.
DON'T "WE'LL SEE" ME!

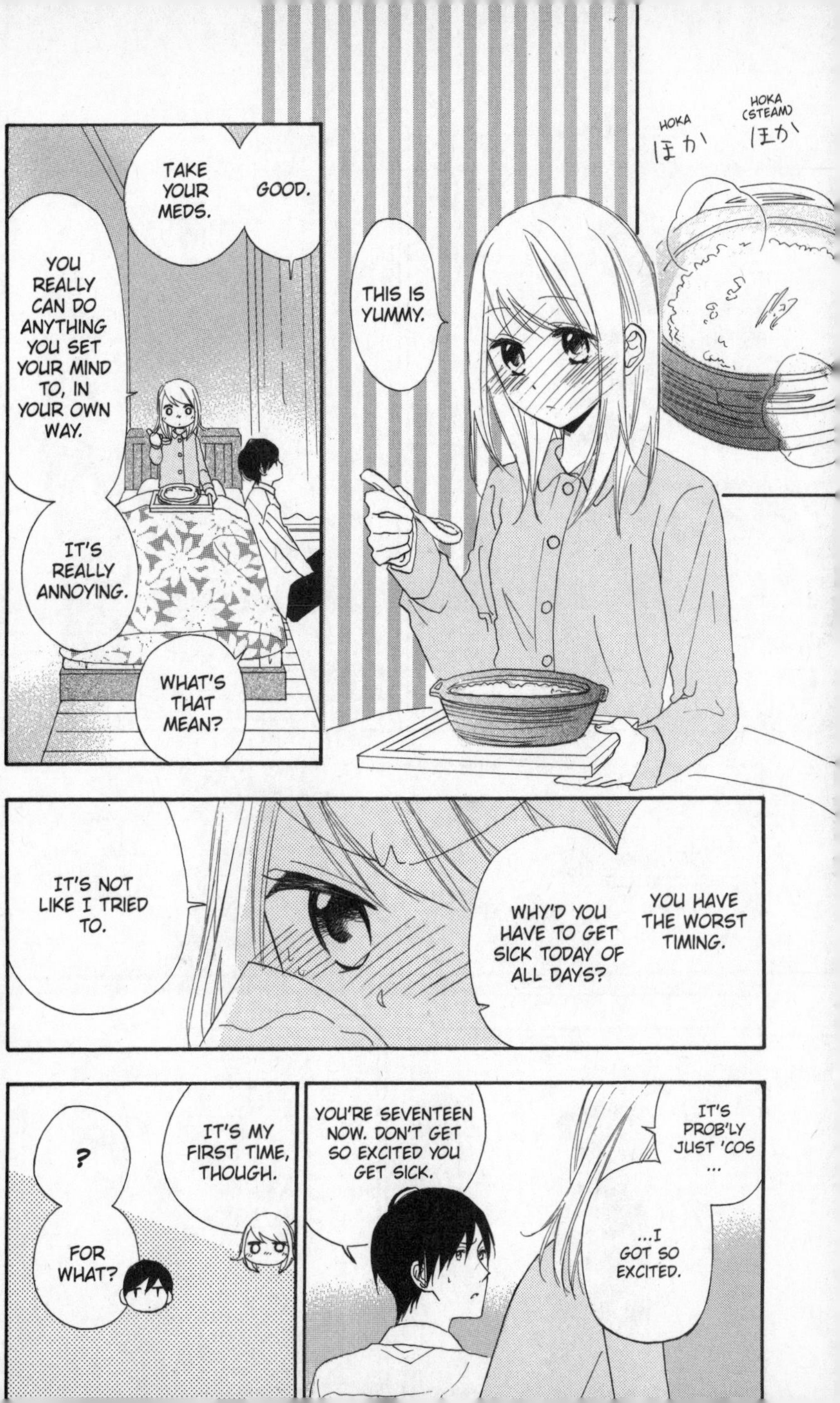
HOKA (STEAM)
ほか
HOKA
ほか
THIS IS YUMMY.
GOOD.
TAKE YOUR MEDS.
YOU REALLY CAN DO ANYTHING YOU SET YOUR MIND TO, IN YOUR OWN WAY.
IT'S REALLY ANNOYING.
WHAT'S THAT MEAN?
YOU HAVE THE WORST TIMING.
WHY'D YOU HAVE TO GET SICK TODAY OF ALL DAYS?
IT'S NOT LIKE I TRIED TO.
IT'S PROB'LY JUST 'COS ...
...I GOT SO EXCITED.
YOU'RE SEVENTEEN NOW. DON'T GET SO EXCITED YOU GET SICK.
IT'S MY FIRST TIME, THOUGH.
?
FOR WHAT?

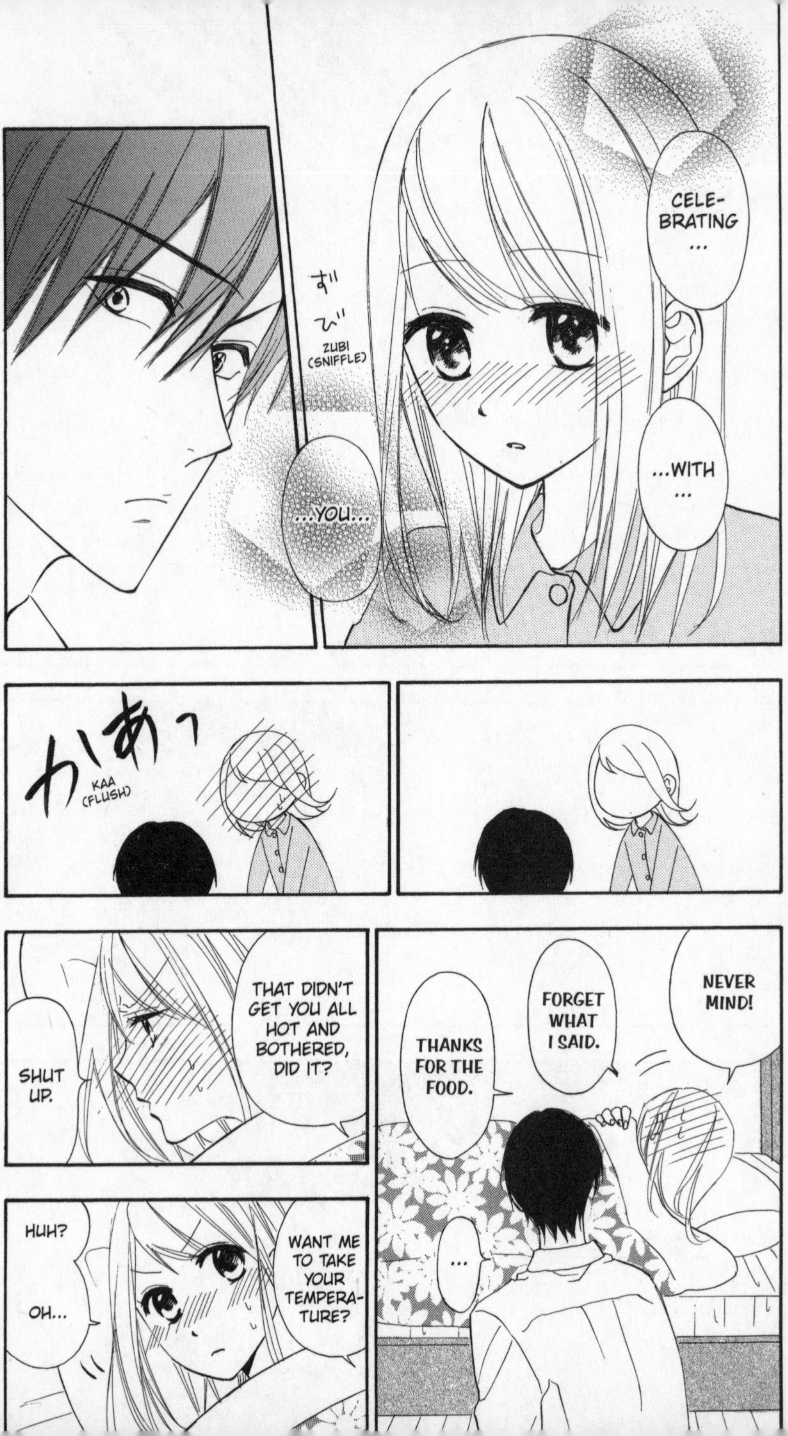
CELE-BRATING...
...WITH...
ずび
ZUBI (SNIFFLE)
...YOU...
かあっ
KAA (FLUSH)
NEVER MIND!
FORGET WHAT I SAID.
THANKS FOR THE FOOD.
...
THAT DIDN'T GET YOU ALL HOT AND BOTHERED, DID IT?
SHUT UP.
WANT ME TO TAKE YOUR TEMPERATURE?
HUH?
OH...

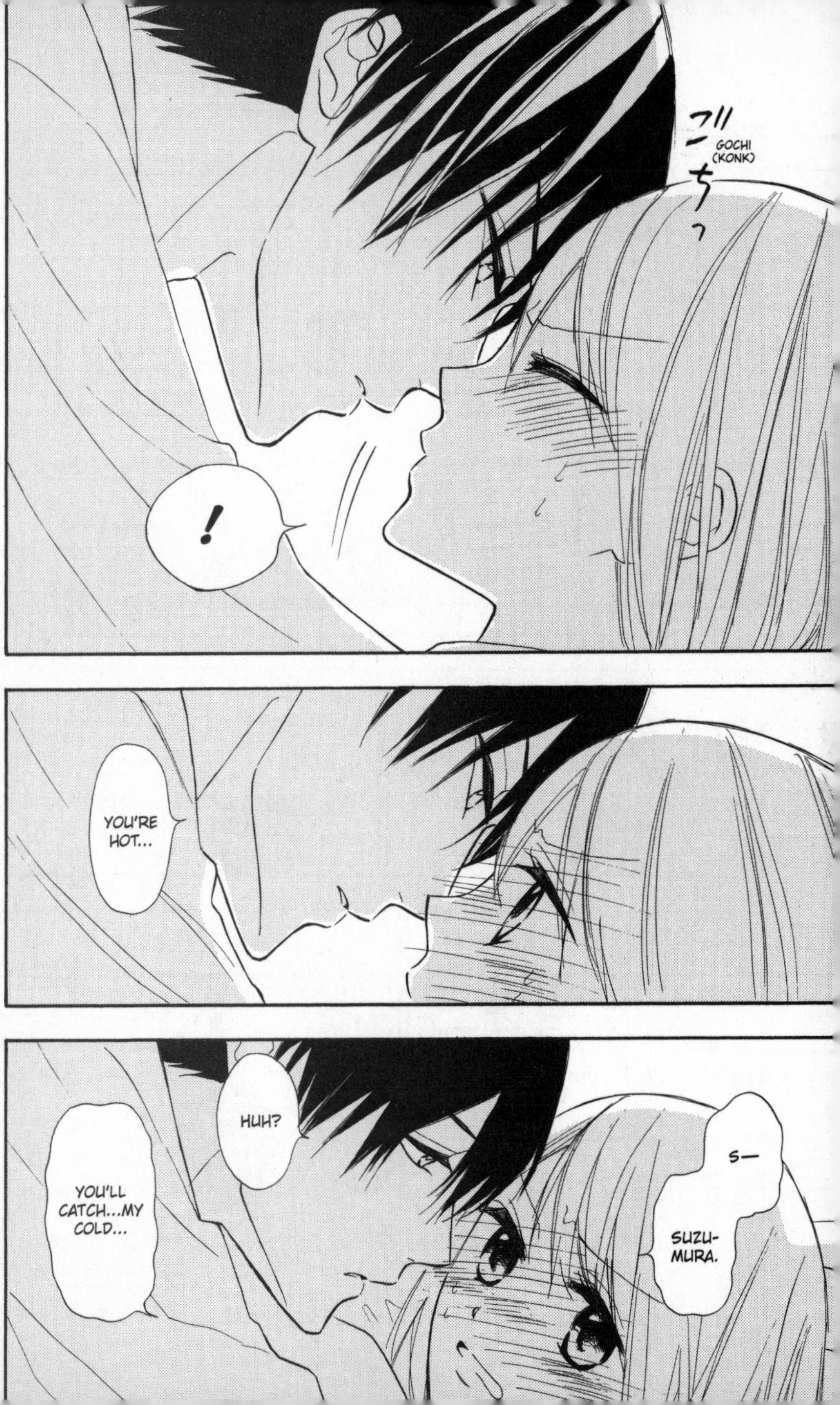
ごちっ
GOCHI (KONK)
!
YOU'RE HOT...
S—
SUZU-MURA.
HUH?
YOU'LL CATCH...MY COLD...

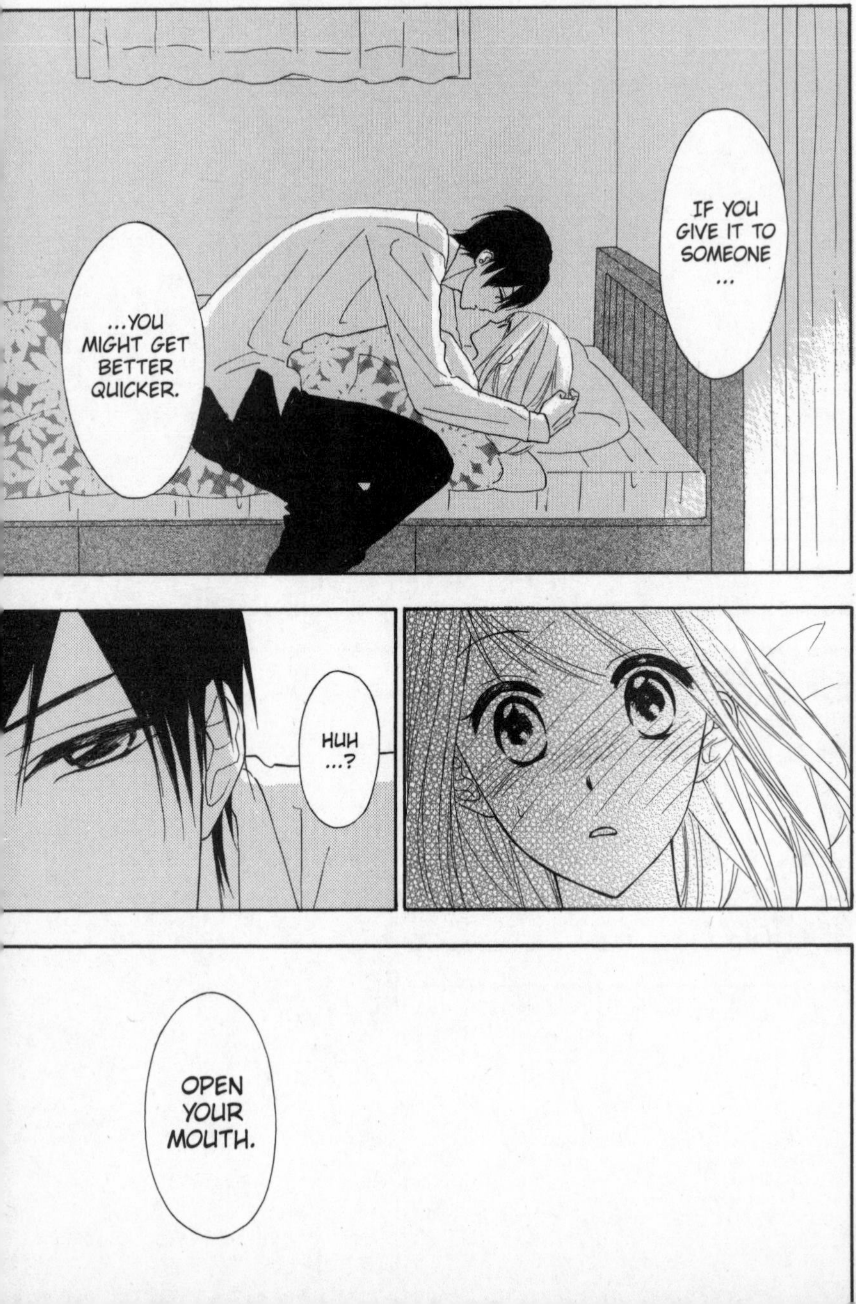
IF YOU GIVE IT TO SOMEONE ...
...YOU MIGHT GET BETTER QUICKER.
HUH ...?
OPEN YOUR MOUTH.

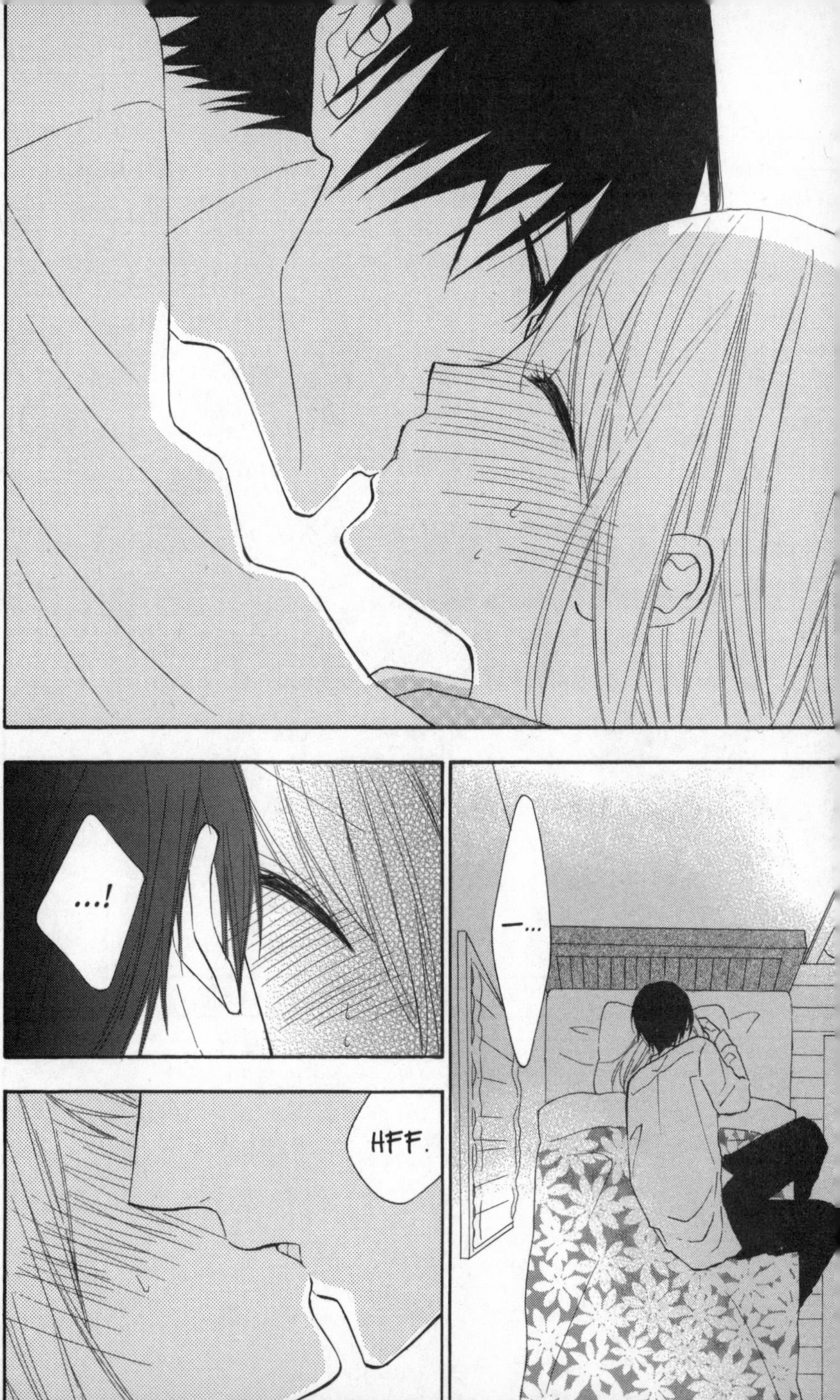
—...
...!
HFF.

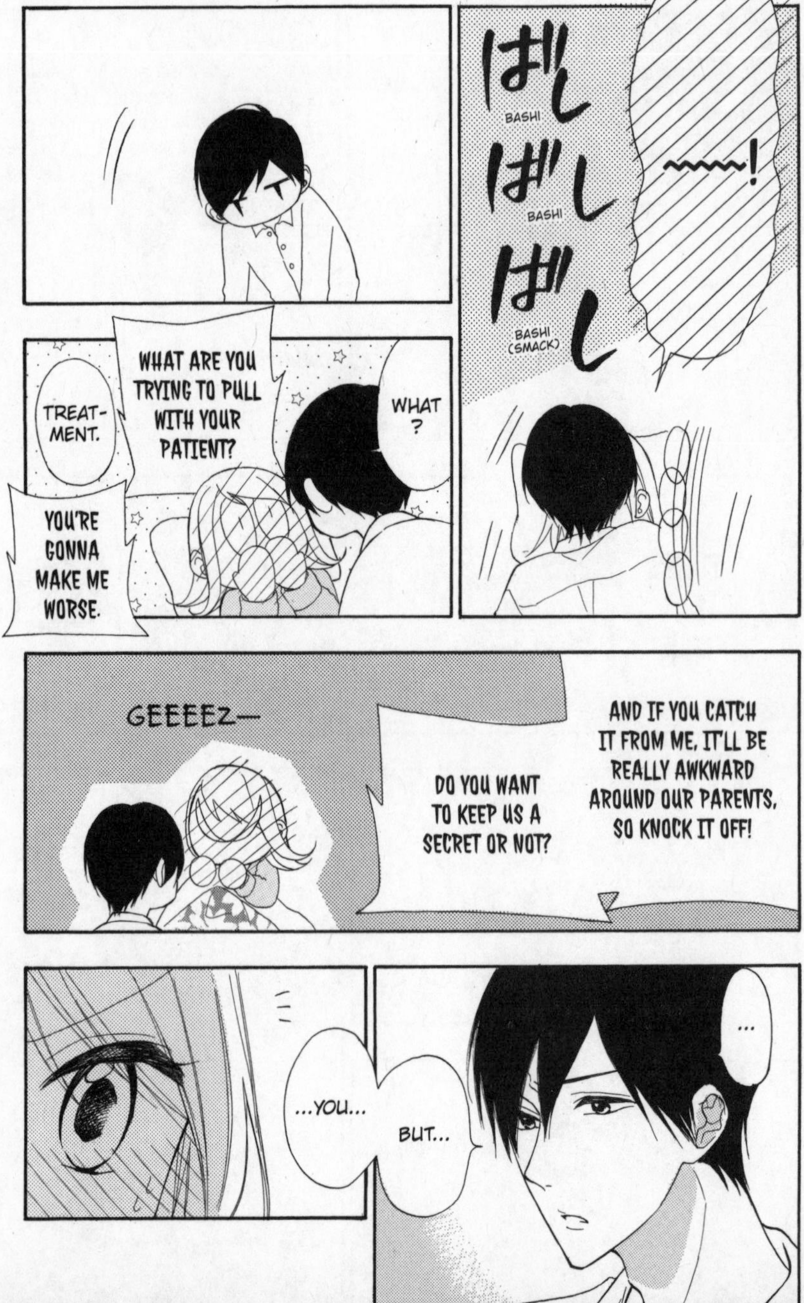
ばし
BASHI
ばし
BASHI
ばし
BASHI (SMACK)
~~~~!
WHAT?
WHAT ARE YOU TRYING TO PULL WITH YOUR PATIENT?
TREAT-MENT.
YOU'RE GONNA MAKE ME WORSE.
GEEEEZ—
DO YOU WANT TO KEEP US A SECRET OR NOT?
AND IF YOU CATCH IT FROM ME, IT'LL BE REALLY AWKWARD AROUND OUR PARENTS, SO KNOCK IT OFF!
...
BUT...
...YOU...
~~~~

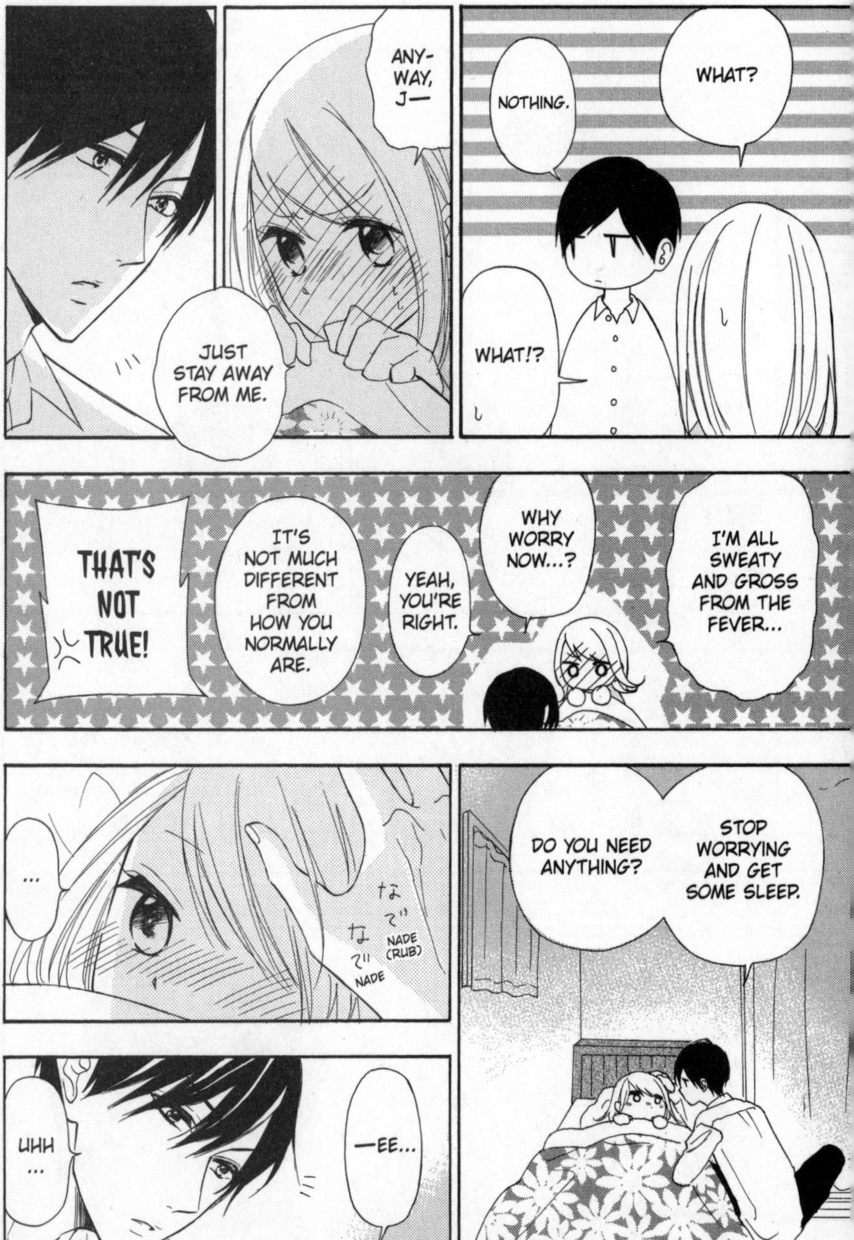
WHAT?
NOTHING.
WHAT!?
ANY-WAY, J—
JUST STAY AWAY FROM ME.
I'M ALL SWEATY AND GROSS FROM THE FEVER...
WHY WORRY NOW...?
YEAH, YOU'RE RIGHT.
IT'S NOT MUCH DIFFERENT FROM HOW YOU NORMALLY ARE.
THAT'S NOT TRUE!
STOP WORRYING AND GET SOME SLEEP.
DO YOU NEED ANYTHING?
なで NADE (RUB)
なで NADE
...
—EE...
UHH ...

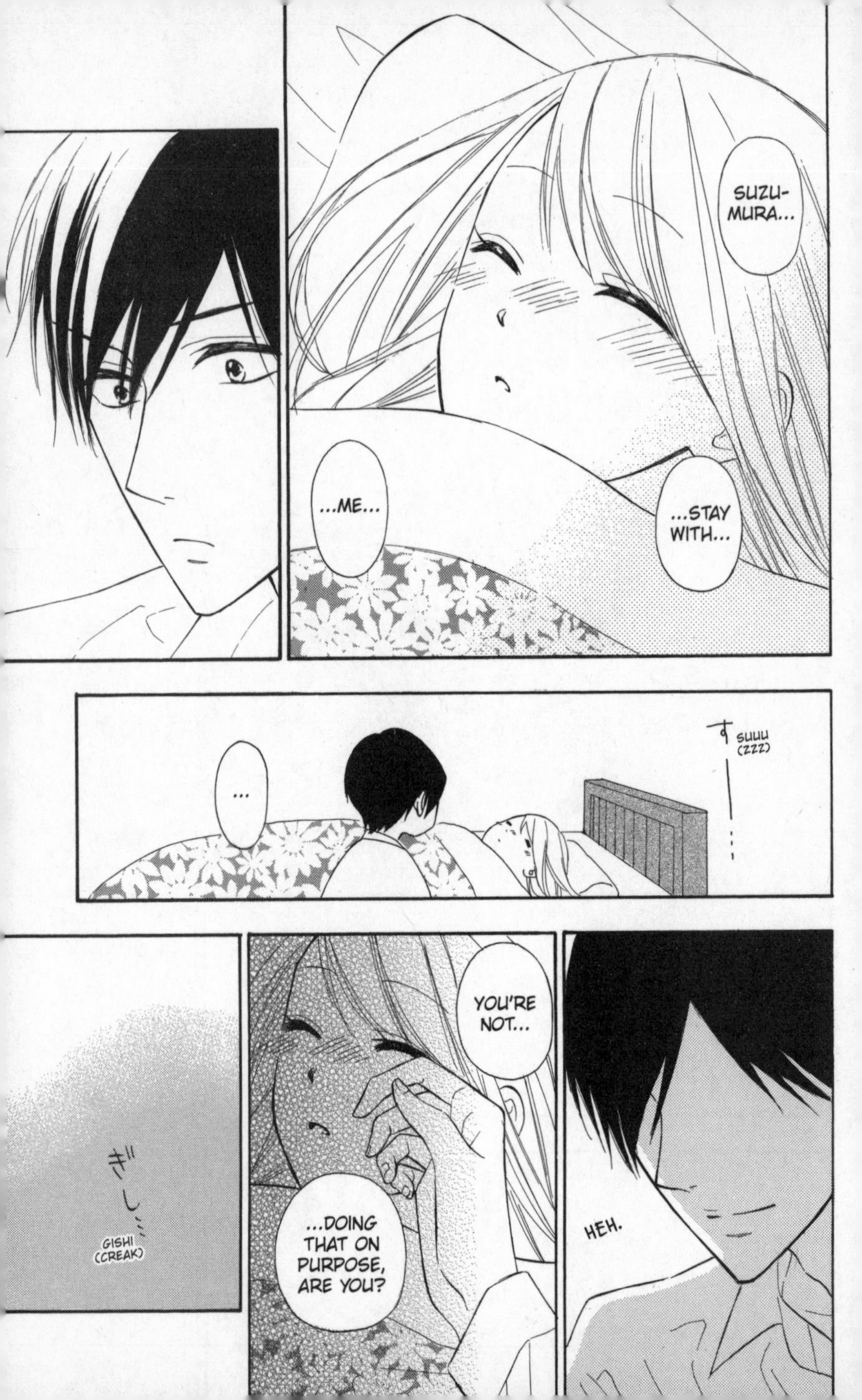
SUZU-MURA...
...STAY WITH...
...ME...
す
SUUU (ZZZ)
...
HEH.
YOU'RE NOT...
...DOING THAT ON PURPOSE, ARE YOU?
ぎし
GISHI (CREAK)

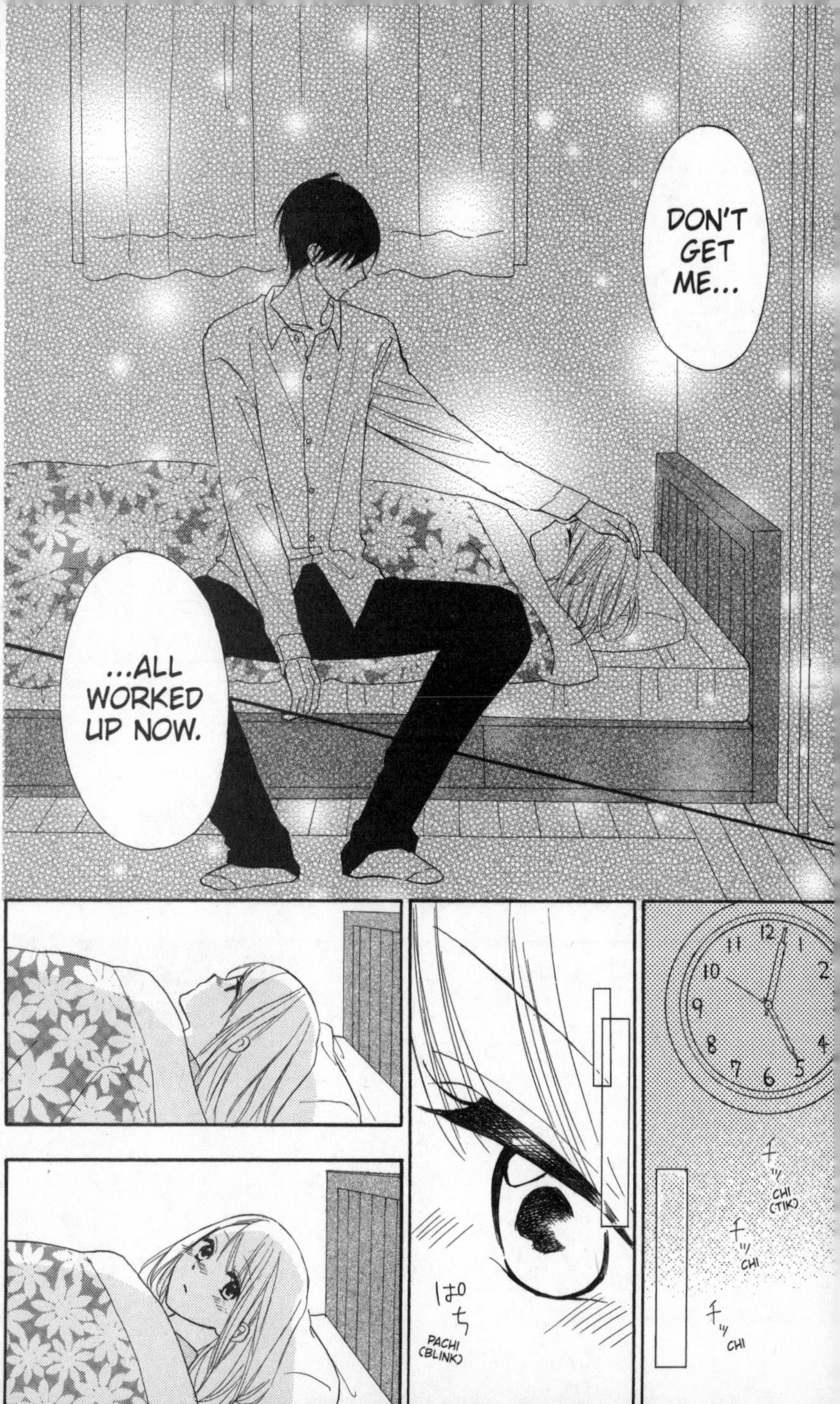
DON'T GET ME...
...ALL WORKED UP NOW.
チッ
CHI (TIK)
チッ
CHI
チッ
CHI
ぱち
PACHI (BLINK)

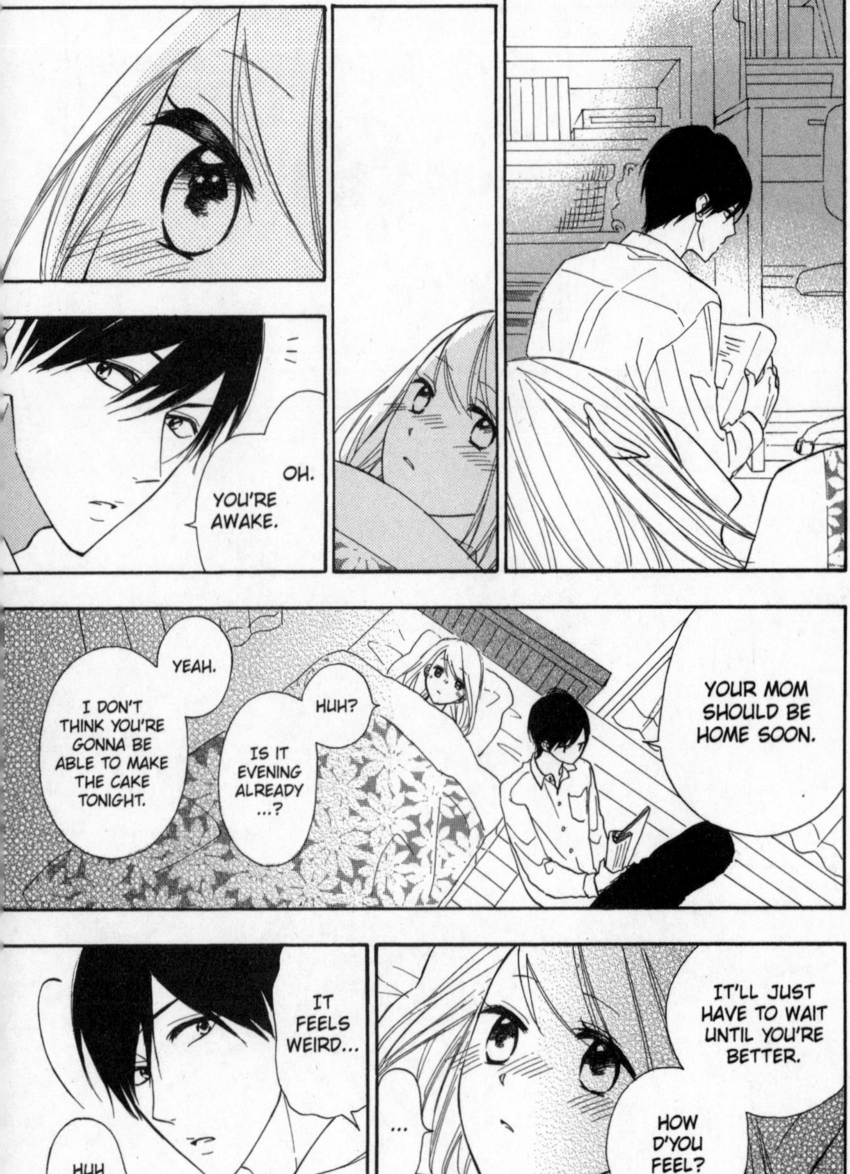
OH.
YOU'RE AWAKE.
YOUR MOM SHOULD BE HOME SOON.
HUH?
IS IT EVENING ALREADY ...?
YEAH.
I DON'T THINK YOU'RE GONNA BE ABLE TO MAKE THE CAKE TONIGHT.
IT'LL JUST HAVE TO WAIT UNTIL YOU'RE BETTER.
HOW D'YOU FEEL?
...
IT FEELS WEIRD...
HUH ...?

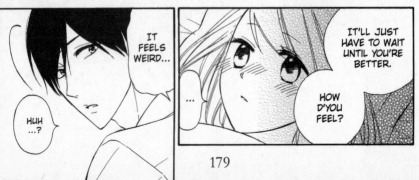

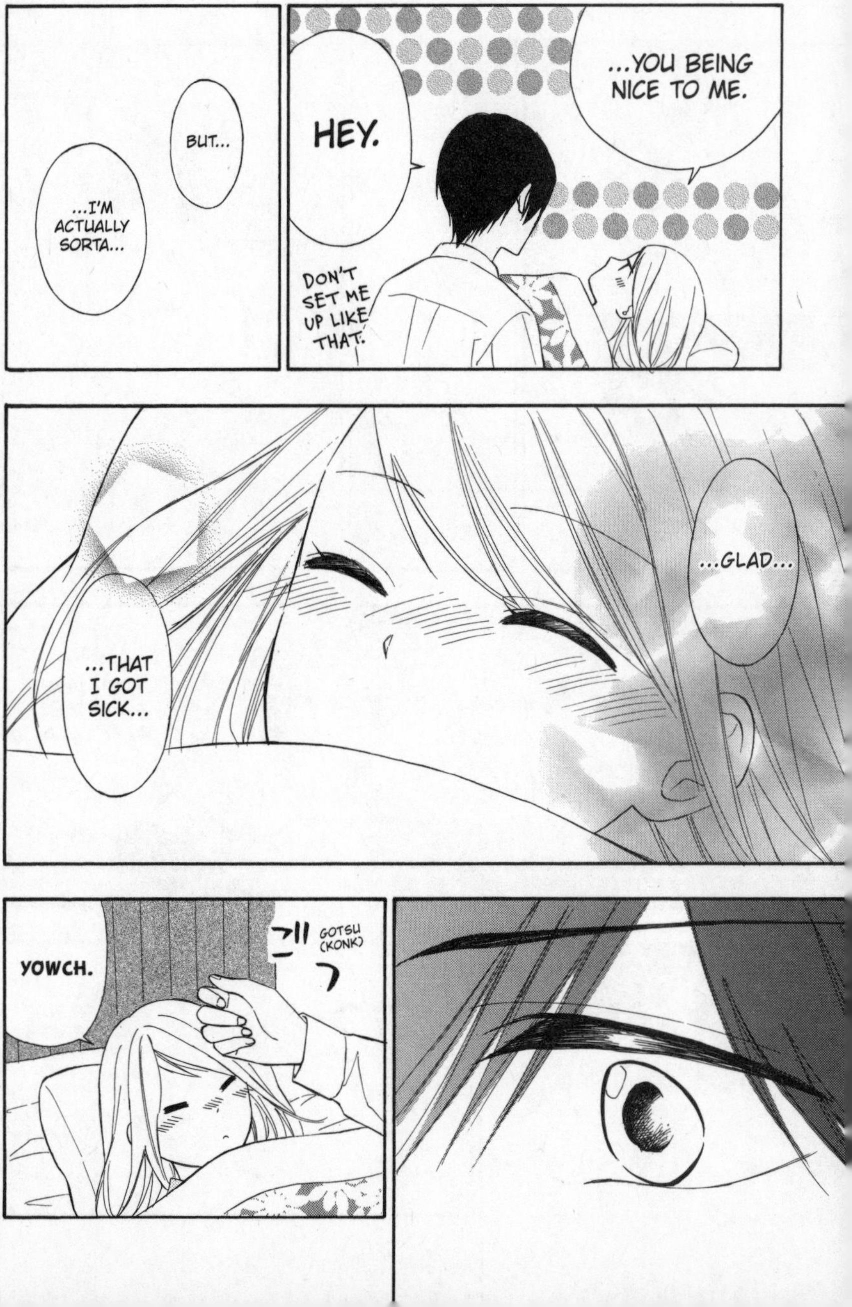
...YOU BEING NICE TO ME.
HEY.
DON'T SET ME UP LIKE THAT.
BUT...
...I'M ACTUALLY SORTA...
...GLAD...
...THAT I GOT SICK...
GOTSU (KONK)
YOWCH.

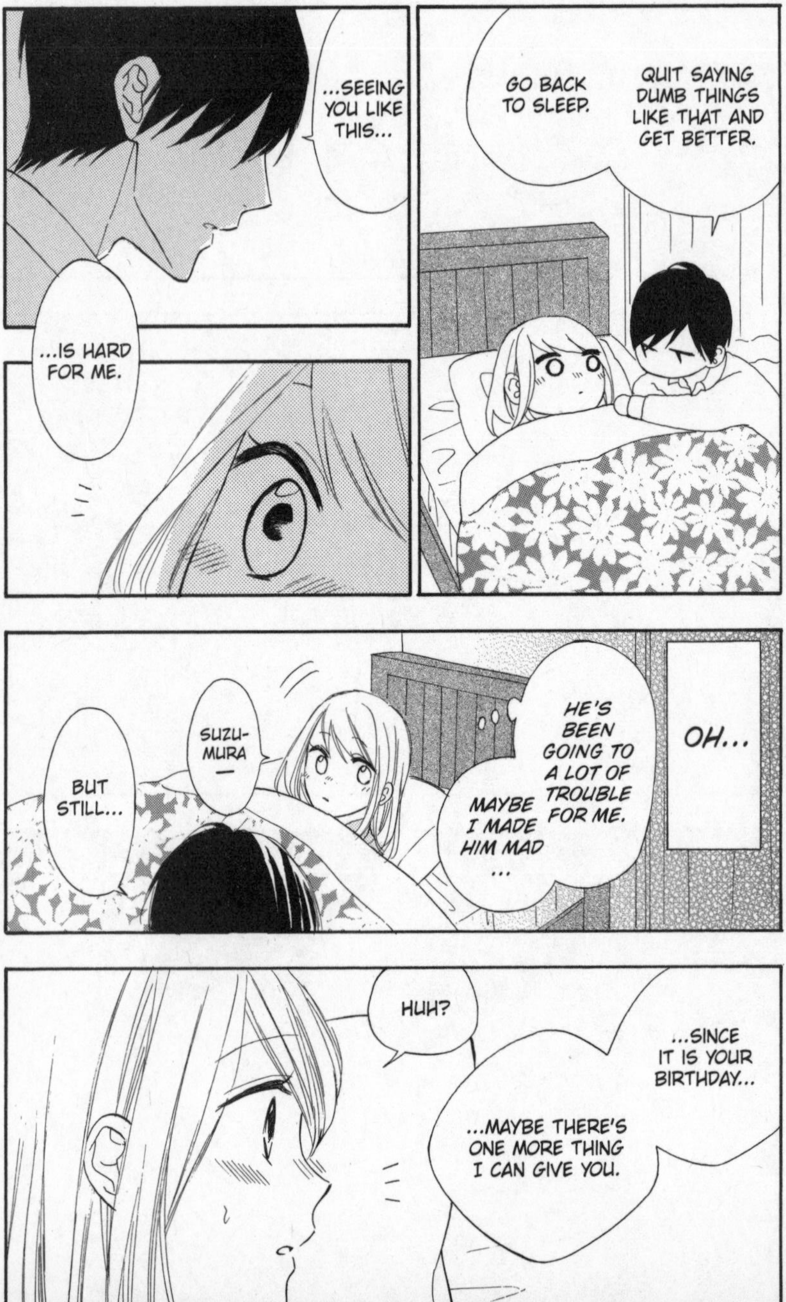
QUIT SAYING DUMB THINGS LIKE THAT AND GET BETTER.
GO BACK TO SLEEP.
...SEEING YOU LIKE THIS...
...IS HARD FOR ME.
OH...
HE'S BEEN GOING TO A LOT OF TROUBLE FOR ME.
MAYBE I MADE HIM MAD ...
SUZU-MURA—
BUT STILL...
...SINCE IT IS YOUR BIRTHDAY...
HUH?
...MAYBE THERE'S ONE MORE THING I CAN GIVE YOU.

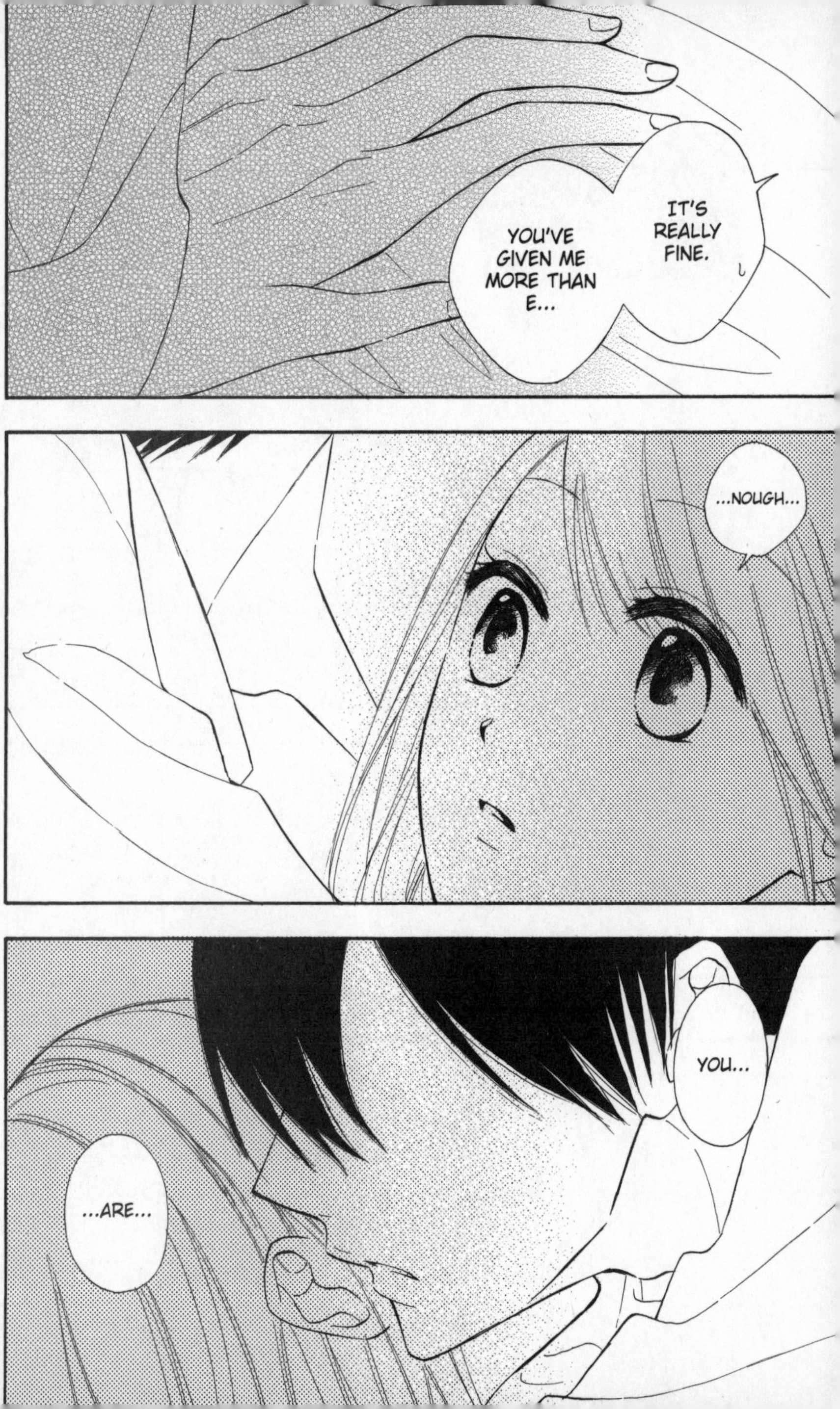
IT'S REALLY FINE.
YOU'VE GIVEN ME MORE THAN E...
...NOUGH...
YOU...
...ARE...

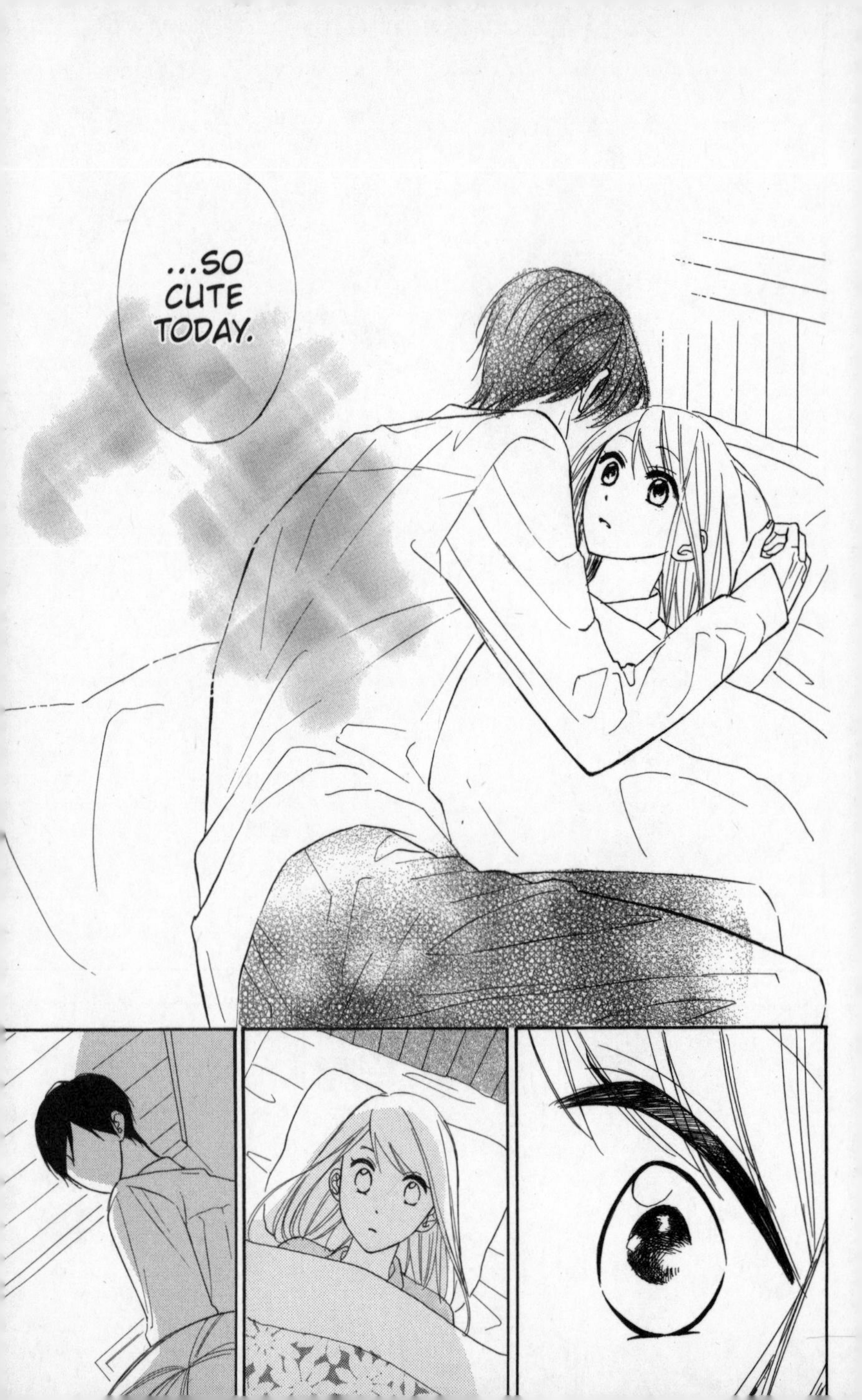
...SO CUTE TODAY.

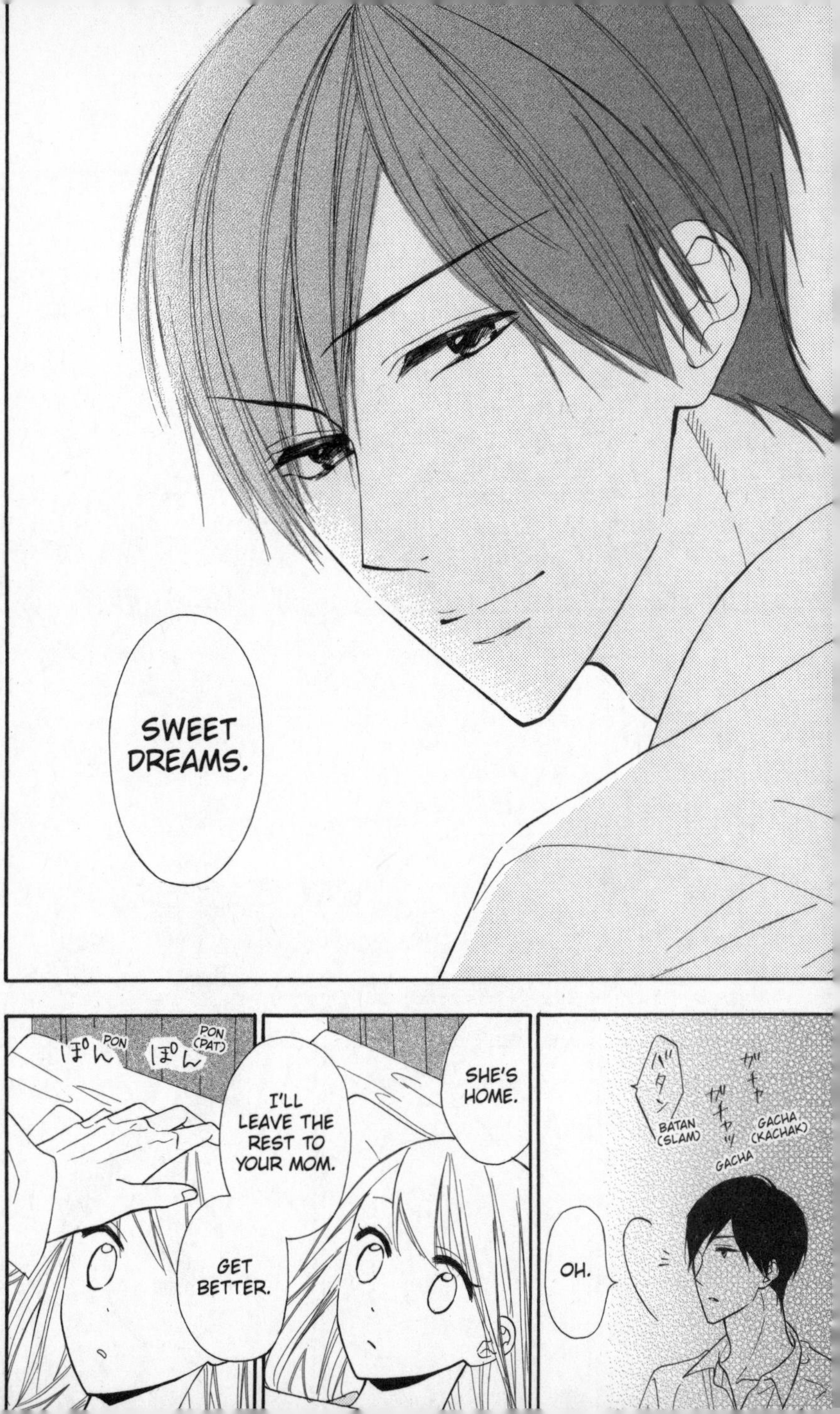
SWEET DREAMS.
バタン
BATAN (SLAM)
ガチャ
ガチャッ
GACHA (KACHAK)
GACHA
OH.
SHE'S HOME.
I'LL LEAVE THE REST TO YOUR MOM.
ぽん
PON
ぽん
PON (PAT)
GET BETTER.

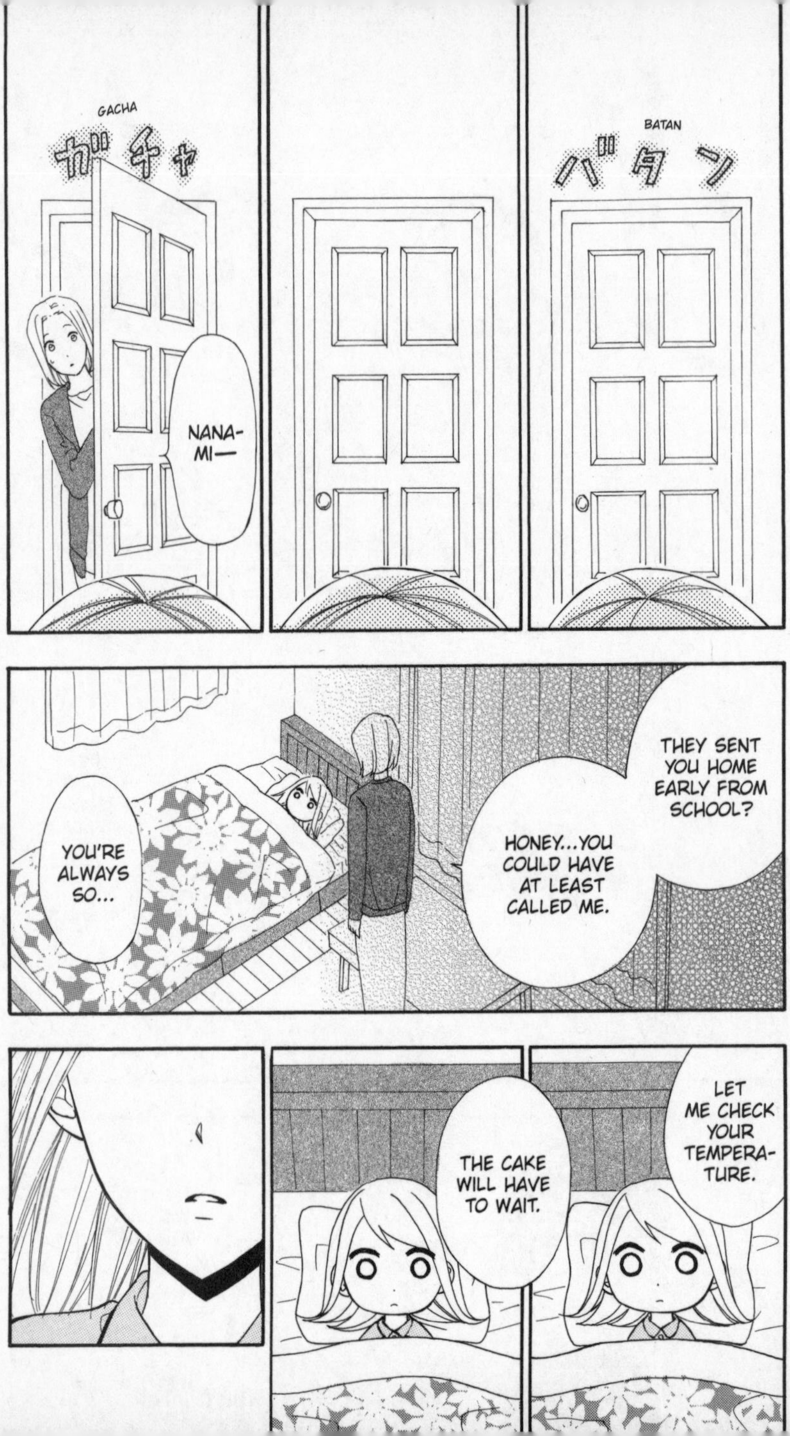
BATAN
バタン
GACHA
ガチャ
NANA-MI—
THEY SENT YOU HOME EARLY FROM SCHOOL?
HONEY...YOU COULD HAVE AT LEAST CALLED ME.
YOU'RE ALWAYS SO...
LET ME CHECK YOUR TEMPERA-TURE.
THE CAKE WILL HAVE TO WAIT.

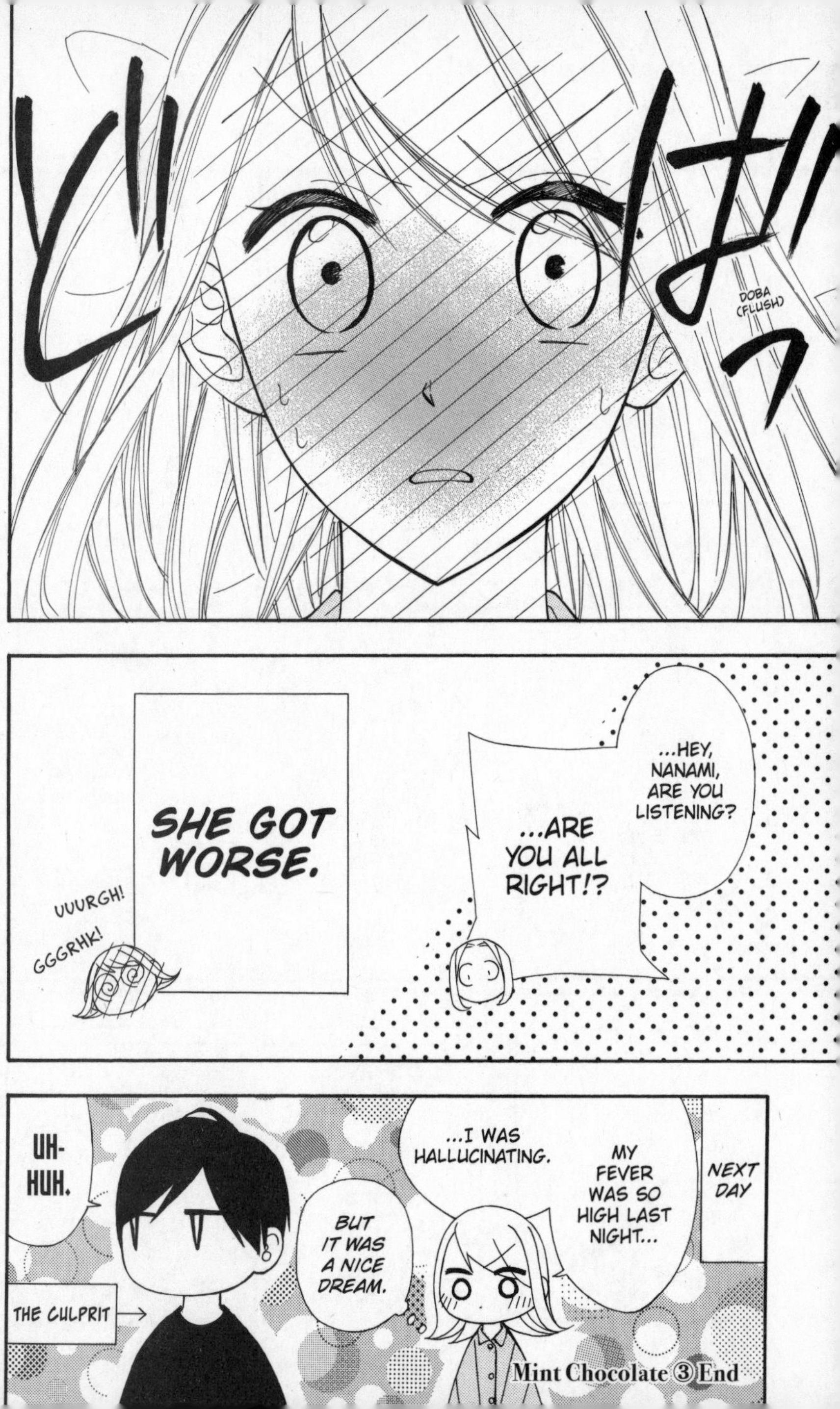
どばっ
DOBA (FLUSH)
...HEY, NANAMI, ARE YOU LISTENING?
...ARE YOU ALL RIGHT!?
SHE GOT WORSE.
UUURGH!
GGGRHK!
NEXT DAY
MY FEVER WAS SO HIGH LAST NIGHT...
...I WAS HALLUCINATING.
BUT IT WAS A NICE DREAM.
UH-HUH.
THE CULPRIT

Mint Chocolate ③ End

Bonus Chapter

After Room: 13

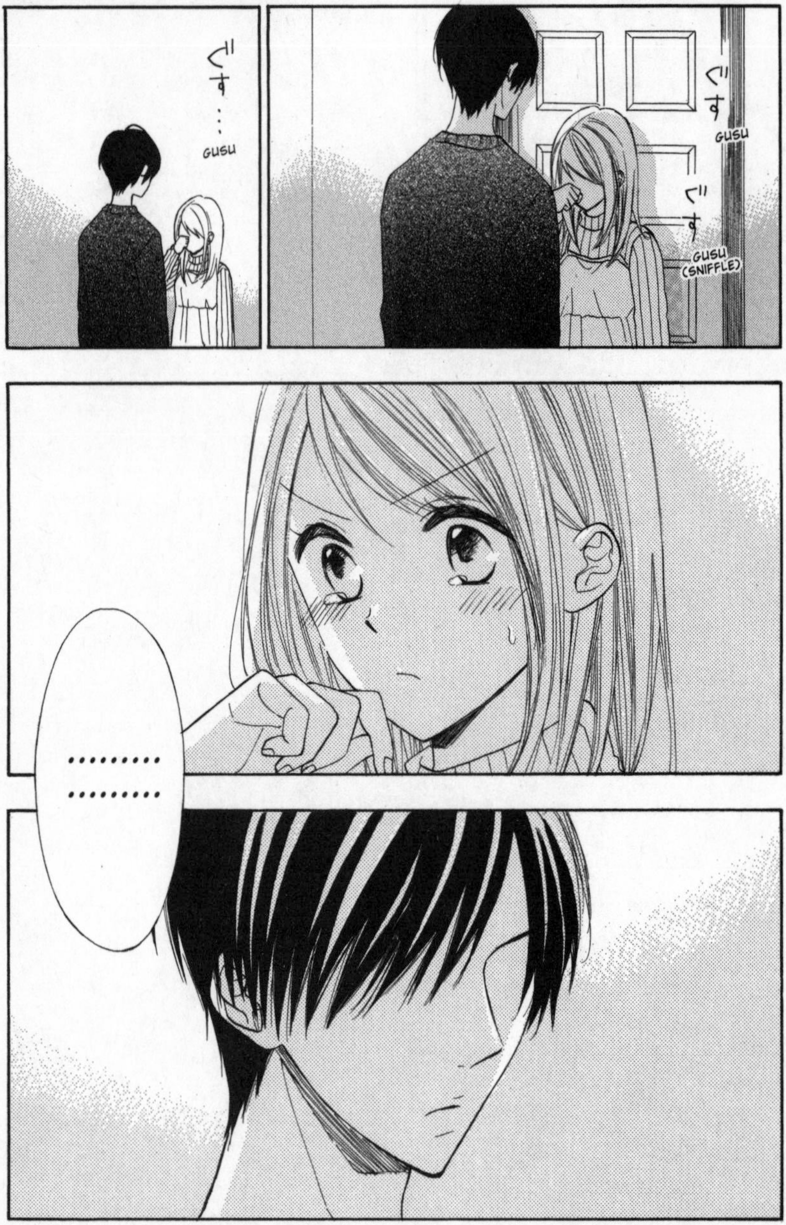
ぐす
GUSU
ぐす
GUSU (SNIFFLE)
ぐす…
GUSU
....
....

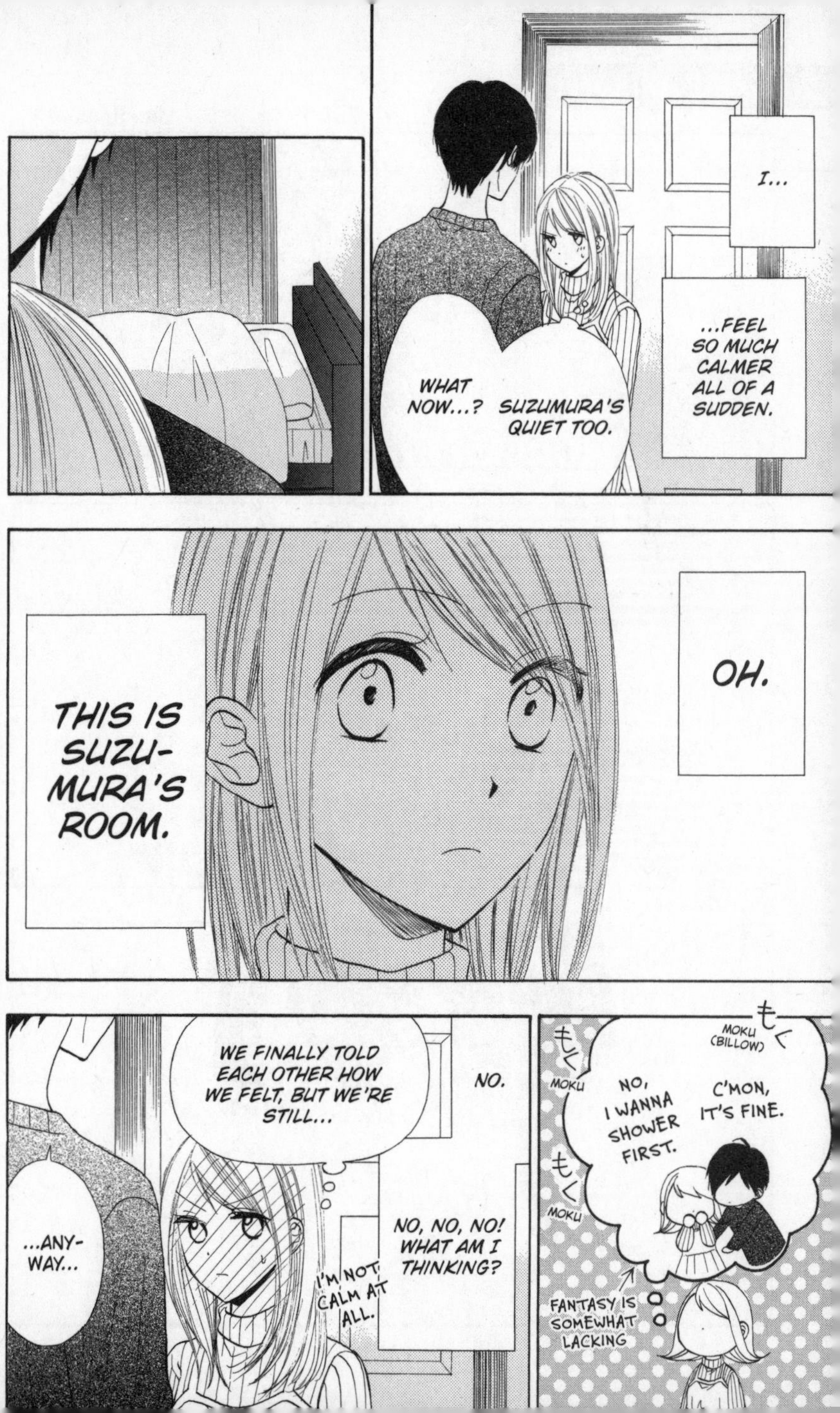

I...
...FEEL SO MUCH CALMER ALL OF A SUDDEN.
SUZUMURA'S QUIET TOO.
WHAT NOW...?
OH.
THIS IS SUZU-MURA'S ROOM.
もく
MOKU (BILLOW)
もく
MOKU
C'MON, IT'S FINE.
NO, I WANNA SHOWER FIRST.
もく
MOKU
FANTASY IS SOMEWHAT LACKING
NO.
WE FINALLY TOLD EACH OTHER HOW WE FELT, BUT WE'RE STILL...
NO, NO, NO! WHAT AM I THINKING?
I'M NOT CALM AT ALL.
...ANY-WAY...

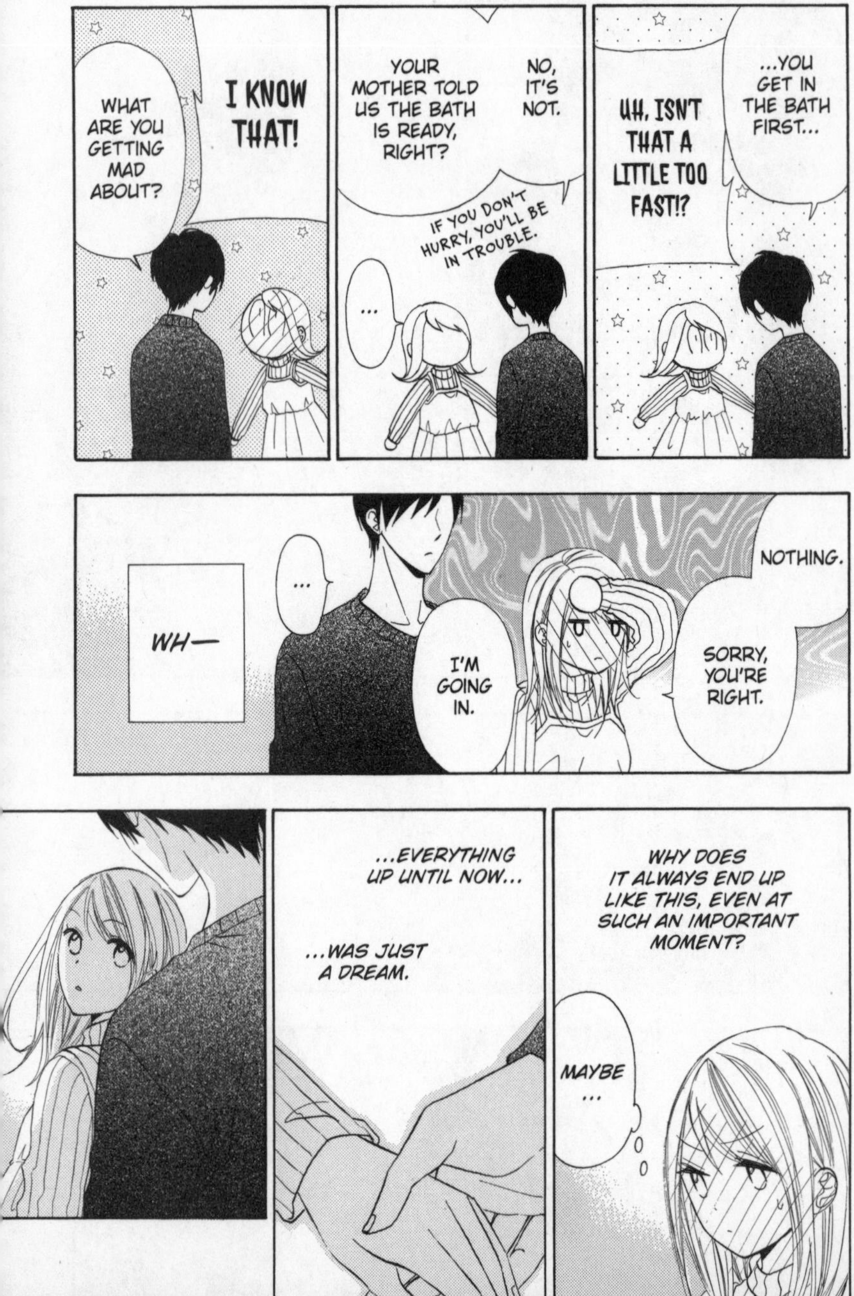
...YOU GET IN THE BATH FIRST...
UH, ISN'T THAT A LITTLE TOO FAST!?
NO, IT'S NOT.
YOUR MOTHER TOLD US THE BATH IS READY, RIGHT?
IF YOU DON'T HURRY, YOU'LL BE IN TROUBLE.
...
I KNOW THAT!
WHAT ARE YOU GETTING MAD ABOUT?
NOTHING.
SORRY, YOU'RE RIGHT.
I'M GOING IN.
...
WH—
WHY DOES IT ALWAYS END UP LIKE THIS, EVEN AT SUCH AN IMPORTANT MOMENT?
MAYBE ...
...EVERYTHING UP UNTIL NOW...
...WAS JUST A DREAM.

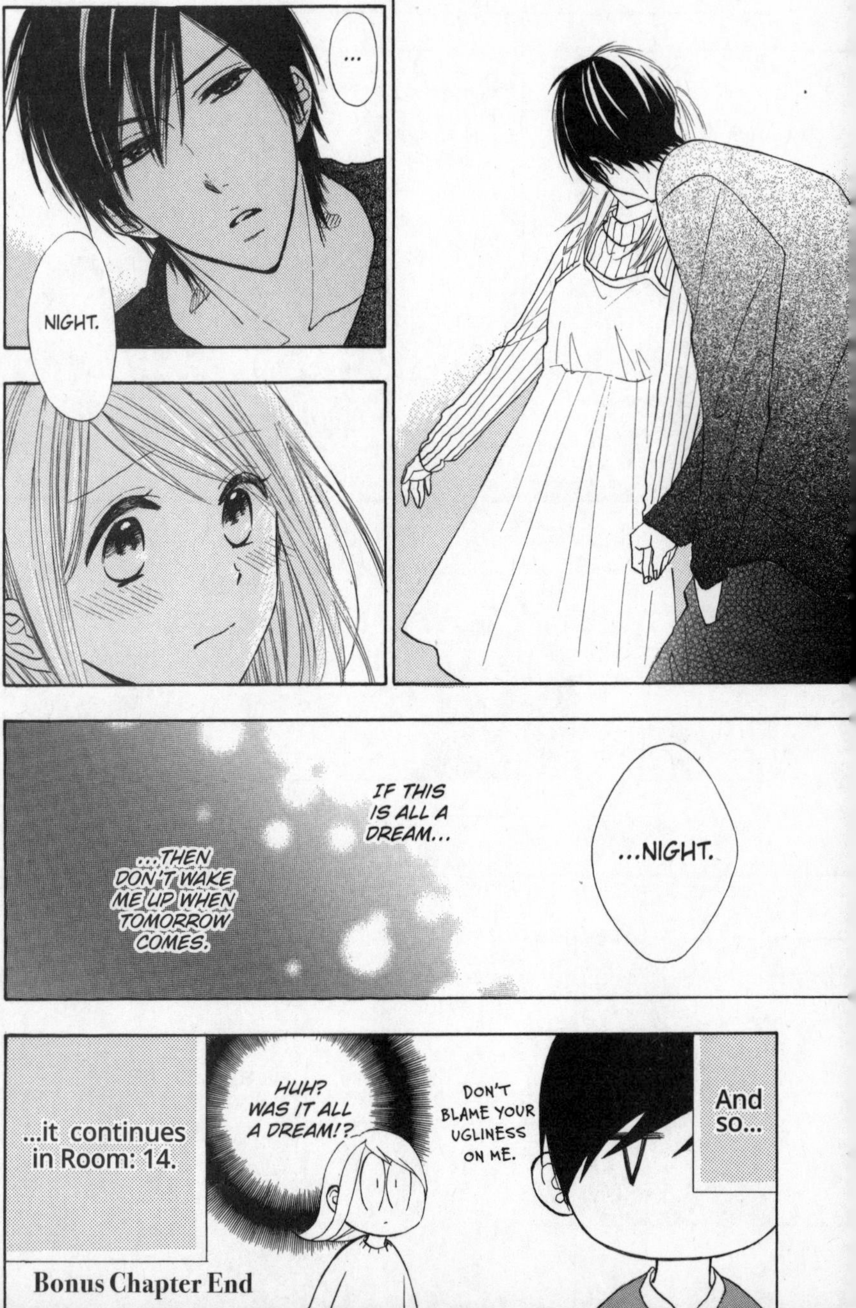
...
NIGHT.
...NIGHT.
IF THIS IS ALL A DREAM...
...THEN DON'T WAKE ME UP WHEN TOMORROW COMES.
And so...
DON'T BLAME YOUR UGLINESS ON ME.
HUH? WAS IT ALL A DREAM!?
...it continues in Room: 14.
Bonus Chapter End

TRANSLATION NOTES

Common Honorifics

-san: The Japanese equivalent of Mr./Mrs./Miss. If a situation calls for politeness, this is the fail-safe honorific.

-kun: Used most often when referring to boys, this indicates affection or familiarity. Occasionally used by older men among their peers, but it may also be used by anyone referring to a person of lower standing.

-chan: An affectionate honorific indicating familiarity used mostly in reference to girls; also used in reference to cute persons or animals of either gender.

no honorific: Indicates familiarity or closeness; if used without permission or reason, addressing someone in this manner would constitute an insult.

Page 12

Birthdays: Japanese school years start on April 1 in Japan, so all children who turn six before April 2 are in the same grade. Since Kyouhei and Nanami are in the same grade, when Nanami says her birthday is in January, Kyouhei immediately knows she was born four months after him.

Page 42

Japanese New Year's: Similar to the special concerts that air in the United States before the Times Square Ball Drop, Japan has a New Year's concert called NHK Kohaku Uta Gassen. It runs for about four hours and takes the format of a song battle between male and female musicians. Only the most popular artists get a chance to appear on the show.

Unlike in the United States, New Year's is usually celebrated at home sitting around with the family, often while eating *toshikoshi soba* which are buckwheat noodles added to a special broth.

Also, since Christmas is considered a romantic holiday, not a religious one, the end-of-year gift-giving commonly takes the form of special allowances presented on New Year's Day.

Page 118

It's illegal: In Japan, it is a violation of citizens' right to privacy, or their "portrait rights," to have their photos taken without permission. For that reason, every phone in Japan makes a shutter sound when a picture is taken. This feature cannot be turned off.

Page 161

38°C: Approximately 100°F.

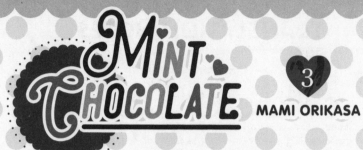

MINT CHOCOLATE

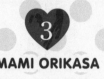

3

MAMI ORIKASA

Translation: Amber Tamosaitis | Lettering: Barri Shrager

This book is a work of fiction. Names, characters, places, and incidents are the product of the author's imagination or are used fictitiously. Any resemblance to actual events, locales, or persons, living or dead, is coincidental.

MINT CHOCOLATE by Mami Orikasa
© Mami Orikasa 2019
All rights reserved.
First published in Japan in 2019 by HAKUSENSHA, Inc., Tokyo.
English language translation rights in U.S.A., Canada and U.K. arranged with
HAKUSENSHA, Inc., Tokyo through Tuttle-Mori Agency, Inc., Tokyo.

English translation © 2021 by Yen Press, LLC

Yen Press
150 West 30th Street, 19th Floor
New York, NY 10001

Visit us at yenpress.com ♥ facebook.com/yenpress ♥ twitter.com/yenpress
yenpress.tumblr.com ♥ instagram.com/yenpress

First Yen Press Edition: July 2021

Yen Press is an imprint of Yen Press, LLC.
The Yen Press name and logo are trademarks of Yen Press, LLC.

The publisher is not responsible for websites (or their content) that are not owned by the publisher.

Library of Congress Control Number: 2020949568

ISBNs: 978-1-9753-2056-0 (paperback)
978-1-9753-2057-7 (ebook)

10 9 8 7 6 5 4 3

WOR

Printed in the United States